GROWTH OF UNPLANNED TOWNS AND CITIES IN THE NORTH EASTERN REGION OF INDIA

About the Editors

Phaiñ Singh Ñianglang D.C.E, M.A, M.Phil, Ph.D, A.I.T.P. (India);born on 22.09.1962 served in different capacities in the MGCC Ltd, Government of Meghalaya and in the North Eastern Council, Shillong. He attended the short-term trainings and workshops in the country and abroad. He superannuated as a Chief Planning Officer & *ex-officio* Joint Secretary in the Planning Department. He qualified in town planning from the Institute of Town Planners, Delhi. His thesis on urban traffic decongestion measures was supervised by Dr. Sanjay Gupta, Professor of Transportation Planning, SPA (Delhi) and Mr. Sazidul Alam, Joint Director, Urban Affairs, Government of Meghalaya as the official adviser. His areas of interest are systems theory in town planning, town planning techniques and urban transport planning.

Siddheswar Sarma M.Sc., M.Phil, Ph.D. born in 1950 started his service carrier as a Lecturer in the Department of Geography, Arya Vidyapith College and subsequently in B. Barooah College, Guwahati. He has retired as Senior Cartographer from the Department of Geography, North Eastern Hill University, Shillong, in 2010. Being a trained geographer in Remote Sensing and GIS, he has completed three projects based on remote sensing techniques. He is the author of two books on Meghalaya and co-editor of three books. After his retirement, he has been engaged with IGNOU, Shillong Study Centre and currently he is the Secretary of NEICSSR, Shillong.

GROWTH OF UNPLANNED TOWNS AND CITIES IN THE NORTH EASTERN REGION OF INDIA

Problems and Alleviation Measures

Edited by

Phaiñ Singh Ñianglang

Siddheswar Sarma

CONCEPT PUBLISHING COMPANY PVT. LTD.

NEW DELHI - 110 059

ISBN: 978-93-5594-622-5

First Published 2025

Published and Printed by

Concept Since 1974

Concept Publishing Company Pvt. Ltd.
A/15-16, Commercial Block, Mohan Garden
New Delhi-110059 (India)
T: +91-11-41101460
E: publishing@conceptpub.com, *W*: www.conceptpub.com

Cataloging in Publication--Courtesy: D.K. Agencies (P) Ltd. <docinfo@dkagencies.com>

"Growth of Unplanned Towns and Cities in the North Eastern Region of India: Problems and Alleviation Measures" (Seminar) (2017 : Shillong, India)
Growth of unplanned towns and cities in the North Eastern region of India : problems and alleviation measures / editors, Phaiñ Singh Ñianglang, Siddheswar Sarma.
pages cm
"North East India Council for Social Science Research (NEICSSR) has taken a bold step by organising a two-day seminar on the 20th & 21st November, 2017 at Shillong Law College, Shillong on "Growth of Unplanned Towns and Cities in the North Eastern Region of India: Problems and Alleviation Measures ..." --Foreword.
Includes bibliographical references and index.
ISBN 9789355946225

1. Cities and towns--India, Northeastern--Growth--Congresses. 2. Urbanization--India, Northeastern--Congresses. 3. City planning--India, Northeastern--Congresses. I. Ñianglang, Phaiñ Singh, 1962- editor. II. Sarma, S., editor. III. North-East India Council for Social Science Research, organizer. IV. Shillong Law College (Shillong, India), host institution. V. Title.

LCC HT384.I42N67 2017 | DDC 307.7609541 23

Dedicated to

Sir Patrick Geddes

The father of Modern Town Planning who at the invitation of Lord Pentland, the then Governor of Madras visited India in 1914 and revolutionised the civic movement and largely contributed to the Development of Town Planning Principles.

Mr. A.K.M. Karim, B.E. (Civil), Dip. T. & C.P., M.C.D.
(Liverpool), F.I.T.P. (India),
Retd. Adviser & Director of Housing,
Government of Meghalaya,
"NISHAT",
Sankardev Road, Kench's Trace, Shillong -793004.
(0364) 2503126
8837287877

Foreword

I am indeed very happy to see that the North East India Council for Social Science Research (NEICSSR) has taken a bold step by organising a two-day seminar on the 20th and 21st November, 2017 at Shillong Law College, Shillong, on **"Growth of Unplanned Towns and Cities in the North Eastern Region of India: Problems and Alleviation Measures"**, in which article contributors, viz., professional planners, architects, geographers, economists, sociologists and other thinkers presented their own viewpoints to mitigate the problems. My knowledge of what makes town planning effective has withstood the test of time. As a town planner who has retired from government service, I had ample opportunity to experiment with planning theories and concepts. My long years of experience indicates the fact that planning is viewed as a management function and significantly moved in the direction of strong decision making at different hierarchies. For example, planning for provision of housing for the poor involves active management and monitoring of quality control during construction to avoid time and cost overruns. Planning does not involve merely planning but it is also a decision-making process. This transpires that for any activity in towns or cities it should involve both planning and management to fructify that activity.

Part A of the book contains the articles contributed by professional planners and architects in their respective areas of interest who suggested corrective measures, deserve implementation to the utmost possible extent. The proposed measures and the way forward given in the article on "Urban Sprawl in Shillong: Unregulated Urban Growth and Considerations for the Future" by Mr. Elangmiki Shullai requires serious attention for reducing congestion through the New Shillong Township. Besides other planned activities, provision of cycling tracts, pedestrians' footpaths, shopping malls, hotels, multilevel parking lots and other facilities as per the Norms and Standards are required to be carried out, urgently to transform this new township into a clean and green city. The article on "Economic and Financial Feasibility of Cable Cars in Hill Cities" by Miss G.D. Laloo merits further feasibility study to make it operative as roads in Shillong city are circuitous and narrow. The article on "Urban Safety in Road Design—Exploring Design Concern" by Miss Namrata Talukdar relates to the urban renewal of the Guwahati city and ways and means should be devised to implement the recommendations as far as practicable for city beautification. The article on "Need for Secured livelihood and Empowerment of Women Street Vendors of Guwahati City: The Challenging Road Ahead for Smart City" by Mr. Parangam Sarma Basistha requires formulation of suitable policy to regulate and formalise the street vendors taking into consideration of the findings. The article presented by Dr. P.S. Ñianglang and Professor Sanjay Gupta, viz., "Planning Strategies for Traffic Decongestion in Hill City: A Case Study of Shillong in Meghalaya" deeply impressed me and it merits special consideration for implementation. When Dr. Ñianglang approached me for recommending him as an Associate of the Institute of Town Planners, India (ITPI); I had the opportunity to read his thesis on traffic decongestion measures submitted to the ITPI. The study *inter alia* found that the volume-capacity (V/C) ratios of the city's arterial roads and intersections were between 0.75 and 1 and some were more than 1 which indicated the heavy and severe levels of traffic congestion. Thus, the recommended multipronged measures which abate morphogenetic transformation of Shillong green city into a red city deserve immediate translation into real action to ease the present level of traffic congestion and as well as for the horizon years. However, the article "Structural Equation Modelling (SEM) for Transport Planning in Towns" by Dr. Ñianglang which is a multivariate statistical technique combining the aspects of factor analysis and multiple regression for analysis and interpretation of qualitative data appears to be a new technique among the transport planners in the country and is yet to gain momentum among the practitioners. The article, viz., "Land Suitability Analysis—A Requirement for the Shillong Master Plan" by Miss Rimeka Dora Ranee which is short and precise acts as a "Guiding Principle" for preparation of Master Plans not only for Shillong urban agglomeration but for any hill city as slope analysis is an essential ingredient of site planning. I hope town planners will carry out this exercise. The article on "Goods Movement Pattern and Planning Imperatives for

Goods Distribution in Gangtok" by Professor Sanjay Gupta which identified the problems, issues and the alternative scenarios for Gangtok city deserves formulation of an effective policy regulating the freight movement in both hilly and plain cities besides the recommendations made in the article since supply of goods to urban dwellers is an indispensable and demand-driven activity of transporters.

Similarly, Part B of the book includes a number of articles presented by the generalists in their respective specialised areas and their valuable contributions merit special consideration since town and country planning is the art and science of the use of land and the character and siting of buildings and communication routes so as to secure the maximum practicable degree of economy, convenience and beauty as defined by Lewis Keeble. Principles, strategies and policies recommended by economists, geographers, sociologists and other thinkers pertaining to solid waste management, urbanisation, environmental consequences, land market, morphology of towns, road safety and accidents, unplanned growth and evolution of cities, problems of slum children, transportation, urban housing demand and others enthuse readers, academicians and policy makers to further their investigations.

I am particularly delighted to see that a book which encompasses a wide range of topics considered for urban renewal in unplanned towns and cities of the North-Eastern Region of India will be published very soon. I believe that professionals will not work in isolation but will increasingly integrate their technical knowledge and skills set within the domain of town planning profession and a larger decision-making process by inducting the generalists and other stakeholders to fructify urban renewal.

16 August 2024 **A.K.M. Karim**

Preface

When the archaeologist's spade unearthed the urban site, it unfolded the origins of city and town planning which evolved in space and time and in consequence of that it manifested the roots of ancient civilisations in the Old World and the New World. Lewis Mumford in his book *The City in History* (1961) tells us that the history of urban settlements sets its base about 5000 years ago and the city of the dead antedates the city of the living. Archaeological remains and carbon dating bear evidence of the existence of ancient cities in the two Worlds. John J. Macionis and Vincent N. Parrillo in their book *Cities and Urban Life, Fifth Edition* (2011), using the Carl Sagan's concept of cosmic calendar crystallised the history of the universe which began with the Big Bang corresponding to 1st January when human species did not exist then. Among the early cities so far unearthed, archaeological ruins substantiated that Jericho (8000 B.C.) was the first city evolved in this planet Catal Huyuk (6000 B.C.) (pronounced Sha-tal Hoo-yook), Uruk (4000 B.C.), Eridu (4000 B.C.), Ur (4000 B.C.), Liangzhu (3400 B.C.), the Great Pyramids (2600 B.C.), Mohenjo-Daro (2500 B.C,), Cheng-Chou (1600 B.C.), Rome (150 B.C.) and other cities evolved along with their civilisations in the Old World. In the New World, the early cities unearthed so far were Monte Alban (500 B.C.), Teotihuacan (100 A.D.), Cuzco (800 A.D.) and Chan Chan (800 A.D.). Arthur M. Sullivan in his book *Urban Economics* (1990) attributed four factors for the evolution of cities namely, (i) comparative advantage, (ii) internal scale economies, (iii) transportation costs and (iv) agglomerative economies. These factors led to the evolution of the first cities in the fertile river valleys in the Near East around 3000 B.C. In the Mesopotamia valley, the city-states of Eiridu, Ur, Lagash and Kish existed and Ur was the largest of these cities which comprised a land area of about 150 acres with a population of about 25,000. In 2000 B.C., the city of Babylon lying 60 miles away from the present Baghdad was founded with a population of about 50,000. Similarly, in the Nile River Valley, Memphis, Heliopolis and Thebes were the prominent cities.

The emergence of modern 'town and country' planning known by its short tittle 'town planning' in the two Worlds did not occur in isolation from the illuminating work of Johann Heinrich von Thünen (1783-1850) who developed his model of agricultural land use in which theories of urban structures such as the Burgess' Concentric Zone Theory, the Hoyt's Sector Theory, the Harris and Ullman's Multiple-Nuclei Theory and other land use theories and models were built upon. The contributions of Robert Owen (1771-1858), J.S. Buckingham (1786-1855), Arturo Soria y Mata (1844-1920), Ebenezer Howard (1850-1928), Patrick Geddes (1854-1932), Raymond Unwin (1863-1940), Barry Parker (1867-1947), Clarence Perry (1872-1944), Ernst May (1886-1970), Le Corbusier (1887-1965), Lewis Mumford (1895-1990) and C.A. Doxiadis (1913-1975) which are land centric; form the theoretical base of modern town planning. They were the seers, pioneers and urban revolutionists who in their cacophony of efforts, developed their theories and models in the last two centuries. They aroused intense interest across the globe and demonstrated the practicable means of alleviating common urban problems such as inner-city decay, overcrowding, twilight zones, slums, traffic congestion, pollution and other forms of urban congestion by way of gentrification, planned dispersal, creation of townships, design of traffic calming measures and other urban planning activities to achieve a more spacious and better civic life. Population explosions, galloping rate of urbanization, industrialization, technological advancement, and persistent increase in car ownership procreated urban problems. Ebenezer Howard in his book *Garden Cities of Tomorrow* (1902), which holds a unique place and is oft quoted in town planning literature sets out his plan for building of a satellite town called the Garden City which he portrays on a grand scale. This plan requires a land use of 6000 acres to accommodate 32,000 persons and a central area of 1000 acres as a town which may be circular in form locating at 1240 yards from the circumference. It comprises six magnificent boulevards each of 120 feet wide extending radially from the centre and dividing the city into six equal parts called wards. In the centre is a circular space about 5½ acres is size where a beautiful and well-watered garden is surrounded by larger public buildings such a town hall, principal concert, lecture hall, theatre, library, museum, picture-gallery and a hospital. The city is envisaged to be a self-sufficient in terms of employment, possessing its own industry, commerce, shops and agricultural production. The remaining portion of the large space encircled by the 'Crystal Palace' has the recreation grounds easily accessible to all the people. The town houses 5500 individual plots of an average size of

20 feet x 130 feet. His plan culminated in the building of Letchworth and Welwyn as the Garden Cities. Though this grand plan is widely known in the town planning literature, however, a great deal of criticism is levelled at it as being unrealistic in its adherence to geometric proportion, the design of concentric circles of varying land use as universal is impractical and it lowers the population density to twelve houses per acre which is crampy as Ratcliffe writes. Although the plan lacks detailed technical accoutrements, however, the Garden City became the model for the modern town planners to harp upon. From the Garden City stems out what is known in modern parlance a 'new town' or a 'satellite town'. Patrick Geddes, the father of Town Planning, though trained as a biologist; his extraordinary mind took him away from the conventional biology into the area of human ecology. He took up a systematic study of the forces that shaped the growth of the modern cities and the civic life of the people which culminated in his masterpiece *Cities in Evolution: An Introduction to the Town Planning Movement and to the Study of Civics*, (1915). Although the book is neither a technical treatise for a town planner nor a manual of civics for a sociologist, but it seeks to express in various ways the essential harmony and cooperation of citizens with concrete arguments and examples in orchestrating their separated aspects of life and affairs. It gives a clarion call for civic awakening and constructive effort capable of survival and fuller cultivation towards fructification in regional and civic literature, history, art and science and social rejuvenation of towns and cities. He developed the theory and concept of town planning and defined town planning as "the development of a local life, a regional character, a civic spirit, a unique individuality, capable of course of growth and expansion, of improvement and development in many ways, of profiting too by the example and criticisms of others, yet always in its own way and upon its foundations." His concept of Survey, Analysis and Plan (SAP) facilitates the study and close analysis of settlement patterns and local economic environment. For most practitioners, planning in those days focuses primarily on the study of civic design at a local level which is a sort of landscape architecture. His concepts of Folk, Work and Place signify the need of a house, work, food, recreation, and social life by the people. His philosophy led to the development of principles and methods of modern town planning. Seeing the suburban decentralisation and the spreading of cities far and wide, he examined certain basic locative factors such as the pull of coalfields in the early nineteenth century, the natural nodality conferred on certain regions by railways, routes and canals, economies of scales and industrial

agglomeration that led to the concentration of urban development in certain regions. He demonstrated that in these regions suburban growth attracted towns to coalesce into gigantic urban agglomeration which he termed *conurbation*. Geddes inferred that under the pressure of economic and social forces such happening would continue and thus town planning must be subsumed under town and country planning which is a planning of whole urban regions encompassing several towns and their spheres of influence.

Town planning which is multidisciplinary in nature and mutable in character makes town planners and urbanologists difficult to provide a single definition acceptable by all. Other titles assigned to town planning are "physical planning", "urban planning", "spatial planning", "land planning" and "land use planning". Planners such as Thomas Sharp (1940), J.B. McLoughlin (1969), Lewis Keeble (1969), John Ratcliffe (1974), Margaret Roberts (1974), J.M. Simmie (1974); F.D. Hobbs and J.F. Doling (1981), Peter Hall (1992), Arthur B. Gallion and Simon Eisner (1986), Amiya Kumar Das (2007) and S.K. Kulshrestha (2016) give their definitions. However, the definition given by Lewis Keeble M.C., B.Sc., M.A., F.R.I.C.S., M.T.P.I., in his book viz., *Principles and Practice of Town and Country Planning* (1964) about town and country planning as "the art and science of ordering the use of land and the character and siting of buildings and communication routes so as to secure the maximum practicable degree of economy, convenience and beauty" is less ambiguous and more expressive because of its technical nature and practice-orientation. Planning discipline in Britain drew out of three 'land-based professions' viz., architecture, engineering and surveying. To meet the clamant demand of the country, the Committee headed by George Schuster in 1950 recommended economics, sociology, and geography as the eligible subjects to study town planning besides civil engineering and architecture. Donald A. Krueckeberg, B.S., M.C.P., Ph.D., in his book *The American Planner: Biographies and Recollections* (1983), discusses the roots and development of modern American planning which begins in the nineteenth and twentieth century Frederick Law Olmsted, Daniel H. Burnham and Charles Mulford Robinson are regarded as the pathfinders of American planning. Among the trio, Frederick Law Olmsted is regarded as the father of the American landscape architecture. He points out that although people carelessly use the term 'professional' to any identifiable occupation, but the fact remains that 'profession' has its own special entity. The evolution of American planning is tied to the older profession of landscape architecture. In reiterating this standpoint, he quotes the unpublished interview with Frederick J. Adams who says, "I think the fact that planning here, as we know it, came from landscape architecture was better than having come from the architects or the engineers. They, in the early days, did try to take over, if not the Institute, at least the claim that they were the logical planners; the architects because they knew about three-dimensional design, and the engineers because they knew how to lay out streets and sewers. But the landscape architects had a better conception of it". Thus, the development of American planning is credited to landscape architecture as its parent academic discipline.

Town planning as a professional field of action is the activity of designing, scheming and arranging or putting together all plots of lands into a number of uses for the proper growth of towns and liveability of townsfolk using the art and technology. The aims of town planning are to ease traffic congestion, minimize air pollution and roadway accidents besides alleviating urban problems such as poor housing, slums and shanties, water pollution, poor sewerage systems, environmental hazards etc. Although town and country planning does not deal directly with economic, social and political planning but it greatly aids in the realization of aims of these kinds of planning due to its correlations with them.

On the other side of the coin, town planning profession faced severe criticisms. Although planning as an activity is an essential function of a civilised society, John Ratcliffe in his book *An Introduction to Town and Country Planning* (1981), expresses the probability of argument about the non-existence of planning as a profession due to the lack of a discernible discipline. Town planning is unkindly defined as hodgepodge of unrelated social sciences with superficial knowledge of quantitative techniques. He reminds planners how David Eversley in his book *The Planner in Society* makes a pejorative expression by calling a planner as a monster, a threat to society, a callous technocrat, a law unto himself and others. Jane Jacobs in her book *The Death and Life of Great* American Cities makes a scathing attack on the principles and aims that shaped the orthodox city planning and rebuilding in America in the 1950s. She questions urban planners about the condition of some streets which are safe and others are unsafe, the function of a neighbourhood within the city's organism and the impoverishment of some slums and the regeneration of others. She writes about the dangers of too much development money and too little diversity and she calls for an assessment of the vitality of cities.

The evolution of modern town planning in India began from the middle of 19th century when insanitary conditions, epidemics and slums occurred in towns and cities. The Sanitary Commission set up in 1864 pressed hard for removal of such urban problems. Consequently, the Bengal Municipal Act 1884, the Bombay Improvement Act 1898, the Mysore Improvement Act 1903 and the Calcutta Improvement Act 1911 were legislated. Besides developing some open areas, provisions were made for improving the badly congested areas of towns and cities as these urban problems were menaces to public health. By the beginning of the 20th century, though actively participated in the World War I (1914-18), India started struggling for independence from the colonial rule. It was during this time that Sir Patrick Geddes, a noted Scottish biologist and sociologist came to India and pioneered the town and country planning activities in the country. He spearheaded the town planning movement and based on the British Town Planning Act, 1909; a catena of town planning laws was enacted in India. The first town planning legislation was the Bombay Town Planning Act 1915. Subsequently, the U.P. Town Improvement Act 1919, the Madras Town Planning Act 1920 and the Andhra Town Planning Act 1920 were legislated and building byelaws were also framed which empowered the State Governments to prepare the master plans and town planning schemes. Thereafter, the concept of town planning began to spread far and wide to other towns and cities. The setting up of the Bhore Committee in the year 1946 to look into the adaptability of the Town Planning Acts gained further momentum.

In the North-Eastern Region of India, the concept of modern town planning was unknown till the early 1950s. It was only after the enactment of the Assam Town and Country Planning Act 1959, modern town planning ushered in this region. This Act empowers town planners to prepare master plans, formulate building byelaws, identify, and declare certain urban settlements as slum areas, etc. Prior to that, towns and cities such as Guwahati, Shillong, Jorhat, Dibrugarh, Agartala, Sivasagar, Imphal, Gangtok, Kohima, Aizawl and other towns already grew in an unplanned manner and hence the problems of traffic congestion, solid waste management, pollution etc. With the rapid rate of urbanisation, unplanned towns and cities, hilly or plain, exhibited their horizontal and vertical expansion. To meet the social, economic and aesthetic needs; urban roads, flyovers, parking lots, parks, EWS housing, educational buildings, public buildings, shopping malls, stadia and other physical amenities were built by the Government and non-governmental agencies. However, such facilities were not proportionate with the demographic profiles. In 1901, the urbanization rate was 11.4% only which rose to 28.53% in 2001 and is currently standing at 31.16 % for the country and 27.72% for the NER as per the 2011 census. The World Population Report 2007 projected that by 2030 India's rate of urbanization would shoot up to 40.76%. Unplanned urban expansion results in the abuse, misuse and under-utility of urban spaces and ultimately deters provision of smart mobility, green buildings, green roads etc. within the urban centres. Townsfolk face common problems such as poor housing, overcrowding, inner city decays, existence of slums, unplanned ribbon developments, lack of green spaces, recreation centres, shopping malls, parking spaces, standard pedestrian facilities, cycle tracks, proper solid waste management, mushrooming of street vendors, hawkers and peddlers besides other negative externalities such as traffic congestion, traffic accidents and pollution. Further, lack of civic sense in caring their own towns and cities begets unclean streets, polluted rivers, unhygienic sewers and other negative externalities. which is unacceptable to a civilised society. It is in this context that John Osman, the former Vice-President of the Ford Foundation told the Americans, "Building a city is a sacramental act on the part of the whole people... For the design of a city is not to be found on the drawing board of the city planner. The forms of the city live in its people. They emerge out of the mind and spirit of its citizens. They reside in the very history of the place."

Physical decay of buildings, transport systems, sewerage systems, power generation systems, parking spaces, green spaces and other urban components caused by high degree of obsolescence, incompatible mixed land uses, poor quality control during construction, archaic roads, ineffectual zoning, increase of vehicles, population growth, irresponsible civic management, financial constraints of ULBs, non-availability of urban spaces and other unplanned activities menaced health, increased crime rates and brought about traffic snarls and injury. Evolution of unplanned towns and cities added by the accelerated rate of physical deterioration of the existing urban inventory and facilities eroded their utility, amenity, and aesthetic beauty. Urban renewal which is a process of rejuvenation of slums, decay and congestion by improving the housing conditions, existing transport systems, sewerage systems etc. is an indispensable means of transforming unplanned towns and cities into green urban settlements. Involvement of traditional institutions, ULBs including town committees, NGOs, firms, companies and other stakeholders in the process of rehabilitation and conservation of green spaces, clearance and redevelopment of squalid CBDs, twilight zones, blighted neighbourhoods, worn-out areas and gentrification is thus considered expedient. It is the bounden duty of the townlings to bear the transitory inconveniences and pains whenever the Government initiates urban renewal programmes and aggressive planning measures so that resettlement plans will not remain merely artists' conceptions and models but are substances of reality and utility.

Realizing the palpable problems of towns and cities and to pre-empt urban decay in future, the North-East Council for Social Science Research (NEICSSR), Shillong unanimously resolved and held the two-day seminar on the 20th and the 21st November, 2017 at Shillong Law College, Shillong. The overall objective of holding this seminar was to devise ways and means to mitigate these urban problems by pooling together the knowledge and skills of professional planners, architects and generalists. Consequently, they recommended suitable alleviation measures and policies for urban renewal and gentrification in towns and cities which exist in this part of the planet. Most of the articles found in this book relate to the modern period of town planning. Though few articles could not be presented and discussed during the two-day seminar, however, they are included in this book for the benefit of readers, professionals, academicians, and practitioners.

We hope that the book is of immense help and a way forward for the officials, policy makers, legislators, investors, students, research scholars, academicians, and the readers to concretise and actualise the recommended measures, strategies and suggestions in furtherance of the agenda of urban renewal and creation of new townships in order to mitigate the gravity of urban problems to the largest possible extent.

Shillong, **Editors**
16 August 2024

Acknowledgements

In producing this book, we offer a deep sense of gratitude to a number of scholars drawn from different universities, institutions, Government Departments and Ministries who presented their articles for the benefits of the readers, policy makers, research scholars and practitioners. Particular mentions are made here for the North Eastern Council (NEC), Ministry of Development of North-Eastern Region, Government of India for funding the seminar, the Principal of Shillong Law College for giving permission to hold the seminar within its premises and also to the officials of Planning Department, Government of Meghalaya for facilitating the proposal to the NEC in a timely manner. We are also thankful to Mr. A.K.M, Karin, a retired Adviser & Director of Housing, Government of Meghalaya, for his consent to give a Forward of this book when we approached him despite his busy schedule and advanced age.

We record our gratitude for the help and advice received from Mr. Ashok K. Mittal of Concept Publishing Company Pvt. Ltd., New Delhi. We deeply acknowledge the kind of technical assistance rendered by the firm in publishing the volume of the book expeditiously.

16 August 2024

P.S. Ñianglang
S. Sarma

Contents

PART B
Principles, Strategies and Policies Recommnded by Economists, Geographers, Sociologists and Lawyers

List of Contributors

Ajit Debnath, Research Scholar, Department of Economics, Rajiv Gandhi University, Rono Hills, Itanagar. **Email:** ajitdebnathrgu@gmail.com

Amitava Mitra, Professor, Department of Economics, Rajiv Gandhi University, Rono Hills, Itanagar. **Email:** amitraau@rediffmail.com

Bibhash Dhar, Superintending Anthropologist (Cul) (Retd.), Anthropological Survey of India, N.E. Regional Centre, Shillong. **Email:** bibhash9@gmail.com

Biswajyoti Das Gupta, Deputy Director of Census Operations, Ministry of Home Affairs, Government of India, Sikkim. **Email:** bdasgupta.rgi@censusindia.gov.in

Dharani Dhar Mali, Director (Retd.), Indian Institute of Entrepreneurship (IIE), Guwahati. **Email:** ddmali@hotmail.com

Daiahunlin Mawlong, Assistant Professor, Shillong Law College. **Email:** daiamawlong25@gmail.com

Donna Rica Diengdoh, Assistant Professor, Department of Sociology, Shillong College, Shillong. **Email:** donnadiengdoh@yahoo.co.in

Elangmiki Shullai, Assistant Urban Planner, Department of Urban Affairs, Government of Meghalaya, Shillong. **Email:** elangshullai@yahoo.com

Gitumoni Rajbongshi, Research Scholar, Department of Economics, North-Eastern Hill University, Shillong. **Email:** gitueco23@gmail.com

Grace Dorathy Laloo, Guest Lecturer, Department of Architecture, North-Eastern Hill University, Shillong. **Email:** grace29dorathy@gmail.com

Kiran Sharma, Research Scholar, Department of Geography, Gauhati University, Guwahati. **Email:** krnsharma05@gmail.com

Nabanita Kanungo, Principal, Paragon Junior College, Karimganj, Assam. **Email:** tia18nabanita@gmail.com

Namrata Talukdar, Assistant Professor, Architecture and Planning, Guwahati College of Architecture & Planning, Guwahati. **Email:** namratatalukdar91@gmail.com

Phibankhamti Ryngnga, Associate Professor, Department of Geography, North-Eastern Hill University, Shillong. **Email:** kryngnga@yahoo.com

Phain Singh Ñianglang, Chief Planning Officer & *ex officio* Joint Secretary to the Government of Meghalaya, Department of Planning, Shillong. **Email:** dr.psnianglang1962@gmail.com

Parangam Sarma Basistha, Assistant Professor in Architecture and Planning, Guwahati College of Architecture and Planning, Guwahati. **Email:** psbasistha32@gmail.com

Phiralin Amy Marsing, Research Scholar, Department of Sociology, University of Science and Technology, Meghalaya. **Email:** amymarsing21@gmail.com

Pranay Jyoti Goswami, Department of Commerce, Assam University, Silchar. **Email:** pranay.jyoti.goswami@aus.ac.in

Rimeka Dora Ranee, Assistant Professor, Department of Architecture, North-Eastern Hill University, Shillong. **Email:** raneerimeka@gmail.com

Sanjay Gupta, Professor and Head, Department of Transportation Planning, School of Planning and Architecture, Delhi. **Email:** drsgupta19@gmail.com

Siddheswar Sarma, (Retd.) Senior Cartographer, North-Eastern Hill University, Shillong. **Email:** sarma.siddheswar54@gmail.com

Sumana Paul, (Retd.) Assistant Professor, Women College, Shillong. **Email:** paulsumana13@gmail.com

Utpal Kumar De, Professor, Department of Economics, North-Eastern Hill University, Shillong. **Email:** utpalkde@gmail.com

Vinitoli H. Zhimo, Research Scholar, Department of Sociology, University of Science and Technology, Meghalaya.

Vitsosie Vupru, Assistant Professor, Dimapur Government College, Dimapur, Nagaland. **Email:** vupruv@gmail.com

PART-A
Principles, Strategies and Policies Recommended by Professional Planners and Architects

1
Urban Sprawl in Shillong

Unregulated Urban Growth and Considerations for the Future

Elangmiki Shullai

Introduction

Indian cities have been undergoing rapid urban growth in the last few decades since our Independence. Our urban fringes are evolving on a regular basis, at a time when basic services are still yet to be fully developed within our core cities. Such unplanned development which lacks infrastructural support is a threat to the future of our cities and citizens. The capital cities of Indian hill states in particular which are witnessing urban growth are facing distinct issues due to their terrain and inadequate infrastructural development. Urban sprawl which is occurring in these cities is largely sporadic and has resulted in a litany of problems ranging from being exposed to hazards like man-made disasters to unregulated construction of buildings and considerable migration into congested urban areas. Urban sprawl can be defined as an uncontrolled expansion of cities from central urban areas into low-density areas. The spread of urban areas into rural area, forests and farmlands in particular influences the physical limits of cities. The economic potential of cities attracts migration from rural to urban areas as people aim to secure better livelihoods and better standards of living. The resulting population expansion can only be accommodated through the physical growth of cities (Brueckner, 2000). In this regard, it has become necessary to understand this phenomenon and question the urban growth so that the future of our cities can be secured (Donella Meadows, 2005).

Urban Sprawl in Indian Hill Towns

Urban sprawl and its related issues pertaining to the capital cities of Shimla, Gangtok and Kohima will be investigated to observe the gamut of factors at play and to identify important observations. As the capital city of Himachal Pradesh, Shimla is an important urban centre for administrative, educational and tourism functions. The concentration of functions has led it to be a primate city in the state of Himachal Pradesh and experiences considerable growth. The Shimla Planning Area was constituted in 1977 to control the future development and growth of the city. Despite this, ribbon development has occurred along major roads branching out from the city as the city core is already congested. Urban sprawl has also claimed the sloping areas of the city where direct access through road networks is impossible. Some of the outgrowths are constructed on slopes which are greater than 45 degrees and are prone to landslides and damage in an earthquake (Town and Country Planning Organisation, 2015). With an urban density of 7600 persons per sq.km and an estimated ninety per cent (90%) of the city being built on such slopes, vulnerability is created as people cannot be tended to or evacuated in emergency scenarios. Inadequate planning has been identified as one of the major causes of the city's uncontrolled sprawl and suitable corrective measures will be required to solve the problems in the city (Shekhar, 2011).

The city of Kohima has experienced physical expansion over several decades. In 1975, the total built up area of the city was 4.83 sq. km which expanded to 11.42 sq. km by 2005, overshooting the present municipal boundary. Urban sprawl has manifested itself in all directions and the town has expanded for various reasons. Urban sprawling has taken place along the main road arteries and the high density of the core area has facilitated the creation of neighbourhoods along the periphery of the municipal area. The city features unplanned growth as a result and the hilly terrain has made it difficult to control the development of the city (Hiese, 2008).

In 1951, the population of Gangtok was a mere 2744 and this Figure has since then grown to 100286 in 2011. This represents a jump of 35.54 per cent in 60 years. The rapid increase in urban growth in Gangtok is creating a demand for urban land to accommodate the additional population. This has resulted in the deforestation of forest areas and has witnessed the encroachment of the urban areas onto vacant land (Yogesh Neopane, 2016). The urban sprawl that has taken over the city has been unregulated and there is little regard for building construction regulations. The augmentation and expansion of the existing infrastructural facilities and the implementation of development schemes in the city has created an additional thrust in urbanization. The migration of unemployed population into the city has created problems of congestion, housing shortages, water scarcity etc. (Sharma, 2016).

Urban Growth and Sprawl in Shillong

Since the British occupation, Shillong has become an important institutional centre with the presence of educational, medical and administrative institutions, some of which were set up during this period. Good schools have been set up here and have drawn students from the entire North-Eastern region. There are also thirty colleges currently under the Directorate of Higher and Technical Education (Education Department, Government of Meghalaya, 2017) and Central Institutions such as the North-Eastern Hill University, the Indian Institute of Management and the National Institute of Technology. The major hospitals in the Greater Shillong Planning Area are NEIGRIHMS (North Eastern Indira Gandhi Regional Institute of Health and Medical Sciences), Civil Hospital, Woodland Hospital, Dr. H. Gordon Roberts Hospital etc. As the capital city of the State of Meghalaya there are many crucial administrative bodies such as the Main Secretariat, High Court and the Meghalaya Assembly. Due to the establishment of these institutional functions over the past century, Shillong has witnessed a considerable growth. In the 1950s after India gained its Independence, the urban growth in Shillong Municipal area was characterized by migration from rural areas into localities with space for development such as Laban, Malki and Laitumkhrah. Gradually this led to an urban sprawl which resulted in the creation of new neighbourhoods beyond the Municipal area. The current towns of Mawlai and Nongthymmai began developing in this period and were considered part of an urban agglomeration by 1961 (Singh, 1992). An urban agglomeration is a contiguous assembly of at least two urban centres with a statutory urban local body and a population of more than 20,000 as per the 2001 Census (Census of India, 2001). To understand the urban sprawl in Shillong since this period, the growth of the municipal area will be examined first. The Shillong Municipal area covers an area of 10.36 sq. km and development has been taking place within its domain since its constitution. Table 1.1 indicates the decadal population growth and density of the Shillong Municipal area. The decadal growth of population from 1971 to 1991 has exhibited an almost constant growth of more than twenty present (20%). In this period, the density of population in the Municipal area has grown from 8461 persons per sq.km to 12714 persons per sq.km. Until 1971, the density within the Municipal area was within the figure of

6000-9000 persons per sq. km for medium hill towns as per the URDPFI Guidelines, 2014. Since 1981 however, this figure rises from 10543 persons per sq.km to 13825 persons per sq.km as of 2011. Considering an upper limit of 9000 persons per sq.km, the density in 2011 has overshot this by almost 54 per cent. Within this time, the decadal growth rate has also slowed down to a mere 7.79 per cent in 2011 (Census of India, 2011). The overshoot in density and decreased decadal growth rate is indicative that the efficiency and productivity of urban infrastructure and services within the Shillong Municipality are approaching an operative ceiling (Florida, 2012). Such a condition has fostered the over spilt population to sprawl onto the neighbouring Census Towns (CTs). Since the Shillong Urban Agglomeration (SUA) was formed in 1961, rural to urban migration as well as urban sprawl have contributed to the growth of the CTs as can be seen in Figure 1.1 and the statistics associated with this are shown in Table 1.2.

Table 1.1: Demographic Statistics of the Shillong Municipal Area (1971-2011)

Year	Population	% Decadal Growth	Area (sq. km)	Density (Persons/ sq.km)
1971	87659	21.01	10.36	8461
1981	109244	24.62		10543
1991	131719	20.57		12714
2001	132876	0.88		12826
2011	143229	7.79		13825

Source: Census of India, 201.

Table 1.2: Decadal Growth Rate and Density of the Census Towns in SUA

Year	Number of Census Towns in Shillong Urban Agglomeration	Population	Decadal Growth (%)	Area (sq. km)	Density (persons per sq. km)
1971	2	30363		9.601	
	Nongthymmai	16103	67.21	3.461	4653
	Mawlai	14260	56.69	6.140	2322
1981	4	58839		14.200	
	Nongthymmai	21558	33.88	3.461	4653
	Mawlai	20405	43.09	6.140	2322
	Madanriting	6165		2.2460	2745

contd...

contd...

Year	Number of Census Towns in Shillong Urban Agglo-meration	Population	Decadal Growth (%)	Area (sq. km)	Density (persons per sq. km)
	Pynthorumkhrah	10711		2.353	4552
1991	4	80571		14.200	
	Nongthymmai	30964	43.63	3.461	8947
	Mawlai	26938	32.02	6.140	4387
	Madanriting	8987	45.77	2.2460	4001
	Pynthorumkhrah	13682	27.74	2.353	5815
2001	5	122620		15.690	
	Nongthymmai	34209	10.48	3.461	9884
	Mawlai	38241	41.96	6.140	6228
	Madanriting	16700	35.82	2.2460	7435
	Pynthorumkhrah	22108	61.58	2.353	9396
	Nongmynsong	11362		1.490	7626
2011	10	199600		77.31	
	Nongthymmai	38004	11.09	3.461	10981
	Mawlai	55012	43.86	6.140	8960
	Madanriting	29194	74.81	2.2460	12998
	Pynthorumkhrah	27219	23.12	2.353	11568
	Nongmynsong	15017	32.17	1.490	10079
	Mawpat	6184		8.250	750
	Umpling	8529		24.560	347
	Nongkseh	4846		12.360	392
	Umlyngka	7381		6.970	1059
	Lawsohtun	8214		9.480	866

Source: Census of India, 2011.

The decadal growth rate of towns has exhibited an upward trend in the past few decades. As is evident from Table 1.2, however, it is observed that once the density of a town overshoots a certain threshold, the decadal growth rate reduces drastically. The three towns of Nongthymmai, Pynthorumkhrah and Madanriting are amongst the oldest census towns of SUA. Nongthymmai demonstrated an average decadal growth of 48.24 per cent from 1971 to 1991. In the same period, the density rose from 4653 to 8947 persons per sq.km. Thereafter, the decadal growth figures decreased to 10.48 per cent in 2001 and 11.09 per cent in 2011. Similarly, the town of Pynthorumkhrah experienced a reduced decadal growth of 23.12 per cent in 2011 from 61.58 per cent in 2001, at which point its density was at

9396 persons per sq. km (Census of India, 2011). For the remaining towns in the SUA where density is low and developable land is available, an accelerated decadal growth continues until the density reaches a threshold.

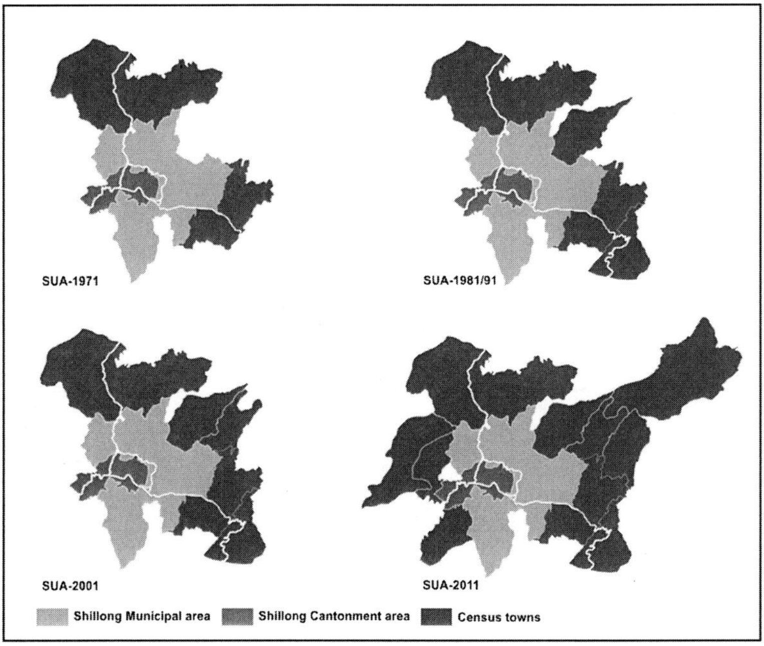

Figure 1.1 Evolution of the Shillong Urban Agglomeration (SUA)

Source: Author.
(Not to scale)

Figure 1.2 shows the decadal growth rate and density of Nongthymmai, Madanriting and Pynthorumkhrah. Looking at Fig. 1.2, it can be seen that the decadal growth rate of the towns reduces when the density is at approximately 10,500 persons per square kilometre. This corresponds to what is seen in the municipal area where the decadal growth rate starts reducing from 1981-91 onwards when the density of the town was 10,543 persons per square kilometre. This figure seems to indicate the threshold density for towns in the urban agglomeration. This is reflected on the ground where the congestion is very high in these towns. Additional population in these towns began to migrate to other census towns and urban fringes where the density is lower. These are the areas where urban sprawl is evident and it appears that a positive growth in population creates urban sprawl (Yogesh Neopane, 2016).

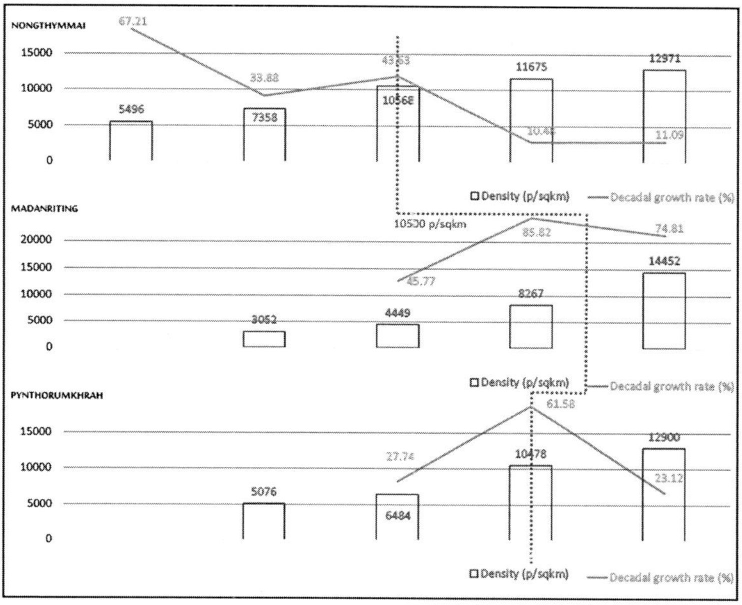

Figure 1.2: Decadal Growth Rate and Density of Nongthymmai, Madanriting and Pynthorumkhrah.

Source: Author.

Urban Development Issues within Shillong Urban Agglomeration

The Meghalaya Urban Development Authority was constituted to enforce the Master Plans for urban areas under the provisions of the Meghalaya Town and Country Planning Act, 1973 and as amended thereafter. MUDA regulates the construction of buildings through the Meghalaya Building Bye Laws 2011. The Byelaws were enforced and published in the Official Gazette of Meghalaya through a notification on the 21st of July 2011 and the extent applies to all Master Plan areas and scheme areas notified and to be notified from time to time as per the Section-A, Sub-Section 1.2 of the Meghalaya Building Byelaws, 2011 (Urban Affairs Department, 2011). However, objections came from the Khasi Hills Autonomous District Council on the ground that the bye laws were to be exempted from being applicable beyond the municipal area in the SUA and a notification to this effect was released on the 5th of November, 2015. This has had an impact on the nature of urban sprawl that has occurred across SUA. Unregulated building construction which had been the norm in the CTs continued unabated. Considering that Shillong lies in Seismic Zone V, it is imperative that urban development is pursued while taking into consideration the possibility of earthquakes and landslides. In view of this and in pursuance of the orders of the Meghalaya High Court, a notification was issued on the 21st of January, 2016, informing the general public on the applicability of the Meghalaya Building Byelaws 2011 within the Shillong Master Plan area. Although this has been a positive step in ensuring the safety of the urban areas, the delayed measure means that the building stock created as a result of the high growth rate requires an assessment and retrofitting measures to ensure that preventive action is taken in the event of natural disasters.

Further, the presence of multiple urban governance institutions in the SUA including the several government line departments, Shillong Municipal Board, Meghalaya Urban Development Authority and the traditional local bodies or Dorbars with only the Shillong Municipal area being a statutory town has resulted in a lopsided distribution of schemes and funds within the SUA. Urban sprawl has contributed to the establishment of the census towns which function without any statutory urban local body and do not receive the same degree of benefits as the municipal area. The prominence of the traditional local institutions known as the "Dorbars" plays an important role in the development of the census towns (Shullai, 2015). Urban development of the municipal area is being pursued through the implementation of various development schemes. The Centrally Sponsored Schemes being implemented in Shillong require the presence of a statutory urban local body which includes the urban development schemes of Atal Mission for Rejuvenation and Urban Transformation (AMRUT) and the Swachh Bharat Mission (Urban). The Swachh Bharat Mission (Urban) is a national programme initiated by the Ministry of Housing and Urban Affairs to solve sanitation and solid waste management issues. It involves the construction of individual households, community and public toilets to eradicate open defecation. Solid waste management becomes one of the primary areas for Indian cities due to the increased generation of waste and a need to improve the overall system. An effective solid waste management system usually includes a segregation of waste at the household level, door-to-door collection, transportation and processing for disposal of the waste depending on the category of waste (Ministry of Housing and Urban Affairs, Government of India). As such, the Mission is being implemented in all the statutory towns of the State. However, in the first meeting of the State High Powered Committee under SBM-Meghalaya, it was decided to include in the Mission all census towns of the SUA through the involvement of the Deputy Commissioner.

Table 1.3 shows the funds allocated to the SUA under the components of Individual Household Toilets (IHTs), Community Toilets (CTs), Solid Waste Management (SWM), Public Awareness with IEC and Capacity Building for the period 2014-15. It categorizes the SUA as including the Shillong Municipal area, the Shillong Cantonment area and the ten CTs as one entity. The first two towns have dedicated ULBs in the form of the Shillong Municipal Board and the Shillong Cantonment Board to implement the components of the Mission. The CTs will be managed by the office of the Deputy Commissioner, East Khasi Hills District which is ill equipped to handle the technical aspects of the Mission. This is reflected in the quantum of funds allocated to the CTs where the per capita allocation is Rs 19.95/person which is smaller than the Shillong Cantonment area's Figure of Rs 74.35/person and the Shillong Municipal area's Figure of Rs. 142.56/person (Urban Affairs Department, 2017).

Table 1.3 Distribution of Funds Under Swatch Bharat Mission (Urban) within SUA (2014-15)

(Rupees in Lakhs)

SUA Towns	Implem-enting Bodies	Popu-lation 2011	IHHL + CT	SWM	Public Aware-ness + IEC	Capacity Building	Total
Shillong Municipal area	Shillong Municipal Board	143229	4.67	184.87	11.61	3.04	204.19
Shillong Cantonment area	Shillong Cantonment Board	11930	0.90	6.75	0.97	0.25	8.87
10 Census Towns	Deputy Commissioner, East Khasi Hills District	199600	8.99	10.48	16.18	4.24	39.89

Source: Urban Affairs Department, 2017.

The AMRUT Mission was launched to ensure that cities have improved and effective urban infrastructure. In Meghalaya, only the Shillong Municipal area has been selected. Under the Mission, the works approved for Shillong includes sewerage management for 2 sub-zones and construction of green spaces and parks. Urban reforms management will also be undertaken which includes e-governance, urban planning, review of building bye laws, municipal tax and fees improvement, energy and water audit. For 2015-16, the Government of India has approved the project funds of Rs. 22.81 crore while for 2016-17 the Ministry has approved Rs. 26.67 crore (Urban Affairs Department, 2017). Apart from the implementation of central sector schemes to improve urban development, the construction of commercial infrastructure such as the Polo Market redevelopment will be an added benefit to the citizens in the municipal area (Urban Affairs Department). Additionally, since the CTs are classified as urban areas, they do not receive any funds from the rural sector, particularly from the Community & Rural Development Department. Thus, there is a need to provide an equitable and inclusive mode of urban development in the areas that have been undertaken by urban sprawl. Urban sprawl itself should be limited to provide control on the efficiency of urban services.

Addressing Congestion through the New Shillong Township

As discussed earlier, Shillong has reached a high level of saturation in density due to urbanization over several decades. The provision of infrastructure and services cannot keep pace with the growth leading to overcrowding and growth of slum-like conditions. This is more prevalent in the CTs which lack a designated ULB to manage urban development. To manage the population growth and unregulated sprawl in the Greater Shillong Planning Area (GSPA), the Shillong Master Plan (1991-2011) was developed. As per the projections of the Master Plan, it was estimated that the population of Shillong by the year 2011 would be 4.93 lakh. To tackle the growth in population of the GSPA, a new satellite township called the New Shillong Township was proposed. The proposed development took into consideration of the integration and distribution of productive forces and population recognizing the spatial and locational aspects of economic growth and desirable physical environment for the need and welfare of the population. The growth of the SUA and the municipal area in particular was headed for stagnation and there was a need for decentralization of administrative functions and channelising investments of infrastructure to a new town which would promote the economic development of the area. Taking advantage of the climatic condition, I.T. based activities and services sector such as education, health centre etc. were prioritized including tourism and urban forestry. Within the New Shillong Township area, there are 6 habitat villages which have been integrated with the overall planning and development of the new town. The implementation of the New Shillong Township involves a controlled mechanism of urban sprawl to address various issues faced within the SUA (Urban Affairs Department, 2015).

The provision of a new satellite township involves the setting up of infrastructural facilities. Presently, the allotment of land to various public-sector organizations has been completed to promote development of the township and henceforth the provision of infrastructure will become a top priority. For provision of infrastructure, there is an urgent need to develop the road network, water supply, sewerage, drainage and power network in the township. The financing options to achieve this include the public sector, private sector or development through a public-private partnership. A sole government funding would be ideal in case there is a land bank available with the Government. However, mobilization of considerable capital investment becomes a constraint and also acceptability of people is low. Private sector investment would be difficult in the present scenario due to the absence of a competent regional private firm to take up the matter. Meghalaya also has a unique land tenure system which becomes a deterrent for private sector investment (Urban Planning Department, School of Planning and Architecture, 2008). The development of housing colonies would be driven by market forces and hence housing for LIG/EWS groups can be marginalised. A PPP mode is desirable from the point of view of policy makers as the control mechanism would be with the government which would act as a facilitator. This attracts private sector investment in housing and commercial sectors while protecting the interests of the marginalised groups. The risk factor for the private investor would also be perceptibly lower. A detailed study is necessary for decision of option which is most feasible for infrastructure development of the township.

Infrastructure development also brings demerits. When urban centres become large with the inclusion of low density sprawling neighbourhoods, they will require an efficient public transport system and an adequate road network, compelling people to depend on motorized transport. Residents of these neighbourhoods would also have to spend more on transportation costs than those that live within the primate city. This leads to social isolation as people spend more time commuting than engaging in social interaction. It also causes health problems such as obesity and asthma. Auto emissions also increase, which in turn causes threats to the environment in the form of global warming (Peter Newman, 1992). Considering the incidences of man-made disasters that have taken place such as urban flooding along Wah Umkhrah in Polo area and landslides in certain localities, an increase in hard paved areas in these urban centres may lead to higher incidences of flooding and erosion. There will also be a loss of valuable open green spaces and forest areas which will aggravate this further (Lyngdoh, 2011).

The Way Forward

Considering the gamut of issues at play, multiple interventions can be explored that may become the statutory solutions in the future. To streamline the multiplicity of governance institutions operating in the SUA, a unified urban development structure is required for the urban management to arrive at a holistic development vision of the city of Shillong which considers all the stakeholders who provide and manage urban services (Shullai, 2015). This may help to ensure an inclusive mode of development for all the ten towns present in the SUA. With the CTs displaying high growth rate and urban densities, the prevailing building regulations may be examined to better manage this. The Meghalaya Building Byelaws, 2011 were amended in 2015 as a result of the orders of the Meghalaya High Court whereby the maximum number of storeys were limited to four. This was done without changing the ground coverage and Floor Area Ratio (FAR) provisions (Urban Affairs Department, 2015). Considering the concentration of improvement schemes for infrastructure in the municipal area, a high-density mode of regulated development may be adopted to preserve the remaining green open spaces. The maximum utilization of land can be achieved by increasing the FAR and ground coverage provisions especially for core commercial areas while retaining the height restrictions. The integration of development policies within the framework of the next Master Plan of Shillong can help propagate this vision further (Leitmann, 1999). Restricting urban sprawl may also be achieved by levying certain charges on the conversion of valuable open space to alternative uses to maintain the quantum of green zones available within the urban boundary. While such alternatives to urban sprawl may not seem to be immediately attractive, they may be the solutions that will help us create an urban environment that is sustainable (Brueckner, 2000). Furthermore, in an effort to provide sustainability within the notified urban areas and to reduce the dependency on city infrastructure, provision of low cost and passive green technologies should be promoted such as the use of solar power and wind energy. A comprehensive investigation into these aspects can further help provide specific measures which are tailor made for the socio-economic and geographical context of Shillong.

REFERENCES

Brueckner, J.K., (2000), Urban Sprawl: Diagnosis and Remedies. *International Regional Science Review*, 160-171.

Census of India, (2011), District *Census Handbook, East Khasi Hills.* Directorate of Census Operations, Meghalaya.

Census of India, (2011), Retrieved from http://censusindia.gov.in/2011-prov results/paper 2/data_files/India2/1.%20Data%20Highlight.pdf

Community and Rural Development Department. (2017). Retrieved from http://megcnrd. gov.in/schemes.htm.

Department of Education, Government of Meghalaya. (2017). Retrieved from http:// megeducation. gov.in/dhte/colleges.html

Donella Meadows, J.R. (2005). *Limits to Growth—The 30 Year Update.* London: Earthscan.

Florida, R. (2012, May 16). Retrieved from https://www.citylab. com/ design/2012/05/limits-density/2005/

Fiese, J. M. (2008). Urban Sprawl Analysis of Kohima town using Multi-temporal remote sensing data. *The Deccan Geographer*, 33-38.

Leitmann, J. (1999). *Sustaining Cities: Environmental Planning and Management in Urban Design.* New York: McGraw-Hill Professional.

Lyngdoh, A.W. (2011, July 2). Retrieved from https://www.telegraphindia. Com/1110702 /jsp/northeast/story_14185383.jsp

Ministry of Housing and Urban Affairs, Government of India. (2017). Retrieved from http://www.swachhbharaturban.in:8080/sbm/content/writereaddata/ SBM_Guideline.pdf

Peter Newman, J.K. (1992). *Housing, transport and urban form.* Canberra: Australian Govt. Pub. Service.

Sharma, K.P. (2016). Post facto, trends and pattern of Urbanity in Sikkim. *Archives of Applied Science Research*, 43-54.

Shekhar, S. (2011). Urban Sprawl and other Spatial Planning Issues in Shimla, Himachal Pradesh. *Institute of Town Planners, India Journal*, 53-66.

Shullai, E. (2015). An integrated approach to Urban Governance in Shillong, India. *Journal for Studies in Management and Planning*, 192-200.

Singh, G. (1992, May). Urban Growth and Changing Landuse Pattern in Shillong. Shillong, Meghalaya, India: North Eastern Hill University.

Town and Country Planning Organisation. (2015, January). Urban and Regional Development Plans Formulation and Implementation Guidelines, 2014, Volume I. Ministry of Urban Development, Government of India.

Urban Affairs Department. (2011). Meghalaya Building Bye Laws 2011. Shillong, Meghalaya, India: Urban Affairs Department, Government of Meghalaya.

Urban Affairs Department. (2015, April). Concept Paper on new Shillong Township Project. Shillong, Meghalaya: Urban Affairs Department, Government of Meghalaya.

Urban Affairs Department. (2015, June 29). Meghalaya Building (Amendment) Bye-Laws 2015. Shillong, Meghalaya, India: Urban Affairs Department, Government of Meghalaya.

Urban Affairs Department. (2017). Retrieved from http://megurban.gov.in/ ongoing.html

Urban Affairs Department. (2017). Brief on Atal Mission for Rejuvenation and Urban Transformation (AMRUT). Shillong: Urban Affairs Department, Government of Meghalaya.

Urban Affairs Department. (2017, October). Note on status of Swachh Bharat Mission—Urban in Meghalaya as on October 2017. Meghalaya, India: Urban Affairs Department, Government of Meghalaya.

Urban Planning Department, School of Planning and Architecture. (2008). *Strategic Development Plan for Hill Capital ; Case Study—Shillong.* New Delhi: School of Planning and Architecture.

Yogesh Neopane, M.K. (2016). Survey paper on Effect of Urban Sprawling on Deforestation and Encroachment of Land using RS and GIS—A Case Study of Gangtok City. *International Journal of Computer Apllications*, 40-42.

2
Economic and Financial Feasibility of Cable Cars in Hill Cities

Grace Dorathy Laloo

Background

Public transport systems bring in economic, social and environmental improvement to an area. However, in hilly areas, the geographical barriers along with high infrastructure cost may not permit the implementation of public transport systems such as bus rapid transit system or light rail. Hill towns require other systems such as aerial ropeways in aid of urban mobility. The IS 5229:1998 defines ropeway as "the system of overhead ropes on which carriers are used for the purpose of carriage of passengers, animals or goods and includes trestles, ropes, carriers, stations, offices, machinery and other works used for the purpose of or in connection with such aerial ropeway" (Kisan *et al.,* 1998). In India, passenger ropeways have been largely associated with tourism and recreation. A few of the ropeways catering to the tourist needs have been set up in Himachal Pradesh, Uttarakhand, Madhya Pradesh, Andhra Pradesh and West Bengal. In India, so far, none of the existing ropeways is used as a means of urban public transportation such as those in Algeria, Columbia, Brazil and London.

One of the main challenges that a growing hill town faces is the non-availability of land. A situation may arise where expansion of the existing road network to solve the traffic problems is no longer possible. The studies conducted by Doppelmayr found that in order to transport 10000 passengers per hour (5000 in each direction), it is necessary to have 2000 taxi cabs, 100 buses and only one cable car (Solutions 2014). Cable cars can safely overcome any topographical or physical barriers as opposed to other systems in improving the mobility of hill cities. They can fill the gap between facilities that generate traffic such as commercial and public and semi-public zones. It is found that cable cars have a minimum impact on the environment and offers a high benefit-cost ratio. Therefore, a city looking for a system that is comfortable, has high capacity and direct links without extensive infrastructure, should invest in cable car system (Ropeways n.d.).

Need of the Study

Cable cars can connect geographically constrained areas without heavy financial investments or alterations of the natural topography. They have the potential to serve as a stand-alone public transport system in smaller cities and hilly areas. In a hill town, a tramway or a Bus Rapid Transit (BRT) with similar transport capacity induces costs for destruction of hundreds of houses, creates a barrier for pedestrian movement and generates greater noise and air pollution. Cable cars are easier to implement and operate than BRT projects for hilly cities. Developing hill cities require public transport systems that can provide greater value-addition and less financial risk. In view of the city's topographic and land ownership pattern, it may not be feasible to go for large-scale widening of roads.

Objectives

The main objective of the study is to evaluate the economic and financial feasibility of cable cars in developing hill cities.

Literature Review

The consideration of whether a cable car or a bus rapid transit system (BRTS) should be adopted in a hill city is based on more than just analyzing the peak hour peak direction traffic (phpdt) of the city. Understanding the physical structure of the city is essential. Cable cars are found to be feasible in places where securing several kilometres ROW for BRT is not possible and when there is no corridor for BRT that provides satisfactory access or priority. Further, BRT that is built cheaply and covers too short a distance will make operations expensive and unattractive. However, a short ropeway at the right place can be relatively inexpensive for implementation and profitable to operate due to its efficiency and unique service (Bergerhoff and Perschon). Aerial ropeway transit is a transportation mode in which passengers are transported in a cabin that is suspended and pulled by cables (Alshalalfah *et al.,* 2012). The available Aerial Ropeway Transit Technology is as follows:

- **Aerial Tramways:** Two passenger cabins are suspended from one or more track cables and are pulled by the haulage cable.
- **Dual Haul Aerial Tramway:** It has two guide ropes and a haul rope loop per cabin. For the study area, the mono gondola system (MDG system) will best suit the requirements of the city. MDG technology as a transit mode exists in Medellin, Caracas and LaPaz. The type of service that is proposed is the continuous system wherein vehicles are launched from terminals at equal intervals of time. Although the frequency of vehicle launch influences the passengers' waiting time, alignment length does not. For long alignments, this system will provide a superior level of service.

Factors affecting the feasibility of cable cars in hill cities are identified as follows:

- **Technology feasibility**: It includes a study on the geological conditions, terrain conditions, climatic conditions and cable car system construction and maintenance.
- **Land acquisition feasibility**: It includes zoning restrictions, air rights and land acquisition costs.
- **Traffic feasibility**: It includes a study on the transportation function, road network integrity and disaster relief needs.
- **Market feasibility**: It requires an understanding of the demand, growth and market competition.
- **Legal feasibility**: It includes a study on public construction, economic taxation and an environmental impact assessment.
- **Social feasibility:** It includes an understanding of the public expectation and public sector policies.
- **Financial feasibility**: It involves a study on the investment scale, return on investment and payback period.
- **Environmental feasibility**: It includes a study of the effects on the cultural environment, natural environment and ecological environment.

In this study, the financial and economic feasibility was explored for the study area. The study on the feasibility of other factors is not considered in this chapter.

Introduction to Shillong

Shillong lies on the deeply dissected central upland of the Meghalaya plateau as shown in Figure 2.1. The relief of the city varies from 1400 m to 1900 m above the mean sea level (MSL). A large part of the area falls within 5 to 10 slope range while a gentle slope range of 0 to 5 is also found in some stretches on the low relief hillocks. Shillong lies in seismic zone V making it highly vulnerable to earthquakes. The boundary of the study area is the Shillong Urban Agglomeration (SUA) which comprises the areas under the Shillong Municipal Board and the Census Towns (CTs) as shown in Figure 2.1. According to the 2001 Census, the population of the study area is 3,07,675 and has a total area of 89.53 sq.km. The population growth trend indicates that there is an increase in the average annual growth rate from year to year. The average decadal growth rate in the past 10 decades is 26.14 per cent. The road network of the study area is shown in Figure 2.2. The per capita trip rate observed in the city is 1.604 including walk and 1.419 excluding walk. The average trip length (ATL) including walk is 3.19 kms and excluding walk is 3.53 kms. ATL for public work and education are 3.27 kms and 3.56 kms respectively and 27 per cent of the trips are made for the purpose of education. ATL by bus and taxi are 4.69

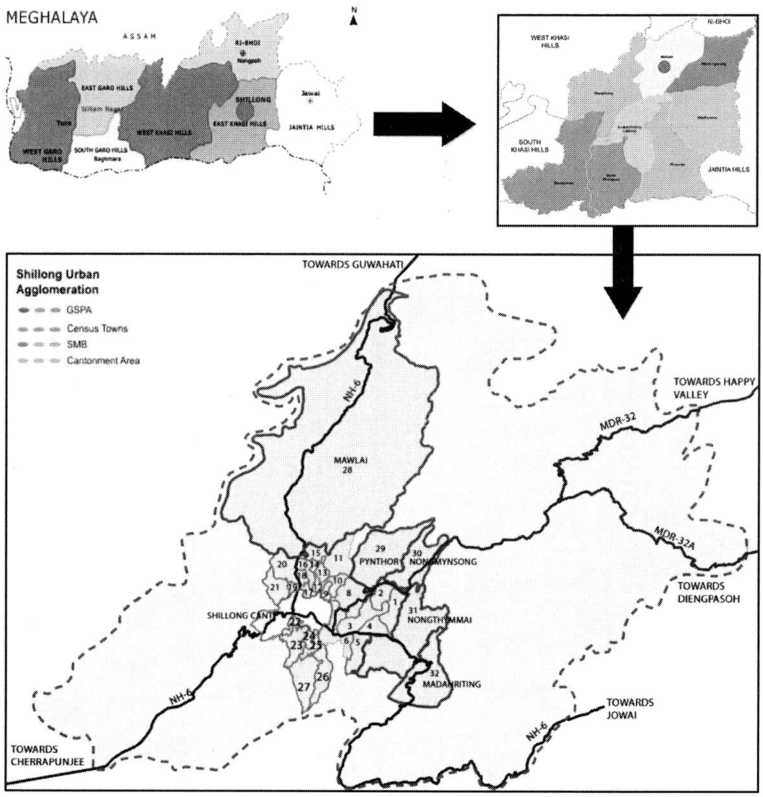

Figure 2.1: Study Area—Shillong Urban Agglomeration

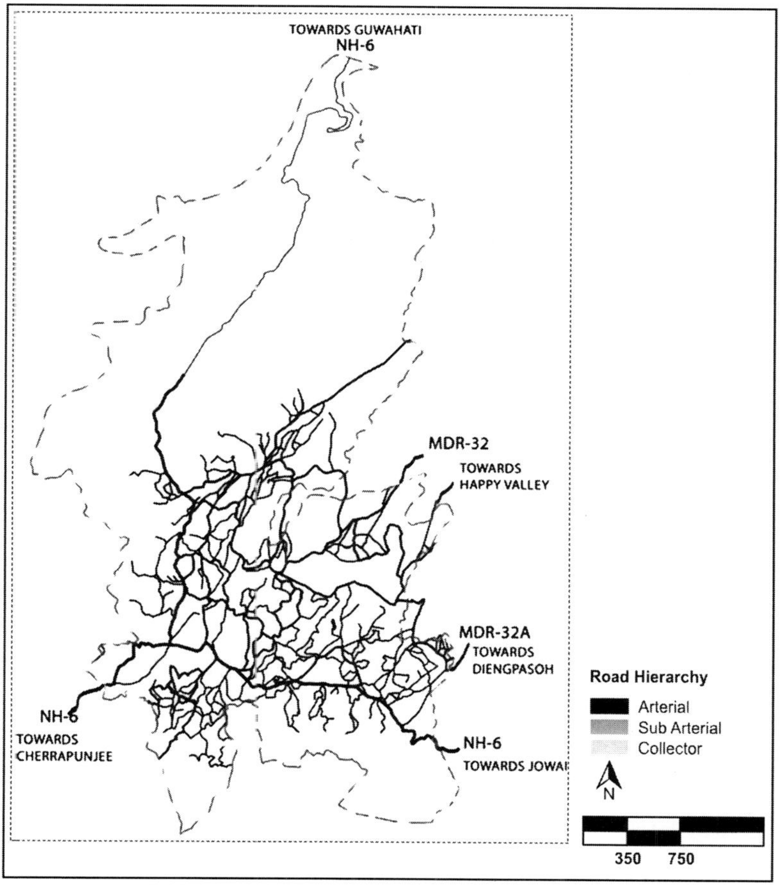

Figure 2.2: Road Network of Shillong

kms and 3.92 kms respectively; 41 per cent of the trips in the city are performed by taxis. The study area has a low average network journey speed with maximum portion of the network exhibiting speeds below 20.00 kmph as shown in Figure 2.3. The average journey speed during peak hours is 14.85 kmph and off peak hours is 23.5 kmph. After carrying out the survey for speed and delay using floating car method, it is found that the various causes of delay are: (i) manual control at intersections, (ii) un-controlled pedestrian movement, (iii) improper location of boarding and alighting points, (iv) bad road condition, (v) limited ROW, and (vi) on-street parking.

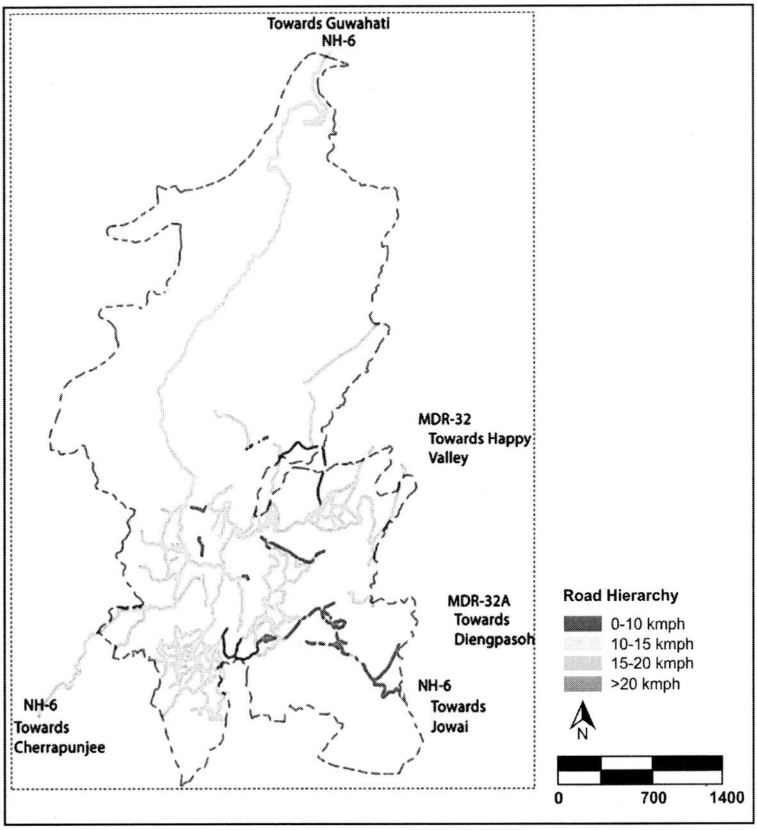

Figure 2.3: Journey Speeds Recorded on the Road Network of Shillong

An analysis of the city shows that the supply of infrastructure has not kept up with the growth of mobility which has led to traffic congestion. It is found that 54 per cent of the roads have right-of-way less than 7 m and the traffic volume or traffic flow in seven critical junctions has exceeded the capacity. According to National Highway Authority of India, on an average, about 35,345 vehicles per day enter/exit Shillong from all the entry points of the city. The rapid growth in private vehicular ownership indicates an increase in the purchasing capacity of the people. The percentage of cabs has been decreasing since 2013 due to the two main reasons, viz. (i) increase in the number of private vehicles and (ii) introduction of the public transport system.Table 2.1 below provides information on the vehicular growth from 2008 to 2016 in Shillong.

Table 2.1: Vehicular Growth

Category of vehicles	2008	2009	2010	2011	2012	2013	2014	2015	2016
Two wheeler	889	1391	1951	2180	2761	2945	3615	3840	2468
Three wheeler	1	2	11	9	1	4	1	2	0
Car	2533	3721	4710	4482	4892	4981	4895	4927	3300
Taxi	446	560	917	788	1155	2030	1080	813	675
Bus	40	26	25	72	125	67	19	24	140
Commercial vehicle	405	524	778	1056	1090	1554	683	590	338
Other non-transport vehicle	59	89	82	69	32	12	21	9	24
Total	4373	6313	8474	8656	10056	11593	10314	10205	6945

Source: City Development Plan 2009.

Cable Car Alignment

The alignment as shown in Figure 2.4 was laid in such a way that the O-D points with the highest demand and tourist areas were given more significance. The guidelines followed in the study while laying down the alignment are as follows:

- Serve the transit corridor, activity centres and tourist areas making use of the existing street and ROW.
- Connect communities to employment centres, shopping/event centres and transit services.
- Connect activity centres over terrain and traffic congestion.
- Service heavy traffic congestion areas where cable cars would be faster than surface bus and vehicles.
- Focus on optimal alignment lengths of half a kilometre with straight alignment section.

The mechanical requirements of the proposed system is given in Table 2.2 below:

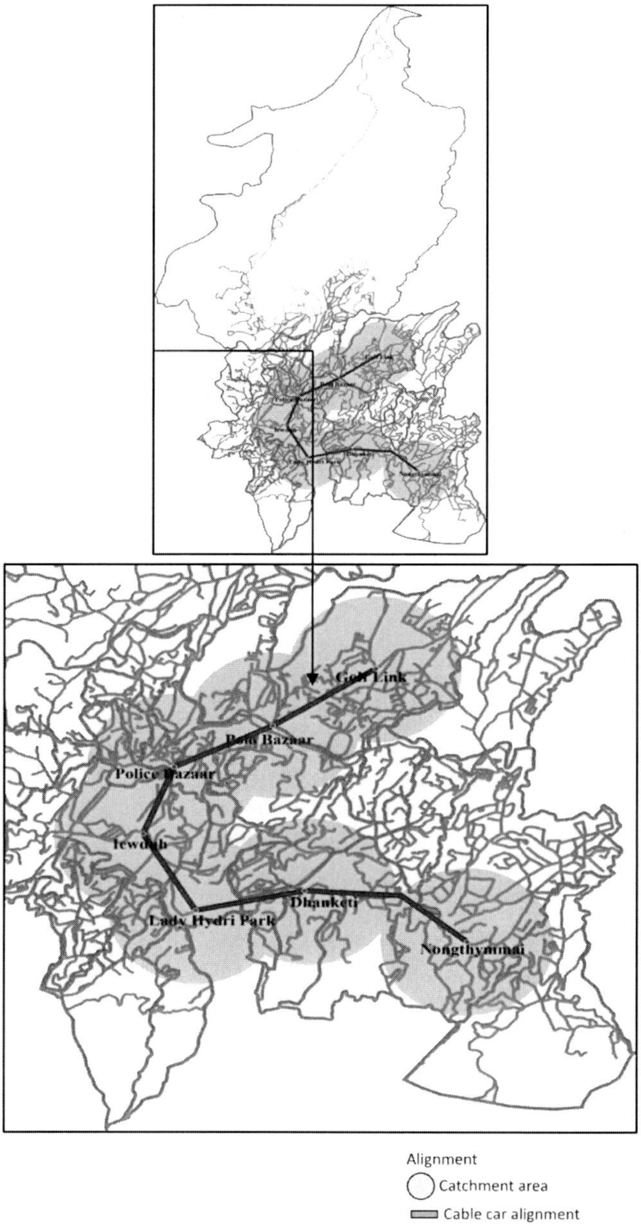

Figure 2.4: Cable Car Alignment

Table 2.2: Mechanical requirements of the proposed system

Sl. No	Mechanical Components of the System	Unit
1	Length	6.8 kms
2	Diameter of the cable	51 mm
3	Cable Speed	21.6 kmph
4	Pylons	9 numbers
5	Diameter of the pylons	1.5 m
6	Height of the pylons	15 m
7	Station with engine	3 numbers
8	Station without engine	4 numbers
9	Cabins	120 Numbers
10	Headway	60 s
11	Operational capacity	1800
12	Cabin capacity	15
13	Propulsion	Electric

The speed at the entry and exit of the station is 1.8 kmph and the minimum distance between the cabins is 0.5 m. The long section chainage from 500 to 1000 along the cable car alignment is shown in Figures 2.5 and 2.6 and the section at chainage 950 is shown in Figure 2.7.

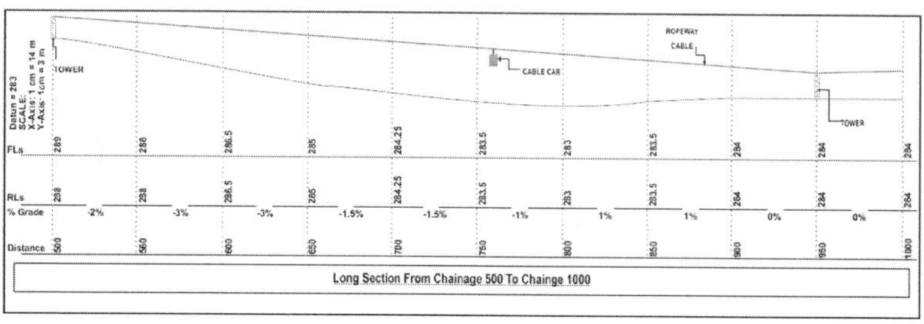

Figure 2.5: Long Section Chainage from 500 to 1000

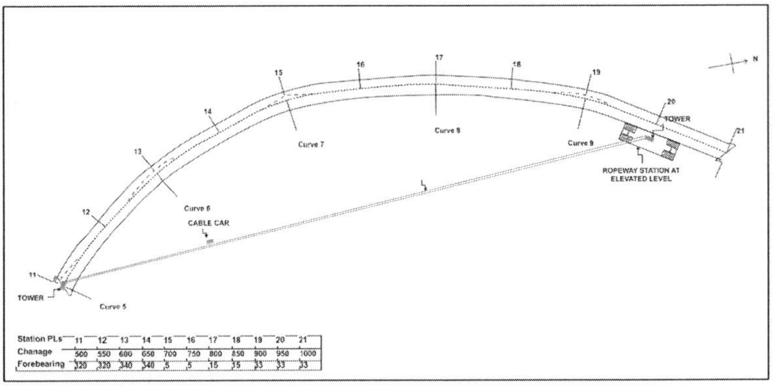

Figure 2.6: Long Section form Chainage 500 to 1000

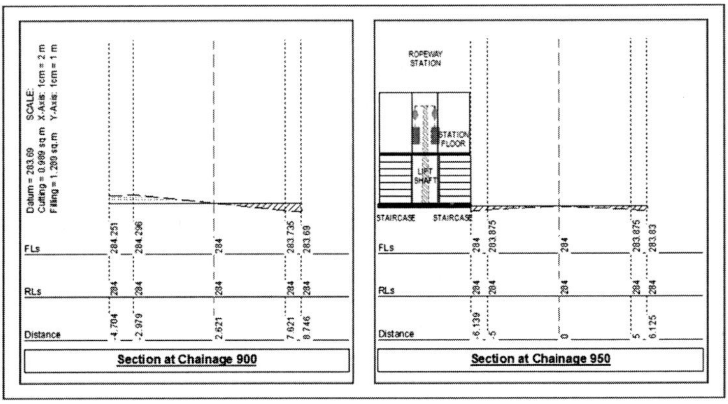

Figure 2.7: Section at Chainage 900 and 950

Financial Analysis

Financial analysis is carried out when a project is expected to generate income. It is necessary to determine the financial profitability of a project in order to know its expected income required for operation and maintenance expenses to make it successful. It also helps to check the long-term sustainability of the project and to come up with cost recovery mechanisms. Financial analysis is always carried out first before proceeding to economic analysis for a clearer understanding. When the comparison of benefits and cost to the investors is carried out, it is called financial analysis but when the comparison is carried out to the entire economy, it is called economic analysis. Due to the non-availability of local or Indian price quotes, estimates from Schneider, Clement-Werny, Transport, 2011 were used to estimate the capital cost of the cable car system at current prices as shown in Tables 2.3 and 2.4.

Table 2.3: Capital Cost of Cable Cars

Cost Estimate	Cost	Quantity	Total cost (in Rs. crores)
Cost of cable/metre	8106.484021	6800	3.810
Cost for pylon	11580691.46	9	3.474
Cost of station with engine	289517286.5	3	86.855
Cost of station without engine	115806914.6	4	46.323
Cost of gondola	3474207.438	120	41.690
Total installation cost			182.153

Table 2.4 Maintenance and Total Cost of Cable Cars

Cost Estimate	Cost	Quantity	Total Cost (in Rs.)
Operation & maintenance	5-10% of Rs. 182.153 crore	–	18.215
Total cost (2017)		–	200.368
Total cost (2021)			262.609

Since the project is proposed for the year 2021, the analysis is carried out in terms of the 2021 prices. Thus, assuming an inflation rate of 7 per cent, the total cost in 2021 becomes Rs. 262.6 crore. The financial cost is calculated using the formula given below:

Financial Cost = Capital Cost + Operation Cost + Annual Maintenance + Periodic Maintenance Cost.

The revenue is the sum of the fare and the advertisement revenue. Thus, revenue is calculated using the formula:

$$Revenue = Fare + Advertisement\ Revenue$$

The fare is taken as Rs. 20 per 3 km and it is assumed that the fare will be increased by 1 per cent every ten years. The advertisement revenue is taken as 10 per cent of the capital cost. The calculation of the financial cash flow statement for the next 30 years is shown in Table 2.5.

Table 2.5: Financial Cash Flow Statement

Year	Total Financial Cost (In Rs.)	Total Revenue (In Rs.)	Net Operating Income (In Rs.)
2021	262.6		-262.6
Start of Operations			
2022	2.63	3.67	1.05
2023	2.81	3.93	1.12
2024	3.01	4.21	1.20
2025	3.22	4.50	1.28
2026	17.21	4.82	-12.40
2027	3.68	5.15	1.47
2028	3.94	5.51	1.57
2029	4.22	5.90	1.68
2030	4.51	6.31	1.80
2031	24.14	6.75	-17.38
2032	5.17	7.23	2.06
2033	5.53	8.51	2.98
2034	5.91	9.10	3.19
2035	6.33	9.74	3.41
2036	33.86	10.42	-23.44
2037	7.25	11.15	3.91
2038	7.75	11.93	4.18
2039	8.30	12.77	4.47
2040	8.88	13.66	4.78
2041	47.49	14.62	-32.87
2042	10.16	15.64	5.48
2043	10.87	18.41	7.53
2044	11.63	19.70	8.06
2045	12.45	21.08	8.63
2046	66.60	22.55	-44.05
2047	14.25	24.13	9.88
2048	15.25	25.82	10.57
2049	16.32	27.63	11.31
2050	17.46	29.56	12.10

Initially, the financial analysis was carried out by considering the revenue from fare box collection and advertisement only. The fare is taken as Rs. 20 per 3kms and it is assumed that the fare will increase by 1 per cent every decade. The advertisement revenue is taken as 10 per cent of the capital cost. The result showed that even after 30 years of operation, the internal rate of return (IRR) would still be negative. Therefore, it is proposed that the Government provides a grant of 40 per cent of the capital cost and levy a tax of 20 per cent on properties along the cable car corridor since the expected property value will increase as a result of increased connectivity. Because a grant of 40 per cent is required, public private partnership is not likely to be feasible for this project. However, for operation and maintenance of the system, PPP appears to be the better option. The financial viability statement of the project is shown in Table 2.6.

Table 2.6: Viability Statement—Financial

Year	Financial Cost	Debt-equity @40% of the cost	Fare + Advertisement Revenue	Property tax @ 20%	Total revenue	NOI after subsidy	FIRR
2021	262.6	105.0				-157.6	
Start of Operations							
2022	2.63	2.63	3.67	6.76	10.43	7.81	
2023	2.81	2.81	3.93	7.23	11.16	8.35	
2024	3.01	3.01	4.21	7.74	11.95	8.94	
2025	3.22	3.22	4.50	8.28	12.78	9.57	
2026	17.21	17.21	4.82	8.86	13.68	-3.53	
2027	3.68	3.68	5.15	9.48	14.63	10.95	
2028	3.94	3.94	5.51	10.14	15.66	11.72	
2029	4.22	4.22	5.90	10.85	16.75	12.54	
2030	4.51	4.51	6.31	11.61	17.93	13.42	
2031	24.14	24.14	6.75	12.43	19.18	-4.96	
2032	5.17	5.17	7.23	13.30	20.53	15.36	-8.07%
2033	5.53	5.53	8.51	14.23	22.74	17.21	-5.00%
2034	5.91	5.91	9.10	15.22	24.33	18.41	-2.71%
2035	6.33	6.33	9.74	16.29	26.03	19.70	-0.89%
2036	33.86	33.86	10.42	17.43	27.85	-6.01	-1.40%
2037	7.25	7.25	11.15	18.65	29.80	22.56	-1.40%

contd...

2038	7.75	7.75	11.93	19.96	31.89	24.13	1.63%
2039	8.30	8.30	12.77	21.35	34.12	25.82	2.71%
2040	8.88	8.88	13.66	22.85	36.51	27.63	3.63%
2041	47.49	47.49	14.62	24.45	39.06	-8.42	3.38%
2042	10.16	10.16	15.64	26.16	41.80	31.64	4.21%
2043	10.87	10.87	18.41	27.99	46.40	35.52	4.95%
2044	11.63	11.63	19.70	29.95	49.65	38.01	5.58%
2045	12.45	12.45	21.08	32.04	53.12	40.67	6.11%
2046	66.60	66.60	22.55	34.29	56.84	-9.76	6.00%
2047	14.25	14.25	24.13	36.69	60.82	46.56	6.49%
2048	15.25	15.25	25.82	39.26	65.07	49.82	6.91%
2049	16.32	16.32	27.63	42.00	69.63	53.31	7.28%
2050	17.46	17.46	29.56	44.94	74.50	57.04	7.61%

Based on the above computations, it is found that the FIRR will initially be negative and will turn positive in the 17th year of operation if the Government contribution to the tune of 40 per cent is provided and a property tax of 20 per cent is levied along the proposed alignment. Without the viability gap funding the FIRR will continue to be negative which is indicative of a non-sustaianble project as it will not be able to generate income. Sensitivity analysis can also be carried out on the risk factors such as the length of the project, costs, discount rates etc. to assess their effects on the expected benefits.

Economic Analysis

Economic analysis is carried out to assess the opportunities that a project will provide. Unlike financial analysis, economic analysis considers other aspects such as the influence of other external factors, the influence of the market, the social and environmental cost etc. The prime objective of economic analysis is to identify and select projects that will benefit a region or a country. This is done by comparing the economic benefits to the economic costs as per calculations shown in Table 2.10 below. The economic cost is calculated using the formula, Economic cost = 0.9 × Financial cost. The system was also examined in terms of travel time savings, fuel cost saving, vehicle operating savings, accident savings and health benefits. Using the wage rate method, the value of travel time is calculated below:

Travel time savings = Savings in delay + waiting + walking time (Hrs/day) × Value of travel time × AADT × 365. The summaries of travel time savings for car, bus and taxi users, fuel savings and health savings are shown in Tables 2.7, 2.8 and 2.9 below.

Table 2.7: Summary of Travel Time Savings for Various Modes

Travel Time savings for Car users	26757373.49	Total (in crores)	4.63	2.68
Travel Time savings for Bus users	5556375.23			0.56
Travel time savings for Taxi users	13937331.87			1.39

Fuel savings = Hours Saved/Day × per cent of vehicles shifting cablecars x fuel price × AADT × 365. The vehicle operating cost (VOC) savings is given by the relation, VOC Savings = 3.1 times fuel cost for heavy vehicles = Fixed cost for car.

Table 2.8: Fuel Savings

	Fuel Saving for Cars		**Fuel Saving for HV**
	Motor Spirit	**HSD**	**HSD**
Hours Saved/Day	101.63	101.63	36
	100%	100%	100%
Fuel Price (%)	86.78	72.74	72.74
Fuel Saving per day (litres)	8820.46	7393.62	2634
Fuel Saving per year (litres)	3219470.442	2698673.753	961291.737
In crores	0.32	0.27	0.10
Total		**0.59**	**0.10**

Health saving is calculated using the following formula:

Health savings = Emission of compound × Vehicle kms × Emission of vehicle per driven km × Health cost. The results of calculations are summarised in Table 2.9 below:

Table 2.9: Health Savings

	CO_2	**CO**	**NO_2**	**SO_2**	**PM**	**HC**	**Total**
PT	0.16	0.008	0.065	0.078	0.0243	0.00029	0.336
IPT	0.11	0.073	0.043	0.009	0.0542	0.00029	0.298
2W	0.06	0.043	0.008	0.006	0.0183	0.00402	0.149
4W	0.45	0.030	0.007	0.019	0.0085	0.00055	0.521

Similarly, accident savings can also be calculated using the following relation:

Accident savings = (Number of serious injuries prevented × 0.25 × 70 × GDP per capita) + (Number of fatalities prevented × 70 × GDP per capita)

Table 2.10: Cash Flow Statement—Economics

(Rs. in Crores)

Year	Economic Cost	Savings in Travel Time	Savings in Fuel	Savings in VOC	Health Benefits	Accident Benefits	Total Benefits	Net Benefits	DF @ 18.47%	EIRR %	Benefits	Costs
2021	236.3						0	-236.3	-236.35		0	236.34
Start of Operations												
2022	2.36	4.63	0.69	0.89	1.31	20.12	27.62	25.26	21.32		23.48	2.01
2023	2.53	5.21	0.79	1.01	1.43	21.52	29.96	27.43	19.55		21.65	1.83
2023	2.71	5.87	0.90	1.15	1.57	23.03	32.52	29.81	17.93		19.98	1.66
2024	2.90	6.62	1.02	1.31	1.73	24.64	35.32	32.42	16.46	-22.97	18.45	1.51
2025	15.49	7.46	1.17	1.49	1.89	26.37	38.38	22.89	9.81	-15.70	17.04	6.88
2026	3.31	8.42	1.34	1.70	2.08	28.21	41.74	38.43	13.90	-7.49	15.76	1.25
2027	3.55	9.50	1.53	1.93	2.28	30.19	45.43	41.88	12.79	-1.83	14.58	1.14
2028	3.80	10.73	1.74	2.20	2.50	32.30	49.47	45.68	11.77	2.28	13.50	1.04
2029	4.06	12.12	1.99	2.50	2.74	34.56	53.92	49.86	10.85	5.37	12.50	0.94
2030	21.73	13.69	2.27	2.85	3.01	36.98	58.81	37.08	6.81	7.07	11.59	4.28
2031	4.65	15.48	2.60	3.25	3.30	39.57	64.20	59.55	9.23	9.10	10.76	0.78
2032	4.97	17.50	2.97	3.69	3.63	42.34	70.13	65.16	8.52	10.70	9.99	0.71
2033	5.32	19.80	3.39	4.21	3.98	45.30	76.68	71.36	7.88	11.99	9.29	0.64
2034	5.70	22.41	3.87	4.79	4.37	48.48	83.92	78.22	7.29	13.05	8.64	0.59
2035	30.47	25.37	4.43	5.46	4.79	51.87	91.91	61.44	4.83	13.69	8.05	2.67

contd...

contd...

Year	Economic Cost	Savings in Travel Time	Savings in Fuel	Savings in VOC	Health Benefits	Accident Benefits	Total Benefits	Net Benefits	DF @ 18.47%	EIRR %	Benefits	Costs
2036	6.52	28.73	5.06	6.21	5.26	55.50	100.76	94.24	6.26	14.45	7.50	0.49
2037	6.98	32.55	5.78	7.08	5.77	59.38	110.56	103.58	5.81	15.09	7.00	0.44
2038	7.47	36.89	6.60	8.06	6.33	63.54	121.42	113.96	5.39	15.63	6.53	0.40
2039	7.99	41.82	7.54	9.18	6.95	67.99	133.48	125.49	5.01	16.10	6.10	0.37
2040	42.74	47.42	8.62	10.46	7.63	72.75	146.87	104.14	3.51	16.40	5.71	1.66
2041	9.15	53.79	9.85	11.92	8.37	77.84	161.77	152.62	4.34	16.75	5.35	0.30
2042	9.79	61.03	11.26	13.58	9.18	83.29	178.34	168.56	4.05	17.06	5.01	0.27
2043	10.47	69.27	12.86	15.48	10.08	89.12	196.81	186.33	3.78	17.33	4.70	0.25
2044	11.20	78.64	14.70	17.64	11.06	95.36	217.39	206.19	3.53	17.57	4.41	0.23
2045	59.94	89.30	16.80	20.10	12.13	102.03	240.37	180.43	2.61	17.74	4.15	1.03
2046	12.83	101.44	19.20	22.91	13.32	109.18	266.04	253.22	3.09	17.92	3.90	0.19
2047	13.73	115.26	21.94	26.11	14.61	116.82	294.75	281.02	2.89	18.09	3.68	0.17
2048	14.69	130.99	25.08	29.76	16.04	125.00	326.87	312.18	2.71	18.24	3.47	0.16
2049	15.71	148.90	28.67	33.93	17.60	133.75	362.84	347.13	2.55	18.37	3.27	0.14
2050	84.07	169.31	32.77	38.68	19.31	143.11	403.17	319.10	1.98	18.47	3.09	0.64
											289.13	271.02

EIRR = 18.47% NPV = 1.63 crores BENEFIT/COST = 1.07

The results show that the returns will be positive in the eighth year and the benefit-cost ratio is 1.07 in the thirtieth year. Since the benefit-cost ratio is greater than 1, the project is economically feasible. Although the financial rate of return is only 7.6 per cent at the end of 30 years, the initial assumption that cable car is more feasible for the mobility in the hill cities holds true because the project has greater benefits for the society.

Conclusion

BRT built cheaply, covering too short a distance, will make operations expensive and unattractive. For 2000 pph, operating costs is 0.8 million euros, therefore, cable cars are more feasible in hill cities. However, a short ropeway at the right place can be less costly to implement and profitable to operate due to its efficiency and unique service. For 2000 pph, operating costs is 0.4 million euros.

Further it is found that cable cars will serve better in a city where the topography and morphology inhibits conventional and higher capacity public transport systems such as light rail and one that serves for the purpose of last mile connectivity. By providing alternative routes and creating new networks, cable cars will help in relieving the traffic congestion in the city. They play a major role in connecting the geographically constrained area as well as the dense areas. They are less affected by terrain and weather and have a short building phase without traffic hindrance and a limited footprint. Since the system runs on clean fuel such as hydropower, it can be considered as a zero emission system. Further research on how to make the system more sustainable, by utilizing clean fuel such as solar power can be carried out.

If cable cars are implemented, the FIRR is found to be positive after 17 years of operation and at the end of thirty years, it will be 7.61 per cent. The economic analysis on the other hand shows that a positive EIRR will be obtained in the ninth year and at the end of 30 years, it will be 18.47 per cent. Although the FIRR is lower, the project is considered to be feasible because of the larger benefits it offers to hill cities, particularly Shillong.

REFERENCES

Alshalalfah, B., Shalaby, A., Dale, S., and Othman, F.M.Y. (2012). *Aerial Ropeway Transportation Systems in the Urban Environment/: State of the Art*. (March), 253-262.

Bergerhoff, J., and Perschon, J. (2013). *The Role of Ropeways to Reshape Urban Mobility in Developing Countries*. (September), 13-21.

By, P. (2016). *Aerial Cable Transit Feasibility Study*.

Kisan, M., Sangathan, S., and Nehru, J. (1998). *IS 5229: 1998*.

Ropeways, L. (n.d.). "Ropeways in urban transport."

Solutions, D.U. (2014). "Is the future of urban mobility above our heads/?" 1-50.

Vegas, L. (1977). "Cable propelled systems in urban environments." (2), 1-9.

3
Urban Safety in Road Design

Exploring Design Concern

Namrata Talukdar

Introduction

A sustainable city must provide its people with the mobility and accessibility to safe and comfortable environment. Assurance to public safety and security in the urban environment demands mitigation of threats facing by people in day-to-day life. Safety relates to protection of life from risk or injury. 'Fear' and 'Risk' are two different but related terms (Matthew *et al.,* 2003). Risk due to crime, illness of health, fast moving vehicles, unsocial building and open space design and even natural disasters create the root of fear in the minds of people. Fear of victimisation occupies people's minds and it begins deciding most of their situations while performing the activities of life in social field. In such cases, women are more victimised than men. Other victims include the old age people, the children as well as the physically challenged people. Hence, a city is called to be safe only when its environment allows people to use, enjoy and move around without any fear and being attacked.

Aim of Research

The aim of this research is to highlight and investigate the issues related to urban safety and security in Indian cities with special reference to the case study areas of Guwahati city.

Objectives

- To identify the problems faced by the people of Guwahati which makes them feel insecure in public spaces.

- To analyse the prevailing safety problems in the city and recommend some measures for mitigation.

Methodology

The study attempts to employ a systematic and logical methodology by identifying the prevailing issues through primary surveys. Three sites within the city were selected for case studies, viz. the Pioli Phukan Path in Rehabari which is nearby the oldest part of the city, the Lakhimi Path in Beltola which is comparatively a newly emerged residential area and the Sundarbari Locality in Jalukbari which is an area dominated by the student-related activities due to the presence of few prominent institutions nearby. The study was conducted by visual observations and analytical approach based on which the findings were recorded. Primary data like on-site videography, photography, discussions with experts, interviews with the residents of the affected sites and secondary data sources such as books, reports, newspaper, electronic media etc. were used for the research paper.

Literature Survey

Urban safety relates to safe environment which refers to a situation in which there is no room for unsafe and uncomfortable activities. In order to ensure safe and security, the public realm should be placed under stronger management and regulation, free from criminal deeds, respect of barrier-free design so that mix culture of different groups of people can happen. The environment should be equitably made available for the poor, the children, the elderly, the pregnant women, the young couples etc. The road design should value the pedestrians also; the built environment should ensure health-promoting conditions and availability for optimum use of all infrastructures. We are living in a primarily urban world with an estimated 3.5 billion people living in urban areas as per the International Centre for the Prevention of Crime report (UN, 2015). Now-a-days, mixed land use development encourages more people and traffic in urban centres which creates conflicts between moving vehicles, moving and static vehicles as well as moving vehicles and pedestrians. The traffic issues in urban areas are mostly complex in nature. In residential areas, pedestrians such as children and elderly persons become the victims of accidents. India produces about 8 million vehicles per year thereby contributing 94.5 per cent of the total volume of CO_2 emitted by road transport in polluting the environment (Sarma R. *et al.,* 2011). Use of motorized vehicles has been increasing tremendously. During the last ten years (2001-2011) the annual growth rate of the registered vehicles was 9.9 per cent and the motorized two-wheelers grew at the rate of 12 per cent annually which indicated their significant rise (Solanki H.K. *et al.,* 2016). During the period 1991-98, the number of vehicles has increased the human deaths at the rate of 4.44 per cent annually as can be seen in Tables 3.1 and 3.2 (Singh S.K. *et al.*).

Table 3.1: Rate of Road Accidental Deaths During 1991-1998

Year	No. of Road Accidental Deaths (in '000)	Estimated Mid-year Population (in millions)	Fatality Risk (Col. 2*100/Col.3)
1991	56.6	849.6	6.7
1992	57.2	867.7	6.6
1993	60.6	883.8	6.9
1994	64.0	899.9	7.1
1995	68.4	916.0	7.5
1996	69.8	931.9	7.5
1997	74.2	955.2	7.8
1998	76.7	970.9	7.9

Source: Solanki, H.K. *et al.,* 2016. Road Transport in Urban India: Its Implications on Health. *Indian Journal of Community Medicine,* Official Publication of Indian Association of Preventive & Social Medicine.

Table 3.2: Growth in Motor Vehicle Population and Road Accidents in India

Year	Road Accidents (in '000)	Persons Injured (in '000)	Persons Killed (in nos.)	Vehicle Population (in '000)	Rate of Accidents per Ten Thousand Vehicles	Rate of Deaths per Ten Thousand Vehicles
1995	214.4	266.5	68351	30286.9	70.8	22.6
1996	272.1	282.2	69800	33782.9	80.5	20.7
1997	290.9	309.5	74204	37231.5	78.1	19.9
1998	300.0	320.5	76732	37231.5*	80.6 (P)	20.6 (P)

Source: Solanki, H.K. *et al.,* 2016. Road Transport in Urban India: Its implications on Health. *Indian Journal of Community Medicine,* Official Publication of Indian Association of Preventive & Social Medicine.

Women are continuously troubled by fear of violence in the male dominated society. In most of the places in India, their mobility in public places at unreasonable time is still questionable which leaves them feel unsafe and thus, hinders from moving around. Cities are not safe for peoples other than the neutral users. In India, a neutral user is a middle or upper class young male, usually a Hindu; a heterosexual who is able-bodied (Phadke *et al.*, 2011). 'Crimes against women' such as rape, murder, cheating, kidnapping, abduction and dowry deaths are brutally killing the confidence of female population to interact with city and work amidst the crowd (NCRB, 2017). The NCRB records show that the annual growth rate of crime against women in India is 9.6 per cent which registered an increase of more than double the crime rate during the period 2004-2015 (Mahadevia *et al.*, 2016) as shown in Figure 3.1.

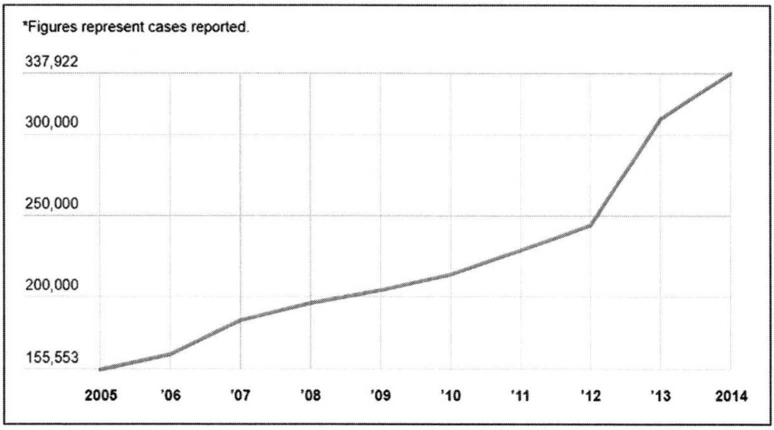

Figure 3.1: Graph Showing the Crime Against Women during 2005-2014
Source: National Crime Records Bureau, 2017.

The data show that Maharashtra has the highest crime record (4803 cases) followed by West Bengal (4073 cases), Bengaluru of Karnataka (3079 cases), South Districts of Delhi (2712 cases), outer Districts of Delhi (2284 cases), Dhubri of Assam (2021 cases) etc. (NCRB, 2015). Hence, the necessity for crime prevention becomes the utmost important topic of concern to achieve a safer and quality city. Crime Prevention Through Environmental Design (CPTED) is the approach to design the built environment to prevent such crimes against people and property as well (The State of Queensland, 2007). This approach believes in the 3 basic philosophies – "crimes against people and property are less likely to occur if other people are around"; "people in adjoining buildings and spaces are able to see what is happening"; and "it is important to give people safe choices about where to be and how to anticipate and respond to problems."

Children are seen to miss the opportunity to be a part of the city design though they are also prominent users of public places. Now-a-days, city fabric has excluded playgrounds meant for children to help them growing physically and mentally. In the year 1999, the British Government through the Department for Culture, Media and Sports has established the advisory body called the Commission for Architecture and Built Environment (CABE) which aimed at building a healthy environment considering the children psychology (UK Government, 2008). Playing outside in nature gives knowledge to a child, enhances the technical skill by stimulating the six senses, encourages the "endless capacity for adventure and imagination" and teaches the "fundamental need for exercise and social interaction; which can never be developed from the inside gaming programmes in today's life style but rather leads a child to an introvert world (Carmona *et al.*, 2003).

Other vulnerable groups of urbanites are the elderly persons, the disabled, the pregnant women etc. Most of the city's public spaces reveal the lack of barrier-free design for these sections of people. While designing the public places designers and planners should consider the fact that disability is not an exceptional phenomenon. The two models of disability viz. 'medical model' which describes disability due to medical issues and the 'social model' which gives the reason for disability in a society should be cognised while designing public spaces (Carmona *et al.*, 2003). In India approximately 10 per cent of the elderly persons suffer from depression and 40 per cent to 50 per cent have psychological issues (Planning Commission Report). The built environment should follow universal design characters to accommodate the disabled people also for their easy mobility.

Indian cities are growing tremendously and are taking away the healthy environment in most of the cases. Due to development pressure the open spaces started vanishing, the hard surfaces are increasing due to road constructions and vehicular burnt fuel is polluting the air day by day. In some parts of the country, the threats of natural disasters due to man-made interventions like earthquake, flood, tsunami etc. are the regular concerns that need to be addressed while designing the public spaces as well as the individual private houses. Absence of street lights, public toilets, inefficient public transport system, improper sidewalks and inactive street life affect the safety factor of citizens in public places.

Profile of the Case City

Guwahati is one of the oldest urban centres of the North-East India. Guwahati as the fastest growing metropolis covers an area of 328 sq. kms with a population of 0.96 million as per the 2011 Census (Hemani *et al.*, 2016). Urban safety in this city is also not an exception. Data presented by the State Home (Police) Department in 2012 revealed that Kamrup Metro had crime cases such as thefts, dacoity and murders (*The Times of India,* 2012). The registered crime records have been increasing in the last few years. The North East Network (NEN), a non-governmental organisation conducted a survey of 1000 samples pertaining to womenfolk. From this sampling size, it was found that 70 per cent of the respondents experienced sexual harassment in public places (Desai *et al.,* 2014). Deteriorated conditions of roads, sidewalks, street lights, furniture and other urban accoutrements encourage street side crimes and leave the pedestrians vulnerable to road accidents. As a part of urban renewal, recently the Government has developed a specific stretch of M.G. Road as a walking zone to promote walk ability of citizens including the disabled, the elderly persons, the children etc. Such measures need to be implemented in other parts of the case city also.

Lakhimi Path-Beltola Tiniali a stretch leading to the residential areas of Beltola like Kailash Nagar connects the Hatigaon area. This stretch covering a length about 200 metres has mixed land use comprising commercial shops, residential flats, post office, hotels, temples etc. as shown in Figures 3.2, 3.3 and 3.4. The target customers of these shops are basically the residents who live in apartments and individual houses. Lakhimi Path has no sidewalks and as such growing numbers of vehicles create hurdles to the mobility of pedestrians. The existence of insufficient numbers of parking lots for motorised vehicle and absence of parking lots for rickshaws exact a lot of movement spaces which results in the conflicts of vehicles and pedestrians.

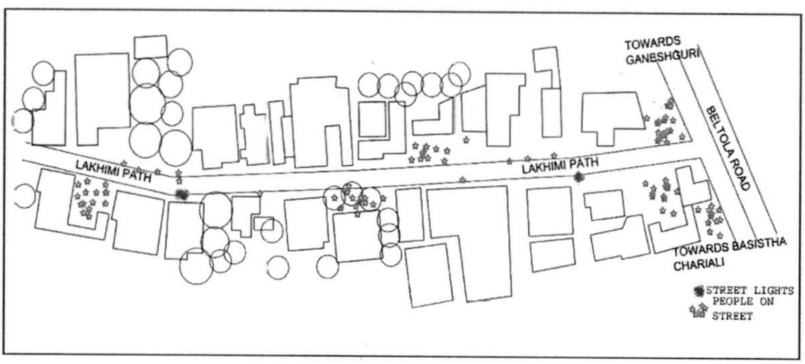

Figure 3.2: Location of Lakhimi Path and Activities Mapping

Source: Field Study.

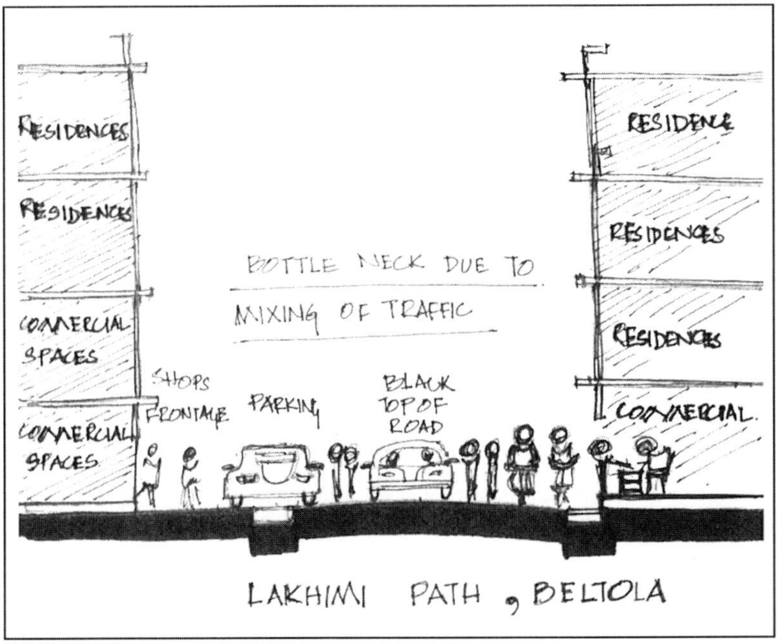

Figure 3.3: Section Showing the Present Road Condition of Lakhimi Path

Source: Field Study.

Figure 3.4: Entry Point, On-road Rickshaw Stand and Car-Parked Footpaths at Lakhimi Path

Source: Field Study.

Pioli Phukan Path-Milanpur-Rehabari is a stretch which connects the Kachari Basti area and the Rehabari area. This area also has a mixed land use consisting of residential apartments, few small institutions, commercial shops, temple, restaurants etc. as shown in Figures 3.5, 3.6, 3.7 and 3.8. Both sides of the road are predominantly residential in character.

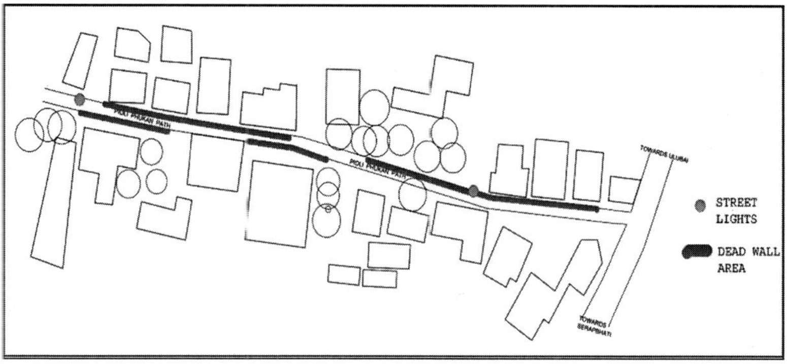

Figure 3.5: Base Map of Pioli Phukan Path-Absence of Stret Lights and Presence of Dead Walls

Source: Field Study.

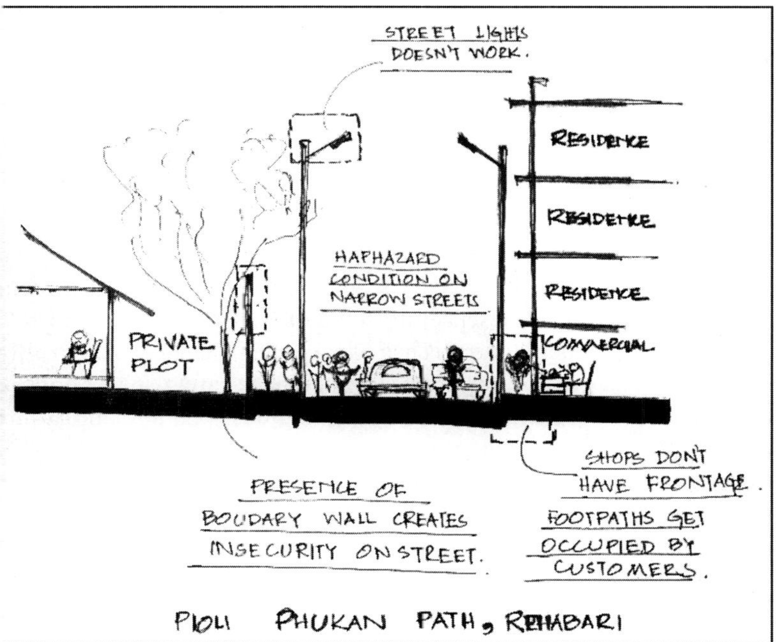

Figure 3.6: A Cross-Section Showing the Present Road Condition

Source: Field Study.

Figure 3.7: Dead Walls Create Insecurity on Road Sides and On-road Parking

Source: Field Study.

Figure 3.8 Absence of Street Lights and Activities on Roads.

Source: Field Study.

During day time, presence of people on roadsides make the street lively but during night time absence of street lights hinders the mobility of people. The bus-stop on the main road has seating spaces for the commuters to wait. But in practice, running buses do not stop at this designated place as a result commuters have to rush to get into it which again creates risk of life. Street vendors belonging to the informal business sector used to erect their stalls on the footpaths. People park their private cars on the sidewalk's space thereby occupying the open spaces of these petty shop-keepers which creates disturbance. Further, absence of street lights creates dark corners at the sharp edges of roads and generates a sense of insecurity and fearsomeness in women's mind after business hours. In the entire residential area, there is not even a single green space for recreation purpose by the children and the elderly persons. Thus children and elderly persons are left with no option but to confine themselves within their houses since the street life is dull and does not attract them. Pioli Phukan Path has footpaths but of insufficient widths. In view of such space constraint it is problematic even for two persons to pass by each other. Parking issues are same as at the Lakhimi Path. The high rise boundary walls of the residential apartments create darkness and dead spaces along the sidewalks. During night time, people do not feel safe to walk on the streets and particularly women become the cynosure of men in front of pan shops. The entrances to apartments are not significant for identification of particular houses as a result visitors sometimes find difficulty to locate the specific addresses they want to visit. Eve teasing and snatching of gold are some common incidents in these two urban localities. Absence of street furniture, open playgrounds, barrier-free measures for disabled and garbage dumping zones results in street violence.

Sundarbari under Jalukbari is one of the oldest urban localities in the case city and in view of the existence of various educational institutions like Assam Engineering College, Government Ayurvedic College and Gauhati University; majority of the residents belong to student community. Buildings are used for commercial purposes such as xerox centres, hostels, rent houses, restaurants or food stalls to cater to the needs of students. Street sides are occupied by informal hawkers who sell food items, vegetables etc. and almost the whole year; activities in this urban locality are student-oriented. On the contrary, the area almost becomes empty during vacation periods of the institutions. Though there is no evidence of any crime record but absence of street lights generates sense of insecurity and fear psychosis among the residents in the institutional zones after sunset.

Recommendations

This survey is an attempt to understand the safety and security factors of the streets of the case city. In order to mitigate the problems captured during the study, the following urban renewal measures are recommended:.

- While promoting the mixed land use development in the city, urban planners and policy makers should take care of the existing conflicts among the motorised vehicles, the non-motorised vehicles and the pedestrians by segregating their routes.
- The built environment should be designed in such a way so as to prevent and mitigate violence and crime.
- Urban design and planning should ensure creation of public spaces with proper infrastructural facilities such as garbage bins, public toilets, street lights and furniture etc.

- Street life should be generated in the case city by providing with dedicated zones for various activities which promotes human interactions.
- Stoppages of public transport and buses should be equipped with barrier-free design elements to ease movement of residents belonging to the weaker sections of society like disabled persons, elderly persons, pregnant women, women with their babies in pushchairs etc.
- Authorities should take responsibility to educate people and sensitise women of their rights and upliftments, pedestrianisation, sustainable growth etc. in order to achieve a safe city.

Conclusion

Indian cities are still far away from being safe cities. Though urbanisation is pushing these cities towards development but the development process affects harshly the environment thereby rendering the cities unsafe. Therefore, urban planners, designers and policymakers should take their utmost care in shaping the cities for the near future by designing public spaces in such a way to bring about optimum benefits to the individuals and this planet as a whole in achieving safer cities.

REFERENCES

Department for Culture, Media and Sport (DCMS), UK Government (2008): *Design for Play: A Guide to Creating Successful Play Spaces*, Downloaded from http://www. playengland. org.uk /media/70684/design-for-play.pdf

Desai, Renu *et al.*, (2014). "City Profile: Guwahati" in *Centre for Urban Equity (CUE)*, CEPT University, Downloaded from http://cept.ac.in/UserFiles/File/CUE/Working%20Papers/Revised%20New/24CUEWP%2024_ City%20 Profile%20Guwahati.pdf

Hemani, Shruti & Das, A.K. (2016). "City Profile: Guwahati" in *The International Journal of Urban Policy and Planning*, Elsevier Publication. Journal homepage: www.elsevier.com/ locate/jci

International Centre for the Prevention of Crime (2015). *Chapter 2: Urban Safety*, http://www.crime-prevention-intl.org/fileadmin/user_upload/Publications/International_Report /CIPC_5th-IR_EN_Chapter-2.pdf, Accessed on 20.11.2017.

Mahadevia, Darshini *et al.*, (2016). *How Safe are Public Spaces for Women in Ahmedabad*?, CEPT University Centre for Urban Equity (CUE).

Matthew, C. *et al.*, (2003). *Public Places Urban Spaces-The Dimension of Urban Design,* Routledge Taylor Francis Group.

Matthew, Carmona *et al.*, (2003). *Ibid., op cit.*

Matthew, Carmona *et al.,* (2003). *Public Places Urban Spaces—The Dimension of Urban Design,* Routledge Taylor Francis Group.

National Crime Records Bureau (2015). *Chapter 5: Crime Against Women,* http://ncrb.nic.in/StatPublications/CII/CII2015/chapters/Chapter%205-15.11.16.pdf.

National Crime Records Bureau (2015), *Ibid., op cit.*

Phadke, Shilpa *et al.,* (2011). *Why Loiter? Women and Risk on Mumbai Streets,* Penguin India.

Planning Commission Report, Important Issues on Ageing in India Recommendations To Planning Commission, Downloaded from http://planning commission.gov.in/data/ ngo/ csw/csw_15.pdf, Last Access: 20.11.2017, 4 pm.

Sarma, Rameswar *et al.,* (2011). "Growth Rate of Motor Vehicles in India—Impact of Demographic and Economic Developments" in *Journal of Economic and Social Studies,* http://eprints.ibu.edu.ba/1073/1/vol1-no2 p JOURNAL. OF. ECONOMIC.AND.SOCIAL STUDIES.-1-2_p137-p153.pdf, Accessed on 19.11. 2017.

Singh, S.K. and Misra, A. (2001). *Road Accident Analysis: A Case Study of Patna City.*

Solanki, H.K. *et al.,* (2016). "Road Transport in Urban India: Its Implications on Health". *Indian Journal of Community Medicine,* Official Publication of Indian Association of Preventive & Social Medicine, 41(1), p. 16.

The State of Queensland (2007). *Crime Prevention Through Environmental Design (CPTED),* Downloaded from http://www.police.qld.gov.au/programs/crimeprevention/, ISBN 978-0-9579910-1-9.

4

Need for Secured Livelihood and Empowerment of Women Street Vendors of Guwahati City

The Challenging Road Ahead for Smart City

Parangam Sarma Basistha

Introduction

One of the central challenges of urban areas in developing countries is to provide formal jobs or income opportunities efficiently to the labour force especially to women. Women who represent almost half of the world's population are always affected by income inequality, exploitation in work areas, gender discrimination and low wage jobs. Despite the growing Indian economy and its development in urbanization, poverty reduction, education, health, information technology, industries sector; a little attention is given towards the inclusive growth and equality in gender relations. The development model of India needs to address the issues of economic empowerment of women by recognizing their important role in socio-economic and sustainable growth of the nation. Economic empowerment of women can contribute to poverty alleviation, zero hunger, gender discrimination, education improvements etc. thereby helping to achieve the sustainable world by 2030 (www.unwomen.org, 2017). Gender gap, discrimination and social segmentation are rooted in Indian societies as manifested in different forms like health, nutrition, education, literacy, employment, social participation, mobility, political awareness and participation, rights exercise and many more. Despite the inclusion of women empowerment and gender equality in the Constitution of India as their fundamental rights, fundamental duties, directive principles and in the preamble part; the struggle for minimizing gender gap is understandable in terms of the World Economic Forum's gender gap index. In this ranking,

India stood at 113th position out of 135 countries participated (World Economic Forum, 2016). Women participation in workforce in India is low comprising only 25.51 per cent of the workforce against 53.26 per cent for males (Census 2011) while economic empowerment is only 0.3 which is quite low when measured from the equality magic Figure, i.e. 1 (one) (Ministry of Statistics and Programme Implementation, 2014). Within the South East Asian countries, the labour force participation for females in India is just ahead of Pakistan (24.6%) and ranks after the neighbouring countries like Sri Lanka (35.1%), Bangladesh (57.4%), China (63.9%) and Nepal (79.9%) as per the latest findings of the World Bank (World Bank Report, 2017). As per the NSS data, the worker population ratios for males in rural areas are 24.8 in 2011 and 54.3 in 2012 whereas in urban areas the ratios are 14.7 for females and 54.6 for males. The urban-rural gap is significant in unemployment rate showing 2.9 in rural areas and 6.6 in urban areas in 2011-12 (Ministry of Statistics and Programme Implementation, 2014). The Global Gender Gap Report, 2017 by World Economic Forum indicates the gender disparity condition in India for indicators, viz. economic participation and opportunity (139 ranks), education attainment (112 ranks), health and survival (151 ranks) and political empowerment (15 ranks) and an overall ranking of 108 out of 144 countries (World Economic Forum, 2016). The rapid growth of urbanization and success in education sector in India has not been able to achieve the desired economic empowerment of women and gender inequality in work environments in cities. The disparity, gender inequality and income differences are more prominent in urban areas than in rural (Ministry of Statistics and Programme Implementation, 2014). In urban areas trade and informal jobs account for an essential source of employment for women. Street vending, the most visible form of informal economy is increasing in urban areas with increasing trend in female participants. The livelihood security, minimizing gender inequality in work sector and economy, sustainable income opportunity for women went missing in the case for India. These issues are some of the central challenges that need to be addressed in the smart city mission (Bhandare, Namita, 2017). Women empowerment and consistent secured livelihood relate to social improvements like child rearing, nutrition of mother and child, better health, education, engagement in social activities, environmental improvements leading towards inclusive and *smart* economic and social development. Despite this prime issue, it is observed that authorities who are responsible for smart city projects did not adequately address the needs of street vendors in "smart city plans". Today, our so called progressive, developmental plans are forcing them to leave their place of business making way forward to their extreme poverty. The eviction of vendors from streets is generally carried out without any proper resettlement or rehabilitation plan or even without prior notice of eviction. In May 2016, over 6000 street vendors in Rachi protested against acquiring lands for smart city proposals and non-rehabilitation of the evicted persons (Dey, Sanjoy, *Hindustan Times*, 2016). In June 2016 street vendors of Delhi protested against the eviction led by the New Delhi Municipal Corporation and put forward demand before the authority to issue vending certificate before eviction (Goswami Sweta, 2016). Thus the research questions arise, whether we can become *"smart"*? To what extent we can become smart by ignoring the vital issue of women's economic empowerment in cities? Can cities become "*smart*" if they ignore one of the visible occupations of informal economy, i.e. the urban women street vendors?

Aim of Research

The aim of this research is to throw light on the issues of livelihood security and economic empowerment of women street vendors in India before the development of smart cities with special reference to the Guwahati city as a case study.

Objectives of the Research

The objectives of the research are:

- To investigate the socio-economic status of women street vendors for establishing a need of secured livelihood and economic empowerment.
- To investigate the issues, problems and prospects of women street vendors and their business activities for envisioning probable challenges, hindrances of smart city development in India with reference to the case city.

Methodology

The data base for the present research work comprises the primary and the secondary sources. The primary data for women street vendors which related to their socio-economic condition, problem and issues were collected from site visits with the help of a semi-structured questionnaire, personal observation, face-to-face interview, photography and discussions with officials. For the purpose of this study, based on the historical significance, varying character and popularity of four marketplaces were chosen, viz. Fancy Bazaar-Paltan Bazaar, Beltola-Tiniali Market, Narengi Bazaar and Azara Godhuli Bazaar. Fancy Bazaar and Paltan Bazaar are the

CBD areas where commercial, wholesale and retail markets exist whereas Beltola-Tiniali market is a traditional market where local foods and vegetables are popularly found. Narengi Bazaar and Azara Godhuli Bazaar situating towards south-west direction of the city, are the traditional fish markets. Using the purposive sampling technique, 10 samples of women vendors which represented the true characteristics of the population were chosen randomly from each market which comprised a total sampling size of 40 numbers. The data were tabulated in the excel sheets for analysis. The secondary data were collected from books, journals, reports and internet sources.

The Context

Street vendors or hawkers constitute an integral part of the urban informal economy, often regarded as "menace" to the planned and organized cities and streets. They are termed them as a "problem" of planned development worldwide (Anjaria Jonathan Shapiro, 2006). Street vending provides livelihood to a section of marginalized, impoverished migrants and unemployed with an opportunity to trade and earn in cities. Street vending provides essential goods and services to consumers especially of low and middle-income categories by supplying foods, clothing, toys, household utilities etc. at cheap and affordable prices and convenience. The informal sectors are defined as activities of the poor for livelihood and not recognized, protected and regulated by any law and authorities [The International Labour Organization (ILO), 1972]. According to ILO, informal sector economy consists of various units which produce goods and services and primarily focused towards the generation of income and employment [Centre for Urban Equity (CUE), 2016]. Street vendors are defined as "*hawkers, peddlers, street vendors, Pheriwalas*" which offer daily household items, vegetables, food, clothing etc. on the streets and footpaths or door-to-door (The National Classification of Occupation 1968, Sonawane, S.T., 2017). Indian researchers like Bhattacharya *et al.*, 1987, define street vendors as people who do not have a permanent place of trade and provide ample amount of goods and services easily available at public spaces. Although street vendors offer direct employment to lakhs of urban poor and provide benefits to thousands of populations, they are at every point blamed for various problems related to planning and development of cities. Proponents of "classy cities" consider street vending as reasons for hue and cries; nuisance in the cities (Rajagopal, Arvind, 2001).

In most cases, authorities consider street vendors as illegal and blame them for use of public spaces and are treated as nuisance. Street vendors are regarded as "black spot" over the planned development of a city (Anjaria Jonathan Shapiro, 2006). They are considered as encroachers of public spaces by police and municipal bodies. They often harass by trying to eliminate them from streets, threatening them, taking bribe and seizing their merchandise. The concept of "ideal", "classic" and "healthy city" has brought challenges and hindrances to street vendors especially to women. For instance, the ban on street vending in Hanoi, evictions of street vending in Mexico City, Peru, removal of street vendors in Delhi during the Commonwealth Games 2010 and the violent demolition drive in Mumbai in the early 1980s (Roever Sally and Skinner Caroline, 2016). Various researchers from India and outside support the existence of street vendors and regard them as essential for efficient functioning of public spaces (Anjaria Jonathan Shapiro, 2006). Classic works of Jane Jacob (1961) argues the alternative use of streets and sidewalks apart from vehicular movement and acknowledge street vendor's importance in cities for happy, safe and livable urban spaces. She identifies people on the streets including the street vendors as "eyes on the street" whose continuous presence helps in reducing crime in cities, ensures safety (Anjaria Jonathan Shapiro, 2006).

Street Vending in India

With the increasing rate of unemployed and underemployed persons in cities, street vending becomes an important part of livelihood among the top job choices. Vending in the streets is a popular job choice among the urban poor as it requires a low level of skill and finance to start up. Urban centres in India ranging from small towns to mega cities faced the challenge of formal employment generation which led to high concentration of informal unorganized sectors of economy especially the street vending. The total number of street vendors in India as per the 2002 data is about one crore [Centre for Urban Equity (CUE), 2016]. Cities like Mumbai, Kolkata, Delhi, Hyderabad, Ahmedabad and Guwahati have large sections of people which rely on street vending activities as the principal source of livelihood. In Delhi alone about five lakhs of street vendors earn their livelihoods from street trading and only 50,000 vendors have licences (indiatoday. intoday.in, 2017). As on 2017 the concentration of regular street vendors in Mumbai is estimated to be 2,50,000 persons, followed by Kolkata (2,00,000 persons) and Ahmedabad about 80,000 street vendors (Sonawane S.T., 2017). The numbers of street vendors are increasing in the case city and as per the 2015 data, the Guwahati municipality area alone has about 45,000 street vendors and majority of them are women (www.business-standard.com, 2017).

In India, the informal sector accounts for more than 90 per cent of the workforce and uses approximate 50 per cent national resources [Centre for Urban Equity (CUE), 2016]. As per the 2009 data, almost 2 per cent of the total city's population is engaged in street vending as indicated by the National Policy of Urban Street Vendors. In urban informal economy, women street vendors comprise a significant percentage among the total street vendors such as migrants, unemployed persons, workers and lay-off women. For women, street vending is a regular source of income to sustain themselves with dignity and respect in the society. For a section of poor urbanites street vending is their "*survival strategy*". Vending in the street is popular job choice among many as it requires less skill, education, low capital and is free in entry and exit. Women street vendors throughout the world face various problems and are vulnerable to issues responsible for livelihood insecurity like workspace erosion, harassment, confiscation, eviction, sexual assault, abuse and other crimes (Roever Sally and Skinner Caroline, 2016).

In the Indian perspective, problems like loss of income, asset erosion, i.e. loss of goods, damage of goods and seizure or confiscation, change in site and mode of work, police beating, and harassment are the prime causes of income insecurity and hinder economic empowerment of women. Many civic organizations and NGOs such as SEWA (Self-employed Women's Association) and National Association of Street Vendors of India (NASVI) worked for legal support, protection of livelihoods and for economic empowerment of women street vendors (www.nasvinet.org, 2017). The Street Vendors (Protection of Livelihood and Regulation of Street Vending) Act, 2014 was enacted in the parliament to deal with the issues of street vendors in India. This Act *inter alia,* includes provision for livelihood protection, regulation of street vending through demarcation of vending zone, formation of Town Vending Committee, formation of State Vendors Plan by the States in every 5 years, eviction with relocation and recommends 2 per cent land in Master Plan and local area plan for demarcation of vending zone (Street Vendors Act, 2014).

Discussions and Findings

Beltola Market Street Vendors

Beltola Market is one of the popular traditional markets of Guwahati where a large number of street vendors sell vegetables, banana, bamboo shoots, poultry products and indigenous species. Vendors from different urban localities, viz. Pukhripar, Birubari, Ulubari, Garchuk etc. and from other regions like Sonapur, Nalbari, Borpeta, Kharupetia, Boko, Dimapur, Bornihat commute to this market. Apart from vegetables and poultry products household products, fish, meat, cloth, cheap used cloth etc. are also sold. Regular vendors occupy the front portions of permanent shops by extending it with plastic roofing sheets whereas others occupy pavements and road spaces. Large numbers of Garo and Bodo women shown in Figure 4.1 are found vending in the market followed by Bengali-Muslim women. Their economic status shows that almost one-third of women vendors earn 400 to 500 rupees per day and work for almost 7 to 8 hours in a day.

Figure 4.1: Women Vendors on Footpaths at Beltola Bazaar

Narengi Market Street Vendors

Narengi is mainly a vegetable market. Now-a-days apart from vegetables, vendors sell clothes, poultry products, milk etc. Women vendors from distant places like Nalbari, Bornihat, Borpeta, Kharupetia, Sonapur, Dimapur etc. come to this market. Hill produces, indigenous products, vegetables are also found in this market as shown in Figure 4.2 and male vendors are more than female vendors. However, majority of the vegetable sellers are women.

Figure 4.2: Vegetable Sellers at Narengi Bazaar

Fancy Bazaar and Paltan Bazaar

This market locates in the CBD of the city. The characters of street vendors and types of their products in this market are different as compared to other markets. Here there are a few numbers of vegetable street vendors while other street vendors shown in Figure 4.3 sell items like cloth, jewellery, decorative items, food items, water bottles etc. Maximum women vendors of this area are Bengali Muslim and Bihari in origin. Very few Assamese speaking women vendors are found in this market.

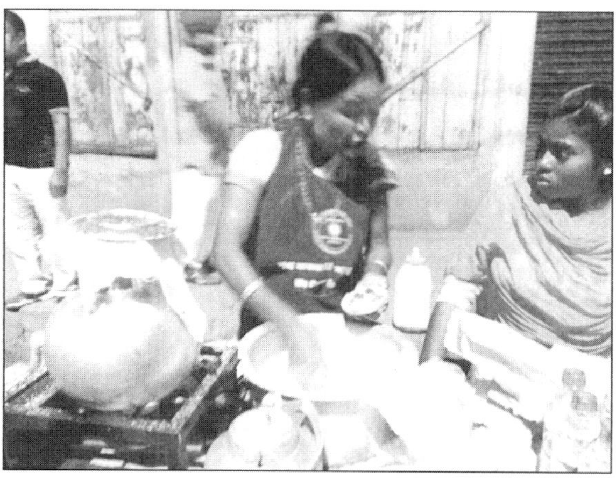

Figure 4.3: Women Street Vendors in Fancy Bazaar during Sunday Walking Zone

Azara Godhuli Bazaar

This is one of the oldest and traditional village markets located at Azara situating towards the South-West side of Guwahati. This is a woman-dominated market where almost 80 to 90 per cent vendors are women selling fishes obtained from Deepor Beel and vegetables as seen in Figure 4.4.

Figure 4.4: Fish Vendors in Azara Godhuli Bazaar

Survey Data Analysis

- Figure 4.5 shows the age groups of women street vendors. It is found that 45 per cent of the respondents were in the age group between 31 and 45, 25 per cent between 46 and 60 years and 10 per cent were above 60 years.
- Figure 4.6 indicates the family sizes of women street vendors. The primary data and information indicated that 50 per cent of households had family members varying from 2 to 5 persons, 42 per cent between 6 and 10 persons and the family sizes of the 8 per cent households were above 10 persons which were large family sizes. Thus economic survival is the vital issue.

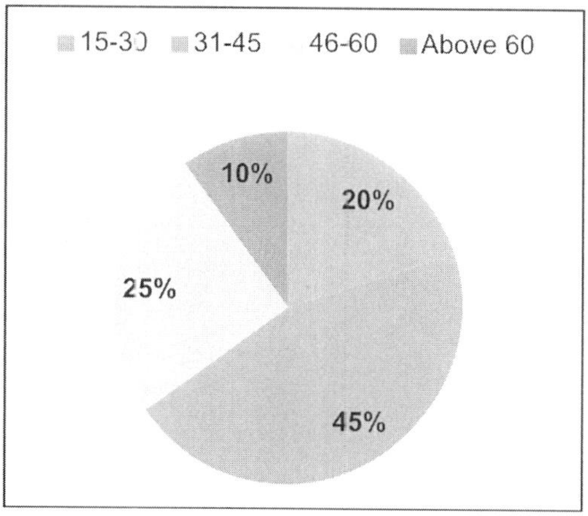

Figure 4.5 Age Groups of Women Street Vendors

Source: Primary Survey, 2017.

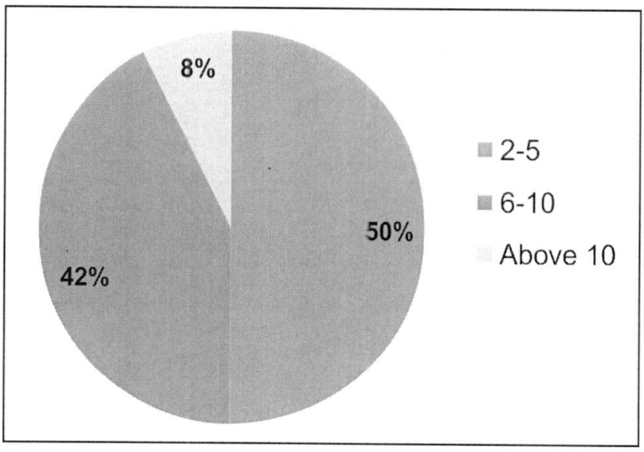

Figure 4.6 Family Size of Women Street Vendors

Source: Primary Survey, 2017.

- Figure 4.7 shows the earning members of the households. The data revealed that 49 per cent of the households had 1 earning member, 26 per cent had 3 earning members, 7 per cent had 4 earning members and 2 per cent had 5 working members. The data show that in most cases (49%) of the vendor families surveyed, the only earning members are the women with average family members of 2 to 4 depend on their day-to-day earning.

- Figure 4.8 shows the different types of commodities sold in the market. The data indicated that 57 per cent of the commodities sold this market were vegetables and the other commodities were milk, sweets, fish, bidi, cigarettes etc. In most of the cases it was found that women vendors' earnings were primarily meant for maintenance of their families.

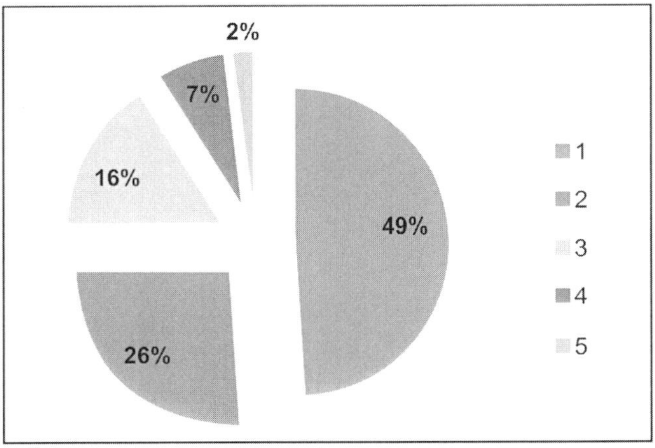

Figure 4.7: Working Members of Vendor Families

Source: Primary Surveys, 2017.

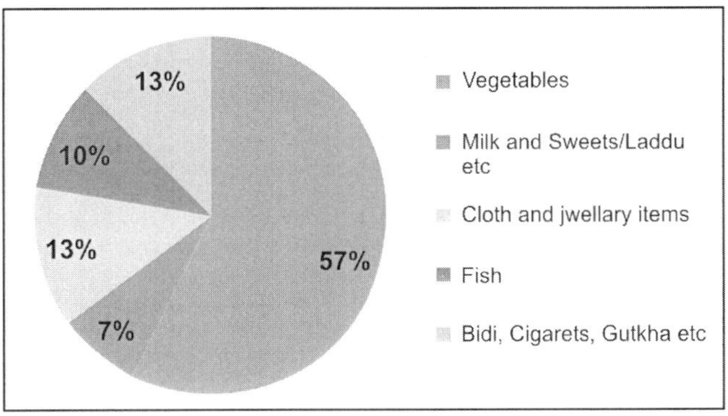

Figure 4.8: Commodities Sold by Vendors

Source: Primary Surveys, 2017.

- Figure 4.9 shows the daily economic earnings of the street vendors. It was found that 41 per cent of the respondents earned their incomes between Rs. 201 to Rs. 300, 30 per cent between Rs. 301 to Rs. 400, 18 per cent between Rs. 101 to Rs. 200, 8 per cent was above Rs. 400 and 3 per cent was between Rs 50 to Rs. 100 per day.

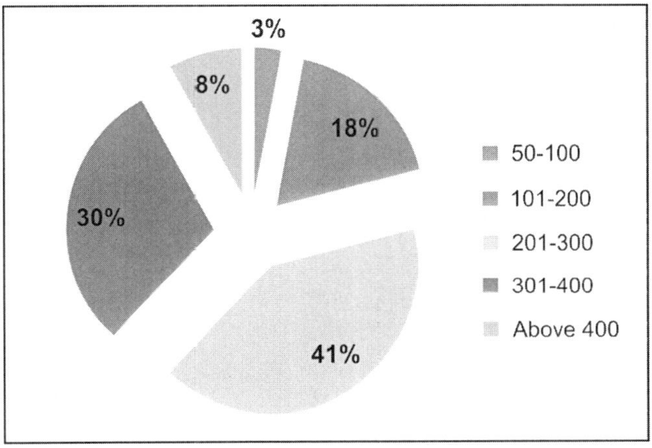

Figure 4.9: Daily Income in Rupees

Source: Primary Survey, 2017.

- Figure 4.10 shows the working hours of the street vendors. It was found that 40 per cent of them worked for six hours whereas the working hours of 51 per cent varied between 7 to 10 hours per day and 9 per cent worked more than 10 hours/day.

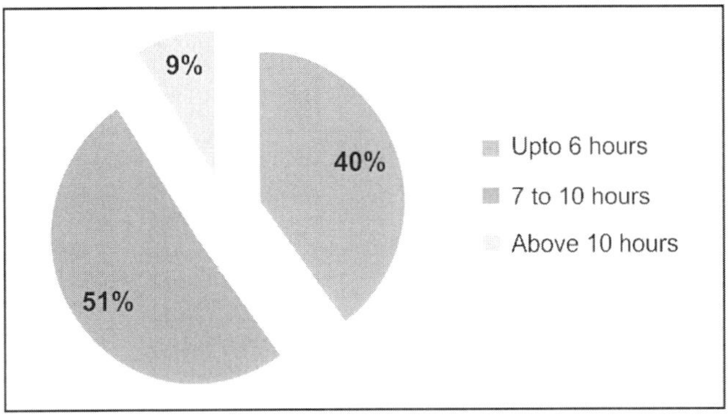

Figure 4.10: Working Hour Per Day

Source: Primary Survey, 2017.

- Figure 4.11 shows the problems and issues associated with the street vendors. It was found that 59 per cent of them responded that the prime problem faced was the absence of public toilet and drinking water, 19 per cent reported the lack of space for storage facilities, 14 per cent faced the vending spaces crisis, 7 per cent faced the problems such as police harassment, payment of tax, bribery and eviction drive and the remaining 1 per cent encountered harassments and abuses from the male customers. Women vendors informed that lack of storage spaces compelled them to dispose of their unsold products either to the customers or to the permanent wholesalers at throw-away prices.

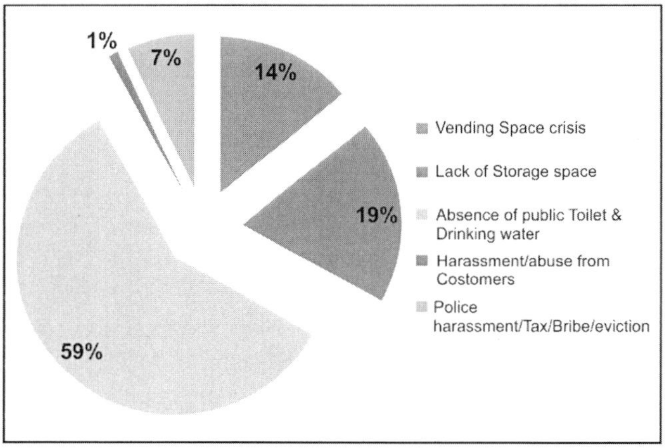

Figure 4.11: Problems and Issues

Source: Primary Survey, 2017.

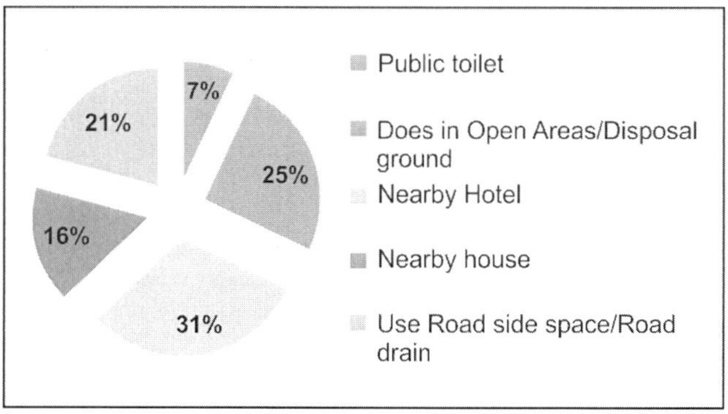

Figure 4.12: Means of Accessing Toilets

Source: Primary Survey, 2017.

- Figure 4.12 shows the means of accessibility or 'ease of reaching' to toilets by women vendors. The data revealed that 31 per cent of them used the nearby hotels, 25 per cent used the open spaces or disposal grounds, 21 per cent used roadside spaces and road drains, 16 per cent used nearby houses and only 7 per cent availed the facility of public toilets.
- Figure 4.13 shows the sources of drinking water availed by street women vendors. It was found that 48 per cent availed their drinking water from the nearby hotels, 24 per cent brought water from their homes, 17 per cent fetched their drinking water from the nearby houses, 9 per cent used public water taps and only 2 per cent used package water.

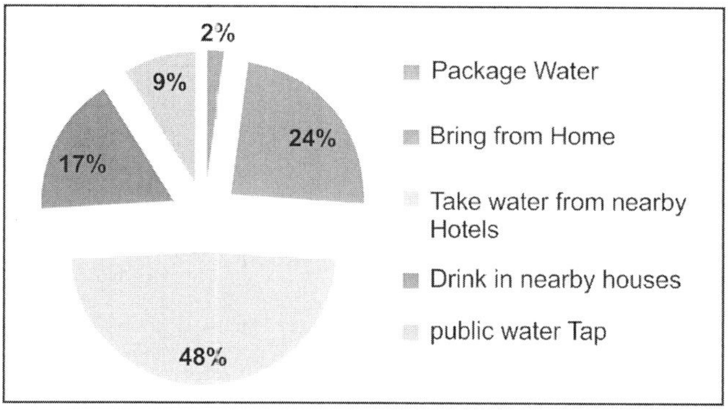

Figure 4.13: Source of Drinking Water

Source: Primary Survey, 2017.

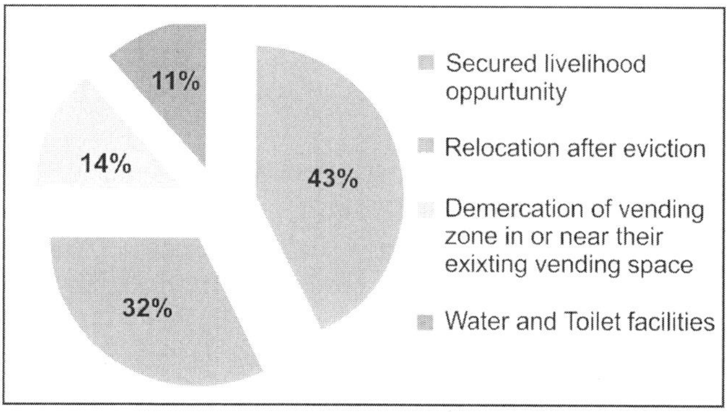

Figure 4.14: Expectations from Smart City

Source: Primary Survey, 2017

Figure 4.14 shows the varied degree of expectations of women vendors from the smart city proposal. After explaining in a nutshell about the benefits of the smart city project and initiatives taken by the Government, almost 43 per cent of the respondents expected secured livelihood opportunities from the smart city for the overall benefit of the society, 32 per cent agreed for relocation planning after eviction, 14 per cent desired for proper demarcation of vending zones in or near their existing vending spaces and 11 per cent of them expected water and toilet facilities.

Figure 4.15 shows the varied degree of expectations of people belonging to the fish community about the impact of smart city proposal on the Deepor Beel. It was found that 76 per cent of them did not have any idea about the smart city proposal and its impact, 16 per cent reported that fish productivity would decrease and 8 per cent expressed their grave concern about their livelihood.

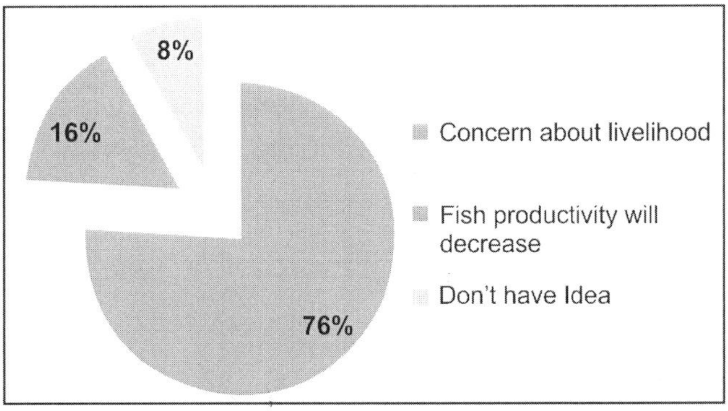

Figure 4.15: Concerns About Smart City Proposals

Source: Primary Survey, 2017.

Major Findings

- Street vendors of Guwahati city lived a very hectic daily life beginning with the collection of products, processing and then carrying to market for sale. On an average, they work for 7 to 10 hours per day and hardly had time for relaxation and leisure activities.
- After market hours, they spent some time with their fellow vendors for gossip and friendly talks each with a cup of tea and then rushed to their homes for domestic works mainly cooking of foods for their family members.

- Most of the women vendors who were young and whose age ranged from 25 to 40 years often faced harassment, abuse, beating by police and municipal authorities.
- Vendors were economically insecure due to their low income and expressed their feelings of insecurity in their workplaces at all times.
- They faced challenges of livelihood insecurity like workspace erosion, harassment, confiscation, eviction. They often moved from one place to another in search of space for fear of eviction and confiscation by authorities.
- Women vendors lived in a very difficult working environment such as exposure to sun, rain, pollution and risk of vehicular accidents.
- About 50 to 60 per cent of the households sustained their livelihoods by earnings of women street vendors which made them to work rigorously without any break or holiday.
- Increased traffic volume affects their sales as the frequency of pedestrian customers' mobility on the roads decreases.
- They also revealed that crisis of vending spaces, storage spaces, lack of toilet facilities, absence of drinking water facilities were some of the problems they faced. Among these, vending space crisis, conflict with fellow vendors over space and absence of toilet and drinking water facilities were the acute problems which required immediate attention.
- Although their education level was low where maximum qualification was class IX or X, their family size was in the range between 2 to 5 persons. Maximum number of street vendors were from outside the Guwahati and they return home in the late evening after the market period.
- Travel expenditure and product transport cost share a significant portion of their daily expenses.
- Almost 70 per cent of the respondents consumed Gutkha, betel nut and smoked bidi or cigarette.
- Women vendors knew little and only 17 per cent of them were aware of the smart city. However, they were not aware of the proposals and initiatives taken by the Government. Almost 75 per cent of the respondents had no idea about smart city Guwahati project.
- With regard to their expectations from the smart city project, almost all revealed their need to have a secure livelihood and safety.
- Women vendors of Godhuli Bazaar were concerned about the shrinking income they derived from fish selling from Deepor

Beel. 96 per cent of the respondents were aware of the smart city proposal in Deepor Beel Wetland and worried about their livelihood. They expressed their deep concern about the aftermath on fish productivity of the wetland due to such developments. They utter, *"Deepor Beelot kiba Korbu buli xunsu, amar nu ki! Khai boi Solba Palli Hol",* which means "they have heard about smart city developments in Deepor Beel and they only concerned about them, their livelihood". They also say *"Juni ji kore korok de! Eman dinor pai maach mari khai aaso. Setu jate korba nora nahou. Ai Beelkhon Aamar"*, that is "Let them do whatever they want. This is our wetland; we will do fishing".

Conclusion

Economic empowerment of women is a prerequisite for enhancing self-respect, role, and confidence in the family as well as in the society. This research investigates the socio-economic condition, income pattern, working condition and economic empowerment of women and their concerns about the smart city Guwahati project. Majority of women street vendors of Guwahati city were facing problems like harassment, abuse, eviction, bribe to authorities and other issues related to work environment like vending space crisis, conflict among vendors, absence of infrastructures, unsafe feeling during night time etc. They also expressed their concern about the smart city proposal and felt insecure about their livelihood sustainability. It is, therefore, mandatory for the smart city project of the case city to address such core issues associated with economic empowerment of women, livelihood security and safety for women on streets. Inevitably, such project should also palliate the problems of urban informal sector to make poor persons accessible to inclusive financing, urban amenities and other programmes of sustainable development. Though the issues relating to street vendors are challenging, however, it is expected that Indian smart city movement will handle them as it is not a matter of impossibility when appropriate urban planning measures are applied.

REFERENCES

Anjaria Jonathan Shapiro, (2006). *Economic and Political Weekly*, "Street Hawkers and Public Space in Mumbai".

Bhandare Namita, (2017). *Why Indian Workspace are Losing Women*: https://thewire.in/165005/ indian-workplaces-losing-women-nationwide/, Accessed on: 19.11.2017.

Centre for Urban Equity (CUE), (2016). "Street Vending in Guwahati: Experiences of Conflict", Downloaded from: http://cept.ac.in/UserFiles/File/CUE/Working%20Papers/Revised%20 New /30CUEWP30_Street%20 Vending%20in%20Guwahati%20Experiences%20of%20Conflict.pdf

Dey Sanjoy, *Hindustan Times*, (2016). Downloaded from http://www.hindustantimes.com/ranchi/ ranchi-hawkers-protest-smart-city-demand-livelihood/story-J1tvcbIdOof1X5ZxNDU71H.html

Goswami Sweta. (2016). Newspaper article, Downloaded from http://www.thehindu.com/news/cities/Delhi/Street-vendors-to-protest eviction/article14393871.ece

Ministry of Statistics and Programme Implementation, (2014). *Women and Men in India.*

Rajagopal, Arvind (2001). "The Violence of Commodity Aesthetics: Hawkers, Demolition Raids, and a New Regime of Consumption" in *Social Text*, 19(3): 91-113

Roever, Sally and Skinner Caroline, (2016). International Institute for Environment and Development (IIED). "Street Vendors And Cities", Downloaded from eau.sagepub.com, Accessed on 12.11.2017.

Sonawane, S.T., (2017). *Problems and Solutions of Vendors–A Case Study*: https://www.ijirset. com/upload/2017/january/62_18_Problems.pdf

Street Vendors (Protection of Livelihood and Regulation of Street Vending) Act, 2014 http://www.indiacode.nic.in/acts2014/7%20of%202014.pdf

The International Labour Organization (ILO), (1972). "Employment, Incomes and Equality: A Strategy for Increasing Productive Employment in Kenya", International Labour Office, Geneva.

The National Classification of Occupation (1968). India (Republic). Occupational Information Unit, 2. Ed. New Delhi.

World Bank Report, (2017). *Reassessing Patterns of Female Labor Force Participation in India* http://documents.worldbank.org/curated/en/559511491319990632/pdf/WPS8024.pdf. Accessed on 19.11.2017.

World Economic Forum, (2016). *Global gender gap report, 2016* http://reports.weforum.org/ global-gender-gap-report-2016/. Accessed on 18.11.2017.

http://indiatoday.intoday.in/story/street-vendors-delhi-aam-aadmi-party-arvind-kejriwal-directive/1/419928.html. Accessed on 18.11.2017.

http://www.business-standard.com/article/pti-stories/assam-guv-express-concern-over-street-vendors-of-guwahati-115112200384_1.html

www.nasvinet.org, (2017). Official website of "National Association of Street Vendors of India"

http://www.unwomen.org/en/what-we-do/economic-empowerment. Accessed on 17.11.2017.

5
Structural Equation Modelling for Transport Planning in Towns

P.S. Ñianglang

Introduction

The profession and practice of town and country planning which is multidisciplinary in nature and mutable in character essentially involve the works of urbanologists and town planners also called physical planners, urban planners, spatial planners, land planners or land use planners. Besides urban housing, urban design, design portfolio, planning theory, town planning techniques and other disciplines; urban transport planning is finely knitted into the fabric of town planning as it deals with urban mobility, etc. Location theory is the foundation in which town planning is built upon for spatial structure, townscape, urban design, landscape architecture and site planning are the tenets of planning process for creation of activities on a geographical space to induce urban growth. Spatial configuration of man's optimising decision and economic behaviour in relation to his regular activities in an ecological setting be it a rustic settlement or a burgeoning town, is always ruled by the locative aspects of a geographic space. Urban activities performed for human needs include basic activities, non-basic activities, weight-gaining activities, weight-losing activities and their variants. Location theory connecting *individual actions* and *urban activity systems* stands behind the planning techniques and analytical methods. The invention of agricultural land-use model by von Thünen, the father of location theory, paved the way for urbanologists to develop their theories of urban structure and among them, the Alonso's Theory of Rent is illuminating. The urban growth theories are also put into practices. Isard, the founding father of regional science, Leontief and

Strout developed the Input-Output Analysis for growth of industries within and outside the urban area (Isard, 1956; McLoughlin, 1970; Ratcliffe, 1981; Balchin, *et al.*, 1995). Among the thinkers of the Old and the New Worlds, it was Geddes the father of modern town planning, who built the epistemological foundation of town planning and pioneered its applications that led the modern town planners to develop and concretise its philosophy. In his *magnum opus* called *Cities in Evolution*, Geddes (1915: 205) defines town planning as "the development of a local life, a regional character, a civic spirit, a unique individuality, capable of course of growth and expansion, of improvement and development in many ways, of profiting too by the example and criticism of others, yet always in its own way and upon its own foundation". It is a veritable orchestration of arts which is higher than the city design. It concerns with haussmannising the towns by improving the landscape, street designs and utility systems to ensure the greatest benefits of citizens. He forewarns, although towns teach a lesson to town planners yet town planning is not something easy which is learnable from one town and imitated in another. Though his *magnum opus* is introductory in character, it revolutionised the town planning movement which culminated his efforts in this discipline. Keeble (1964: 8) defines town and country planning as "the art and science of ordering the use of land and the character and siting of buildings and communication routes so as to secure the maximum practicable degree of economy, convenience and beauty". This definition is more expressive as it is practice-oriented, scientific and technical in nature. By analogy, as a geomorphologist is common to a geologist and a geographer, so also an urban designer to a civil engineer and a town planner. Intuitively, a town planner is involved in a wider process of planning. In America, the achievements in civic design made by Frederick Law Olmsted, the father of American landscape architecture paved the way for the successive urban planners, site planners, architects and designers to develop urban planning. Urban planning is credited to landscape architecture as F.J. Adams affirms, "I think the fact that planning here, as we know it, came from landscape architecture was really better than having come from the architects or the engineers. They, in the early days, did try to take over, if not the Institute, at least the claim that they were the logical planners; the architects because they know about three-dimensional design, and the engineers because they know how to lay out streets and sewers. But the landscape architects had a better conception of it." Robinson's writings, professional activities and artistic bent, all reinforced landscape architecture as the progenitor and technical base of planning profession (Krueckeberg, 1983). In Great Britain, the emergence of town and country planning known by its short title "town planning", is attributed to the skills of two classes of persons, viz., men who had great interest in the subject and technical men such as architects, civil engineers and surveyors. Considering the clamant demand for town planning studies, Schuster presented his Report in 1950 which expressed a strong preference for persons with university education in civil engineering, architecture, economics, geography and sociology as eligible candidates for planning profession. The infusion of persons from geography, economics and sociology induced some changes of attitude among town planners, however, the legacy of construction and design still precedes (Keeble, 1964; McLoughlin, 1970). Researchers recognise landscape architecture, agriculture, surveying, traffic engineering, operations research, statistics, behavioural science or any specialist profession as essential elements of town planning.

A town planner who is professionally different from a general planner employs specific techniques for his work. In practice, when he enters a 'solution space' of analysis, he applies the models and quantitative techniques to obtain an answer. Quantitative techniques permeate into the theoretical insights of town planning as they are the scientific and technical methods of solutions. Use of instruments and quantitative techniques makes town planning a technical process as Roberts (1974) put it, "Since some of the instruments of land use planning are technical, people are able to convince themselves that they are engaged in a technical process." Thus, town planning is a technical science of measurement, visual representation of mixed land uses to scales in two- or three-dimensional spaces and an analysis of data using scientific techniques and models for configurations of stand-alone activities to spatial structure to achieve legibility, imageability, aesthetic beauty, clean environment, convenience, safety, economic growth, and other goals befitting to and making the townsfolk liveable. Data including spatial data, *observed variables* called *indicators* or *manifest variables* or *measured variables* (MVs) and *constructs* or *concepts* or *unobserved variables* or *latent variables* (LVs) are collected, presented, analysed, and interpreted using the appropriate quantitative techniques capturing the qualitative and quantitative aspects of human population and urban land-use activities. Town planning undergoes a sequence of operations enveloping implementation, monitoring and evolution to achieve its objectives, targets, and goals and its approach is holistic and land-centric. Ratcliffe (1981:14) writes, "In a democracy it should be the practical and technical implementation of the people's wishes operating within a legal framework, permiting the manipulation of the various urban components such as transport, power, housing and employment, in such a way as to ensure the greatest benefit to all." The physical entity of transport planning as an associated discipline of town planning is visualized in a master plan, or a blueprint plan. The oft-quoted Buchanan Report (1963) called *Traffic In Towns* asserts transport planning as an ingrained component of town planning and is a technical profession. When town planners design for car-free towns, provisions of certain urban roadways for designated vehicles, walkways, railings, parking lots and other facilities for pedestrians and cyclists are the mandatory requirements to accomplish the trip purpose and hence the need of urban transport planning.

Quantitative techniques and models are scientific methods and tools used in the process of data analysis, constructs, and information such as estimation, forecast, evaluation, calibration, optimisation, simulation, etc. The techniques which are technical in nature are efficacious and powerful. Their applications in town planning began during the buoyant years of 1960s. The igniting minds for empirical analyses and surging interests for heuristic investigations facilitated by the advancement in computer science paved the way for researchers to develop theories and models in the 1970s. It is evident from planning literature that the evolution of town planning techniques are the results of tireless efforts and seamless researches made by professionals in the fields. If the neologism, viz., technometrics given by the ECOOM is acceptable in English lexicon, quantitative science is a synonym of the same genre for technometrics is defined as a discipline that measures and evaluates technological change. .. It is characterised by the combination of several disciplines such as econometrics, engineering, applied mathematics, mathematical and multivariate statistics for big data analyses (https://www.ecoom.be, 2002). The upsurge of interest and the rediscovery of the Wrightian path analysis (WPA), confirmatory factor analysis (CFA) and the multiple regression analysis (MRA) by Jöreskog in the early 1970s created a revolutionary effect on the statistical modelling system which came to be known as the structural equation modelling (SEM). SEM is also known by the name, Analysis of Covariance Structures. Analysis of Moment Structures (AMOS) and LISREL (Linear Structural Relationships) are the names of the computer software developed for specifying, fitting, and evaluating the SEMs. The robustness of SEM culminates in its applications in technical professions such as town planning, transport planning and natural systems too. Following the LISREL approach, the mechanics of SEM is presented in this article.

Definitions and Concepts of SEM

Researchers offer their definitions on SEM according to their perceptions and analytical insights. For example, Johnson and Wichern (2001) define

SEMs as sets of linear equations used to specify phenomena in terms of their presumed *cause-and-effect* variables. Hoyle (1995) defines SEM as "a comprehensive statistical approach to testing hypotheses about relations among observed and latent variables". Similarly, Grace (2006) defines SEM in its most basic sense as "the use of two or more structural equations to model multivariate relationships". The full LISREL model for single samples, for deviations about their mean, defined by Jöreskog and Sörbom (2001) is expressed in terms of three equations (5.9), (5.10) and (5.11). By multivariate relationships he refers to a series of equations that involve simultaneous influences and responses. An example of SEM is specified as

$$y_1 = \alpha_1 + \gamma_{11} x_1 + \zeta_1 \tag{5.1}$$
$$y_2 = \alpha_2 + \beta_{21} y_1 + \gamma_{21} x_1 + \zeta_2 \tag{5.2}$$
$$y_3 = \alpha_3 + \beta_{32} y_2 + \gamma_{31} x_1 + \zeta_3 \tag{5.3}$$

Equation (5.1) is a single univariate equation representing the effect of a single x on y and is called the *structural equation*, if theory and sufficient evidence support the interpretation that x_1 has a *causal effect* on y_1 so that the parameter γ_{11} is an estimate of the magnitude of such influence or effect. For example, if an average annual daily traffic (AADT) measured in PCU is a function of pavement or carriageway width measured in metres, then it is sufficient to infer that a pavement or carriageway width produces a *causal effect* on AADT. Omitting the alphas (αs) which are the intercepts of the Cartesian plane, the equations can be pictorially represented through the path diagram where boxes represent the observed variables, arrows between boxes are the directional relationships which are the equality signs in the equations, gammas (γs) indicate the effect of x variables on y variables, betas (βs) represent the effects of ys on other ys and zetas (ζs) represent the error terms for response or endogenous variables. Byrne (2016) defines SEM as a "statistical methodology that takes a confirmatory (i.e., hypothesis-testing) approach to the analysis of a structural theory bearing on some phenomenon". Hair *et al.* (2015) describe SEM as a "multivariate technique combining aspects of factor analysis and multiple regression that enables a researcher to simultaneously examine a series of interrelated *dependence relationships* among the *measured variables* and *latent constructs* (*variates*) as well as between several latent constructs". Thus, the structure of interrelationships expressed in a series of equations, portrays the relationships among the constructs comprising the dependent and the independent variables which is akin to multiple regression equations. The definitions elucidate SEM as a comprehensive and mature statistical modelling framework comprising a *measurement model* and a *structural model* for hypothesising the relations among the MVs and the LVs using the confirmatory factor analysis (CFA) approach. Fornell (1982) calls principal components analysis (PCA), cluster analysis (CA), discriminant analysis (DA), canonical correlation (CC), canonical correspondence analysis (CCA), MANOVA and other multivariate statistical methods as the "first generation" multivariate statistical methods while SEM as the "second generation" statistical methodology due to its capability for analysing the models involving LVs and MVs (Grace, 2006).

The two components of SEM make it a robust model capable of handling intricate modelling challenges such as indirect measurement of LVs, minimisation of measurement errors and reciprocal causation involving simultaneity or interdependence using the MLE method. SEMs contain both recursive and non-recursive systems which are pictorially represented by path diagrams (Grace, 2006, Byrne, 2016). In a *recursive* or *triangular* or *causal* system, βs of endogenous variables form a triangular array and the diagonal of βs contains units and βs do not appear above the main diagonal. For this type of model, parameters are estimable using either OLS technique or ML method which yields unbiased and consistent estimates (Koutsoyiannis, 1977; Intriligator, 1980; Johnston, 1984; Kmenta, 1986; Greene, 2003; Gujarati *et al.*, 2012). In a non-recursive system which shows a reciprocal relationship, i.e. simultaneity or interdependence, the LVs appear not only as *causes* but also as *effects* of the MVs. For example, Duncan, Haller and Portes present a simultaneous model in which the choice of occupation by a person is influenced by his peers. If a person's friend influences his choice, he also influences his friend's choice. The ambition of a student is measured using two indicators namely, educational choice and occupational choice and a reciprocal causation between the ambitions of two persons is specified. For non-recursive models, estimates can be obtained using the main estimating techniques, viz., ILS, 2SLS and LIML which are essentially single equation methods and 3SLS and FIML which are simultaneous equation system methods and not OLS technique. For non-recursive models, ML and 2SLS methods are advantageous because they are capable of handling the correlations between residuals (errors) and exogenous variables without violating the basic assumptions as other estimation methods are untenable (Johnston, 1984; Jöreskog and Sörbom, 2001; Grace, 2006). Factor analysis (FA) intends to gain insight into psychometric measurements using constructs such as intelligence, analysis of scores on mental tests and other LVs. Although from the same family, unlike PCA, FA is based on a specific statistical model which describes a covariance matrix Σ of the relationships among many variables in terms of a few underlying but unobservable and latent quantities called *common factors* k which are statistically sufficient to represent the original candidate variables p. The aim of FA is to reduce the number of p original candidate variables to a smaller set of sufficient number of $k < p$ elected LVs. Initially, the technique is widely used by psychologists and behavioural scientists. FA sets out and explains a typical population correlation in a symmetric matrix denoted by ρ_{ij} to distinguish from a sample correlation denoted by r. The regression matrix Δ of such *factors* will contain many zero elements to make the matrix simple. The correlation between the two factors is equal to the cosine of the angle between them. When the axes are orthogonal, the factors are uncorrelated and the cosine of the angle is 90° and its numerical value is 0 (since cos 90°= 0). *Schwarz inequality* satisfies $-1 \leq \cos\theta \leq 1$, then any angle lying between 0° and 180° is computable. When correlation values are expressed in terms of angles between the observed vectors, acute angles (< 90°) represent positive correlation values whereas obtuse angles (> 90°) represent negative correlation values. The two vectors a and b are orthogonal if their scalar product vanishes, i.e. $a'b = |a|\,|b| \cos\theta = 0$ (Hadley, 1962; Ayres, 1974). FA is such a powerful and elegant multivariate statistical method and is called the queen of analytical methods (Kerlinger, 1973). The orthogonal factor model is developed based on certain assumptions and these are $E(F) = 0$, $Cov(F) = E(FF') = I$,

$$E(\varepsilon) = 0 \text{ and } Cov(\varepsilon\varepsilon) = \Psi = \begin{bmatrix} \psi_1 & 0 \ldots & 0 \\ 0 & \psi_2 \ldots & 0 \\ 0 & 0 \ldots & \psi_p \end{bmatrix}$$

where Ψ is a diagonal matrix and that F and ε are independent so that $Cov(\varepsilon F') = E(\varepsilon F') = 0$. The orthogonal FA model expressed in matrix form is given as:

$$(X-\mu)_{(px1)} = L_{(pxm)} F_{(mx1)} + \varepsilon_{(px1)} \tag{5.4}$$

where X is the observable random vector with p-components has a mean μ and a population covariance matrix Σ, L a matrix of p *factor loadings*, F is a matrix of m unobservable random variables or LVs and ε is a column vector of p *random errors* or *specific factors*. The fundamental difference between the orthogonal FA model (5.4) and the multivariate linear regression model is that the former expresses the p deviations $X_1-\mu_1$, $X_2-\mu_2$, $X_3-\mu_3$, ... $X_p-\mu_p$ in terms of p + m random LVs f_1, f_2, f_3, ... f_m and ε_1, ε_2, ε_3, ... ε_p whereas the latter contains the independent MVs (Johnson and Wichern, 2013). In confirmatory studies, a modeler has obtained the knowledge about the variables measured and he is in a position to formulate a hypothesis specifying the relationships between the LVs and the MVs whereas in exploratory studies, he has not obtained such knowledge but he is yet to find a simple and meaningful interpretation of the experimental results. Conceptually, exploratory factor analysis (EFA) explores the data and informs a researcher about the number of factors needed to best represent the data whereas CFA specifies a number of factors from a set of variables and identifies each variable will load on *before* computing the results based on the theory being tested. CFA tests the effectiveness of the MVs in representing a smaller number of constructs (Jöreskog, 1979; Hair *et al.*, 2013). In practice, the distinction between the EFA and CFA is vague for many investigations are both exploratory and confirmatory in nature as they involve some variables of known and other of unknown composition. A CFA incorporated in SEM is a measurement model that determines how well various variables load on a number of factors or LVs.

Superiority

SEM occupies a unique position in the smorgasbord of computationally intensive methods. In his legitimate and heuristic quest for superiority of SEM over the other multivariate linear statistical methods such as PCA, CA, DA, CC, CCA, MANOVA, regression trees (RT), multiple or multivariate regression (MR), etc.; Grace (2006) affirms Fornell's classification of these methods as the "first generation" (1G) multivariate methods and the methodology of SEM as the "second generation" (2G) multivariate statistical method. There are some similarities between the 1G methods like CA, MR and ANOVA and the 2G method such as linearity of statistical models, testing of significance of coefficients, reliance on certain plausible assumptions, models of statistical tests for *necessary* but not *sufficient* evidence of *causality* and post *ad hoc* adjustments to statistical hypotheses tested by any statistical model. However, SEM as an advanced statistical method differs from the 1G techniques in some aspects which makes it superior to them. For comparing the efficacy of SEM with the 1G techniques, he assigns seven attributes in tabular form, viz. (i) include measures of absolute model fit, (ii) user can specify majority of relationships, (iii) capable of including LVs, (iv) able to address measurement error, (v) allows evaluation of alternative models, (vi) examines networks of relationships and (vii) can be used for model building. It is found that DA, RT, PCA and MR are compatible with the *seventh* attribute and SEM is the only technique which is capable and best suited for all the seven attributes. Additionally, PCA is compatible with the *third* attribute and so also does the MR for the *fifth* attribute. Thus, PCA and MR are useable for two attributes, DA and RT for one and SEM for all the seven attributes.

The following aspects amplify that SEM is superior to other multivariate statistical techniques. *First*, other multivariate statistical techniques are capable to examine only a single relationship between the dependent and the independent variables at a time. In SEM, with a specific theory, a prior experience and objectives of the study; model specification, estimation, evaluation of fit, model modification and interpretations of results are performed simultaneously using a set of multiple equations representing *cause-and-effect* relationship. For example, if urban commuters find that a robust public transport (PT) system creates utility and utility creates demand then utility is both a dependent and an independent variable in the same theory. When this law of demand is expressed into a simultaneous equations system with multiple relationships, the parameters of such system are estimable. Although, the use of LVs in SEM may sound like a "black box" approach, but it has both theoretical and practical justifications. The methodology validates an analysis for LVs by using several MVs (usually not less than three) for each LV simultaneously which enables an analyst to infer on the influence of LVs while other multivariate statistical techniques are incapable of measuring the LVs. *Second*, in regression analyses, logistic model and multinomial logit (MNL) model are mostly used for dealing with categorical variables where discrete numbers 0, 1, 3, ... (k-1) are assigned for measuring the qualitative or categorical or indicator variables. In SEM, the probit model and multinomial probit model are mostly used for parameters estimation involving such variables. When observed variables are ordinal or discrete, the matrix of polychoric correlations is analysed with the help of WLS method using the correct weight matrix. Although these models deal with the behavioural aspects of individuals they do not measure the LVs as the SEM does. Treatises on these models abound in literature (Meyer and Miller, 1984; Ben-Akiva and Lerman, 1985; Papacostas and Prevedouros, 2001; Washington *et al.*, 2011; Sabouri *et al*, 2020). PCA and FA which deal with psychometric measurements reduce the number of p original candidate variables to a smaller set of k elected variables where $k < p$ using a specific statistical model or otherwise. SEM deals with several intricate modelling challenges in which the exogenous and endogenous LVs are indirectly measured through indicators. Thus, other multivariate statistical techniques use MVs and discrete variables while SEM incorporates MVs and LVs and as such it is the most capable model in all behavioural sciences. Measuring abstract entities such as people's behaviour, attitudes, feelings, motivations, etc., using a set of indicators as per the designed questionnaires, tests, etc., begets observational errors and measurement errors due to erratic behaviours of human beings and imperfections of instruments. The technique is reliable in accounting the measurement errors by explicitly including variables for the measurement error portions of the MVs. When LVs are defined and parameters are identified, a *measurement model* evaluates the extent of measurement error called *reliability* and the estimates of residual covariance matrix and measurement error covariance matrix are obtained. When multicollinearity is present, estimates of individual parameters is obtainable using the multisample analysis which is computable by LISREL 8. Even when real data deviate far from multivariate normal distribution, the mechanics of SEM provides a scope for robustification of variances and covariances in sample variance-covariance matrix S before the analysis. Thus, SEM is more fitting for evaluation of multivariate hypotheses. *Third*, SEM addresses the statistical issue of endogeneity when multicollinearity is present while such capacity is not available with the conventional multivariate techniques. *Fourth*, these techniques do not offer alternative methods for modelling multivariate relations and for estimating point or interval effects whereas the methodology of SEM offers such promising features (Grace, 2006; Washington *et al.*, 2011; Hair *et al.*, 2015; Byrne, 2016).

Development

Beginning from the 1960s, researchers and traffic engineers in UK and USA studied the significance of human factors on roadways and developed a number of traffic capacity specifications, methods of traffic surveys, models, traffic simulation techniques, traffic flow theory, etc. Since transport system comprising the *fixed facilities*, the *flow entities* and the *control system*; co-operation and close co-ordination among the behavioural scientists, traffic engineers and transport planners are manifested explicitly. Qualitative human dimensions, viz., human factors and human behaviour play a very significant role in the system. In India, road safety studies involving human factors are carried out in engineering institutions and universities to minimise and eliminate road traffic injury and deaths and for formulation of concrete measures and policies. The *Transportation Research & Injury Prevention Programme* (TRIPP) at the Indian Institute of Technology, Delhi, an interdisciplinary programme, focuses on the minimisation of adverse health effect of road transport and endeavours to integrate all transport-related issues for promoting safety, cleaner air and energy conservation. The regular activities included under this programme are applied research projects, conduct of special courses and workshops, supervision of student projects, publications of papers presented by faculty members, Ph.D. scholars and M.Tech. students (HMSO, 1965; TRB, 1975; Shinar, 1978; Papacostas and Prevedouros, 2001; Khisty and Lall, 2003; ICoRSI, 2016).

Psychometric measurements of human dimensions comprising human behaviour and human factors such as ability, attention, perception, decision, attitude, willingness, interest, tastes, etc., require some standard models for fitting into the data of MVs and LVs to ascertain their variations and covariations. Psychometricians use concepts, constructs, mediators, moderators, independent, dependent, confounding variables and other operational variables for study of human factors in highway traffic accidents, safety and other transport-related phenomena involving human behaviour and decisions (Kerlinger, 1973; Shinar, 1978). FA technique mostly applied in behavioural sciences, is also used in diverse fields such as urban planning, regional planning, transport planning, meteorology, political science, medicine, geography, economics and business (Roberts, 1974; Glasson, 1978; Jöreskog, 1979; Washington, *et al.*, 2011; Wheelwright, M. *et al.* 2020). During the buoyant years of 1950s and 1960s some writings ignited the minds of clinical sociologists, psychologists and behavioural scientists to make *causal* interpretations of the non-experimental data. Quantitative studies in psychology unravelled various models for analysis of qualitative data and psychometric literatures abound in. The structural analysis of covariance matrices evolved as the most useful method for confirmatory studies although it could be used for exploratory analysis too. SEM originally developed by Jöreskog in the 1970s is powerful and illuminating. It is primarily meant for indirectly measuring the hypothetical concepts and constructs called LVs like social status, occupational aspiration, motivations, attitudes, etc., by sociologists; intelligence, verbal ability, spatial ability, etc., by psychologists and price level, permanent income, economic expectations, etc., by economists using a number of MVs. SEM is a multivariate statistical technique which combines the modern path analysis the FA and the MR analysis. It examines simultaneously the structure of interrelated *dependent relationships* among the endogenous LVs, the exogenous LVs and the latent errors of endogenous LVs of the *structural* or *LV model* in (5.9) besides examining the relationships between the LVs and MVs in the *measurement models* in (5.10) and (5.11). For example, using SEM, researchers took up different studies such as change in ability between two occasions for a group of individuals, relationships among depression, functioning of immune system and physical illness, relationships among social support network structure, perceived adequacy of social support and depressive symptoms (Sörbom, 1979; MacCallum, 1995; Marsh and Grayson, 1995) are other examples of applications of SEM. Though LVs are not directly measurable, they have operational implications for relationships among the MVs which are the indicators of LVs. In practice, when more indicators are assigned for measurement of each LV, the analysis yields satisfactory results. The practice of assigning only one indicator resulting in poor measurement of LV should be avoided. Analysis of SEM in the LISREL programme developed by Jöreskog and Dag Sörbom used mostly Greek letters and matrix notations. Nowadays, Mplus and AMOS programmes which are used worldwide, provide more familiar statistical models without compromising the mechanics and effectiveness of the LISREL model.

Path Diagram and Symbology

Path analysis originally developed by Sewell Wright (1918) explains the *causal* relations in population genetics. This technique assesses the direct *causal* contribution of one variable to another in the analysis of non-experimental data. The method of path coefficients is a flexible means of relating the correlation coefficients between variables in a multiple system and the functional relations among them. A system of variable quantities with notation V_s is ramified into a sequential order with which such quantities meet at some points of confluence representing the functional relations as portrayed by a path diagram. The *causal* or *associative* relations or correlations between the exogenous variables V_4, V_5 and V_6 are pictorially represented by curved lines with double-headed or bidirectional arrows whereas the *causal* or *cause-and-effect* relations between the exogenous variables and the endogenous variables V_1, V_2 and V_3 are shown by straight lines with single-headed or unidirectional arrows. A system of functional relations among the variables is shown in Figure 5.1 where an arrow denotes a linear relation. Path analysis is not a method of examining the *causal* or *associative* relationships between variables as the correlation analysis does but is akin to regression analysis which examines the *causal* relations of variables. The strength of each relationship or path is pictorially represented in the diagram using only a correlation matrix as input.

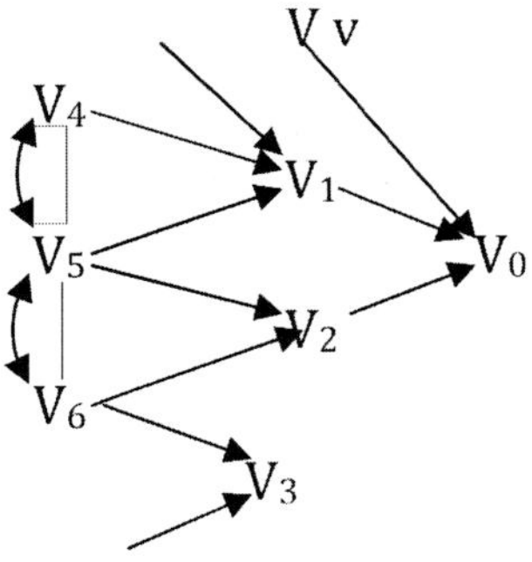

Figure 5.1: Path Diagram of a System of Variables and Their Functional Relations.

Source: Wright—The Method of Path Coefficient.

Following the Wrightian notations, if a variable V_0 is functionally related to variables V_1, V_2, V_3...V_n, i.e. $V_0 = f(V_1, V_2, V_3...V_n)$, then small deviations from the mean values are approximated to the first order terms of Taylor's Theorem of expansion of a polynomial function and the directional arrows are drawn to it. In standard normal distribution, the random variable Z is formally standardized corresponding to the original or unstandardized variable x using the relation $Z = \frac{x - \sigma_x}{\sigma_x}$ to obtain the mean E(Z) = 0 and variance Var (Z) = 1. The standardized random variables are shifted and the scaled versions of the original variables are obtained. Path analysis measures the deviations of each variable by its standard deviation. A correlation analysis is applicable for all paths in the diagram either directly or through common factors by which the two variables are connected such that the value of each contribution is the product of the coefficients pertaining to the elementary paths. Besides, the paths shown in the diagrams, Wright used an extension of a system of symbols to deal with the compound paths (Wright, 1934).

In correlation analysis an analyst measures the strength of suspected or hypothesised association between the variables x and y whereas in regression analysis he examines the influence or prediction of an independent variable x on a dependent variable y. The existence of a *causal* relationship or correlation between two variables x and y does not necessarily warrant a *causal* or cause-and-effect relationship between them. If a correlation between the two variables is observed merely on the basis of their sample data and without any theoretical foundation it simply reveals a typical case of *spurious* or *non-sense* correlation. For example, a *casual* relationship between road width and speed of vehicles, passenger emplanements and prices per litre of aviation fuel, tensile strength and hardness of aluminium, density of a highway sub-base material and road's durability, traffic flow and amount of rainfall, etc., are all supported by theories and therefore, are correlations (Benjamin and Cornell, 1970; Washington *et al.*, 2011). Axiomatically, a meaningful relationship between two variables is compatible with a theory. The objective of path analysis or structural equation analysis is to provide plausible interpretations of the observed correlations by constructing models of *cause-and-effect* relations among variables. For example, in demand and supply, an increase in the price of vehicle results in the decrease of its demand. The two variables representing demand and supply are the causes of changes in vehicle prices. In a simple linear regression analysis, when x and ε are assumed uncorrelated, the relation is given in (5.5).

$$y = \beta_o + \beta_1 x + \varepsilon \tag{5.5}$$

where y is the dependent or endogenous variable, x the independent or exogenous variable, β_o is the intercept, β_1 the slope of the regression line and ε is the error term or the white noise as engineers and scientists call it. The error term is a surrogate of random behaviour of human actions, incorrect specification of model, errors of aggregation, errors of measurement, omission of variables from the model, etc., which collectively influence y. The model (5.5) transforms into a statistical or stochastic model when an error term is included in it otherwise it is a mathematical equation of a straight line. When physical activities such as surveys for new roads, parking lots, PT, commercial vehicles, new towns, residential densities, site planning, designs of colonies, etc., are carried out; errors do crop up. In real life, statistical models are more efficacious than mathematical models since the significance of ε paves the way for statistical investigation such as residual analysis, treatment of outliers, cointegration, error correction, etc. In regression analysis, the units of regression parameters β_j are expressed as the ratios of y_i units to x_j units. Scaled variables are sometimes obtained to produce *dimensionless* or *standardised regression parameters* using the two popular scaling techniques, namely (i) the Unit Normal Scaling and (ii) the Unit Length Scaling (Draper and Smith, 1998; Montgomery *et al.*, 2003; Chatterjee and Haidi, 2012). When one variable x precedes another y in time, then x causes y that is x is the *causal* or exogenous variable and y is the *effectible* or endogenous variable. If the relationship between x and y has an error ε, it can be written as x → y with ε. The path diagram of such relationship is shown in Figure 5.2. Holding the OLS assumption of no correlation between the error term and the *causal* variable x, ε has a *cause-and-effect* relationship on y. In the path diagram, ε is connected by a straight arrow to y and not to x. Centering and scaling the intercept regression model, $y = \beta_o+\beta_1x+\varepsilon$ in the standardised form we obtain the relation in (5.6).

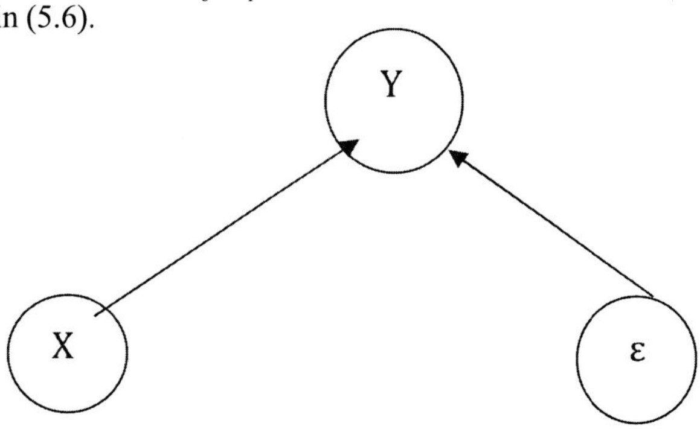

Figure 5.2: Path Diagram with an Error.

Source: Author's Construction.

$$Z_y = p_{yx} Z_x + p_{y\varepsilon}\varepsilon \quad (5.6)$$

where Z_x is a scaled regressor or scaled exogenous variable which has a *cause-and-effect* relationship on Z_y, a scaled regressand or scaled endogenous variable. Z_x is a *causal* variable and p_{yx} and $p_{y\varepsilon}$ are the parameters or *path coefficients* of the standardized model (5.6). The path diagram for the MR model is shown in Figure 5.3. It portrays the utility of PT denoted by y which depends on the two exogenous LVs, viz. passengers' ability to read a book, newspaper or carry out minor jobs denoted by x_1 and comfort in terms of passenger capacity, noise level, closed-circuit television, boarding, alighting, etc., denoted by x_2 (Simpson, 1994; White, 1995).

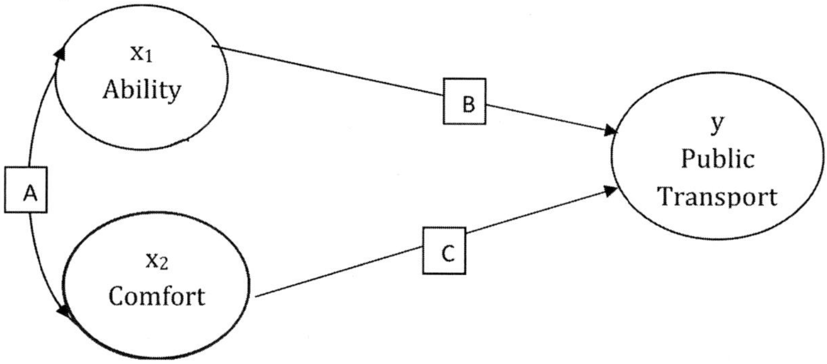

Figure 5.3: Path Diagram for Multiple Regression with Two Exogenous Variables

Source: Author's Construction.

The upsurgence of interest in the 1970s led to the rediscovery of WPA and the development of *modern path analysis*. In WPA, correlations are used as statistical frameworks of analyses whereas in *modern path analysis* covariance matrices are used. WPA used only a correlation matrix as input whereas *modern path analysts* employ a covariance matrix or a variance-covariance matrix to calculate the strength of relationship between variables. A distinction between the two is available in SEM literature. Path analysis models used in the analysis of hypothetical constructs or LVs have operational implications on MVs. MVs appear only as *effects* or *indicators* of LVs in some models and as *causes* or *components* or as both *causes* and *effects* in others. The models operate within the domain of structural analysis of covariance matrices as this is a general method for analysing the measurements to detect and assess the latent sources of variation and covariation in observed measurements. The Coster model with correlated measurement errors, the Hauser-Goldberger model with multiple causes and multiple indicators of a LV and the Jöreskog general model for analysing the multitest-multioccasion correlation matrices are illustrations of *modern path analysis* models. In *modern path analysis*, a population variance-covariance matrix or more simply a variance or a covariance or a dispersion matrix of MVs denoted by Σ (capital sigma) is used (Jöreskog, 1979). Path analysis has two components namely, (i) the path diagram and (ii) the decomposition of observed correlations into a sum of path coefficient terms comprising simple and compound paths. Path diagram is used to depict a model of SEM in graphical equivalence of its statistical representation of a set of equations relating the independent variables to the dependent variables.

SEM uses particular configurations comprising mathematical symbols, geometric symbols and variables which represent structural relations. A directly MV such as speed of vehicle, transport cost, traffic volume, etc., is represented by a square (□) or a rectangle (▭); a LV such as attitude towards PT, convenience of private car, opinion towards HOV lane, etc., which is a psychological underpinning of utility theory is represented by a circle (○) or an ellipse (⬭), a *composite variable* is represented by a circle (○) or an ellipse (⬭) with no indicators and zero error represents a LV. A *composite variable* represents a collective effect of a group of LVs such as convenience, comfort, individual freedom and social superiority which collectively influence upon the individual's decision to buy a car. An *error variable* which is unenclosed between the single-headed or one-way arrow and the curved double-headed or curved two-way arrow or behind the single-headed or one-way arrow is a true variable representing an unknown or unspecified effect on MV and endogenous LV. An *error variable* is usually presumed to represent a collective effect of a random measurement error and unmeasured variables that produce *causal* influences on an *endogenous variable*, a single-headed or one-way arrow (→) pointing a variable x to variable y shows a *causal* influence of an exogenous variable x on an endogenous variable y. The direction of an arrow is assumed to coincide with the direction of influence from an exogenous to an endogenous variable. When only one arrow links the two LVs, a *direct relationship* which is equal to the parameter estimate exists. An *indirect relationship* exists when an exogenous variable x does not influence an endogenous variable z directly but through another exogenous variable y. A curved double-headed or curved two-way arrow (↔) between x and y signifies the symmetrical nature of a *casual* association which may be a correlation or covariance of a pair of variables (Jöreskog, 1979; Grace, 2006; Byrne, 2016). When multiple arrows linking one LV to another exist, for example, $x \rightarrow y \rightarrow z$, then the effect of x on z is equal to the product of the parameter estimates for each arrow that are *causally* related to endogenous LV. In Figure 5.3, the correlational path A shows the *casual* relation between x_1 and x_2, paths B and C show the respective effects or *causal* relations of x_1 and x_2 on y. This is the standard convention of symbology used in SEM. From Figure 5.3 and equation (5.6), *identification* of direct and indirect paths and *estimation* of relationships of model can be done. Variances, covariances, correlations and regression coefficients constitute a set of statistical procedures of SEM. Grace (2006) presents eight *rules of path coefficients* for MV models and one *rule of path coefficients* for LV models. The *causal* relation of three variables is akin to the MR model which passes through the origin of the 1st quadrant, i.e., where the intercept term (b_0) is absent. Although LISREL 8 does not employ MR method but performs any of the seven methods viz., VI, TSLS, ULS, GLS, ML, WLS and DWLS, however, a glimpse on the MR method is necessary due to its identicalness with the ML method. The MR model (5.7) extended to a k-variable linear model is expressed as

$$Y_i=\beta_0+\beta_1X_{1i}+\beta_2X_{2i}+\beta_3X_{3i}+...+\beta_kX_{ki}+\varepsilon_i \tag{5.7}$$

where β_0 = intercept, β_1 to β_k = partial slope coefficients, i = i^th^ observation, n = population size and $\boldsymbol{\varepsilon}_i$ = stochastic disturbance term or white noise.

Model (5.7) is expressed in matrix form along with the order of matrix and vectors as

$$Y_{(n\times 1)} = X_{(n\times k)} \quad \beta_{(k\times 1)} + \varepsilon i_{(n\times 1)} \tag{5.8}$$

with $E(\varepsilon_i) = 0$; $Var(\varepsilon_i) = \sigma^2$ (constant); $Cov(\varepsilon_i, \varepsilon_k) = 0$ for $j \neq k$ and $Cov(\varepsilon_i) = E(\varepsilon\varepsilon') = \sigma^2 I$. Equation (5.8) identifies k-1 explanatory variables or regressors namely, $X_1, X_2, X_3 ... X_k$ which collectively influence Y, the dependent variable or regressand. When the regressors are not linear, they are transformed into semilog transformation, double-log transformation, reciprocal transformation, logarithmic transformation, etc., and in such a process the regressand, the regressors or both are transformed. The prime objective of *transformation* is to *linearise* the variables as long as βs are linear so that simple techniques like *Time Series Plot*, *Scatter Plot*, *Correlation Analysis*, *Least Squares Estimators,* etc., can be applied to obviate complex relations.

Undeniably, *modern path analysis* is overwhelmingly advantageous over the WPA. Paths *identification* and relationships *estimation* are the two basic processes of path analysis. Once all relationships connecting the two variables are identified, an analyst decomposes the simple or bivariate correlation between any two variables into the sum of simple and compound paths connecting them. Analysts oftentimes use Chi-Square (χ^2) as the GoF test to evaluate the overall model fit. Inclusion of GoF tests is a significant advance of *modern path analysis*. The efficacy of path diagram is weighed in terms of its capability to depict either (a) a model originally specified and estimated by the investigator; (b) that portion of the original model for which parameter estimates are significant or (c) a model that resulted from one or more modifications and re-estimations of the original model (Hoyle, 1995). A path diagram is powerful if it can present the hypotheses and describe the initially specified and estimated model. A path diagram which depicts all parameters in the original model is a bridge between the full and the partial diagrams.

Specification of Structural Equation Models (SEMs)

A model represents a statistical statement which indicates the relations among the variables. The relations among the LVs can be either *cause-and-effect* relations or correlational or covariance relations. Researchers in quantitative methods for town and country planning develop new theories, models, hands-on techniques, etc., to sharpen the knowledge of planners and practitioners. For teaching SEM, some academicians start with a conceptual framework (CF) involving abstract constructs and their interrelationships and then translates it into a casual path diagram using operational variables (Park *et al.*, 2020). Model specification which fits in theory is an exercise of identifying and including the right number of *cause-and-effect* variables in models to obtain significant estimates for a meaningful inference. Models and their variants are either simple or complex. For example, simple correlation analysis is a simple model which specifies a non-directional relation between two variables whereas multiple correlation, partial correlation, canonical correlation are complex models. MR and ANOVA models directional relations. Although statistical tests for directionality cannot be done by correlation analysis, regression analysis and ANOVA, however, they are widely used for estimation of parameters. In SEM, model specification is a formulation of statement about a set of parameters which hypothesises the nature of relations between the two sets of variables to be analysed. It is a process of confirming the existence or non-existence of relationships of MVs or LVs and an arrow is drawn if it exists and no arrow is drawn otherwise. Specification of relationships between the MVs and LVs is a necessary condition. Model specification is central in SEM for a researcher cannot set off his analytical process until this exercise is carried out. In this article unless specifically expressed, the original notations η (eta), B (capital beta), Γ (capital gamma), ξ (xi), ζ (zeta), Φ (capital phi), Ψ (capital psi), Λ (capital lambda), δ (delta), ε (epsilon) and Θ (capital theta) used as the LISREL language for SEM; are retained for easy reference of readers (Jöreskog, 1979; Jöreskog and Sörbom, 2001; Johnson and Wichern, 2001; Grace, 2006). The assumptions made are ε is uncorrelated with η, δ is uncorrelated with ξ, ζ is uncorrelated with ξ and as per the ordinary least squares (OLS) assumptions ζ, ε and δ are mutually uncorrelated. The assumptions for covariance matrices are Cov (ξ) = Φ (nxn), Cov (ζ) = Ψ (mxm), Cov (ε) = $\Theta\varepsilon$ (pxp) and Cov (δ) = Θ_δ (qxq). It is also assumed that B has zeros on the diagonal, I-B is a non-singular matrix, E (ξ) = 0 and E (η) = 0. The zeros on the diagonal of B imply that any given η has a direct effect on itself. The full LISREL model comprising the *structural equation model* and the *measurement models* developed by Jöreskog and Sörbom are the three matrix equations given in (5.9), (5.10) and (5.11).

$$\eta = B\eta + \Gamma\xi + \zeta \quad (5.9)$$
$$x = \Lambda_x\xi + \delta \quad (5.10)$$
$$y = \Lambda_y\eta + \varepsilon \quad (5.11)$$

The SEMs in (5.9), (5.10) and (5.11) are collectively called the *general model*. Equation (5.9) which describes the relationships among the m endogenous LVs collected in a vector $\eta_{(mx1)}$, n exogenous LVs collected in a vector $\xi_{(nx1)}$ and m latent errors collected in a vector $\zeta_{(mx1)}$ is called the *structural equation model* or LV model. A vector of m endogenous LVs denoted by $\eta = (\eta_1, \eta_2, \eta_3, \ldots \eta_m)$, a vector of n exogenous LVs denoted by

$\xi = (\xi_1, \xi_2, \xi_3, \ldots \xi_n)$ and a vector of m errors for endogenous LVs denoted by $\zeta = (\zeta_1, \zeta_2, \zeta_3, \ldots \zeta_m)$ have *causal* relationships and encapsulate all variables which are latent in nature. The two coefficient matrices in (5.9) are $B_{(mxm)}$, a matrix of structural coefficients which describes the relationships among the endogenous LVs and $\Gamma_{(mxn)}$, a matrix of structural coefficients which describes the effects of exogenous LVs on the endogenous LVs. Expounding in terms of path diagram, endogenous variables are the dependent LVs with an arrow pointing towards them from another LV and exogenous variables are the independent LVs. Specification of *structural equation model* is incomplete unless structures of covariance matrices of exogenous LVs and errors of LVs are described. By assumptions, $\Phi_{(nxn)}$ is a matrix of covariances among the exogenous LVs and $\Psi_{(mxm)}$ is a matrix of covariances among the errors of LVs which implies that the model (5.9) implicitly contains these two matrices. The elements of B on the diagonal side are all zeros and I-B is a non-singular matrix where I is the identity matrix.

Unlike equation (5.9) which specifies the *causal* relationships among the LVs only, the *measurement equations* (5.10) and (5.11) specify how LVs are indicated by the MVs. This model has four vectors of variables i.e., $X_{(qx1)}$ is a vector of observed indicators of the exogenous LVs contained in ξ, $Y_{(px1)}$ is a vector of observed indicators of the endogenous LVs contained in η, $\delta_{(qx1)}$ is a vector of measurement errors for the indicators of the exogenous LVs in X and $\varepsilon_{(px1)}$ is a vector of measurement errors for the indicators of the endogenous LVs in Y. The *measurement model* encapsulates two coefficient matrices Λ_x and Λ_y where $\Lambda_{x(q\,x\,n)}$ is a matrix of coefficients which explains the influence of ξ, the vector of exogenous LVs on X and $\Lambda_{y(p\,x\,m)}$ is a matrix of coefficients which explains the influence η, the vector of endogenous LVs on Y. Although Θ_δ and Θ_ε are not explicitly shown in the *measurement model*, by assumptions, $\Theta_{\delta(qxq)}$ is a matrix of covariances among the measurement errors for indicators of the exogenous LVs in δ and $\Theta_{\varepsilon(pxp)}$ is a matrix of covariances among the measurement errors for indicators of the endogenous LVs in ε. The *structural equation model* differs from the *measurement model* in that it introduces additional constraints on the relations among the LVs. The distinctive feature of LISREL model provides a scope to postulate a complete system of *causal* relationships given in (5.9) which holds among the factors where ηs are treated as the jointly dependent or endogenous variables and ξs as the independent or exogenous variables.

Structure of Covariance Matrix

The covariance structure $LL'+\Psi$ of the model (5.4) may not be tenable if the p observable random variables $x_1, x_2, x_3, \ldots x_p$ are non-linearly related to the *m* unobservable random variables $f_1, f_2, f_3, \ldots f_m$. The statistical framework of LISREL system given in (5.9), (5.10) and (5.11) relating them with (5.12) describes $\Sigma(\Theta)$ and expresses the relationship between the data and the model. It provides an insight into the mathematical underpinnings of modelling covariances in which ε is ramified into sub-matrices that construe the practical significance of the model.

$$\Sigma = \Sigma\,(\Theta) \qquad (5.12)$$

where Σ is the population covariance matrix of observed variables and $\Sigma\,(\Theta)$ is the model-predicted covariance matrix sometimes denoted as $\hat{\Sigma}$. Specifically, Σ is a well-defined collection or set of sub-matrices of covariances among ys, among xs, between xs and ys, ys and xs. Clearly, Σ is a symmetric matrix. The expressions of covariance sub-matrices into equations using the LISREL language give an insightful learning to the nitty-gritty of SEM technique (Johnson and Wichern, 2001; Grace, 2006). Each sub-matrix has variances as elements in its principal diagonal and covariances as elements in the lower and upper triangular matrices. With the Cartesian coordinates x and y in a two-dimensional space, the covariances between x and y which are the sub-matrices of Σ are expressed in matrix form as shown in (5.13).

$$\text{Cov}\begin{bmatrix}\frac{Y}{X}\end{bmatrix} = \Sigma_{(p+q)x(p+q)} = \begin{bmatrix}\frac{\Sigma_{11}}{pxp} & \frac{\Sigma_{12}}{pxq} \\ \frac{\Sigma_{21}}{qxp} & \frac{\Sigma_{22}}{qxq}\end{bmatrix} = \begin{bmatrix}Cov(Y) & Cov(Y,X) \\ Cov(X,Y) & Cov(X)\end{bmatrix} = \begin{bmatrix}(\sigma_{yy}) & (\sigma_{yx}) \\ (\sigma_{xy}) & (\sigma_{xx})\end{bmatrix} \qquad (5.13)$$

The *structural equation model* and the *measurement model* in (5.9), (5.10) and (5.11) contain a series of equations and notations that describe the main parts of the LISREL model. When these model ingredients are expressed as a complete set of expectations for a full structural model, equations (5.12) and (5.13) emerge into a magnified form of $\Sigma\,(\Theta)$ as

$$\Sigma = \Sigma\,(\Theta) = \left[\frac{covariances\ among\ ys}{covariances\ between\ xs\ and\ ys} \Big/ \frac{covariances\ between\ ys\ and\ xs}{covariances\ among\ xs}\right] \qquad (5.14)$$

Derivations and expressions of four sub-matrix elements of (5.14) in the form of individual equations are available in SEM literature (Hayduk, 1987; Johnson and Wichern, 2001). Using the LISREL symbols and notations with their assigned meanings and significance, the individual equations of four sub-matrices are presented here. Beginning with the lower right sub-matrix of xs, the first equation is expressed as

$$\mathrm{Cov}(X) = \Delta_x \Phi \Delta_x' + \Theta_\delta \tag{5.15}$$

where Φ, the matrix of covariances among the exogenous LVs denoted by ξ is pre-multiplied by Δ_x, the coefficients which describe the influence of ξ on x in the *measurement model* and post-multiplied by its transpose Δ_x'. The covariance matrix among variables xs is thus, equal to the product $\Delta_x \Phi \Delta_x'$ plus Θ_δ, the matrix of covariances among the measurement errors for indicators of the exogenous LVs in δ. For the upper left sub-matrix of ys, the second equation describes the covariances among the endogenous variables collected in a vector η is first expressed as

$$\mathrm{Cov}(Y) = \Delta_y\,[\text{covariances among } \eta\text{s}]\,\Delta_y' + \Theta_\varepsilon \tag{5.16}$$

Substituting the words occurring in (5.16) with covariances among ηs $= A(\Gamma\Phi\Gamma' + \Psi)A'$, the second sub-matrix equation is obtained as,

$$\mathrm{Cov}(Y) = \Delta_y\, A(\Gamma\Phi\Gamma' + \psi)A'\Delta_y' + \Theta_\epsilon \tag{5.17}$$

where $A = (I-B)^{-1}$, is the inverse of the beta matrix of the *structural equation model* which subtracts the identity matrix and A′ is the transpose of A. The sub-matrix of covariances between xs and ys of the lower left quadrant is given by the third equation as

$$\mathrm{Cov}(X, Y) = \Delta_x \Phi \Gamma' A' \Delta_y' \tag{5.18}$$

This gives the expected cross-products between xs and ys of the *measurement model*. The sub-matrix for the covariances between ys and xs of the upper right quadrant is given by the fourth equation as

$$\mathrm{Cov}(Y, X) = \Delta_y A \Gamma \Phi \Delta_x' \tag{5.19}$$

This encapsulates the transpose of the equation in the lower left quadrant of (5.18). Fitting the equations (5.15), (5.17), (5.18) and (5.19) into (5.14); finally, Σ contains the quadrantal equations in (5.20) which is the original form developed by Jöreskog.

$$\Sigma = \begin{bmatrix} \Delta_y A(\Gamma\Phi\Gamma' + \psi)A'\Delta_y' + \Theta_\epsilon & \Delta_y A\Gamma\Phi\Delta_x' \\ \Delta_x \Phi\Gamma' A' \Delta_y' & \Delta_x \Phi \Delta_x' + \Theta_\delta \end{bmatrix} \tag{5.20}$$

Using the matrix approach, (5.20) is a lucid expression of covariance expectations of the LISREL model from a full *structural equation model*. Derivations show that covariances are non-linear functions of the model parameters Δ_x, Δ_y, Γ, Φ, Ψ, Θ_x and Θ_δ. From (5.12), it is seen that $\Sigma = \Sigma(\Theta)$ and the model parameters of $\Sigma(\Theta)$ can be estimated using S. With n multivariate observations of two variables x and y given in a row vector $[y_j', x_j']'$ where j = 1, 2, 3 ... n, S is constructed and partitioned to conform to Σ as shown in equation (5.21)

$$S_{(p+q)x(p+q)} = \left[\begin{Bmatrix} S_{11\,(pxp)} & S_{12\,(pxq)} \\ S_{21\,(qxp)} & S_{22\,(qxq)} \end{Bmatrix}\right] \tag{5.21}$$

Overtly, from (5.12) and (5.21), a relation is obtained as

$$\Sigma\,(\Theta) = S \tag{5.22}$$

Using the information of the covariance structure provided by S, the model parameters are estimated by specifically setting Σ (Θ) equal to S as shown in (5.22) and solve the resulting equations.

It may be recapitulated that the partition of Σ and S in (5.14) and (5.21) is necessary to address the heterogeneity in the characteristics of MVs by clustering into distinct homogeneous groups holding the conformability in (5.22). For example, from the survey of 261 commuters conducted in the Seattle metropolitan area to know the commuters' opinions or attitudes about the HOV lanes, the heterogeneity in characteristics of respondents necessitated the grouping of variables (Washington *et al.*, 2011). The total 42 candidate variables are classified into three groups, namely (i) travel behaviour variables, (ii) HOV attitude variables and (iii) socio-demographic variables. Using the PCA and FA, the two methods yielded 6 components (factors) with 9 variables under the first group and 5 under the second group. In the third group, the PCA yielded 8 variables and the FA distilled only 6 variables which means that the elected variables given by the PCA are 22 and FA are 20. The remaining candidate variables are insignificant and are thus discarded from the analysis. Clearly, 42 candidate variables are distilled into subsets or groups of elected variables. The results given by PCA and FA are used for SEM specification. The three LVs, namely travel behaviour variables, HOV attitude variables and socio-demographic variables are presumed to define the structure of HOV data. Since η and ξ involve the LVs, the model parameters in (5.21) cannot be estimated directly. SEM relies on the S and the orthogonal factor model using the ML technique. A *Conceptual Framework* shows the *causal relations* between the abstract constructs and the operational variables. For example, the number of children using the park is influenced by the three constructs, namely (i) user characteristics or behaviour, (ii) neighbourhood characteristics, and (iii) Park characteristics. Altogether 21 candidate variables are identified in which 4, 8 and 9 variables are classified into the first, the second and the third group respectively (Park *et al.,* 2020). Clearly, the heterogeneous nature of respondents collected in S attracts grouping of the indirectly measured LVs or constructs using the indicators or manifest variables. These examples crystallise our perceptions about the need of partitioning the matrix S into distinct groups or subsets of compatible ordered matrices.

Identification of Parameters

In a simultaneous equations system, a model is said to be complete if it contains at least as many independent equations as the endogenous variables and each equation is said to be identified if consistent estimates of parameters of a structural equation are obtained from the estimated reduced-form coefficients. The problem of estimating the parameters of a structural equation presumed to have generated the observations on the endogenous variables from the parameters of the likelihood function is called *identification*. The two rules for identification are: (i) the order or the necessary condition and (ii) the rank or the sufficient condition. Treatises on identification and estimation methods of simultaneous equation models abound in econometric literatures where econometricians and students use in economic planning and research.

In SEM, assuming that the distribution of MVs is multivariate normal and is well described by the *first order* and the *second order* moments, identifiability depends on the model choice and specification of *fixed*, *constrained* and *free* parameters. Identification is the process of ascertaining the fixed parameters from the number of observed variances and covariances in a matrix and the path coefficients representing the known values or information that will be used for estimating the *free* or *unknown parameters* using the t-rule, the necessary and the sufficient conditions. A model is said to be identified if for each of its *free parameter*, a unique value is obtainable from the observed data collected in a vector θ. If a unique estimate is obtained for each *free parameter* through one and only one manipulation of the observed data, the model is said to be *just-identified* and has zero degrees of freedom denoted by the Greek letter υ. A *just-identified* model has a one-to-one correspondence between the data and the structural parameters which means that data variances and covariances are equal to *free parameters* to be estimated. If a unique estimate is obtainable for one or more *free parameters* in multiple ways from the observed data, the model is said to be *overidentified* and υ are equal to the number of observed variances and covariances minus the number of *free parameters*. If a unique estimate is not obtainable from the observed data for one or more *free parameters*, the model is said to be *underidentified* and in such a case the model is inestimable (Hoyle, 1995). That means if the information matrix is not positive definite, the specified model is said to be unidentified. This stipulates that a model is estimable only if it is *just identified* or *overidentified*. $\Sigma(\theta)$ contains p elements or simultaneous equations and some are redundant leaving only $p^* = \frac{1}{2}p(p-1)$ non-redundant and independent equations. Restriction entails two necessary and sufficient conditions for SEM identification. The *necessary condition* restricts the number of p* elements or simultaneous equations which must be equal to or greater than the number of *free parameters* q, i.e. $q \leq p^*$. The *sufficient condition* is that each and every *free parameter* is identified (Chou and Bentler, 1995). Consider a vector θ of s order containing all the *independent*, *free* and *constrained parameters*. Identification problem concerns with the question whether θ is uniquely determined by $\Sigma_{(pxp)} = \sigma_{ij}$, where σ_{ij} are the variances which are the diagonal elements of a matrix. LISREL model has been refined and modern SEM relies on a comparison between observed and model-implied covariances. Then hypothesising to generate $\Sigma(\theta)$ which relates the Σ, variances are functionally related to parameter vector θ and is expressed as

$$\sigma_{ij} = f_{ij}(\theta) \text{ for } i \leq j \tag{5.23}$$

Conditionally, for estimating the model parameters, the number of equations should be > the number of unknown parameters. The parameters vector θ contains $\frac{1}{2}(p+q)(p+q+1)$ equations and t total unknown parameters or elements. Therefore, a *necessary condition* for identification of all parameters stipulates p and q must be such that

$$t \leq \tfrac{1}{2}(p+q)(p+q+1) \tag{5.24}$$

where p is the number of variables or equations and q is the number of parameters. The weak inequality in (5.24) means that the total number of parameters to be estimated must be less than or equal to the number of known values. If S contains known values of four MVs, viz. x_1, x_2, y_1 and y_2 tabulated as a lower triangular matrix pictorially shown in a *saturated* model, then identification process begins by calculating the number of known values denoted as p* either countable by hand or using a simple formula, $p^* = \frac{1}{2}p(p+1)$ where p* is the number of known variances and covariances in the matrix representing the elements of S. The t-rule for solving the SEMs stipulates that the number of parameters to be estimated should be ≤ to the number of known information given by S. Grace (2006) illustrates the procedure of parameter estimation with *saturated* and *unsaturated* path diagrams.

The discussions on identification problem illuminate the fundamental aspects of parameter estimation. It involves calculation of known parameters and estimation of *free parameters* for model identification. This explains the specifications of variances and covariances of matrices, namely $\Lambda_{y\,(pxm)}$, $\Lambda_{x\,(qxn)}$, $B_{(mxm)}$, $\Gamma_{(mxn)}$, $\Phi_{(nxn)}$, $\Psi_{(mxm)}$, $\Theta_{\varepsilon\,(pxp)}$ and $\theta_{\delta\,(qxq)}$ as *fixed parameters*, *constrained parameters* and *free parameters*. Clearly, a *fixed parameter* is not estimated from the data but its value is fixed by an analyst and a *free parameter* which is estimated from the non-zero data shows the strength of specific relationship, magnitudes and signs. In practice, since parameter values are unknown, variances or covariances are obtained from the sample data or observations. When estimates match with the sample values of variances or covariances closely a solution is obtained. Thus, a *free parameter* is a function of variances or covariances. An *underidentified* model cannot be put into practice because estimates are arbitrary and inexplicable. The *just identified model* fits the data very well, however, assessment of model plausibility by evaluation of fit is meaningless. The model does not generate scientific interest as it has no υ thereby disabling an analyst to reject or accept a model. The υ for an *overidentified model* are equal to the number of observed variances and covariances minus the number of *free parameters*. A model with *overidentified* parameters usually does not fit the data exactly since the known values are more than the unknowns. An analyst uses the surplus information or known values to test the overall model fit. Thus, an *overidentified model* with one or more *free parameters* is of primary interest to an analyst for it is possible to find a poor fit and a good fit of the model. Using the results in positive υ, an analyst decides to reject or accept the fitted model (MacCallum, 1995; Byrne, 2016).

Estimation

Parameter estimation process in SEM dated back to the early parts of 1970s where the search for a synthetic approach to solve the structural equation models reached its highest trajectory. The robust method of analysing the covariance structures known as LISREL model, presented by Jöreskog stood out among the heuristic ventures as the illuminating work. The LISREL model and its metaphysics produced a revolutionary effect on the statistical modelling system. Such synthetic approach of model building which evolved as entropy of advancement in scientific researches made the LISREL technique a robust measure of psychometric effects of latent constructs on the endogenous and exogenous aspects. Estimation methods such as ML, FA, PCA, ULS and GLS are developed, among which ML is the most popularly used method. The methods have their respective fitting functions and each function is to be minimised with respect to Δ, Φ and Ψ. The ML technique minimises the fitting function involving a logarithmic term or maximises the likelihood of the observations under multinormality of x. Among the three important rotation methods, viz. (i) the Varimax Rotation, (ii) the Quartimax Rotation and (iii) the Equamax Rotation; the first method is widely used in FA. The *varimax* rotation technique selects the orthogonal transformation T and maximises the sum of variances V of *factor loadings* ℓ_{ij}. Computer programmes are employed since rotation methods involve *iterations*. When estimates are obtained, variables with high factor loadings are taken as statistically competent and influential in describing the original candidate variables whereas variables with low factor loadings are eliminated for analysis. A *factor loading* ℓ which is close to 1 implies that a variable x is greatly influenced by a factor f whereas a *factor loading* ℓ which is close to 0 implies that the influence of a factor ℓ on a variable x is insignificant. By convention, *common factors* with *eigenvalues* which are > 1 are retained for analyses as they account for higher *communality* while *eigenvalues* which are < 1 are discarded (Johnson and Wichern, 2001; Washington *et al.*, 2011; Wheelwright *et al.*, 2020).

SEMs evaluate theories or hypotheses using empirical data contained in $S_{(pxp)}$. This S is an unstructured estimator of Σ. Hypothesizing SEM to be a function of q unknown structural parameters contained in vector Θ, will generate $\Sigma(\Theta)$. When Σ is ramified into sub-matrices shown in (5.13) and (5.14), finally the relation between $\Sigma(\Theta)$ and S is obtained using (5.22). This general equation has S which contains a series of derived equations in (5.15), (5.17), (5.18) and (5.19). S is used to represent the fundamental consequences of modelling covariances using the ML technique. Intuitively, the structures of Σ, $\Sigma(\Theta)$ and S contain a series of simultaneous equations for parameter estimation. From (5.22), it transpires that Σ can be described and understood in terms of $\Sigma(\Theta)$ and S. In practice, variances and covariances of MVs containing estimates or known values in S are compared with those contained in $\Sigma(\Theta)$ and a statistical inference for Σ is drawn. Such comparison process entangles a model-fitting procedure that seeks to minimise the deviations between S and $\Sigma(\Theta)$ by selecting the most commonly used fitting function in ML estimation. Since an analyst does not know Σ, he uses the known S which yields the best estimate. While comparing S with $\Sigma(\Theta)$, an analyst chooses the numerical values for the structural coefficients in θ in such a manner making S as close as possible to $\Sigma(\Theta)$. The estimation problem is the fitting of $\Sigma(\Theta)$ imposed by a model to S. Robust methods such as ML, GLS, asymptotic distribution free (ADF), Scale-Free Least Squares (SLS), ULS and WLS and their respective discrepancy functions are preferred in SEM (Chou and Bentler, 1995; Washington *et al.*, 2011). In structural analysis of covariance matrices, Jöreskog recommended the use of GLS and ML as the techniques for estimating the unknown parameters of $S_{(pxp)}$. The fitting function or discrepancy function in SEM is a criterion selected for parameter estimation and is expressed as F= F[S, Σ(Θ)]. It is a guideline of minimising the difference between Σ yielded by the estimated S and the covariance matrix derived from Σ(Θ). The GLS which minimises the GLS fitting function is given as

$$F_{GLS} = \tfrac{1}{2}\,\mathrm{tr}\,(I\text{-}S^{-1}\Sigma)^2 \qquad (5.25)$$

where I is the identity matrix and other symbols carry usual meanings. The ML technique which minimises the fitting function is expressed as

$$F_{MLE} = \log[\Sigma(\Theta)] + \mathrm{tr}\,[\Sigma(\Theta)^{-1}S] - \log\,[S] - (p + q) \qquad (5.26)$$

where tr is the trace of a matrix, p and q are the indicators of endogenous LVs and exogenous LVs respectively. Assumptions made are S and Σ(Θ) are positive definite matrices, sample data follow a multinormal distribution and the observed covariance matrix is a Wishart distribution. ML method is more advantageous due to its better statistical properties, viz. (i) consistency, (ii) asymptotic normality, (iii) asymptotic efficiency, (iv) invariance and (v) the score yielded by this method has zero mean and variance which are tenable under fairly general conditions as sample size increases (Johnston and DiNardo, 2007). The robust estimation technique most commonly used in SEM is the ML method and the log likelihood ratio is used as a fitting function. This fitting function is a family of LS methods because it hinges on the principle of squared deviations. The exercise compares the likelihood for a given model to the likelihood with perfect fit. When sample matrix and model implied matrix in (5.26) are identical, the first and the third terms cancel each other out so also do the second and the fourth terms. When model and data match perfectly, the expected value of F_{MLE} is 0. Oftentimes, equations in (5.22) cannot be solved explicitly and requires an iterative process. Using S to estimate the parameters of Σ(Θ) involves solving of a number of resulting equations. The ML technique iteratively cruises about the significant estimates until a set is found which maximises the likelihood so that the differences between S and Σ(Θ) are caused by normal sampling errors only. When ML estimates are obtained, the computer programme calculates the information matrix at the estimates.

Evaluation of Fit

The model-fitting strategy in SEM is of interest to an analyst as he concerns with the parameter values and their concomitant effects. It stipulates to (i) apply estimation techniques such as ML and MR and compare the consistency of signs and magnitudes, positivity of variance estimates and residual matrices of sample covariance matrix S and sample correlation matrix R; (ii) analyse $\Sigma(\Theta)$ and S and examine the effect of MVs on the outcome and (iii) to bifurcate large data sets, complete the estimation process and compare the results of the two sets with the complete data set to check the solution stability. If a model yields results which are compatible with these criteria then it is acceptable otherwise for incompatible results, model modification or re-specification is necessary (Johnson and Wichern, 2001). The Chi-square (χ^2) test or Pearson test and the likelihood-ratio test or Neyman-Pearson test are the most commonly used GOF tests of hypotheses. The two tests yield similar values and have approximate χ^2 distributions if a model selected for the test fits the data well. The χ^2 GOF test is mostly used for evaluating the overall fit. The most commonly used χ^2 GOF index test of model adequacy, indicates the degree to which the pattern of *fixed* and *free parameters* specified in the model is consistent with the pattern of variances and covariances from a set of observed data. The GOF measures confirm the model fitness to data and compare the estimated covariance matrix which represents a theory with the observed covariance matrix which represents a reality. They are classified into three broad groups, viz. (i) absolute measures, (ii) incremental measures and (iii) parsimony fit measures. The Absolute Fit Indices are the direct measures of testing model fits comprise the χ^2 statistic, the Goodness-of-Fit Index (GFI), the Root Mean Squared Error of Approximation (RMSEA) and the Normed Chi-Square (χ^2). The Incremental Fit Indices embrace the Normed Fit Index (NFI), the Tucker-Lewis Index (TLI), the Comparative Fit Index (CFI) and the Relative Non-centrality Index (RNI). The Parsimony Fit Indices include the Adjusted Goodness of Fit Index (AGFI) and the Parsimony Normed Fit Index (PNFI). For descriptions of these GOF measures, readers may like to read multivariate statistics by Hair *et al.* (2013). A best-fit model is a model which has a right number of predictors needed to explain the data well. Fitting a model is a trade-off between parsimony and explanatory power called GoF because high parsimony models i.e. models with few parameters tend to produce a worst fit to the data than low parsimony models. A model is said to fit the data if

$\Sigma(\Theta)$ is equivalent to S i.e. the elements of the residual matrix, $\varepsilon = (\varepsilon_1, \varepsilon_2, \varepsilon_3, \ldots \varepsilon_p)$, are insignificant and are almost equal to zero so that $\Sigma(\Theta)$ closely approximates S. The χ^2 test is applied on the LISREL model given by the null hypothesis. When ML estimates are obtained, the GOF of a model for large samples is tested using the likelihood ratio technique. Consider the null hypothesis of a model with given specifications of *fixed*, *free* and *constrained parameters* denoted by H_0 and the alternative hypothesis for $\Sigma(\Theta)$ denoted by H_1 where $\Sigma(\Theta)$ and S are assumed as positive definite matrices. The maximum likelihood fitting function in (5.26) follows a χ^2 distribution such that

$$\chi^2 = (n-1)F_{MLE} \tag{5.27}$$

where n is the sample size. For a *saturated model*, the variance-covariance structure is completely unconstrained and no υ are available for tests and it perfectly fits to the data. For models with υ, the χ^2 test is the most suitable measure of overall model fit. Then υ for the χ^2 measure are

$$\upsilon = \tfrac{1}{2}(p+q)(p+q+1) - s \tag{5.28}$$

where p is the total number of MVs, q is the equations and s is the number of *free* or *identified parameters* estimated under H_0 and these s *independent parameters* are the elements of S. If H_0 is tested against another general model H_1, the estimates of the two models are obtained separately and their χ^2 values are compared. If a χ^2 GOF value obtained is large as compared to the number of υ, the fit is examined by inspecting the residuals i.e. the discrepancies between the observed and the reproduced variances and covariances. When more parameters are included a new model produces a smaller χ^2 value. A large drop in χ^2 value as compared to the difference in υ indicates that the changes made in the model represent a real improvement. Conversely, a drop in χ^2 which is close to the difference in number of υ implies the low effects of the added parameters (Jöreskog, 1979).

The GOF test statistic for hypothesis testing is equal to the product of minimised discrepancy function (F_{MLE}) and (n-1), i.e. F= (n-1) F_{MLE}, where $F_{MLE} = F[S, \Sigma(\hat{\theta})]$, $\hat{\theta}$ is an estimator for the parameters and n is the sample size. When the sample size increases, the product of the minimised F_{MLE} and (n - 1) converges to χ^2 variate as given in (5.27) with $(\dot{p} - q)$ υ where $\dot{p}$ is the number of non-redundant elements in S and q is the number of *free parameters*. The asymptotic GOF χ^2 test statistic evaluates the SEM null hypothesis which expresses as H_0: $\Sigma(\Theta) = \Sigma$. The test statistic is χ^2 distributed if certain assumptions of large sample, model specification and distribution of variables are tenable (Chou and Bentler, 1995). The issue of fit is a statistical one which should capture the three ingredients of data analysis viz., data features, the model and the estimation method. For example, as *free parameters* increase, it is more likely that the model fits the data well. The GOF test indicating the difference of residuals between S and $\Sigma(\Theta)$ is expressed as

$$\chi^2 = (n - 1)\ [(S - \Sigma(\Theta)] \quad (5.29)$$

where n is the sample size. In statistical analyses υ signify the amount of information available to estimate the parameters. The practice of subtracting the *free parameters* from the total amount of information generated by $\Sigma(\Theta)$ is like in other multivariate methods. In SEM the fundamental difference is the calculation of ½(p+q) (p+q+1) which is the sum of the covariances below the diagonal matrix plus the variances that lie on the diagonal matrix. The two GOF tests serve as measures of fit although the "best" measure from the two still remains an unsettled topic.

Researches reveal that growing dissatisfaction with the χ^2 test led to the development of *adjunct fit indexes* pioneered by Bentler and Bonett. The indices which are descriptive in nature, instead of comparing the $\Sigma(\Theta)$ and S, they compare the fit of a specific model and the fit of an *independence* or *null model*. In this approach, only variances are estimated since all relational paths are fixed to zero. The adjunct fitness of these indices shown by the improvement in fit of a specified model which includes *fixed* and *free structural parameters* over the independence model, fixes all structural parameters at zero. Since adjunct fit indexes are not statistics and therefore, they are not used for statistical tests of model fit. The indices are accepted as the global indices for model adequacy checking in which a model with a value lying between 0.90 and 1.0 is accepted as consistent with the data. Weighing the value that gives the acceptable fit of a model clearly distinguishes between the χ^2 GOF and the adjunct fit indexes. Since a zero value gives a perfect fit and smaller values indicate a better fit, the χ^2 is, indeed, a "badness-of-fit" (BAF) index. On the contrary, Adjunct Fit Indexes are, in reality, "goodness-of-fit" (GOF) indexes because the overall model fit is weighed in terms of larger values (Hoyle, 1995).

Results and Interpretations

Although, due to the existing unanimity among the researchers the GOF measures in SEM remain the area for further research, however, the first results of interest to a SEM user are the paraphernalia that quantify the overall GOF. The philosophy behind this is because SEM is a model-centric methodology. A proximity or deviation between $\Sigma(\Theta)$ and S gives a scope for better interpretations of SEM results. LISREL programme uses residuals that represent discrepancies between S and $\Sigma(\Theta)$ for generating the modification indices (MIs). When the ML estimates are reported, the standard errors (SEs) and the t-values printed together with parameter estimates (βs, γs, ηs and λs) indicate the accuracy of estimation. Small values of *free parameters* show that the parameters are estimated accurately. The ratio of the parameter estimate divided by its standard error yields a t-value which is distributed as a z-statistic. If each *free parameter* yields a t-value between -1.96 and 1.96, so fixing it to zero does not significantly worsen the model. Intuitively, a t-value which is more than 1.96 only is acceptable before the estimate can be considered reliably different from zero. Other estimates (Θ_ε and Θ_δ) derived from the parameter estimates tell us how well the observed variables measure the constructs. If multiple correlations for observed variables are all high, it indicates that they are the good measures of LVs. Values above 0.80 are treated as very high values of squared multiple correlations for the structural equations and thus a very high proportion of variance in the endogenous variables is accounted for by the variables. Residuals compare the observed variances and covariances with the parameter estimates. Small values of residuals show that the model fits well and large values show the badness of fit. The stem-leaf plot is another way of examining the standardised residuals. A plot which is shallower than the diagonal line indicates that a model fits poorly while a plot which is steeper than the diagonal line shows that the model fits well since the standardised residuals are very small. When a model does not fit well, the MIs are the most often used measures for improving the model fit. When a fixed parameter is freed and χ^2 values are decreased, it yields an estimate which ensures the model fitness. When the stability index is used for non-recursive models, i.e. models with reciprocal or circular paths, the *sufficient* condition for convergence is that the largest eigenvalue of BB′ is less than 1. This ensures the stability of the system and the finiteness of the total effects of ξ on η. If it is more than 1, then the system is unstable and the model is unacceptable.

When a new relationship is included in the model, MIs indicate a decrease in χ^2 values and therefore, their influences need precise interpretations. The overall model fit is evaluated and specific parametric hypotheses are tested using large sample χ^2 tests. The difference in χ^2 values of a model or its variants, the υ and the significance level is examined and a model is either accepted or rejected. LISREL parameters yield estimates of factor variances and squared correlations between factors and covariance matrices of errors. When R_i^2 values are high, it shows a very high stability of the quantitative factor over time and conversely, R_i^2 low values show little stability. This version can perform any of the seven methods mentioned earlier to obtain the estimates of *free* and *constrained parameters* from S. Parameter estimates and entries in the residual matrix $S - \hat{\Sigma}$ which are the benchmarks for interpretations of the fitted LISREL model need careful examination. Parameter estimates should have appropriate signs and magnitudes.

The standard LISREL 8 output captures all the GOF measures discussed in the literature. The χ^2 GOF test or Pearson test, the likelihood-ratio test or Neyman-Pearson test, the adjunct fit indices and other measures are used for tests of fit and among these the χ^2 GOF test and the AGFI are mostly used. The χ^2 should not be regarded as a test statistic but as a GOF measure if large χ^2-values correspond to bad fit and as a BOF if small χ^2-values correspond to good fit. The χ^2 GOF index is judged in terms of measures, viz., υ, χ^2, $\chi^2\upsilon$, parsimony ratio, AIC, Brown-Cudeck Criterion and PNFI. When a χ^2 value is obtained and an inspection of the magnitudes of the first derivatives F with respect to fixed parameters is examined, it suggests ways to add more parameters in the model. A significant drop in χ^2 value as compared to the difference υ, shows a real improvement of the model while a drop in χ^2 close to the difference in the number of υ indicates that the fit is obtained by "capitalising on chance" and the exercise of adding more parameters is insignificant (Jöreskog, 1979).

When a model yields a poor fit to a set of data, obviously such statistical model is deficient and the structural coefficients are inconsistent. To overcome such problem, an analyst rejects it and a discovery of a revised model or a new compatible model is made. In SEM, the fundamental tenet of model evaluation is a *confirmatory process* in which a χ^2 test is designed to serve as a yardstick for accepting or rejecting a hypothesised model. It is an exercise of formulating *strictly confirmatory models*, specification of *alternative models* and generating *new model* and in each stage, substantive interpretations should be made. An analyst does not recommend that paths are judged insignificant merely on the arbitrary p-value of 0.05 unless such paths are decided unimportant and when making modifications only the minimum changes are necessary to avoid *overfitting*.

The smoking model given by Hayduk (1987) is a good illustration of SEM's results and interpretations. The model hypothesises the potential *causal links* between smoking behaviour, antismoking (AS) views and AS actions as the three endogenous concepts and sex, age, education and religion as the four exogenous concepts. Thus, η_1, η_2 and η_3 constitute a random vector (η_{mx1}) of endogenous LVs or concepts, ξ_1, ξ_2, ξ_3 and ξ_4 a random vector (ξ_{nx1}) of exogenous LVs or concepts and ζ_1, ζ_2 and ζ_3 a random vector (ζ_{mx1}) of equation errors in the structural relationship between η and ξ. The results show that the model with reciprocal effects fits well and is acceptable since $\chi^2 = 3.07$ with 2 υ and $p = .22$. Each coefficient estimate in B and Γ indicates a basic direct effect of exogenous LV or concept on the endogenous LV or concept. An amount of change in an endogenous eta (η) variable is expected to follow a unit change in the *causal* variable (ξ or η) if no effects are transmitted through indirect routings or cycled through the loop. Thus γ_{33} shows that increasing educational level by "one diploma" is expected to increase by .046 the number of AS bylaws with which one agrees assuming no effects are transmitted through AS views (η_2) or smoking behaviour (η_1). The model containing numerous modifications, grounded the discussions and yielded interesting results and lucid interpretations. When the basic direct and indirect effects are allowed in the absence of looping, a unit change in η_1 (smoking) on η_1 (acts) yields an effect which is the sum of direct and indirect effects. The loop yields a negative value which is -.0339 for this model and if it is allowed to operate, the total expected effect is reduced. The total effects of endogenous concepts (ηs) on one another is mathematically expressed as

$$T_{\eta\eta} = B^1 + B^2 + B^3 + \dots B^{\infty} \tag{5.30}$$

where $T_{\eta\eta}$ is the *total effects* of the endogenous concepts on one another, B^1, B^2, B^3 ... B^{∞} are the power matrices representing the path lengths 2, 3, 4 and so on and B is a matrix defined in structural equation (5.9). The indirect effects of exogenous concepts (ξs) on endogenous concepts (ηs) is mathematically expressed as

$$I_{\eta\xi} = B^1\Gamma + B^2\Gamma + B^3\Gamma + B^4\Gamma + \dots B^{\infty}\Gamma \tag{5.31}$$

where $I_{\eta\xi}$ is an *m* x *n* identity matrix of the structural coefficients of exogenous and endogenous concepts and Γ is the value of the first path coefficient. The total effects of exogenous concepts (ξs) on endogenous concepts (ηs) is mathematically expressed as

$$T_{\eta\xi} = (I - B)^{-1}\Gamma \tag{5.32}$$

where $T_{\eta\xi}$ is an *m* x *n* matrix representing the total effects of exogenous concepts on endogenous concepts.

LISREL works well when the model is consistent with the data. The programme yields good initial estimates and a solution after certain iterations. But in practice, deviations from the ideal situation do occur and as such procedures for resolving the problem cases are provided in LISREL 8 (Jöreskog and Sörbom, 2001).

The salient features of interpretations given by LISREL are discussed here in a nutshell. However, LISREL results centering on the MIs, χ^2 GOF, standardised parameters and other aspects or criteria associated with SEM stipulate careful interpretations. For using SEM, Kline (2005) listed 44 errors and classified them under four broad groups, viz., (1) errors of specification, (2) improper treatment of data, (3) errors of analysis and (4) errors of interpretation. The common errors of interpretations are (1) relying solely on indices of overall model fit, (2) interpreting good model fit as proving validity of model, (3) interpreting good fit as suggesting model is good at explaining variance, (4) relying solely on statistical criteria for model evaluation, (5) relying too heavily on p-values, (6) inappropriate interpretation of standardised parameters, (7) failure to consider equivalent models, (8) failure to consider alternative non-equivalent models, (9) reification of LVs, (10) equating a LV with its label, (11) considering SEM's ability to compensate for either poor data or weak theory, (12) failure to report sufficient information to permit proper scrutiny and (13) interpreting significant results as proof of causality (Grace, 2006).

Applications of SEM in Transport Planning

Besides supplying the demand-driven infrastructure and regulatory measures, transport planning deals with four problems caused by automotive industry, viz. traffic congestion, air pollution, water pollution and traffic accidents. Travel behaviour approach encompasses a wide range of studies enveloping observations, analysis and interpretations of trip makers' attitudes towards transport policies such as petrol and diesel taxes, congestion pricing, vanpooling, HOV lanes, mass transit, role of education, socio-economic status, drivers' decision making, etc. SEM as a robust technique is applied for parameter estimation and fitting to the sample data involving LVs. For example, in the study of the efficacy of PT to wean away people from using their private cars; a researcher might want to determine the impact of LV such as passengers' attitude or perceptions towards PT. Since the attitude towards PT itself is a LV; a researcher is required to formulate indicators and ask a series of questions with an intent to indirectly measure the LVs.

Travel behaviour analysis began with the work of Liepmann (1945) when he analysed the 1930s data on workers' travel in England. Today, many of the insights on mode choice such as time spent, ride sharing, etc. are found in his work. Researches on road traffic safety in the early 1950s evolved traffic engineering. Systematic investigations developed traffic models including statistical models, Lighthill-Witham theory of traffic flow, use of computers in traffic flow studies, design of road capacities, etc. They applied Poisson model in the study of random arrivals of vehicles at a particular road section, Pascal or negative binomial distribution model for a left-turn lane at traffic light, binomial distribution model for urban traffic dispersion, etc. Human behaviour has discrete components of performance juxtaposed between neuromuscular and cognitive time lags which are the parameters of performance of person-motor vehicle relations. Such components are perception-reaction time, control movement time, responses to traffic control devices, responses to movements of other vehicles, handling of hazards on the roadway and many other associated factors (HMSO, 1965; Benjamin and Cornell, 1970; TRB, 1975; Papacostas and Prevedouros, 2001; Khisty and Lall, 2003). Probit and logit models are widely used in modal split analyses (Hutchinson, 1974; Sarkar *et al.,* 2015). Extensive researches on behavioural analyses for urban travel demand by modelling the discrete choices were carried out by Domencich and McFadden. They estimated the parameters of linear probability models on the OLS and logit models using MLE for simple types of trips such as home-based work trips and home-based shop trips involving mode choices. They found that statistical results of empirical analyses were highly encouraging. The theory of mode choice in the face of discrete alternatives including its application to travel demand is illuminating (Domencich and McFadden, 1975). Behavioural theories are mind-boggling which reorient the thinking process of car users despite its advantages such as comfort, speech and flexibility. First, strategies designed for reducing car use are structural strategies which require *financial-economic simulation* through instruments such as subsidies, discounts, taxes, fines, tolls, etc.; second, *provision of physical alternatives and arrangements* such as preventing vehicles from entering certain area, alternating the geographic configuration of popular destinations, etc.; third, *regulations and enforcements* of the extant laws and standards and fourth, *organisational change* such as working partly through physical changes and partly through changes in the financial or social payoff structure. Cognitive-motivational strategies are *provision of information, education and communication* and *social modelling and support.* It is observed that structural strategies are generally more effective than the cognitive-motivational strategies (Steg and Tertoolen, 1998). Shinar (1978) elaborates the role of human factor in an operations system which transports people and goods from the traffic safety's standpoint. He examines the role of psychology in highway safety enveloping traffic safety, driver education, civil and industrial engineering permeating into the experts' domain such as physicians, system engineers, civil engineers, optometrists, educators and psychologists of various orientations. In outlining the conceptual basis of injury control pertaining to the relations between transport systems and human error, Mohan (2016) observes that road traffic injury is a new disease of the twentieth and twenty-first centuries and victims contracting such disease should not be blamed if solution is to be found. This disease results from an acute exposure of human body to a transfer of energy from the environment around it. The outcome of events which cause injury are predictable and in many cases are subject to human control. The occurrence of the physical event itself is oftentimes a result of man's activity as may be evident from causes of floods resulting from human activities such as deforestation, faulty design of dams, chocking up of drainage in cities, etc. He infers that accidents and injuries are not the "Acts of God" but are the effects of human errors. Thus, studies of human behaviour in relation to transport systems are more than seventy-five years now.

In recent years, the applications of SEM in transport planning attracted traffic engineers, transport planners and researchers due to its capability to measure the LVs indirectly. Attitude, satisfaction, comfort, convenience, etc. which are latent in nature strongly influence mode choice and decisions of trip-makers besides other MVs such as price, distance, time, household size, etc. Volume-capacity (v/c) ratios on road segments of towns which are > 1 indicate that provision of physical infrastructure such as roads, bypasses, flyovers, parking lots, termini, etc. is only one of the measures for solution of traffic congestion problem. Effective measures and solutions demand changes in car-owning behaviour to make a paradigm shift to PT. Putting in place the right type of PT to wean away commuters from using their private cars does not exclusively confine within the domain of researchers including psychologists but active involvement of road users is indispensable. SEM analysis involves applications of softwares such as AMOS, Mplus, LISREL, R and Stata. IBM SPSS AMOS is more convenient and is being widely used for modelling including drawing of path diagrams and permitting an analyst to focus on science (Miller *et al.*, 2020). The procedure for applying AMOS-25 is described in 12-steps. Fillone *et al.* (2005) used SEM approach for assessing the urban travel in Manila city. They divided the morning trip-makers into three groups, namely (a) private car users, (b) PT users with their own cars or with vehicles of their households, and (c) captive riders. The study revealed that for the private car users, the LVs relating to the socio-demographic characteristics of the travellers loaded positively while the LVs for the car users loaded negatively on urban travel assessment. For PT-using but car-owning travellers, both the socio-demographic characteristics of the traveller and the generalised cost of travel loaded positively on urban travel assessment. For the latter group it showed that household characteristics were more important than individual characteristics. Using the theory of planned behaviour, Warner and Aberg (2006) applied SEM for the study of drivers' everyday speeding behaviour to determine the effect of four LVs, viz. tendency to speed as an outgrowth of attitudes towards speeding, subjective norms regarding speeding, perceived behavioural control and self-reported speeding. It was found that the independent variables stipulated in the theory afforded a level of prediction of drivers' self-reported speeding as well as of their logged speeding. Attitude towards speeding, subjective norm and perceived behavioural control were significant determinants of self-reported speeding. Silva and Goulias (2009) carried out a study of relation between travel behaviour and land use patterns using SEM framework by comparing Seattle, Washington with Lisbon, Portugal. The number of trips and trip scheduling were included as the behaviour variables for the short-term while home location, car and pass ownership and mobility decisions as the variables for the long-term. The study revealed that land use variables were influenced by socio-economic variables which were indicative of self-selection effects. Younger women and people with medium and higher levels of income belonging to smaller and younger households tend to work in denser and central areas. In the study of HOV lanes in Seattle metropolitan area, the three important LVs identified were attitude towards HOV lanes and their use, the socio-economic status which reflected the relative level of personal wealth combined with relative social status and HOV experience. It revealed that HOV experience was influenced positively by a respondent who regularly engaged in HOV use either through carpooling, bus or some other HOV qualifying use and that HOV experience and HOV attitude were not mutually endogenous as initially expected and instead HOV experience directly influenced HOV attitude (Washington *et al.*, 2011). Eboli and Mazzulla (2012) employed SEM for analysing passengers' perceptions about railway services in Northern Italy. SEM is formulated to explore the impact of the relation between global customer satisfaction and service quality attributes, viz. safety, cleanliness, main and additional services, information and personnel. The services offered by rail operators were analysed with a sample size of 16,000 passengers. The main findings were that service characteristics like punctuality, regularity, frequency of runs and cleanliness had the highest positive effect on service quality. Pavlina (2015) analysed the factors influencing satisfaction with PT in Czech Republic using SEM approach. The main findings were that the model was optimal. Logistic parameters including service continuity and frequency and service including information rate, station proximity and vehicle cleanliness were the factors which influenced passengers' satisfaction on a large scale. Following SEM approach for measuring perception of pedestrian level of service (PLOS) of sidewalks, Bivina and Parida (2018) found that perceived PLOS of sidewalks was most influenced by pedestrian satisfaction in terms of "Security" followed by other factors such as "Comfort and Convenience", "Safety" and "Mobility and Infrastructure". The study of bus transit as one of the transfer modes at high-speed railway (HSR) stations was carried out by Cheng *et al.* (2018) using the SEM evaluation approach. It focused on the passengers' transfer experience and used a methodology for evaluation of bus traffic transfer service. Based on perceptions, factors such as convenience, comfort, safety, service and economy which affected the passengers' satisfaction were analysed. SEM results revealed that economy and convenience were the critical influential factors of passengers' satisfaction among which bus fare preferential policy and transfer distance were the most significant factors. Their findings helped transport planners and managers to improve the services of the existing HSR facilities and for guidance of the planning of new ones.

The applications of SEM in diverse areas of transport planning are indicative of the fact that SEM is the most powerful technique among the extant multivariate statistical methods which captures the endogenous and exogenous MVs and LVs in simultaneous equations system. In India, SEM approach started recently in some institutes and universities and is yet to gain momentum among the practising town planners, traffic engineers and transport planners.

REFERENCES

Ayres, F. Jr. (1974). *Theory and Problems of Matrices, SI (Metric) Edition,* McGraw-Hills Book Company, New York, p.101.

Balchin, Paul N. *et al.*, (1995). *Urban Land Use Economics and Public Policy, Fifth Edition*, MacMillan Press Ltd., London, pp. 50-55.

Ben-Akiva M. and Lerman S.R. (1985). *Discrete Choice Analysis: Theory and Application to Travel Demand,* The MIT Press, Massachusetts, pp. 100-130.

Benjamin, J.R. and Cornell, C.A (1970). *Probability, Statistics and Decision for Civil Engineers*, Dover Publications, Inc., New York, pp. 170-75, 207, 231-32, 421-26 & 562-66.

Bivina, G.R. and Parida, M. (2018). Modelling of Perceived Pedestrial Level of Service of Sidewalks: A Structural Equation Approach. In https://www. google. com. journals.vgtu.ithttps: // dated 03.10. 2019, pp. 339-49.

Byrne, B.M. (1995). One Application of Structural Equation Modelling from Two Perspectives: Exploring the EQS and LISREL Strategies. In Hoyle (ed.), *Structural Equation Modelling: Concepts, Issues and Applications*, SAGE Publications, California, pp. 144-57.

Byrne, B.M. (2016). *Structural Equation Modelling With AMOS: Basic Concepts, Applications and Programming,* Third Edition, Reprinted 2019, Routledge/ Taylor and Francis Group, New York, pp. 3-4, 7, 10-11 & 40-43.

Chatterjee, S. and Hadi, A.S. (2012). *Regression Analysis,* Fifth Edition, Reprint 2017, Wiley India Pvt. Ltd., New Delhi, pp. 64-67 & 279-88.

Cheng, X. *et al.* (2018). Modelling the Satisfaction of Bus Traffic Transfer Service Quality at a High-Speed Railway Stations. In *Journal of Advanced Transportation,* Volume, 2018, Article ID 7051789.google.com/ pdfs. semanticscholar.org dated 28.08.2019.

Chou, C. and Bentler, P.M. (1995). Estimates and Tests in Structural Equation Modelling. In Hoyle (ed.), *Structural Equation Modelling: Concepts, Issues and Applications*, SAGE Publications, California, pp. 37-55.

Domencich, T.A. and McFadden, D. (1975). *Urban Travel Demand: A Behavioural Analysis. Reprinted 1998*, North-Holland Publishing Company, Amsterdam, pp. 47-99.

Draper, N.R and Smith, H. (1998). *Applied Regression Analysis,* Third Edition, Wiley India Pvt. Ltd., New Delhi, pp. 59-69, 181-198, 205-14, 371-75 & 387-400.

Eboli, L. and Mazzulla, G. (2012). Structural Equation Modelling for Analysing Passengers' Perceptions about Railway Services. In *Procedia-Social and Behavioural Sciences 54*, pp. 96-106. science.direct.com/science/article dated 28.08.2019.

ECOOM In https://www. ecoom.be, 2022.

Fillone, A.M. *et al.* (2005). Assessing Urban Travel: A Structural Equations Modelling (SEM) Approach. In *Proceedings of the Eastern Asian Society for Transportation Studies,* Vol. 5, pp. 1050-64.

Geddes, P. (1915). *Cities in Evolution: An Introduction to the Town Planning Movement and to the Study of Civics*, Williams, London, p. 205.

Glasson, J. (1978). *An Introduction to Regional Planning,* 2nd Edition, Reprinted 1983, Hutchinson, London, pp. 41-43.

Grace, J.B. (2006). *Structural Equation Modelling and Natural Systems*, Cambridge University Press, Cambridge, pp. 10-19, 37-42, 46-56, 115-40, 198-203 & 275-88.

Greene, W.H. (2003). *Econometric Analysis,* Fifth Edition, Dorling Kindersley (India) Private Limited, New Delhi, pp. 383, 411, 468-524 & 719-35.

Gujarati, D.N. *et al.* (2012). *Basic Econometrics,* Fifth Edition, Tata McGraw Hill Education Private Limited, New Delhi, pp. 753-55.

Hadley, G. (1962). *Linear Algebra,* Reprinted 1987, Addition-Wesley/Narosa Publishing House, New Delhi, p. 33.

Hair, Joseph F. *et al.* (2015). *Multivariate Data Analysis*, Indian Edition, Reprinted 2017, Dorling Kindersley India Pvt. Ltd., pp. 92-93, 546-47, 554-61, 576-81 & 600-37.

Hayduk L.A. (1987). *Structural Equation Modelling with LISREL: Essentials and Advances*, The Johns Hopkins University Press, Baltimore, Maryland, pp. 106-17 & 244-72.

HMSO (1963). *Traffic in Towns: A Study of the Long-Term Problems of Traffic in Urban Areas,* Third Impression 1964, pp. 33-163 & 201.

HMSO (1965): *Research on Road Traffic*, Department of Scientific and Industrial Research, Road Research Laboratory, Harmondsworth, Middlesex, pp. 178-89.

Hoyle, R.H. (1995). The Structural Equation Modelling Approach: Basic Concepts and Fundamental Issues. In Hoyle (ed.), *Structural Equation Modelling: Concepts, Issues and Applications*, SAGE Publications, California, pp. 1-15.

Hutchinson B.G. (1974). *Principles of Urban Transport Systems Planning*, McGraw-Hill Company, Washington D.C., pp. 64-80.

ICoRSI, (2016). In *Readings in Road Safety*, Indian Institute of Technology, New Delhi.

Intriligator, M.D. (1978). *Econometric Models, Techniques and Applications*, Reprinted 1980, Prentice-Hall of India Private Limited, New Delhi, pp. 14-28, 88-112 & 358-61.

Isard, W. (1956). *Location and Space-Economy,* Reprinted 1968, The MIT Press, Cambridge, Massachusetts, pp. 24-30, 172-206 & 254-87.

Johnson, R.A. and Wichern, D.W. (2001). *Applied Multivariate Statistical Analysis,* Third Edition, Prentice-Hall of India Private Limited, New Delhi, pp. 397-99, 419-29 & 443-51.

Johnson, R.A. and Wichern, D.W. (2013). *Applied Multivariate Statistical Analysis,* Sixth Edition, Prentice-Hall of India Private Limited, New Delhi, pp. 482-87.

Johnston, J. and Dinardo, J. (2007). *Econometric Methods,* Fourth Edition, McGraw-Hill Book Co., Singapore, pp. 53-56, 63-64 & 143-45.

Johnston, J. (1984). *Econometric Methods,* Third Edition, McGraw-Hill Book Co., Singapore, pp. 467-69.

Jöreskog, K.G. (1979). Basic Ideas of Factor and Component Analysis. In Jöreskog, K.G. and Sörbom, D., *Advances in Factor Analysis and Structural Equation Models*, Abt Books, Cambridge, pp. 5-20.

Jöreskog, K.G. (1979). A General Approach to Confirmatory Maximum Likelihood Factor Analysis with Addendum. In Jöreskog, K.G. and Sörbom, D., *Advances in Factor Analysis and Structural Equation Models*, Abt Books, Cambridge, pp. 21-29.

Jöreskog, K.G. (1979). Analyzing Psychological Data by Structural Analysis of Covariances Matrices. In Jöreskog, K.G. and Sörbom, D., *Advances in Factor Analysis and Structural Equation Models*, Abt Books, Cambridge, pp. 45-49 & 90-97.

Jöreskog, K.G. (1979). Structural Equation Models in the Social Sciences: Specification, Estimation and Testing. In Jöreskog, K.G. and Sörbom, D., *Advances in Factor Analysis and Structural Equation Models*, Abt Books, Cambridge, pp. 100-22.

Jöreskog, K.G. (1979). Statistical Models and Methods for Analysis of Longitudinal Data. In Jöreskog, K.G. and Sörbom, D., *Advances in Factor Analysis and Structural Equation Models*, Abt Books, Cambridge, pp. 129-68.

Jöreskog, K.G. and Sörbom, D. (2001). *LISREL 8: User's Reference Guide*, SSI, Inc., Lincolnwood, USA, pp. 1-36, 138-39, 143-70, 188-95, 239-43, 321-37.

Keeble, L. (1964). *Principles and Practice of Town and Country Planning,* Third Edition, Reprinted 1967, The Estates of Gazette Limited, London, pp. 8 & 19-26.

Kerlinger, F.N. (1973). *Foundations of Behavioural Research,* Reprinted 2009, Surjeet Publications, Delhi, p. 659.

Khisty, C.J. and Lall, B.K. (2003): *Transportation Engineering: An Introduction,* Third Edition, Pearson India Education Services Pvt. Ltd., Noida, pp. 97-115.

Kmenta, J. (1986). *Elements of Econometrics*, Second Edition, Reprinted 2018, Khosla Publishing House, New Delhi, pp. 585-86.

Koutsoyiannis, A. (1977). *Theory of Econometrics,* Second Edition, Reprinted 1993, ELBS with Macmillan, pp. 340-42.

Krueckeberg, D.A. (1983). *The American Planner: Biographies and Recollections*, Methuen, New York, pp. 10-24.

Liepmann, K.K. (1944). The Journey to Works, Its Significance for Industrial and Community Life. In google.com.https://Meghalaya dated 09.10. 2019.

MacCallum, R.C. (1995). Model Specification: Procedures, Strategies and Related Issues. In Hoyle (ed.), *Structural Equation Modelling: Concepts, Issues and Applications*, SAGE Publications, California, pp. 16-36.

McLoughlin, J.B. (1970). *Urban and Regional Planning: A Systems Approach,* Second Edition, Reprinted 1978, Faber and Faber, London, pp. 23-24 & 58-70.

Marsh, H.W. and Grayson, D. (1995). Latent Variable Models of Multitrait Multimethod Data. In Hoyle (ed.), *Structural Equation Modelling: Concepts, Issues and Applications*, SAGE Publications, California, pp. 177-98.

Meyer, M.D. and Miller, E.J. (1984). *Urban Transportation Planning: A Decision Oriented Approach,* McGraw-Hill Publishing Company, New York, pp. 257-73.

Miller, M. *et al.* (2020). Structural Equation Modelling. In R. Ewing and K. Park (eds.), *Advanced Quantitative Research Method for Urban Planners*, Routledge Taylor and Francis Group, New York and London, pp. 185-214.

Mohan, D. (2016). Road Traffic Injury as a Public Health Problem. In ICoRSI *Readings in Road Safety*, Indian Institute of Technology, New Delhi, pp. 3-13.

Montgomery, D.C. *et al.* (2003). *Introduction to Linear Regression Analysis,* Third Edition, Reprint 2007, Wiley India Pvt. Ltd., New Delhi, pp. 50-52 & 112-17.

Park, K. *et al.* (2020). Conceptual Frameworks. In R. Ewing and K. Park (eds.), *Basic Quantitative Research Methods for Urban Planners*, CRC Routledge, New York, pp. 76-87.

Papacostas, C.S. and Prevedouros, P.D. (2001). *Transportation Engineering & Planning,* Third Edition, Reprinted 2009, PHI Learning Private Limited, New Delhi, pp. 29-42 & 385-400.

Pavlina, P. (2015). The Factors Influencing Satisfaction with Public City Transport: A Structural Equation Modelling Approach. In *Journal of Competitiveness,* Vol. 7, Issue 4, pp. 18-32. journal.cz/files/203.pdf dated 28.08.2019.

Ratcliffe, J. (1981). *An Introduction to Town and Country Planning,* 2nd Edition, Reprinted 1989, Hutchinson, London, pp. 14 & 115-17.

Roberts, M. (1974). *An Introduction to Town Planning Techniques,* Reprinted 1982, Hutchinson Education, London, pp. 7 & 250.

Sabouri, S. *et al.* (2020). Logistic Regression. In *Basic Quantitative Research Methods for Urban Planners*, edited by R. Ewing and K. Park (eds.), CRC Routledge, New York, pp. 270-304.

Sarkar P.K. *et al.* (2015). *Transportation Planning: Principles, Practices and Policies*, PHI Learning Private Limited, Delhi, pp. 121-27.

Shinar, D. (1978). *Psychology on the Road: The Human Factor in Traffic Safety,* John Wiley & Sons, New York.

Silva, J. de A. and Goulias, K.G. (2009). Structural Equations Model of Land Use Patterns, Location Choice, and Travel Behaviour. In *Journal of Transportation Research Board, No. 2135*, Transport Research Board of the National Academies, Washington D.C., pp. 106-13. In https://www. google. co.in.

Simpson, B.J. (1994). *Urban Public Transport Today,* First Edition, E & FN Spon, London, p. 3.

Sőrbom D. (1979). Detection of Correlated Errors in Longitudinal Data. In K.G. Jöreskog and D. Sörbom (eds.), *Advances in Factor Analysis and Structural Equation Models*, Abt Books, Cambridge, pp. 171-84.

Steg, L. and Tertoolen, G. (1998). Sustainable Transport: Assumptions on Behavioural Change, Social and Cultural Planning Office, University of Groningen & Ministry of Transport, Public Works and Water Management, Transport Research Centre (AVV), U.K. Government, pp. 203-10. In https google.com

TRB (1975). *Special Report 165*, Transportation Research Board, U.S. Department of Transportation, Federal Highway Administration, Washington D.C, pp. 3-1 and 3-29.

Warner H.W. and Aberg L. (2006). Drivers' Decision to Speed: A Study Inspired by the Theory of Planned Behaviour. In *Transportation Research Part F: Traffic Psychology and Behaviour,* Volume 9, Issue 6, November 2006, pp. 427-33.

Washington, S.P. *et al.* (2011). *Statistical and Econometric Methods for Transportation Data Analysis,* Second Edition, CRC Press, Taylor & Francis Group LLC, Boca Raton, pp. 8-9, 13-14, 241-44, 249-55 & 303-43.

Wheelwright, M. *et al.* (2020). Principal Component and Factor Analysis. In R. Ewing and K. Park (eds.), *Advanced Quantitative Research Methods for Urban Planners*, CRC Routledge, New York, pp. 95-119.

White, P. (1995). *Public Transport: Its Planning, Management and Operation,* Third Edition, UCL Press Limited, University College, London, pp. 46-64.

Wright, S. (1934). The Methods of Path Co-efficient. In *Annals of Mathematical Statistics,* Volume 5, Issue 3, pp. 161-215. Google.com, fitelson.org/269/.

6
Planning Strategies for Traffic Decongestion in Hill City

A Case Study of Shillong in Meghalaya

P.S. Ñianglang and *Sanjay Gupta*

Introduction

Transport is the movement of people, materials, goods and other tangible objects from one place to another. It is an essential infrastructure of service sector which ensures flows of people and goods from one place to another. Improved means of urban transport enable the urbanites to achieve the above objectives without time and cost overruns. Planning of strategies and issues for traffic decongestion is one of the objectives of urban transport planning. The rapid growth of urban population, towns and cities, planned or unplanned, hilly or plain, exhibit their horizontal and vertical expansions so as to meet the social, economic and aesthetic needs of the urbanites. Unplanned expansion results in the abuse, misuse and under-utility of urban space which ultimately impinges on the urban growth and also on the urban mobility.

The problems in hill towns and cities are of two types, viz. (1) nature-made problems and (2) man-made problems. Both nature-made and man-made problems are the extreme limitations of physical development in hill towns and cities. Most of the hill towns grow in an unplanned and haphazard manner and very little thought is given on the planned physical development. Alam (1986) enumerates the problems of hill towns such as rigorous topography, extreme limitations of accessibility networks, geographical, social and economic constraints, unplanned physical development, planning based on norms and standard meant for towns in plains, lack of proper planning legislation, indequate building bye-laws, unplanned use of flat lands available for development, etc. Increasing population and activities resulted in mounting demand for space. Unavailability of additional building spaces resulted in congestion and haphazard growth, mushrooming of structure and environmental degradation. Many hill towns, especially the ones lying in the North India, Himalayas and the hilly areas of the North-Eastern Region lie in the seismic zone or belt V. The National Institute of Urban Affairs (1988) carried out the study on the *Urbanisation and Urban Development Policy Issues of the North-Eastern Region* and *inter alia*, found that street lighting was deficient in about 50 per cent of the sample urban centres. Aizawl, Kohima and Shillong were burdened with narrow roads and streets which strongly impeded vehicular movement. Traffic flow was further constricted by haphazard building construction which abutted on the main roads and streets due to the absence of proper building byelaws. Most of the urban centres including state capitals faced severe shortage of parking facilities for both public and private vehicles. The extremely high volume of *through traffic* causing traffic congestion at major intersections had affected the orderly movement of both motorised and non-motorised traffic. The study team which foresaw the impending traffic problems of urban centres in the Region thirty years ago, made concrete suggestions for urban renewal and development in transport sector. It drew the attention of the public authorities to put in place the regulatory measures including repairs and reconstruction of major urban roads, resurfacing of state highways and rehabilitation of bridges and culverts in major urban centres such as Aizawl, Kohima, and Shillong. Mitigation of urban transport bottlenecks through the provision of by-passes for *through traffic*, creation of Transport Nagars at designated locations for inter-state movement of people and goods, provision of new parking facilities, bus terminals, remodelling and redesign of major traffic junctions and widening of urban roads. Thus, transport and its associated negative externalities such as traffic congestion, air and water pollution, traffic accident and deforestation constituted the major problems of hill towns and cities and hence the need of the study with focus on traffic decongestion measures. An interested reader in *negative* and *positive externalities* produced by *public goods* including transport systems and their effects on third parties may like to refer to the literature (Koutsoyiannis, 1985; Button, 1993; Balchin *et al.,* 1995; Vuchic, 1999; Hyman, 2005).

The Context

In Shillong which is a large hilly city and the state capital of Meghalaya, traffic congestion is, *inter alia*, one of the problems faced by the urban dwellers. The transport networks in the city are already overloaded beyond their designed capacities and are insufficient to meet the pressing demand. There has been a sharp rise in the number of vehicles (both public and private) especially after the year 2000 and this trend continues to rise in the near future. The road network is inadequate as evident by the presence of narrow roads, non-vehicular road areas, missing links and inadequate parking facilities. During the last two decades, urban sprawl in the city grew beyond its absorptive capacity which resulted in frequent traffic congestion. People regularly face the menace of traffic congestion while carrying out their day-to-day activities such as commuting to workplaces, schools, colleges, shops, etc. This calls for immediate attention of the urban transport planners, traffic engineers, urban economists, psychologists and urbanologists to evolve suitable traffic decongestion measures to mitigate this compounded problem at the earliest possible.

Literature Review

Traffic congestion is the traffic flow phenomenon or traffic impedance caused by traffic-influencing events, traffic demands and physical highway features where vehicular speeds on a particular road section at a particular period of time decelerate slower and frequently much slower than the operating speeds. When the level of traffic congestion is severe i.e., the V/C ratio exceeds 1, such traffic flow phenomenon is called traffic jam. The concentration or density of vehicles on a particular section of road space known as the degree of traffic congestion or congestion level is assessed using some measures. The multiple effects of traffic congestion are economic effects, societal effects, environmental effects, engineering effects, accidental effects, inefficient effects and psychological effects (Ñianglang, 2016).

Downs (2004) mentions five measures of traffic congestion, viz. (i) the travel time index, (ii) the percentage of all daily travel occurring during those hours when major roadways typically experience congestion, (iii) the percentage of all daily travel occurring under actually congested conditions, (iv) the number of hours of delay per peak-hour road traveller and (v) the roadway congestion index. The higher the travel time index the greater the congestion it indicates. Also, congestion levels are assessed by using the prevailing measurable average journey speed observed on major corridors. Traffic congestion depends on the level of service (LOS) of a roadway capacity. LOS is defined as a qualitative measure indicating the operational conditions within a traffic stream as perceived by motorists and passengers. Besides the pedestrian and the bicycle LOS services, the Highway Capacity Mannual (HCM) classifies the LOS for freeways and multilane highways into six categories, viz. category A, B, C, D, E and F. Using the prescribed indices, when the congestion thresholds of urban roads, viz. urban expressways, arterial roads, sub-arterial roads, distributor/ collector roads, local streets and access streets are measured and placed in the D, E or F category the traffic congestion starts. When the V/C ratio is greater than 1 = severe congestion, V/C ratio of 0.75 to 1.00 = heavy congestion, V/C ratio of 0.5 to 0.74 = moderate congestion and V/C ratio of less than 0.5 = low congestion.

Table 6.1: Recommended DSVs (PCUs per hour)

Sl. No.	Type of Carriageway	Total Design Service Volume for Different Road Categories		
		Arterial	**Sub-Arterial**	**Collector**
1	2-lane (One-Way)	2400	1900	1400
2	2-lane (Two-Way)	1500	1200	900
3	3-lane (One-Way)	3600	2900	2200
4	4-lane Undivided (One-Way)	3000	2400	1800
5	4-lane Divided (Two-Way)	3600	2900	–
6	6-lane Undivided (One-Way)	4800	3800	–
7	6-lane Divided (Two-Way)	5400	4300	–
8	8-lane Divided (Two-Way)	7200	-	-

Source: UDPFI Guidelines, 1996.

In India, as per the UDPFI Guidelines (Government of India, 1996), normally the 'C' LOS is adopted for design of urban roads. At this level the traffic volume will be around 0.70 times the maximum capacity and is taken as the design service volume (DSV). The recommended DSVs (PCUs per hour) for different categories of urban roads are presented in Table 6.1.

Traffic decongestion strategies are classified into three broad categories *firstly* supply-driven strategies are provision of roads, transit systems, bypasses, flyovers, pedestrian footpaths and subways, intelligent transportation system (ITS) and bus system coordination. *Secondly,* demand-driven strategies comprise the fiscal measures such as congestion pricing, vehicle and fuel tax, parking charges, road pricing, multi-mode ticket systems, etc. *Thirdly*, administrative or regulatory measures include formulation of an appropriate urban land-use planning and policy for supply, use and management of land, physical restraint banning the entry of vehicles into pedestrian precincts or regulation of reserved bus lanes where the street space is reserved exclusively for buses, designation of HOV roads/lanes, etc. restrictions of mushrooming of private vehicles, staggering of working hours, introduction of sliding times, encouragement to non-motorised transport such as walk, cycling, use of rickshaws, etc. application of a wide range of traffic regulations, parking, waiting controls, etc. They are classified as short, medium and long-term traffic decongestion measures.

Arnott *et al.* (2005) discuss some measures to alleviate urban traffic congestion such as mass transit, pedestrian traffic, restriction of shopping hours, development of activity-based models for non-commuting trips, staggered work hours, land use controls, promotion of bicycle commuting, suitable parking policy and the implementation of multi-mode ticket and recommend multimode ticket as a pragmatic solution for alleviation of urban traffic congestion. Papacostas and Prevedouros (2009) recommend the bus and High Occupancy Vehicle (HOV) or High Occupancy Toll (HOT) lanes policy as one of the effective traffic decongestion measures. This strategy envisages that HOV/HOT lanes allow vehicles/cars to travel toll-free if they carry a minimum of three occupants and are tollable if the numbers of occupants are below three. The rationale of this policy is to encourage sharing of vehicles and to travel by public transport (PT) so as to optimize the utilization of bus and HOV/HOT lanes. Sen (1995) in her study on the demand for PT for the case city proposed some traffic decongestion measures such as strengthening of PT, reservation of lanes exclusively for buses, efficient regulation of public transport system, provision of tracks for pedestrians, differential pricing for private cars during peak hours, imposition of congestion tax in Central Business District (CBD) and other congested areas, establishment of small shopping centres in different localities, construction of flyovers at major traffic intersections, decentralization of workplaces and institutions to suburbs, construction of ring road, adoption of improved traffic management methods, educating the general public and drivers, fixing different timings for different organizations, review of the existing road laws, effective enforcement of law, designation of more CBDs and undertaking of appropriate town and traffic planning measures.

The traffic congestion mitigation measures which broadly come under short-term improvement plans within 1-5 years period are called traffic calming measures or traffic taming measures. Traffic calming measures such as road humps, speed tables, raised junctions, reduced carriageway width, changed road surfaces and others; slow down traffic flows and encourage drivers to use 'suitable' links in the road network or alternative modes (Ratcliffe, 1981; Button, 1993; Vuchic, 1999; Papacostas and Prevedouros, 2001; Jain, 2012). Traffic calming measures control traffic accident which is a *causal factor* of traffic congestion besides promoting the use of green modes. Such measures are widely applied in USA, Canada, UK, Japan, Australia, European countries and other parts of the world (Hanna, 1997; Odani and Yamanaka, 1997; Vuchic, 1999; Sipes and Sipes, 2013). They involve least cost burden and are relatively easy to implement and give quick relief. Germany and Austria tested the effectiveness of traffic calming measures and the results were positive and frugiferous (Monheim, 1997; Sammer, 1997). In India too, a gamut of traffic calming measures and green modes are being implemented in urban systems.

Profile of the Study Area

Shillong, the capital of Meghalaya situates at an average altitude of 1496.00 metres above the mean sea level. The Master Plan (1991-2011) shows that the Greater Shillong Planning Area (GSPA) is 174.00 km^2 and the city comprises seven urban components, viz. the Shillong Municipal Board (SMB), the Shillong Cantonment Board (SCB), Nongthymmai, Mawlai, Madanrting, Pynthorumkhrah, Nongmynsong and the 32 urban villages. It locates in the East Khasi Hills District at 25°34′ N Latitude and 91°53′ E Longitude. Due to its rapid expansion, the 32 numbers of villages located in the suburbia are included in the GSPA. A large part of the Master Plan area falls in between 5° and 15° slope range whereas the gentle slope ranges between 0° and 5° is found in Happy Valley.

Table 6.2: Growth Rate in SUA Area from 1901 to 2011

Year	Population	Decadal Growth (%)	Annual Growth (%)
1901	9,621	–	–
1911	13,639	41.76	4.18
1921	17,203	26.13	2.61
1931	26,536	54.25	5.42
1941	38,192	43.92	4.93
1951	58,512	53.20	5.32
1961	92,314	57.77	5.78
1971	1,22,752	32.97	3.29
1981	1,74,703	42.32	4.32
1991	2,23,366	27.85	2.79
2001	2,67,662	19.83	1.98
2011	3,54,759	32.59	3.25
Average		**39.32**	**3.98**

Source: District Census Handbook, 1991 & Statistical Abstract, 1978 and 2018.

The existence of an age-old institution known as *shnong* in any urban system in Khasi and Jaintia Hills, Meghalaya is analogous to the concept of *neighbourhood* or *neighbourhood unit* popularised by Clarence Perry or Howard's *ward* in his conception of *Garden City* (Howard, 1965; Gallion and Eisner, 1986). An agglomeration of *neighbourhood units* constitutes an urban system including an urban village. For urban planning, the census definition of a town is acceptable.

As per the 2011 census, the population of SMB area is 1,43,229 persons and that of the Shillong Urban Agglomeration (SUA) is 3,19,605 persons. Table 6.2 highlights the decadal growth rate in SUA area from 1901 to 2011. The city's land use distribution indicates its administrative and educational standpoint and the presence of defence establishment besides residential use. While residential areas take away nearly 50 per cent of the total developed land, areas under security, defence and public use account for 14.2 per cent and 15.4 per cent respectively. A land use of 14 per cent comes under circulation which is indicative of the hilly terrain. The population growth and decadal variations from 1901 to 2011 showed that the decadal growth rate in the SMB area dropped down drastically to 0.87 per cent which implies that the old inner areas of the city are already saturated.

Table 6.3: Numbers of Registered Vehicles in the DTO's Office, Shillong

Year	Year-wise Total of Vehicles (Y)	% of Vehicular Growth
2004	4502	–
2005	4853	7.79
2006	4448	–8.34
2007	3490	–21.53
2008	4256	21.94
2009	6028	41.63
2010	8180	35.70
2011	8466	3.49
2012 (P*)	9970	17.76
1013 (Q**)	10313	3.44
2014 (A***)	10536	2.16
Overall	**75042**	**10.4**

Source: District Transport Office, Shillong.

The city has a number of meandering roads and steep slopes which limit the provision of parking facilities. Presently, about 45.00 km^2 of the city's area is a valley which is bounded on the south by the Shilllong range, on the north east by the Mawpat hill, on the east by the tributaries of Umkhrah and Umkhen rivers, on the north by the Umkhrah-Umshing water divide and on other sides by the lower minor water divides. It is spatially linked to Guwahati, Assam and to Nongpoh town, Ri Bhoi district at a distance of 103.00 km and 53.00 km respectively by the N.H. No. 6. This road is converted into a four-lane highway and the construction is completed. It is linked to Nongstoiñ town, West Khasi Hills district at a distance of 93.00 km by the N.H. No.106 and to Jowai town, West Jaintia Hills district at a distance of 66.00 km by N.H. No. 6. The time-series data for different categories of registered vehicles during 2004-14 are given in Table 6.3.

Field Surveys and Database

The databases on characteristics of various sub-components of transport sector such as road network, transport system, traffic and travel patterns, parking, PT and terminals were identified. The information was identified and was largely supported by secondary data and supplemented by limited primary surveys as per the designed questionnaire. The study area was divided into thirty-three internal traffic analysis zones (TAZs) and three external zones.

The primary road network system comprising the city's arterial, sub-arterial roads and collector streets were identified on which road network inventory primary survey was carried out on 12 roads to observe the elements such as road width, road length, density, etc. Further an assessment of the city's highly congested and busiest roads besides PT routes was also carried out. Using the moving car observer method, speed and delay surveys were carried out on the road network on 12 roads for off peak, morning peak and evening peak hours. Primary surveys of the JNNURM and the Shillong City Bus Syndicate (SCBS) buses, their depots/parking areas were carried out and secondary data were collected. Primary surveys were carried out for parking areas including bus and truck terminals. In all 25 locations/sections of arterial, sub-arterial roads and collector streets were identified where on-street parking behaviour was observed.

The latest available secondary data related to traffic volume counts for outer cordon (24 hrs) and screen line locations (16 hrs) were collected for 4 outer cordon locations and 4 screen line locations. Secondary data on the classified volume counts of the major intersections were collected at 24 locations for 16 hours duration. The data for on-street and off-street parking surveys at 26 on-street locations covering 12 hours besides 17 locations near terminals were also collected. Data on 39 bus routes were collected for about 76 buses of JNNURM. Further, secondary data were also collected on 28 maxi cab routes for 117 maxi cabs. Household travel survey data of 1500 households forming 2 per cent of the total number of households (2001 census) were collected from the designated TAZs which included all the SMB Wards and other urban agglomerations of the GSPA.

Base Line Traffic and Transport System Characteristics

Traffic Characteristics and Level of Service

Capacity analysis is fundamental to planning, design and operation of roads and helps in determining the carriageway width in respect of traffic composition and volume. The volume-capacity (V/C) ratios are low at the Gauhati-Shillong (G.S.) Road (Near NEDFi Office) and at Polo Road. It is seen that most of these roads have exceeded the highest level of service in 2007 (Table 6.4). Except for the roads at serial number 5 and 7, where the moderate level of congestion existed, the actual PCU/hour and the capacities on these arterial roads and sub-arterial roads showed that the actual traffic flow or volume of vehicles on the major intersections has exceeded the designed capacities of roads.

Table 6.4: V/C Ratios of City's Major Roads in 2007

Sl. No.	Name of Road	Traffic Characteristics			
		Total Volume	Peak Hour Volume (V)	Road Capacity $(C) = \frac{DSV}{0.70}$	V/C Ratio
1	2	3	4	5	6
1	Dhankheti Road	30958 (12 hrs)	3450	2143	1.60
2	Fire Brigade Road	23017 (12 hrs)	2416	2143	1.12
3	G.S. Road (Near Centre Point)	22967 (12 hrs)	2535	2143	1.18
4	G.S. Road (Near IGP)	25853 (24 hrs)	3201	2143	1.49
5	G.S. Road (Near NEDFI Office)	16539 (24 hrs)	1712	3429	0.50
6	Secretarial Road	37249 (24 hrs)	5668	3429	1.65
7	Polo Road	12204 (12 hrs)	1432	2143	0.67
8	Rhino Point	22320 (12 hrs)	2427	2143	1.13

Source: SCDP, 2007 & Field Study.

Similarly, the V/C ratios of the arterial and sub-arterial roads given in Table 6.5 indicated the existence of heavy congestion on all the roads and a severe congestion for roads mentioned at serial number 10 and 11 and a moderate congestion for road at serial number 9 in 2012. Thus the capacities of these arterial and sub-arterial roads are no longer capable to bear the traffic flows during peak hours and hence congestion frequents. The realized ADT values during the peak hour are higher than the recommended ADT values.

Table 6.5: V/C Ratios of City's Major Roads in 2012

Sl. No.	Name of Road	Volume (V) PCU/ Hr	Carriageway Width (m)	Road Capacity $(C) = \frac{DSV}{0.70}$	V/C Ratio
1	G.S. Road (Near Centre Point)	1649	9.0	1714	0.96
2	G.S. Road (Near IGP Point)	3003	11.0	3429	0.88
3	G.S. Road (Near Bimola Pharmacy)	1417	9.5	1714	0.82
4	G.S. Road (Near District Council Point)	2190	10.0	2714	0.80
5	N.H. 40 (Near Mawlai Petrol Pump)	1808	9.50	2143	0.84
6	N.H. 40 (Near Rhino Museum)	1877	9.5	2143	0.88
7	Polo Road	1347	8.0	1714	0.79
8	Dhankheti Road	1799	9.5	2143	0.83
9	Fire Brigade Road	1595	9.5	2143	0.74
10	Don Bosco School to Laitumkhrah Road	2151	9.5	2143	1.00
11	N.H. 40 (Near MES Point)	3641	10.5	3429	1.06

Source: CMP for GSPA—Support Document, 2012 & Field Study.

Public Transport System Characteristics

As on 2007 the motorized share of bus and intermediate public transport (IPT) was about 10-20 per cent which was far below the recommended share of 25 per cent in Indian cities. In 2009 prior to the JNNURM buses, the modal share of bus and IPT rose to 42 per cent of which the bus' share is only 2 per cent. After the operation of JNNURM buses (32-seater capacity) and maxi cabs (10-seater capacity) a market competition between the PT and the private operators arose. The buses run by four Non-Governmental Organisations (NGOs) operated on the 38 designated intra-city and intra-region routes. Before the operation of the JNNURM buses, the Meghalaya Transport Corporation operated around 46 buses on 10 intercity routes. Private buses were given permits for operating in the city on some routes—some are mini buses and a large number operated as chartered buses hired by Assam Rifles, ICAR, NEHU, NEIGRIHMS, NIFT, Army Schools and MeSEB. Presently, the SCBS which is the city's oldest transport organisation issues permits/licences to the 32-seater bus operators for transport of passengers, goods and other tangible entities from exurbs to city and *vice versa*. The SCBS controls 70 bus operators which ply on the routes, viz. (1) Tynring-NEIGRIMS-Bara Bazaar route, (2) Nongkrem-Smit Bara Bazaar route, (3) Mylliem-Laitkor-Bara Bazaar route, (4) Zero Point-Garikhana route and (5) Bhoilymbong-Garikhana route. The frequency for routes (1) to (3) is 3 to 4 trips per day and for routes (4) and (5) is only two trips per day and the operation is viable. The fares for various embarking and disembarking points are approved by the government. The maxi cabs operate on 12 hours basis from 8:00 a.m. to 8:00 p.m. everyday on the 29 arterial and sub-arterial roads connecting various TAZs. The SMB leases the operation of maxi cabs and other cars, viz. ACE MAGIC, MAXIMO, VENTURE and WINGER to the NGOs.

The IPT mode commonly found in the city are the two-wheeler, the three-wheeler and the four-wheeler systems. The two-wheeler consists of bikes, motorcycles and scooters. The three-wheeler (passengers) and the three-wheeler (goods) ply on various routes with varied utilities. Prior to the JNNURM, shared taxis (four-wheeler) were run by private operators with least competition from the PT. Cars, taxis, vans, jeeps, maxi cabs, etc. are of great utility, the city being hilly and rainy. Over time, the shared taxis gradually replaced the buses due to high frequency of service as they reduced the waiting time. This has encouraged the cabbies to operate as stage carriers. This modal shift from PTS to IPT resulted into unacceptable levels of congestion, increased pollution, accidents, etc.

Parking Characteristics

The on and off-street parking demand-supply gap analysis shows that on-street parking demand exceeds parking supply by 1673 ECS and off-street parking demand exceeds the peak demand by 594 ECS. The overall situation for on-street and off-street parking shows the shortage of supply of parking lots by 1079 ECS. This indicates a clamant demand for supplying extra multilevel parking spaces to ease parking congestion.

Transport Demand Forecast

The short-term and medium-term forecasts for transport demand (registered vehicles) are 16015 and 21493 vehicles respectively. Taking an annual growth rate of 6 per cent observed between 2009 and 2014, the number of buses estimated by 2019 and 2024 will be 1302 and 1603 respectively. Assuming the same modal share of 4.7 per cent, the modal share of PT will increase to 12.51 per cent by 2019 and to 15.47 per cent by 2024. If IPTs are included the total PT's share is worked out. The total strength of the IPT by 2019 and 2024 will be 9719 and 11700 respectively assuming an annual growth rate of 10.4 per cent. As calculated, assuming the average annual growth rate of traffic on city roads system at the rate of 10.38 per cent per annum, the likely traffic volume/hour for the horizon years 2019 and 2024 on the city's busy roads along with V/C ratio are given in Table 6.6.

Table 6.6: Expected Traffic Volume and Impact on Major Roads in 2019 and 2024

Sl. No.	Name of Road/ Intersection	Traffic Characteristics				
		Volume (PCU/ Hr) in 2019 (V)	Volume (PCU/ Hr) in 2024 (V)	Road Capacity $(C) = \frac{DSV}{0.70}$	V/C Ratio in 2019	V/C Ratio in 2024
1	G.S. Road (Near Centre Point)	3361	4216	1714	1.96	2.46
2	G.S. Road (Near IGP Point)	6120	7679	3429	1.8	2.23
3	G.S. Road (Near Bimola Pharmacy)	2888	3623	1714	1.69	2.11
4	G.S. Road (Near District Council Point)	4463	5600	2714	1.64	2.06
5	N.H. 40 (Near Mawlai Petrol Pump)	3685	4623	2143	1.71	2.16

contd...

contd...

Sl. No.	Name of Road/ Intersection	Traffic Characteristics				
		Volume (PCU/ Hr) in 2019 (V)	Volume (PCU/ Hr) in 2024 (V)	Road Capacity $(C) = \frac{DSV}{0.70}$	V/C Ratio in 2019	V/C Ratio in 2024
6	N.H. 40 (Near Rhino Museum)	4029	5055	2143	1.88	2.36
7	Polo Road	2745	3444	1714	1.60	2.00
8	Dhankheti Road	3666	4600	2143	1.71	2.14
9	Fire Brigade Road	3251	4078	2143	1.51	1.90
10	Don Bosco School to Laitumkhrah Road	4384	5500	2143	2.05	2.57
11	N.H. 40 (Near MES Point)	7420	9310	3429	2.16	2.71

Source: CMP for GSPA—Support Document, 2012 & Field Study.

It can be seen that the projected traffic volume is beyond the traffic design/geometric design capacity of these urban roads which will induce multiple effects or impacts such as economic effects, societal effects, environmental effects, inefficient effects, etc. on the lives of the urbanites. Thus, unless appropriate traffic decongestion measures are put in place, the traffic flow phenomenon during the peak hour periods will come to a standstill.

Proposed Traffic Congestion Countermeasures

Bearing in mind the causes or sources of traffic congestion, the demand, supply and administrative or regulatory measures/strategies are proposed to ease the city's traffic congestion/traffic jam. Short-term, medium-term and long-term traffic congestion countermeasures provide a safe, efficient and environmentally sustainable green transport system for smart mobility of people and goods (Ñianglang, 2016).

Short-Term Measures

Supply-Side Measures

The following short-term supply-driven strategies comprising the traffic engineering measures are recommended for implementation.

Traffic Engineering Measures

To pacify the immediate needs of urban commuters, the UMTCL (2012) and the authors recommended to implement the following short-term strategies on the busy sub-arterial and arterial roads.

(1) *Pavement Markings:* Centre line, dotted line, direction arrow, stop line, pedestrian crossing, chevron and diagonal markings in core area of physical traffic, parking area and restricted entry/exit is required to be carried out as per IRC specifications. Proper pedestrian marking with stop line in the road segment designated for pedestrian crossings is essential.

(2) *Traffic Control Devices:* Installation of speed tables, traffic signals, stop signs, pedestrian crossings, no stopping/no-standing, no parking, overtaking prohibited, left turn prohibited, right turn prohibited and other devices at the designated road portions is mandatory. Direction signs and advance direction signs should be installed at 150.00 m and 500.00 m apart before approaching the intersections. Traffic signs like T-Intersection, Y-Intersection and round-about sign, etc. are required to be installed at 50.00 m before the junction. Similarly, provision of one-way/two-way traffic direction hazard marker signs on traffic islands, separators and traffic rotaries is necessary.

(3) *Traffic Signals:* Traffic signals need to be made functional and movement timing to be synchronized as per priority movement of peak hour traffic. Traffic signals on some major intersections like MES Point, Rhino Point, Polo Bazaar, Police Bazaar, Anjali Cinema, Howel Point, Barik, IGP Point, Dhankheti, etc. may be installed on try basis to control the traffic flow during the peak hours. Provision of amber blinkers near small road junctions and pedestrian crossings is necessary.

(4) *Barricades and Channelisers:* Barricades, traffic separators and channelisers are required to be provided at major 'X' and 'T' intersections to effectively segregate and divert the traffic flows to their respective directions.

(5) *Traffic Marshals:* Deployment of traffic marshals at different intersections is also considered expedient in order to control the wrong traffic entry and misconduct of some cabbies and drivers so as to maintain continuous traffic stream.

(6) *Reflective and Solar Studs/Cat Eyes:* Traffic studs/cat eyes are required to be installed at hazardous locations to direct the traffic

to their right directions. Provision of reflective cat eyes at both ends of pedestrian pavement marking to indicate the pedestrian crossings is essential.

(7) *Roadway Delineators:* To have a clear view of the hazardous areas by commuters or road users, it is essential to provide the roadway/traffic delineators at all hazardous locations like island, hairpin/sharp curve locations, near-sharp turnings, separators, etc.

(8) *Construction/Renovation of Pedestrians' Footpaths:* Construction of new footpaths and renovation of the existing footpaths is necessary to incentivize and boost the morale of pedestrians and to direct them to the nearest pedestrian crossing locations. At steeper terrains, cantilever footpaths and skywalks may be constructed as done in Gangtok and other hill towns. This will increase the percentage of 'walk' from all modes.

(9) *Renovation of Existing Roads, Potholes and Patches:* Some urban roads are partly serviceable as pavements are damaged. Potholes and patches have developed on the top surface of these roads and hence they need to be rectified for safe and smooth traffic flow.

(10) *Improvement of Intersections:* Intersections strongly influence the overall traffic flow and the DSVs of roads and their improvements lead to orderly traffic movement. For example, improvement of Police Bazaar intersection carried out few years ago eased the traffic congestion to a large extent. Improvement of some intersections such as Ganesh Das Hospital Junction, Polo Junction, Nongmynsong Junction and others is considered expedient. Some could be identified and converted into rotaries or traffic islands which are also a part of urban renewal for greening the city's transport systems. Lack of traffic sense by road users adds problems to a traffic police. Thus, it is expedient to install the road signs and pavement markings in all the busy arterial and sub-arterial roads. Traffic signals installed earlier at the intersections, viz., Police Bazaar, I.G.P. Point, Barik Point, Dhankheti, Anajalee Petrol Pump Point, Rhino Museum Junction, Civil Hospital Junction, Nongrim Hill, etc. needs to be made functional. Hence, a separate city's Intersections Improvement Plan is necessary.

Provision of School and College Buses

One of the most effective decongestion strategies is to provide buses to schools and colleges existing in the city's core areas on minimum payment of transport charges. To actualize this purpose, supply of information relating to routes, frequency of trips and timetables for boarding and alighting students going to St. Edmund's School, St. Anthony's School, Loreto Convent, Step-by-Step School, All Saints School etc. is essential.

Demand-Side Measures

The demand-driven measures some of which are regulatory in nature are given below.

Parking Management

Organized on-street parking needs to be provided near activity areas to prevent traffic congestion on narrow stretches and to allow smooth movement of traffic. Organisation of on-street parking serves the purpose for a small period but development of off-street parking facility is extremely essential for a long-term.

(1) *Restrict or Ban On-Street Parking:* On-street parking is required to be restricted in some locations and banned in certain locations as they hinder movement of vehicles thereby causing traffic congestion.

(2) *Integration of Parking with the City's PTS System:* Construction of parking lots in all the proposed bus depot locations, bus termini and truck termini to integrate and maintain seamless multi-mode traffic of goods and freight with the city's PTS system and freight carriers is recommended.

(3) *Off-Street Parking:* Land acquisition for construction of additional parking lots at business centres/shopping centres such as Police Bazaar, Bara Bazar needs to be explored to ease traffic congestion. The study team also recommended provision of off-street parking lots at Nongthymmai, Laitumkhrah, Dhankheti, Nongmynsong, Madanryting, Laban, Umpling Bazaar and improvement of Taxi Stand at Golf Link.

(4) *Rationalization of On-Street Parking:* The on-street parking, which is presently very disorganized in some road spaces, needs to be rationalized and organized and laid out in consonance with the proposed circulation system. The recommended guidelines with reference to road width and traffic circulation are (i) no on-street parking up to 15 m from an intersection edge on all arms, (ii) no parking near entry to public utility buildings, hospitals, schools, etc., (iii) no parking near entry gates to properties and (iv) no parking near bus stops up to 15 m on either side. Table 6.7 shows the general recommendation for on-street parking facilities.

Table 6.7: Guidelines for Traffic Circulation and Parking Organisation

Circulation Type	Parking Organisation
Traffic one-way, road width ≤ 5.00 m	No on-street parking.
Traffic one-way, road width between 5.00 m and 11.00 m	On-street parking on one side only alternatively on either side on odd and even dates. Parking type to be perpendicular for 2-wheelers and parallel for other modes.
Traffic one-way, road width > 11.00 m	On-street parking on both sides.

*Source:*Ñianglang AITP (India) Thesis.

(5) *Levying Parking Fees:* The most important component of the parking policy is levy of parking fees for on-street and off-street parking within central area to begin with and extends it over the entire city in due course of time. It is recommended to implement a differential parking fee policy with increasing fee structure in the CBD areas/activity areas and in the traffic-sodden city centres in comparison to non-activity areas. Suitable parking policy for the off-street parking facilities needs to be formulated based on costs of development, operation, maintenance and management. Similar differential policy amongst the parking sites in different zones needs to be adopted.

(6) *Municipalisation of Parking Spaces:* Parking areas could be created within the individual sites through prescribed zoning regulations and parking norms within SMB area and in case of stand-alone multi-storey car parks, FAR/FSI relaxation may be granted as per the provisions of the extant Meghalaya Building Byelaws. This is analogous to the TDR concept of land pooling technique in which parking spaces will remain under the ownership of the individual site developer/owner. A general tendency observed is that if the built-up area remains unbridled, there is a chance of misusing such parking spaces for commercial and other uses. This will not only reduce the parking spaces but adds additional demand for parking. Constant enforcement by the civil agency is difficult, costly and ineffective. To prevent this misuse and ensure availability of parking spaces for parking, 'municipalisation' of parking spaces created as part of building byelaws is recommended. The management of parking spaces will be vested with the SMB or

Meghalaya Urban Development Authority (MUDA) or any other authorised agency which will manage these spaces for parking purposes. The agency will levy a fee for parking and contract out the service.

(7) *Compounding Fee:* Another concept recommended is the levy and collection of a compounding fee in lieu of parking fee provision under the existing building byelaws. A charge per parking space may be fixed at different locations and types of uses and the site developer charged the equivalent sum based on the car spaces required to be provided as per building byelaws. The SMB or MUDA will collect this fee and will pool the resources and develop, maintain and manage off-street parking facilities at different locations for use by public. The compounding fee may be fixed and collected for development within activity areas/CBD areas in the first instance. It may judiciously be extended to other areas over a period of time.

(8) *Better On-Street Management:* Parking issues require better on-street parking management, strict enforcement of traffic rules, creation of more off-street parking facilities and other ameliorating measures.

Car Pooling for Government Officials

As many of the commuters are government employees, pooling vehicles and pool subsidies could be introduced. We propose that a government employee who has an official car is required to pay Rs. 1000 per month as a conveyance charge. If the concerned officer pools with other officials for high occupancy vehicle (HOV) use, a waiver could be introduced.

Staggering of Work Hours

Staggered time management lessens the traffic pressure on a road space. Availing the early sunrise, we propose that all central government offices will function at 8:30 a.m. and close at 5:00 p.m. whereas State Government's offices will function at 9:30 a.m. and close at 4:30 p.m. Thus, there will be a staggering effect of one hour. We propose that the city's commercial centres, viz. Police Bazaar, Bara Bazaar, Polo Bazaar, Laitumkhrah Bazaar, etc. will open at 7:00 a.m. and will close at 10:00 p.m. to enable the consumers to make their shopping trips as per their conveniences and not necessary during the peak traffic hours. Besides police personnel, installation of ITS tools, viz. CCTV, digital cameras, etc. at designated commercial places and shops is required to be carried out as a security measure/strategy.

Staggering of Time Schedule for Goods Vehicles

Goods vehicles are the people's lifelines. Due to space constraint for truck termini, a suitable time schedule say from 9:00 p.m. to enable the goods vehicles to load/download the goods for shifting to godowns and storage facilities needs to be chalked out by stakeholders, viz. SMB, KHADC, MUDA, DTO, District Administrator and SP (Traffic). A Goods Transport Monitoring Committee comprising the stakeholders under the Chairmanship of the Deputy Commissioner, Shillong to monitor the inflow and outflow of goods is required to be put in place.

Prohibition of Certain License Numbers from Driving on Specific Days

As a part of traffic management, all officials and functionaries working in public offices, courts, institutions, hospitals, etc. may be prohibited from using their private cars on certain days during peak hours. This measure is more effective if a robust PT in city's major accessible routes is provided. The practice of allowing even and odd plate numbers may be enforced on alternate basis. For example, private cars with even plate numbers can ply during peak period on Monday to be followed by the private cars with odd plate numbers in the following day. Violation of such regulation is liable for congestion pricing. However, they may be permitted to use their private cars in any day if they resort to carpooling or adhere to the 'car-freeness' principle. This measure may be exempted for patients, medical doctors, magistrates, employees pertaining to emergency services and other functionaries as may be decided by the government.

Alteration of Existing Work Laws

The existing rules and regulations mandating government employees to work from their offices needs to be revisited since they are directed to arrive at their working places in a timely manner at 10:00 a.m sharp which adds a heavy traffic volume to the already overloaded urban roads during peak traffic hours. The existing rules may be revised/amended and professionals such as architects, engineers, planners and interior designers may be allowed to work from their homes and send the information to their offices through e-office, e-proposal, etc. This may be extended to other categories of employees too.

Banning of On-Street Hawkers

Street vendors and hawkers mushroomed especially on the Old G.S. Road connecting Bara Bazaar (Ïewdub), Police Bazaar, Mawlong-Anjalee Petrol

Pump Road, Motphran-Garikhana Road and other parts of the city. These are the arterial roads of the city's CBD. Vendors and hawkers occupy sizeable portions of road space and footpaths that reduce the carriageways, footpaths and pedestrian crossings meant for the pedestrians, wheelchair travellers, etc. To avoid accidents, a slight manoeuvring of vehicles towards the camber results in traffic congestion and jams. A robust law enforcement mechanism involving the stakeholders, viz. Dorbar Shnongs, Mylliem Syiemship, SMB, KHADC, DTO and District Administrators could be evolved to ban all street hawkers and vendors and to find out suitable locations for them.

Congestion Pricing

Fiscal measures such as congestion pricing, vehicle and fuel tax, parking charges, pollution charges, road pricing, etc. may be applied for private vehicle users/motorists to orient their travel habits towards PT and discourage the use of private vehicles. To begin with, a road pricing may be imposed on private vehicles/motorists that use the bus routes to (i) divert commuters to other IPT modes of travel such as car pools, shared taxis, auto rickshaws, (ii) cancel the non-essential trips during peak periods and change the departure time or route of vehicular trips, (iii) mobilize resources for construction/upgradation of flyovers, arterial roads, parking facilities, etc. and (iv) to cross-subsidize the PT modes. For example, increasing the parking fee for private vehicles at Police Bazaar parking lot discourages them from using their cars. A committee may be constituted to evolve a suitable 'Pricing Package' to make the proposal socially and politically acceptable.

Multi-Mode Ticket

In the late 1980s, the Stockholm Urban Traffic Committee came up with the idea called the multi-mode ticket in which each driver entering the inner city by car during the workdays between 6:00 a.m. to 6:00 p.m. should provide a valid ticket for the Stockholm PT system either on daily or monthly basis. This could be a monthly ticket for commuters or a single return ticket for occasional travellers. However, the London cordon toll system introduced in 2003 was more promising, the multi-mode ticket was appealing and was replicated in some cities around the world such as Hongkong, Oslo, etc. (Arnott *et al.*, 2005). In Singapore, the former ALS was replaced by the current Electronic Road Pricing (ERP) System in 1998 with which charges are automatically deducted from a pre-paid card as the vehicle drives past the gantry. The charge/levy is varied in accordance with the congestion levels on each road and at different times of the day (Soon *et al.,* 2009). Applying the tenets of behavioural economics to towners, a robust multi-modal ticket system for PT system could be evolved for Shillong city which should be socially, politically acceptable and economically viable.

Implementation of Vehicle Quota System

Since 1990, the Vehicle Quota System was implemented in Singapore to manage the growth of vehicle population. The *modus operandi* is that the number of new vehicles allowed, i.e. the quota is pre-determined every year, considering the prevailing traffic conditions and the number of vehicles taken off the roads permanently. The quota for a given year is administered through the monthly release of Certificates of Entitlements (COEs). An aspirant for a new vehicle is required to bid for and acquire a COE before buying a vehicle. It was found that this system has capped the growth rate of vehicle population at 3 per cent per annum (Soon *et al.,* 2009). It is recommended that a traffic volume survey on quarterly or monthly basis may be carried out and the Vehicle Quota System may be considered for capping the growth rate of vehicles in the state. This may be started first for private cars.

Supply-Type and Demand-Type Measures

Conversion of City's Existing CBDs into Car-Free City Centres

Urbanologists and spatial planners evolved a broader concept of car-free city. 'Car-free' means only 'qualified traffic' and qualified traffic is a vehicle which carries not less than three occupants including a driver. Vehicles such as ambulance, fire extinguisher, disaster-rescue vehicle, emergency service vehicle, hotel-guest or tourist-carrying vehicle or any special purpose vehicle may be exempted to ply during peak traffic hours. Buses, taxis, hired cars, vanpools, carpools, cavalcades, convoys which carry not less than three occupants during peak period are declared 'qualified traffic' and special parking permits or licenses are given. Under the extant car-free principle, unqualified vehicles or single occupancy vehicles (SOVs) are tollable, i.e. they are allowed to enter in a car-free city centre during peak traffic hours only if they pay the toll prescribed by the government as done in the cities of Lubeck, Aachen, San Diego and others (Brunsing, 1997; Monheim, 1997). To begin with, CBDs such as Police Bazaar and Bara Bazaar could be explored for conversion into car-free city centres.

Conversion of City's Existing Roads into HOV/HOT Lanes

Arterial roads with V/C ratios more than 1 may be identified and explored for conversion into HOV/HOT lanes called 'diamond' lanes. The speeds on the HOV/HOT lanes which are faster than the speeds on the regular lanes save time and money thereby incentivising the travellers to shift to HOV/HOT lanes. Since the road space per traveller for HOVs is lower than the road space for regular lanes, reduction in the road's overall average V/C increases the average speed of travel on the HOV lane (Mohring, 1999). In practice, traffic engineers and transport planners adopt either the "Covert-a-lane" approach, i.e. conversion of one or more existing general-purpose lanes or roadways or the 'Add-a-lane' approach, i.e. construction of new HOV facilities. In USA, public authorities used both approaches for implementing this concept in cities like New York, Seattle metropolitan area, Portland, Houston, Chicago and others (Vuchic, 1999; Washington *et al.*, 2011; Khisty and Lall; 2017). Based on the car-free principle, unqualified vehicles or single occupancy vehicles (SOVs) are tollable, i.e. they are allowed to ply on a HOV/HOT lane or roadway during peak traffic hours only if they pay the prescribed toll. As a maiden venture, a techno-economic feasibility study for the Motphran-Police Bazaar-IGP-Barik road may be carried out for conversion into a HOV/HOT lane.

Installation of Intelligent Transport Systems (ITSs)

Supply type ITS tools such as early incident detection, optimised signal operation based on real-time demand, freeway management with ramp metering, accident avoidance with variable message signs warning of impending congestion, fog, bad weather, etc. could be explored for installation. Similarly, demand type ITS tools such as real-time traffic congestion information at homes, workplaces, shopping centres, etc. enabling car users to postpone or delay or change their trips to alternative modes of travel and in-vehicle devices to divert drivers from congested roads alleviate traffic congestion. The scope and applications of ITS tools is available in the literature (Kumar, 2022). After the operation of the PTS under the JNNURM programme, there is an immediate need to install the ITS tools and control system facilities in vehicles, bus stops, control stations, electronic road pricing (ERP), electronic fee collection (EFC) and the automatic fare collection (AFC) systems meant for PT and IPT. To actualize this objective, a separate ITS plan configuring to the case city's road landscape, private vehicles and PTS systems could be explored.

Medium- and Long-Term Measures

The following medium- and long-term measures including some measures recommended by the UMTC Ltd. (2012) are proposed and reiterated.

Shifting of Offices to NST and Conversion of Deserted Spaces into Downtown Ecology, etc.

Shifting of some offices such as offices of the Executive Engineer, PWD (NH) at Barik, District Transport Officer and others may be explored and shifted to the NST and proposed Integrated Townships to decongest the city's core areas. The deserted open space at Barik may be converted into downtown ecology applying the theory of 'island biogeography' as done in Singapore, Bracknell in UK and other cities for counteracting ecological imbalances, research activities and for tourism (Schilthuizen, 2018). Other deserted built-up spaces may be redeveloped, modified and converted into water reservoirs, green spaces or any other alternative uses.

Formulation of Area Development Plan for Bara Bazaar (Ïewduh)

The present Bara Bazaar (Ïewduh) which is multi-faceted in nature attracts townlings within the city and people from outside due to its proximity from the existing parking lots, availability of goods at wholesale prices, its legacy as an age-old market centre, etc. With the increase in human and vehicular populations, it became congested which frequents traffic congestion on the roads circumjacent to it. A redevelopment may be prepared by MUDA after taking decision and signing the MoU/MoA with the Syiem of Mylliem Syiemship and his Durbar.

Provision of Parking Facilities, ISBTs, ISTTs, Cycle Parks, etc.

Wherever feasible, landowners may also be allowed to develop parking lots for public according to designs, specifications and conditions prescribed by the MUDA utilizing the full built-up area equal to FSI available on the plot for purpose of providing parking space. It is proposed that construction/retrofitting of (1) inter-state bus terminus (ISBT) at Mawïong with park-and-ride facility, (2) underground/roof car parks in residential, commercial and public buildings, (3) multi-level Shillong City Centre at the MTC land, Police Bazaar as per the existing plan and design, (4) multi-level parking facility in the SCBS land at Mawlonghat and (5) multi-storey car parks in all CTs of SUA under the management of the respective Town Committees may be explored. Outside the SUA, construction of (1) inter-state truck terminus (ISTT) at

Umbang area or any new site on the city's north direction, (2) inter-state bus termini equipped with full-scale facilities at Laitkor, Upper Shillong and near NST, (3) buildings with in-house parking facilities in the NST and (4) construction of ISTTs, ISBTs, bus depots, bus bays, cycle parks, multi-level car parks and automated multi-level parking systems in NST, new townships and in suburbia could be explored.

Provision of Attractive Public Transport System

Provision of PT is one of the robust measures to ease the traffic congestion thereby weaning car users away to it. After the operation of minibuses and ten-seater vans, proper planning measures are necessary to augment their operating system in the face of competition with private transport operators. It is necessary to integrate properly the primary, secondary and tertiary route networks to ensure smooth functioning of the bus operating system. To encourage urban commuters to travel by PT systems, we propose to designate the city's arterial and sub-arterial roads for PT systems as shown in Figure 6.1. Mode-wise travelcards renewable on weekly or monthly basis to dissuade motorists from using their cars may be introduced (Simpson, 1994; White, 1995).

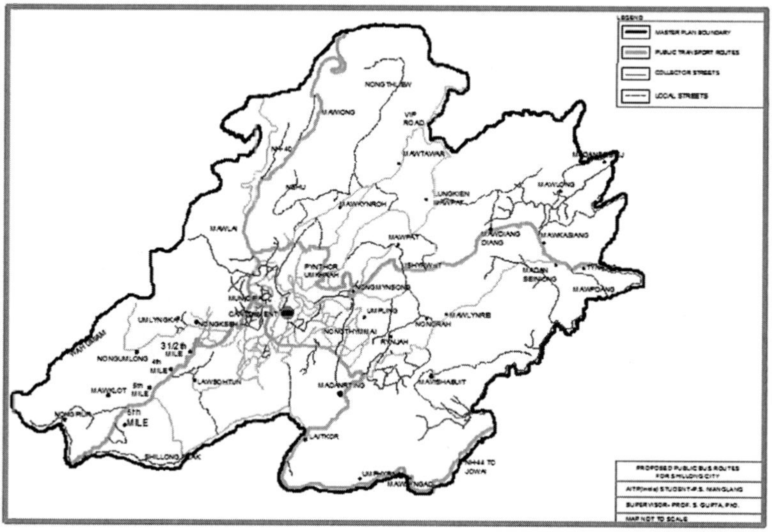

Figure 6.1: Proposed Public Transport Routes

Source: Ñianglang AITP (India) Thesis.

Construction of Bus-Bays

Provision of properly designed bus-bays including bus shelters at the curbs of roadways with hotel/restaurant facilities and shops enable the flowing vehicles to temporarily recess for loading and unloading of passengers without producing any backflow on the traffic stream. Thus, provision of bus-bays in all bypasses and NHs at a minimum spacing of 75.00 m from intersections in case of urban roads and 300.00 m in case of regional roads is necessary.

Provision of Ramp Metering System

Vehicles surging from link or transit routes of the regional and urban transport network systems tend to move onto the major overloaded freeways or expressways in bunches and slow down the existing traffic flows. To avoid such platooning of vehicles, at-grade or grade-separated ramps are constructed at designated segments of freeways or expressways and meter systems are provided to admit new entrants onto such roadways one at every interval of 5 to 20 seconds between entries. Ramp metering system is also used to limit the total number of vehicles using an expressway or freeway in a given period to keep traffic flows at high speeds to ensure transportation of maximum through-puts, goods, etc. The system is integrated with traffic signals and traffic signs to guide drivers for their mode choices. The MUTCD provides general guidelines for successful application of ramp control. The common methods used for controlling freeway entrance ramps are (1) closure, (2) simple metering, (3) traffic response metering and (4) the integrated systems control. The two methods of traffic response metering, viz. (i) the demand capacity control and (ii) the occupancy control are used for determining the metering rate (Papacostas and Prevedouros, 2001; Garber and Hoel, 2002; Downs, 2004). The signal timings on ramps are adjusted applying either a fully restrictive, a partially restrictive or a non-restrictive metering method, depending on the current LOS of roadways. Although, it is primarily used on expressways and freeways but experience in some cities like Seattle and Twin Cities regions shows that this traffic decongestion tactic is more effective for city streets rather than expressways.

Depending on the availability of land, provision of ramp metering systems on the following road locations is therefore recommended for control and regulation of traffic flows into the city:

(1) NH-6 at Mawïong near Umïam Lake (Dam Site), Umsning, Laitkor, Lad Smit and Sohryngkham.
(2) NH-106 at Sanmer, Umdiengpun and near Mawkriah.

Improvement of Roads for By-passable Traffic

The traffic congestion/jam of the case city warrants improving or constructing the following arterial, sub-arterial, collector roads and state roads for by-passable vehicular traffic.

(1) Widening and improvement of the Police Bazaar-Jail Road leading to Polo Traffic Police Point for one-way downward flow of all cars and small vehicles coming from Police Bazaar and other areas for diversion of traffic directly to Polo areas without passing through the overloaded segment of the Police Bazaar-Kasheri-Raj Bhawan Road.

(2) Widening of the existing link road connecting Laitkor and Sanmer, Upper Shillong through Shillong peak for through traffic. This serves as the bypass of the regional traffic coming from Jowai, Sohra (Cherrapunjee), Nongstoin, etc.

(3) Designation and improvement of the existing road as the link road between Nongthymmai and Shillong New Township.

(4) Conversion of the existing road from Mawmaram to Umïam (Bara Pani) on the west of the city as a state highway. This serves as the bypass for the Nongstoiñ-Guwahati traffic.

(5) Construction of bypass outside the GSPA from Sohryngkham to Laitlum connecting the NH-6 and NH-206 on the south. The two bypasses will carry the regional traffic flows/by-passable traffic volumes coming from Silchar, Mizoram Jaintia Hills destined to Goalpara *via* Nongstoin, Tura and those exuding from South-West and West Khasi Hills destined for Guwahati and other parts of the country.

Provision of Cycle/NMT Tracks

Provision of cycle/NMT tracks of 2.00 m width either on one side or both sides of some city's routes, viz. Mawlai-Polo-Demseiñïong-NST road, Mawlai-Mawroh-Golf Link-Polo Road, NST roads and others as per the URDPFI Guidelines 2014 (Government of India, 2015) could be explored. Provisions of cycle/NMT tracks, parking lots for cycles, walkways along with shops, restaurants, tea stalls, etc. at regular intervals promoting uses of green modes is essential. Existing steep gradients in some portions of roads are required to be brought down to the IRC recommended gradients.

Provision of Electric Ropeways

In India, provision of electric ropeways in hill towns and cities like Simla,

Gangtok, etc. is on the top of the government's agenda. Such means of transport are eco-friendly as the pollution rate is minimal. Thus, feasibility studies for the provision of electric ropeways on the western part of the city connecting Lummawbah to Upper Mawprem, Lower Mawprem to Mawlai Nongkwar, etc. may be explored. This will also boost and showcase the city's tourism.

Construction of Link Roads

The proposed link roads, viz. (i) Mawlai-Umroi Airport Road (VIP road), (ii) Mawtawar-Mawpat-NST and (iii) NST-4-lane road linking the existing Umïam-Mawryngkneng bypass needs to be started immediately. These will ease the pressure on the city's prime mobility corridors such as the NH-6 and NH-106. The roads need to be upgraded/constructed to a minimum of two-lane road with suitable road markings and barricaded intersections to avoid accidents and pedestrian conflicts and to decongest the city.

Development of Wholesale Logistics Hubs

Shillong does not have even a single well-planned wholesale logistics hub to house the freight vehicles. Absence of wholesale logistics hubs necessitated the goods trucks to load and unload goods at Bara Bazaar (Mawlonghat and Garikhana) near the city's heart. Movement of goods vehicles into the city is a seamless process and is throughout the day. As vehicles tread through the narrow hilly terrain, i.e. a portion of NH-6 between Umïam (Barapani) and Shillong they frequently tend to overtake each other. This produces a traffic backflow affecting the movement of other vehicles which results in congestion. This situation warrants the construction of by-passes and wholesale hubs at the proposed ISTTs to prevent heavy goods vehicles from entering in the city's commercial areas.

Creation of Integrated Townships

Integrated townships are large self-sufficient enclaves with homes, schools, offices, workplaces, malls, multiplexes, private security and high-quality water, sewerage and solid waste management systems (Joshi, 2009). To alleviate congestion in the old city and to prevent any possible urban decay i.e. the process by which the functioning city falls into decrepitude in the future, setting up of integrated townships near Nongkrem, Mawphlang, Mawsiatkhnam or any other feasible area could be explored.

Laws and Policy Measures

Formulation of Meghalaya Urban Mixed Land-Use Planning and Policy

Land is the scarce resource which is fixed in supply. Hitherto, there is no Urban Mixed Land-Use Planning and Policy meant for multifarious uses such as residential, commercial, transport, public, urban agriculture, etc. Absence of such policy results in the misuse of land. For example, due to lack of technical guidance, people at Pynthorumkhrah and other parts of the city use agricultural lands for residential purposes which are incongruous with the land use tenets of a physical planner. Such use abuses urban agriculture which contributes to the city's economy besides deteriorating its landscape and downtown ecology. Moreover, urban agriculture becomes the neglected component of town planning. Formulation of this Policy is expedient to evade land abuses in the city.

Formulation of Meghalaya Integrated Land-Use and Transport Planning Policy

One of the most important traffic congestion countermeasures is the recognition of the close link between land use and transport to optimise the planning system for control of transport growth. The principal objective is to maximise accessibility and minimise trip lengths. These twin policy objectives guarantee the greatest levels of demand for PT, cycling and walk modes. Ensuring mixed land uses specifically for transport sector, availabilities of local facilities and employment and attractive PT system; sustain minimum levels of pollution and energy consumption per trip and per person even in the TAZs where trip generation is high and yields the greatest efficiency in TDM (Banister, 1994). Formulation of Meghalaya Integrated Land-Use and Transport Planning Policy is, thus, considered expedient.

Formulation of Meghalaya Urban Transport Policy

As urban systems expand it is expedient to formulate the Meghalaya Urban Transport Policy in tandem with the National Urban Transport Policy 2014. Such policy shall *inter alia*; encompass a background, a vision and objectives for provision of urban transport systems and interactive components/amenities. With the elapse of time, such policy shall be periodically updated to keep pace with the needs of the people and development.

Formulation of Urban Parking Policy

Parking policy does not promise an unending supply chasing an unsatisfied demand but is an instrument to articulate demand and supply to achieve a desired balance. The major components of such a policy could be (i) development and management of off-street parking facility at appropriate locations, (ii) identification, organisation and regularization of on-street parking facilities, (iii) Pricing of parking space, (iv) Institutional arrangement for planning, development and management of parking facilities and (v) parking norms/standards to be incorporated as part of building byelaws and zoning regulations. Considering the increasing traffic intensity and inadequate road network capacity particularly in central areas, an urban parking policy needs to be framed which could be used as a tool or guide document for formulation and implementation of transport demand management (TDM) measures (IRC, 1994).

Enactment of the Meghalaya Transport Efficiency Act

To curb traffic congestion and provide smart mobility to all users, drastic measures like physical restraint banning the entry of vehicles into pedestrian precincts, reservation of some roads exclusively for PT and HOVs, application of car-freeness principle, equitable allocation of road space, road pricing, etc. are inevitable. Thus, enactment of MeTEA, 2018 is considered expedient.

Inter-Modal Coordination

Common experience tells us that travellers exercise their mode choices based on costs, time and convenience for their trip ends. To make this process more effective, development of routes and pedestrian facilities for transit, taxi-sharing, carpools, auto rickshaws, walk, bicycles, etc. is essential. A few possibilities can be created at the city's periphery for intermodal coordination such as general-purpose modes with HOV lanes, park-and-ride, park-and-walk facilities enabling the motorists to park their vehicles and reach at the CBDs or city centres by other modes such as walking, auto cycling, carpooling, rickshaws, buses, HOV lanes, etc. in time. Thus, it is expedient to construct link roads and parking facilities near the proposed ISBTs, ISTTs, urban fringes and exurbs to prevent private cars from going into the city's core areas.

Reform Measures in Urban Transport

The UMTC Ltd. (2012) proposed to set up a Unified Transport Authority (UTA) which will principally function as a nodal authority to plan and decide the development of urban and regional transport. The UTA to be chaired by the Principal Secretary or Commissioner and Secretary, Urban Affairs Department comprising the Dorbar Shnongs, KHADC, SMB, SCB, MUDA, MTC, Traffic Police, Planning, Transport, Urban Affairs and PWDs as the stakeholders along with town planners and transport planners needs to be vested with powers and functions. Amendment of the Meghalaya Town and Country Planning Act, 1973 empowering the UTA is, thus, proposed.

Conclusion

The study of traffic congestion of the case city culminated in the finding of urban traffic congestion levels and formulation of possible planning strategies for traffic decongestion based on various issues of concern (CIRT, 2009). It is observed *inter alia* that rapid increase in the share of private vehicles and IPT, limited road capacities, lack of parking facilities, absence of bypass in the south-west and north-west directions of the city are the prime causes of traffic congestion. In most cases the existing ROWs of urban roads are below the recommended ROWs and have no traffic separators/medians. The capacity analysis shows most arterial and sub-arterial roads carry vehicles beyond their designed capacities. The V/C ratios of the city's major arterial and sub-arterial roads are indicative of the traffic flow phenomena of heavy and severe traffic congestion.

Although the above traffic decongestion measures are not exhaustive and new measures may be evolved as may be required, however, unless these countermeasures are implemented in right earnest, mobility in the city during peak periods will lead to a clogging of the arteries of transport systems which may result in a general thrombosis.

REFERENCES

Alam, S. (1986). *Development Strategies for Hill Towns: Case Study-Shillong*, An unpublished M.R.P. Thesis, Department of Architecture and Regional Planning, Indian Institute of Technology, Kharagpur, pp. 8-18.

Arnott, R. *et al.* (2005). *Alleviating Urban Traffic Congestion*, The MIT Press, Cambridge, pp. 34-37, 101-28, 135-81 & 187-222.

Balchin P.N. *et al.* (1995). *Urban Land Economics and Public Policy,* Fifth Edition, Macmillan Press Ltd., Hampshire, Great Britain, pp. 211-29.

Banister D. (1994). *Transport Planning, First Edition*, E & FN Spon, London, pp. 212-13.

BCEOM India Private Limited (2007). *City Development Plan for Greater Shillong Planning Area, Final Report.* Directorate of Urban Affairs, Government of Meghalaya, Shillong, pp. 4.101 to 4.105 & 10.7 to 10.8.

Brunsing, J. (1997). A Car-Free Lubeck? In R. Tolley (ed.), *The Greening of Urban Transport, Edition II*, John Wiley & Sons Ltd, Chichester, England, pp. 435-40.

Button K.J. (1993). *Transport Economics,* 2nd Edition, Reprinted 2003, Edward Elgar, Cheltenham, UK, pp. 93-121 & 148-70.

Central Institute of Road Transport (2009). *DPR for Procurement of Buses, Shillong*, Urban Affairs Department, Government of Meghalaya, p. 27.

Downs, A. (2004). *Still Stuck in Traffic*, Brooking Institution Press, Washington DC, pp. 76-90, 107-09, 341-42 & 348.

Gallion A.B. and Eisner, S. (1986): *The Urban Pattern: City Planning and Design,* Fifth Edition, Indian Reprint, 1986, CBS Publishers & Distributors Pvt. Ltd., New Delhi, pp. 297-301.

Garber N.J. and Hoel, L.A. (2002). *Traffic & Highway Engineering,* Third Edition, Thomson Learning, Toronto, Canada, pp. 321-27 & 354-66.

Government of India (1996). *Urban Development Plans Formulation & Implementation (UDPFI) Guidelines,* Volume-1, Ministry of Urban Affairs and Employment, Government of India, Centre for Research, Documentation & Training, Institute of Town Planners, India, New Delhi, p. 172.

Government of India (2015). *Urban and Regional Development Plans Formulation & Implementation (URDPFI) Guidelines 2014,* Volume-1, *Main Guidelines*, Ministry of Urban Development, Town and Country Planning Organisation, New Delhi, pp. 70-75 & 285-86.

Government of Meghalaya (1991). *Master Plan of Shillong (1991-2011),* p.18.

Government of Meghalaya (2021). *Meghalaya Building Byelaws 2021*, Urban Affairs Department, Government of Meghalaya, pp. 21-22 & 41-51.

Hanna J. (1997). Putting People at the Centre of Planning in Britain: From 'Feet First' to 'Streets for People'. In R. Tolley (ed.), *The Greening of Urban Transport,* Edition II, John Wiley & Sons Ltd., Chichester, England, pp. 275-84.

Howard E. (1965): *Garden Cities of To-Morrow*, Faber and Faber Limited, Great Britain, 51, 71, 98 & 103.

Hyman D.N. (2005). *Public Finance: A Contemporary Application of Theory to Policy,* Eighth Edition, Reprinted 2007, Krishna Offset, Delhi, 97-134 & 140-167.

Indian Roads Congress (1994). *Guidelines on Low-Cost Traffic Management Techniques for Urban Areas: Indian Roads Congress Special Publication 43*, Indian Roads Congress, Jamnagar House, Shahjahan Road, New Delhi, pp. 3-6.

Jain A.K. (2012). *Planning, Design & Engineering of Sustainable Urban Transport & Systems*, Khanna Publishers, New Delhi, pp. 566-77.

Joshi, R. (2009). Integrated Township as a Policy Response to Changing Supply and Demand Dynamics of Urban Growth. In N. Mohanty *et al.* (eds.), *India Infrastructure Report 2009*, Oxford University Press, New Delhi, p. 169.

Khisty C.J. and B.K. Lall (2017). *Transportation Engineering: An Introduction,* Third Edition, Pearson India Education Services Pvt. Ltd, Noida, pp. 649-50.

Koutsoyiannis A. (1985). *Modern Microeconomics,* Second Edition, ELBS, Hong Kong, pp. 541-45.

Kumar R.S. (2022). *Intelligent Transportation Systems*, University Press (India) Private Limited, Hyderabad, pp. 8-11, 57-66 & 98-129.

Mohring H. (1999). Congestion. In J. Gômez-Ibâñez *et al.* (eds.), *Essays in Transportation Economics and Policy: A Handbook in Honor of John R. Meyer*, Brookings Institution Press, Washington D.C., pp. 181-219.

Monheim R. (1997). Policy Issues in Promoting the Green Modes in Germany. In R. Tolley (ed.), *The Greening of Urban Transport,* Edition II, John Wiley & Sons Ltd., Chichester, England, pp. 192-95.

Monheim R. (1997). The Evolution from Pedestrian Areas to 'Car-Free' City Centres in Germany. In R. Tolley (ed.), *The Greening of Urban Transport,* Edition II, John Wiley & Sons Ltd, Chichester, England, pp. 253-64.

Ñianglang, P.S. (2016). *Planning Strategies for Traffic Decongestion in Hill City: A Case Study of Shillong in Meghalaya*, An unpublished A.I.T.P. (India) Thesis, Institute of Town Planners, India, New Delhi, pp. 10-13 & 82-97.

National Institute of Urban Affairs (1988). *Urbanisation and Urban Development Policy Issues of the North Eastern Region,* Research Study Series Number 39, Volume-I, New Delhi, pp. 71-72.

Odani, M. and Yamanaka, H. (1997). The Practice of Improving the Neighbourhood Street Environment through Traffic Calming in Japan. In R. Tolley (ed.), *The Greening of Urban Transport,* Edition II, John Wiley & Sons Ltd., Chichester, England, pp. 391-96.

Papacostas, C.S. and Prevedouros, P.D. (2001). *Transportation Engineering & Planning,* Third Edition, Reprinted 2009, PHI Learning Private Limited, New Delhi, pp. 78-82, 148-50, 276-81 & 304-06.

Ratcliffe, J. (1981). *An Introduction to Town and Country Planning,* 2nd Edition, Reprinted 1989, Hutchinson, London, pp. 225-30.

Sammer G. (1997). A General 30 km/h Speed Limit in the City: A Model Project in Graz, Austria. In R. Tolley (ed.), *The Greening of Urban Transport,* Edition II, John Wiley & Sons Ltd., Chichester, England, pp. 387-88.

Schilthuizen M, (2018). *Darwin Comes to Town: How Urban Jungle Drives Evolution*, Quercus Editions Ltd, London, pp. 33-44.

Sen, S. (1995). *An Econometric Analysis of Demand for Public Transportation in Shillong*, An unpublished Ph.D. Thesis, Department of Economics, North-Eastern Hill University, Shillong, pp. 227-31.

Simpson B.J. (1994): *Urban Public Transport Today*, E & FN Spon, London, pp. 112 & 175.

Sipes J.L. and Sipes M.L. (2013). *Creating Green Roadways: Integrating Cultural, Natural and Visual Resources into Transportation*, Island Press, Washington DC, pp. 45-48.

Soon T.Y. *et al.* (2009). *Clean, Green and Blue: Singapore's Journey towards Environmental and Water Sustainability*, Institute of Southeast Asian Studies, Singapore, pp. 44-46.

Urban Mass Transit Company Limited (2012). *Comprehensive Mobility Plan for Greater Shillong Planning Area, Final Report.* Directorate of Urban Affairs, Government of Meghalaya, Shillong, pp. 72-131.

Urban Mass Transit Company Limited (2012). *Comprehensive Mobility Plan for Greater Shillong Planning Area, Support Document.* Directorate of Urban Affairs, Government of Meghalaya, Shillong, pp. 36-37.

Vuchic V.R. (1999). *Transportation for Liveable Cities,* Reprinted 2000, Centre for Urban Policy Research, New Jersey, pp. 47, 51-52, 124, 149, 177, 208-09, 215, 252 & 288-90.

Washington, S.P. *et al.* (2011). *Statistical and Econometric Methods for Transportation Data Analysis,* Second Edition, CRC Press, Taylor & Francis Group LLC, Boca Raton, pp. 238-40.

White P. (1995): *Public Transport: Its Planning, Management and Operation,* Third Edition, UCL Press, London, pp. 132-34.

7
Land Suitability Analysis
A Requirement for the Shillong Master Plan

Rimeka Dora Ranee

Introduction

The two main life support systems on Earth are land and water. Throughout history, it has been observed that the origin of civilizations has been associated with these two elements and their abundance. Land resource has been subjected to a variety of pressures due to land being used in an abusive manner thus robbing it of its resilience. Land is viewed in terms of its utility, meaning the capability to meet human-perceived needs and wants. The most easily categorized varieties of land from the utility point of view are—land fit for use, land with potential for use and land which appears useless at least in the foreseeable future. This is where problems of land degradation and erosion of ecosystems begin. With the advent of modern age, there has been an exponential misuse of land resources due to consumerism, materialistic value systems, short-term profit-driven motives and greed of the users. As a result, land has degraded, soil fertility depleted, the rivers polluted and the forests destroyed (Kanda, n.d.).

Land in general has always been a scarce resource, but more so in hill areas due to other problems like having fragile eco-systems, limited availability of land for development, highly vulnerable to irreversible damages caused by overuse, deforestation or rapid changes in the characteristics of land and vegetation resources, landslides, erosion, flooding, destruction of scenic capacity and environmental degradation (Department of Land Resources, n.d.). Hence, it is of prime importance to manage land resource in this area.

Background

Land resource management is defined as "the actual practice of the use(s) of the land by the local human population, which should be sustainable". Land resource management is crucial to minimize land degradation, rehabilitate degraded areas and ensure the optimal use of land resources for the benefit of present and future generations (Food and Agriculture Organisation, 1991). Land resource management is important in general, but it is even more crucial in hill areas.All hill areas face general issues that are related to the environment like large scale deforestation, soil-erosion, dry water bodies, soil acidity, high intensity rainfall increasing risk and lack of infrastructure in the hostile topography and transportation facility for movement of goods and services (Barah, 2010). Thus, it is imperative to plan for hill areas in a sustainable manner. This approach to sustainable development needs to be applied at various scales—regional, sub-regional and local, which are listed below:

- Watershed Management—Regional Level Scale
- Land Suitability Analysis—Regional and Settlement Level
- Carrying Capacity Analysis—Settlement Level
- Climate Conscious Building Designs—Settlement and Building Level (Settlements, 2014). GIS-based land suitability analysis techniques are useful for decision makers, engineers and planners to provide a framework for land development in a holistic manner.

Methodology

Based on a case study of Alaknanda basin where land suitability analysis was carried out for agriculture, five parameters were identified to be used for this research focusing on those which might have an impact on development.

Study Area

Shillong is the capital of the state of Meghalaya and the second largest urban centre of North East India. In terms of its economic, administrative and commercial importance, it is perhaps second to Guwahati. According to Census of India 2011, the city is supporting about 60 per cent and about 96 per cent of the total urban population of the State and East Khasi Hills District respectively. The city of Shillong has been experiencing a high pace of urbanization. The Census of India 1981 and 1991 indicated phenomenal growth rate of 40 per cent and 70 per cent respectively. This has led to increasing pressure on land resource due to its limited availability and nature of the terrain. This rapid urbanization coupled with unscientific construction carried out all over the city begot a number of problems including landslides and flooding.

Risk Assessment

The Greater Shillong Planning Area (GSPA) has an area of 17400 hectares out of which 5494.10 hectares (31.58%) has been developed. An analysis of the existing development was carried out to identify the landslide-prone areas in GSPA. Two categories of risk were identified, viz. high risk areas with slope of >45° and low risk areas with slope >30° upto 45°. It was found that about 647 ha (5%) of the existing built up falls under high risk areas and 3237.27 ha (25%) under low risk area prone to landslides as shown in Figure 7.1.In order to establish the quantum of land available for development, five parameters were taken and land suitability analysis was done,, viz. Slope, Watershed, Soil Type, Vegetation and Accessibility as shown in Figure 7.2. These five parameters were given a scoring and analysis was carried out with the help of GIS. The scoring criteria for these parameters are given in Table 7.1.

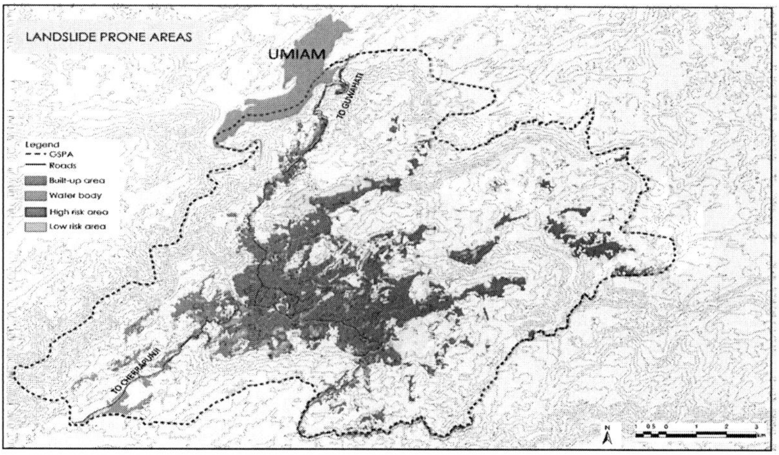

Figure 7.1: Landslide Prone Areas of GSPA

Source: Author.

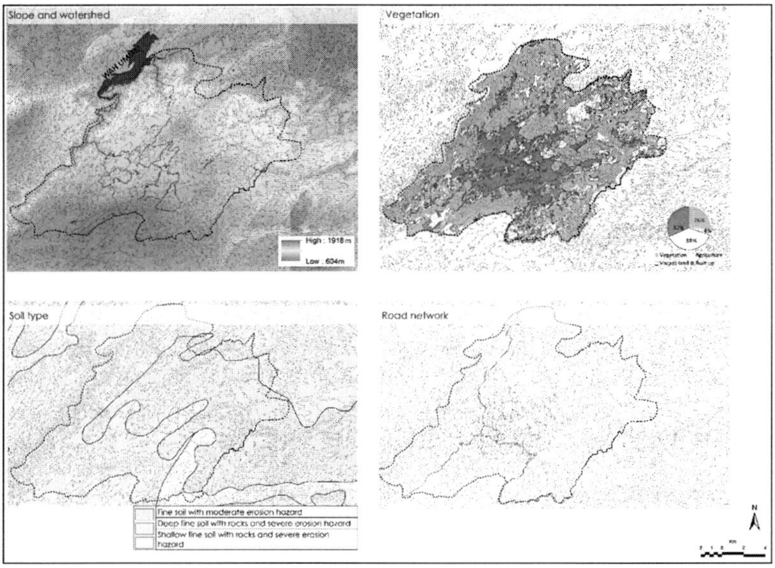

Figure 7.2: Maps Generated for Land Suitability Analysis

Source: Author.

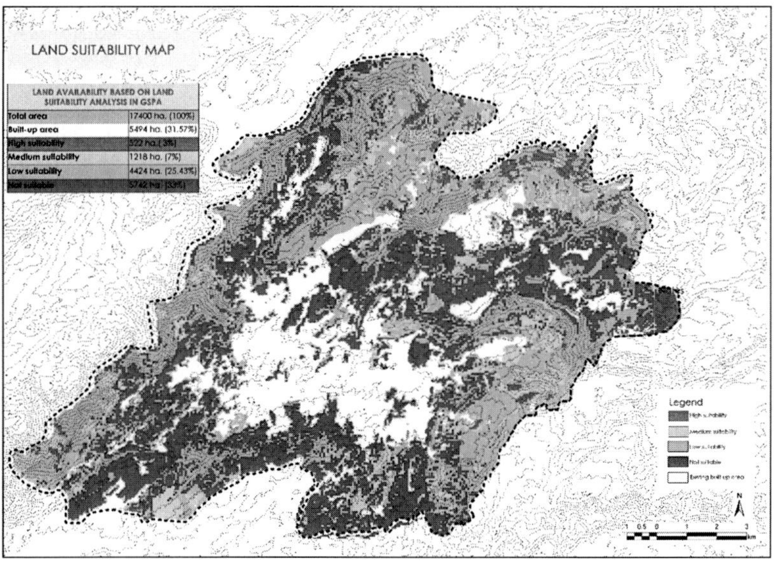

Figure 7.3: Land Suitability Map of GSPA

Source: Author.

Table 7.1: Parameters for Land Suitability Analysis and Their Scoring

Parameters		**Slope**	**Watershed**	**Soil Type**	**Vegetation**	**Accessibility**
Scoring	0	>30	No buffer from waterbody	Fine soil with moderate erosion hazard	Presence of forest	> 1.5 km from road
	1	5-30°	<500 from waterbody	Deep fine soil with rocks and severe erosion hazard	Absence of forests	500m-15 km from road
	2	<5°	500m from waterbody	Shallow fine soil with rocks and severe erosion hazard		<500m from road

Results and Discusion

On combining these five parameters, a land suitability map was generated as shown in Figure 7.3. The suitability categories identified were four in numbers, viz. high suitability, medium suitability, low suitability and not suitable for development. It was found that only 3 per cent of the land was highly suitable for development whereas up to 33 per cent of the land is not suitable for development purposes. This land suitability map can act as a guide for future development that shall be planned in a scientific and logical manner to ensure holistic development of Greater Shillong Planning Area.

REFERENCES

Bandooni, S.K. (2004). *Land resource management and development in hill areas*. Research India Press.

Barah, B.C. (2010). Hill agriculture: Problems and Prospects for mountain agriculture. *Indian journal of agricultural economics*, 596.

Barah, B.C. (2011). Census of India.

Chakraborty, S. (2006). *Growth of Shillong urban agglomeration and its impact on the geo-environment with special reference to solid waste disposal and water supply*.

Das, P.K. (2013). North-East, 'The Power House of India': Prospects and Problems. *IOSR Journal of Humanities And Social Science* (IOSR-JHSS), 37.

Das, P.K., Department of Land Resources. (n.d.).

Das, P.K. (2011). *District Census Handbook East Khasi Hills*. Directorate of Census Operations, Meghalaya.

Das, P.K. *Food and Agriculture Organisation*. (1991).

Kanda, M. (n.d.). *Land Resource Management in India*. Retrieved from Press information bureau: http://pib.nic.in/feature/feyr2000/fsep2000/f120920001.html

Meghalaya Urban Affairs Department. (n.d.). *Master Plan of Shillong*, 2015.

Misri, B. K. (1999). *Country Pasture/Forage Resource Profiles*. Retrieved from FAO: http://www.fao.org/ag/agp/agpc/doc/counprof/india.htm

Planning Commission. (2014).

Planning Commission. (n.d.). *6th Five Year Plan*. Retrieved from Planning Commission, Government of India: http://planningcommission.nic.in/plans/planrel/fiveyr/6th/ 6planch25.html

Settlements, E.C. (2014, 05-13). *Human Settlement Planning in Hill Areas. Retrieved from ENVIS Centre on Human Settlements*: http://spaenvis.nic.in/index1.aspx? lid=1205& mid=1&langid=1&linkid=408

Singh, J.P. (n.d.). *Problems of Hill Area Development.*

8
Goods Movement Pattern and Planning
Imperatives for Goods Distribution in Gangtok

Sanjay Gupta

Introduction

The ability to transport goods quickly, safely, economically and reliably is seen as vital to a nation's prosperity and capacity to compete in a globalizing economy.The movement of goods within urban areas is vital since cities are the centres of economic and social life. The timely and smooth movement of such freight is crucial to the well-being of the people and the viability of the economic activities they undertake. Freight movement in the cities often puts considerable strain on urban transport infrastructure and imposes high social costs. Cities are now facing global competition for investment and trade when an efficient transport system is necessary for sustained economic prosperity. Urban freight transport has become an important issue in urban planning.There are many challenges and problems relating to increasing levels of traffic congestion, negative environmental impacts and energy conservation. It is widely appreciated that in the present state-of-the-art of city planning and practice, there is very little importance attached to understanding the characteristics, problems and potentials of goods movement to, from and within urban areas. Moreover, the methodology and techniques for freight infrastructure planning is generally insensitive to the diverse nature of goods movement.

Indian cities are on the move witnessing good economic growth and notably a momentum set in. Cities are now facing global competition for investment and trade when an efficient transport system is necessary for sustained economic prosperity. With all the rising economy on the anvil India's key cities are focusing on building their infrastructure development plans to cater to the rapid urban sprawl phenomena and governance mechanism to handle the same. As part of this effort while there has been significant efforts made in discussing and solving urban passenger transport issues in order to achieve overall city transport sustainability it is imperative to understand the vital role of urban freight transport which is often neglected in our planning and policy making process. The explicit consideration of urban goods movement has the potential to contribute towards achieving the goals of urban transport. The objectives of city planning in general and city transport system planning, in particular, is to enable goods movement at desired levels of efficiency of goods movement.

Trends of Goods Movement in Indian Cities

Goods vehicles constitute an importantc omponent to the traffic flow on the road system in urban areas. According to the study carried out by the CRRI in 1998 it is observed that goods traffic generally tends to vary consistently with respect to city size, its economic base and its location (Table 8.1).

Table 8.1 Daily Goods Flow in Selected Cities In India

Cities	Population (Lakhs)	Intercity Inbound		Intercity Outbound		Intra-cityflow	
		Vehicles	Tonnes	Vehicles	Tonnes	Vehicles	Tonnes
Ahmedabad	32.97	7060	42994	2087	12811	7019	13996
Nagpur	16.61	2754	18556	1112	6501	8517	8234
Indore	11.04	3699	23236	1183	11988	1863	4237
Vishakhapatnam	10.52	2604	18026	267	829	1244	645
Agra	9.56	2934	17103	1551	5873	3185	2888
Asansol	7.64	798	4115	423	143	1677	556
Nashik	7.22	2731	16558	348	1854	879	1715
Bhubaneswar	4.16	2206	15494	118	660	185	215
Yamunanagar	2.20	2648	14956	1294	10805	210	1567
Adoni	1.36	642	2884	517	2329	501	528
Darjeeling	0.73	140	557	39	66	524	326
Samastipur	0.58	1650	6319	134	237	242	302
Chickballapur	0.47	210	943	79	154	27	43

Source: CRRI study (1998).

In Delhi the goods traffic increased from 46,148 vehicles to 63,058 vehicles at a rate of 10.97 per cent per annum during 1993 to 1996 while the quantity of goods moving in and out of Delhi at outer cordon increased from 1,84,946 tonnes in 1993 to 2,65,807 tonnes in 1996, registering a growth rate of 12.9 per cent per annum (Gupta *et. al,* 2007). According to the study by Wilbur Smith (2008) on traffic and transportation policies in urban areas in India based on 30 cities cordon points OD and traffic counts revealed that nearly 40 per cent of the goods vehicles entering the city are through in nature. The goods vehicle traffic intensity observed in an 8 hours traffic count varied from a low of 3650 vehicles observed in cities with population less than five lakhs to a high of 41,907 vehicles in cities exceeding population size of 80 lakhs. Moreover the share of goods vehicles out of total vehicles entering or leaving the city varied from a low of around 10 per cent in smallest category city, i.e. below 5 lakhs to a range of 23 per cent to 26 per cent in higher category cities, i.e 20 lakhs and above indicating the growing importance of freight traffic as cities increase in size.Table 8.2 shows the trends of freight traffic in hill towns of Shimla and Guwahati which shows that the daily inter- city freight tonnes vary between 1610 tonnes in Shimla to 6194 tonnes in Guwahati which are relatively much less than comparable cities in the plains. The share of through traffic in total inter-city goods movement varies between 21 per cent and 34.4 per cent. Further from Table 8.1 it is seen that in Darjeeling the daily inter-city freight movement is 326 tonnes excluding the through traffic.

Table 8.2: Inter-City Daily Freight Traffic in Hilly Cities (1994)

City	Population 1991 (Census)	Daily Freight Traffic (Tonnes)	% share of Through Traffic
Shimla	1.1	1610	34.40
Guwahati	5.84	6194	21.00

Source: RITES Report 1994

Profile of Freight Generating and Handling Areas in Gangtok

In Gangtok the goods transport within the city and through the city forms a major component of traffic which affects the traffic flows on the roads and poses problems with regard to parking and obstructions on kerb side occupied for loading and unloading operations. At the same time, intra-city goods transport is very important for proper functioning of trade and commerce. This sector generates economy for the area and also generates goods movement in the urban area, due to the local demand. The main wholesale markets are at Indira bypass and Tadong. In all about 35 wholesale shops existed in the city. The main retail markets are M.G. road, new market, Lal bazaar, NH 31 market, Deorali market. In all, about 547 retail shops existed in the city. The maximum loading and unloading activity takes place at three places, namely M.G. Road, Lal Bazaar and

Deorali area. In terms of tonnes these areas attracted about 195 tonnes in a day (1994). Other places like Kazi Road, Lal Bazaar, Zero Point, Tibet Road also have loading/unloading activities but far less in terms of quantity (Fig. 8.1). The places being used as truck terminals are near truck driver's association office (Tadong) and Tata stand (Deorali).

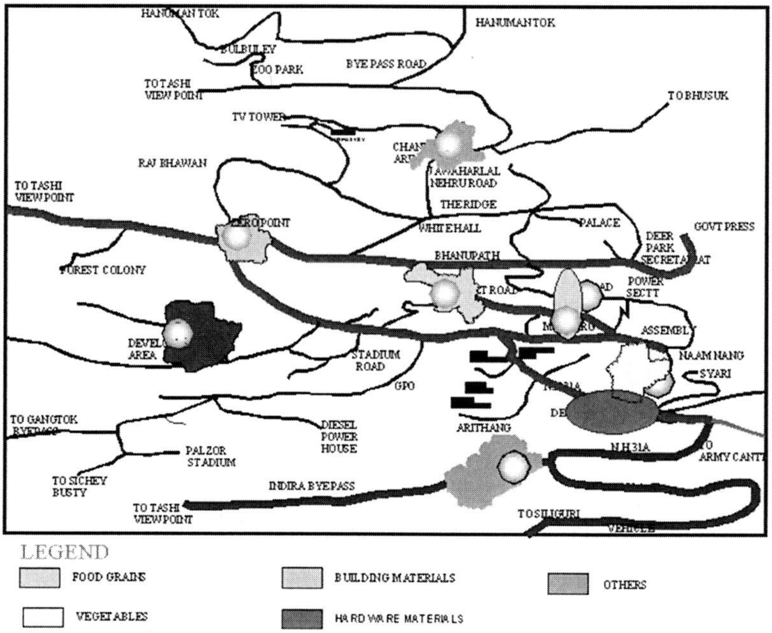

Figure 8.1: Goods Loading and Unloading Areas in Gangtok

There is a restriction on entry of goods vehicles in areas such as M.G. road, NH 31A, Kazi Road, Lal Bazaar, Tibet Road, Zero Point, the operation time for the heavy vehicles in the city is from 7:00 A.M. to 8:00 P.M. The entry time of goods carriers during day like TATA 407 and utility is from 1 P.M. to 3 P.M. Special permits are issued by the traffic police for entry of goods carriers during the day in the core areas of the Gangtok city. M.G. Road, by and large, summons food grains and related items as majority of the shops fall in the category of departmental stores, hotels and shops of groceries. Development Area and Zero Point are the unloading points for building materials as there is on-going construction activity in the area, Lal Bazaar area has the only sabzimandi of Gangtok hence commodities like vegetables, fruits and food grains item get unloaded there. Most of the wholesale markets of wood, liquor and building materials are on the Indira Bypass Road so most of such items get loaded/unloaded here.

Primary Surveys Conducted

The following Table 8.3 describes various primary surveys conducted in the study area in 2006 to understand the characteristics of goods movement.

Table 8.3 Details of Primary Survey

Sl. No.	Primary Survey	Location	Duration of Survey/ Coverage	Method Used
1	Truck Terminal Survey	Tadong and Deorali (Tata Stand)	4 Hours	Interview Method
2	Wholesale Survey	Indira Bypass, M.G. Road and Tadong	49%	Interview Method
3	Goods Handling Agent Survey	MG Road, NH 31 A and Lal Bazaar	60%	Interview Method
4	Retail Survey	MG Road, NH 31 A and Lal Bazaar and Deorali Baazar	20%	Interview Method
5	Truck Parking Survey	Tadong and Deorali (Tata Stand)	4 Hours	Interview Method
6	Truck Operator	Truck Driver's Association		Interview Method
7	Origin snd Destination Survey	Referral Hospital, Tashi View Pcint and Nathula Check Post	9 Hours	Road Side Interview Method
8	Commercial Use Inventory	MG Road, NH 31 A and Lal Bazaar	5 Markets	Observation
9	Loading/ Unloading Survey	M.G. Road, Zero Point, Metro Point, Tibet Road, Kazi Road, Development Area, Chanmari Road	47 Covered	Interview Method
10	Porter's Survey	MG Road, Lal Bazaar	15 Captured	Interview Method

Source: Field Study.

Goods Traffic Generation Characteristics

Market Characteristics

M.G. Market

M.G. Market the main market of Gangtok, is centrally located and one of the main loading/unloading points of Gangtok. But due to time restrictions on heavy vehicles loading/unloading operations take place at night or in early morning. It was found that food grains and building materials are the main commodities being loaded/unloaded at M.G. Market. In terms of quantity out of an estimated daily inflow of 64 tonnes nearly 83 per cent share is accounted by foodgrains.

Lal Bazaar

Lal Bazaar is the main vegetable mandi of Gangtok. The operation of loading and unloading takes place at night or in early morning hours. Out of an estimated daily inflow of 76 tonnes in the market the share of vegetables and foodgrains account for 58 per cent and 35 per cent share respectively.

Kazi Road

Kazi Road is one of the markets of Gangtok, which caters to daily domestic needs of the population. Out of an estimated daily inflow of 34 tonnes in the market the share of foodgrains and hardware building materials account for 71 per cent and 13 per cent share respectively.

Zero Point

Zero Point is the northern most point of Gangtok, where the urban area ends. A lot of new development has been taking place in this direction as the city is growing. Out of an estimated daily inflow of 35 tonnes in the market, the share of hardware building materials accounts for 75 per cent share.

Development Area

A lot of new development has been taking place in the Development Area as the city is extending in this direction. Out of an estimated daily inflow of 10 tonnes in the market, the share of hardware building materials accounts for 75 per cent share.

Chanmari Area

It is in the northern part of the city. This area is relatively a new development and a lot of new development has been taking place. Out of an estimated daily inflow of 5 tonnes in the market the share of hardware building materials accounts for 75 per cent share.

Goods Traffic Pattern

Daily Intensity of Flow

The results of the surveys indicate that the percentage of vehicles that come for unloading goods are much higher (71.4%) than the vehicles for loading (28.6%) indicating that Gangtok is a consuming city rather than a producing one, which is substantiated by the economic activities of the area which are basically tertiary in nature. The main commodity that enters Gangtok daily is food grains (117 tonnes) having a share of 48 per cent out of the total commodities being loaded/unloaded. Building materials come second (58 tonnes) at about 24 per cent indicating at the development taking place in and around Gangtok, followed by vegetables (20 tonnes) and building material (19 tonnes) which come at a close third with about 11 per cent share. About 66 per cent of total goods quantity is procured from Siliguri showing heavy dependence on Gangtok of Siliguri. Maximum procurement (84%) share is through trucks.

Haulage Length

Among the commodities coming into Gangtok, vegetables and others have an average haulage length of around 80 kms, food grains have an average haulage length of 70 kms, while hardware materials have an haulage length of 55 kms and building materials which is mostly sand brought in from Singtham is around 25 kms haulage length.

Transport Operators Characteristics

The salient findings from the transport operator survey reveal the following salient findings:

(i) In terms of vehicle ownership about 57 per cent of the truck operators have only one vehicle followed by 28 per cent having 2 vehicles.
(ii) About 57 per cent of the truck operators were owner –cum-driver.
(iii) LCV's are most commonly used, i.e. 38 per cent, followed by HCV's 36.5 per cent.
(iv) Maximum trucks carry 8 to 10 tonnes.
(v) About 41 per cent of trucks are between 1 to 5 years while 34 per cent are between 5 to 10 years.

(vi) Trucks operate about 8 hours per day and the average vehicle utilization comes about 80 kms per day.

Problems and Issues

The analysis of data on freight characteristics revealed that seasonality is a major factor affecting goods movement particularly in rainy seasons. The movement of heavy commercial vehicles with heavy load becomes hazardous. The city does not designate place for terminal in the entire city which is a major drawback. There is absence of designated place for loading/unloading which often results on overspill leading to inconvenience. The regulation restricting the entry of loaded vehicles to wait for long before entering the city results in loss of productivity. The whole freight operations is disorganized and is at disposal of individual operators with no coordination between various stakeholders. Moreover there is no agency that manages and controls the movement of goods in and out of Gangtok.

Goods Traffic Forecast and Alternate Scenarios of Goods Distribution

Goods Traffic Forecast

A volume of 382 tonnes of goods traffic was estimated to be generated in the city in 2011 for an estimated population of 38,232 persons in Gangtok city assuming goods consumption rates of 10 tonnes per day per 1000 persons based on consumption patterns observed in hilly regions.

Alternate Scenarios Description

Four alternate scenarios were worked out for movement of goods traffic coming into the city for future. These scenarios were compared with each other and evaluated based on various parameters chosen and one strategy was finalized for implementation. The scenarios are :

(i) Business as usual (BAU).
(ii) Market-wise zoning and day specific distribution.
(iii) Change in modal mix.
(iv) Market consolidation with change in modal mix.

Business as Usual (BAU)

In this scenario it was assumed that the increase in demand for goods movement in future would be proportionate to the present market-wise distribution. Further there would not be any change in the present modal mix of goods traffic and they would in future too adhere to the existing time restrictions. It was also assumed that the average payload would remain the same.

Market-wise Zoning and Day Specific Distribution

In this scenario the distribution system has been clubbed in three major zones, based on their locational proximities. It is assumed that the demand of a week for a market will be supplied twice in the duration of the week. Delivery of perishable items and essentials like medicines will be allowed everyday. It was also assumed that the increase in demand in future would be proportionate to the present market-wise distribution. Further there would not be any change in the present modal mix of goods traffic and they would in future too adhere to the existing time restrictions. It was also assumed that the average payload would remain the same.

Change in Modal Mix

In this scenario the basic assumption was that the vehicle for distribution would be loaded to its optimal capacity and the modal mix of the goods movement would be changed to eliminate HCVs from the distribution chain. There would be a consolidation centre assisting in this modal shift, at the entrance into the city. It was also assumed that the increase in demand in future would be proportionate to the present market-wise distribution. Further the goods traffic would in future too adhere to the existing time restrictions.

Market Consolidation with Change in Modal Mix

In this scenario the basic assumptions were that the vehicle for distribution would be loaded to its optimal capacity and the modal mix of the goods movement would be changed to eliminate HCVs from the distribution chain. There would be a consolidation centre assisting in this modal shift, at the entrance of the city.The distribution system has been clubbed in three major market zones, based on their locational proximities. The demand of a week for a market will be supplied twice in the duration of the week. Delivery of perishable items and essentials like medicines will be allowed everyday. It was also assumed that the increase in demand in future would be proportionate to the present market-wise distribution.Further, the goods traffic would in future too adhere to the existing time restrictions.

Evaluation of Alternate Scenarios

Comparing the four alternatives, the scenario option of market consolidation with change in modal split comes across as the most viable in terms of cost per km and cost per tonne km as observed from Table 8.4. Various necessary actions and facilities are required to be put in place for the successful implementation of this strategy. These include development of new facility to provide for consolidation centre at Indira Bypass with facilities for change of modes. Further, traffic management actions in terms of entry prohibition of HCV is needed and permits to be given to all the vehicles which will be used only for distribution inside the city. Wayside amenities need to be provided with basic infrastructures at terminals.

Table 8.4: Comparative Evaluation of Alternate Scenarios

Parameters	BAU Scenario	Market Consolidation Scenario	Modal Mix Scenario	Modal Mix Change with Market Consolidation Scenario
Total Truck Trips	74	76	99	115
Total Tonnage (Tonnes)	381.9	381.9	381.9	381.9
Fuel Cost (Rs.)	2571.2	2731	2049.3	2501.7
Cost of loading/ unloading (Rs.)	9025	9149	8275	9548
Total cost (Rs.)	11596.2	11880	10324.3	12049.7
Total Veh. KM	315.4	337	419.5	514
Total Tonne KM	1597.5	1775	1619.5	1970.5
Cost per KM	36.8	35.3	24.6	23.4
Cost per tonne KM	7.3	6.7	6.4	6.1
Total emissions produced				
SPM	0.27	0.29	0.16	0.2
SO_2	0.42	0.44	0.03	0.03
NO_x	6.16	6.52	0.77	0.92
Fuel Consumption (litres)	82.3	87	67.9	82.9

Source: SPA Study (2006).

Summing Up

It can be concluded that in the present state-of-the-art of city planning and practice in Indian cities in general and hilly regions in particular there is very little importance attached to understanding the characteristics, problems and potentials of goods movement to, from and within urban areas. Moreover, the methodology and techniques for freight infrastructure planning is generally insensitive to the diverse nature of goods movement as reflected in the present study of Gangtok. In view of the growing importance of goods movement and the major impact it has on the urban economy and life, it is important that a more in-depth appreciation of its characteristics and potential is made. It is very evident that freight movements eventually impact the city mobility and efficiency besides in turn also getting affected by efficiencies of various freight handling facilities such as truck terminals etc. In order to achieve sustainable urban mobility environment in urban areas and particularly in hilly regions such as Gangtok it is imperative that informed policies on urban freight logistics are evolved based on empirical studies related to its movement pattern and supply chain networks facilitating freight movement.

In view of the growing importance of goods movement it is proposed that a coordinated sustainable urban freight policy be framed by better co-operation among various city departments and local organisations. It is also imperative that integration of urban freight in town planning and land-use/ infrastructure planning (construction and development regulations, access to installations etc.) needs to be ensured along with the integration of urban freight in transport policy and mobility planning (mobility management) in hilly regions. The local government in Gangtok needs to explore modern concepts of urban freight distribution such as Urban Consolidation Centres (UCC), to ensure sustainable urban distribution environment in the city. Further, the city government bodies should have special impetus on maintaining data base on urban freight logistics related activities for informed policy decisions.

REFERENCES

Central Road Research Institute, (1998), *Estimation of Short Haul Urban and Suburban Freight Traffic, Study Report*, New Delhi.

Gupta, A., (2013), Urban Freight – An essential but neglected component of a comprehensive urban mobility policy in India' at *61st Annual Town Planners Congress*, organized by Institute of Town Planners, India, 8th February, 2013, Ahmedabad.

Gupta, S. and N. Ranganathan, (1996), Characteristics of Goods Movement into and Out of a Metropolitan City: Case Study-Delhi, *Spatio-Economic Development Record Journal*, Vol. 3 No. 5, September-October 1996.

Gupta, S. and N. Ranganathan, (2007), 'Urban freight movement in Delhi – Characteristics, Issues and Policy directions', *Journal of Institute of Urban Transport (India)*, Delhi.

Gupta, S., (2004), Temporal Changes in Urban Goods Movement in a Metropolitan City; Case Study – Delhi, *Proceedings on International Conference on Transportation,* TRANSPO2004, IIT Chennai, February, 2004.

RITES, (1994), *Comprehensive Transport Study of 21 Cities in India*, Delhi.

School of Planning and Architecture, (2006). *Planning of Goods Movement in Gangtok*, Department of Transport Planning, Delhi (unpublished).

PART-B

Principles, Strategies and Policies Recommnded by Economists, Geographers, Sociologists and Lawyers

9
Municipal Waste Management in Itanagar

Municipal Corporation Area of Arunachal Pradesh

Ajit Debnath and *Amitava Mitra*

Introduction

Urbanisation can be defined as an increase in the proportion of the urban population to the total population over a period of time. It is a phenomenon which is a part and parcel of economic development in general. For example, some economists like Colin Clark (1940) go so far as to assert that the acid test of development lies in the shift of population from rural to urban areas. Simon Kuznets (1966) in his Nobel Prize winning work on measurement and analysis of historical growth of national income of developed countries has identified the high rate structural transformation as one of the six basic characteristics of modern economic growth. "Some of the major components of his structural change include the gradual shift away from agricultural to non-agricultural activities and more recently away from industries to services and a corresponding shift in the spatial location and occupational status of the labour forces away from rural agricultural and related non-agricultural activities towards urban-oriented manufacturing and service pursuits" (Tadaro, 1985, p. 52).

Thus, urban development is no doubt a natural outcome of economic development. But it has a number of adverse effects. For example, rapid urbanization may lead to rapid growth of slum settlements, informal sectors as well as environmental problems like solid waste accumulation etc. Solid waste can be defined as a non-liquid waste material arising from domestic, trade, commercial, agricultural and industrial activities and from public services. It is a combination of various heterogeneous waste materials. It is commonly known as garbage, refuse, rubbish or trash. Its main sources are residential premises, business establishments, street sweepings, hospitals etc. Solid wastes in urban areas popularly known as municipal solid waste (MSW) refers to materials discarded in the urban areas which municipalities are responsible for collection, transportation and final disposal. The Ministry of Environment and Forests, Government of India defined MSW as commercial and residential wastes generated in urban areas or notified areas in either solid or semi-solid form excluding industrial hazardous wastes but including treated bio-medical wastes (The Ministry of Environment and Forests, Government of India, 2000). Solid waste is one of the most important sources of environmental pollution in Indian cities and towns.

Around 1.3 billion metric tonnes of MSW are generated in the world at present (Kawai and Tasaki, 2016). It is anticipated that the world generation of MSW would increase to around 2.2 billion metric tonnes by 2025. But the MSW generation in Organisation for Economic Co-operation and Development (OECD) members has been decreasing (Kawai and Tasaki, 2016). However, in India per capita municipal waste generation was not very high but there was a significant increase in solid waste generation in the last few decades. This is largely because of rapid population growth and economic development in the country resulting in an increase in migration of population to towns and cities, changing life style and consumption pattern etc. Indian cities and towns generated, on an average, 300-400 gms per capita, per day of solid wastes, translated into approximately 80,000 MT/day or 30 Million MT/annum of urban solid wastes. Out of this, nearly 8.5 million MT/annum came from nine major metropolitan centres alone. Only about 60-80 per cent of these wastes are collected on a daily basis and the rest was left to decay on the roads, streets and drains, etc (Singh, 2001). Cities and towns in India had generated an estimated 6 million tonne of waste products in 1947 whereas in 1997, it was about 42 million tonne per year (TERI). It was estimated that by 2047, waste generation in Indian cities would be increased by five-fold to touch 260 million tonne per year, entailing that the recent solid waste generation is over 50 million tonne per year (Asnani, 2006). It was found that India's annual generation of municipal solid waste would be somewhat lower, that is, range of 35 to 45 million tonne, amounting to about 1,00,000 to 1,20,000 metric tonne everyday (World Bank, 2006). Asnani (2006) estimated the annual increase in the quantity of solid waste in India's cities to be at the rate of 5 per cent per annum. Disposal practices at the solid waste open dumping sites are highly unsatisfactory. Poor management of solid waste has led to the contamination of groundwater and surface water through leachate and pollution of air through unregulated burning of waste. Unscientific practices in processing and disposal compound the environmental hazards by solid waste. More than 25 per cent of the MSW was still not being collected at all and 70 per cent of the Indian cities lacked adequate capacity to transport it. The waste quantities are estimated to increase from 46 million in 2001 to 65 million in 2012 (Kumar and Gaikward, 2004).

The Central Pollution Control Board (2016) stated that around 141064 tonne of solid waste is generated in India per day. Out of the total solid wastes 127531 tonne (90%) were collected and only 34752 tonne (27%) of wastes were treated per day. It was found that Maharashtra was the largest generator of solid wastes around (15.99% of India) followed by Tamil Nadu (10.28% of India) of total wastes generated. However, it was found that only 24.66 per cent of wastes in India were treated. The Figure was much less than in selected industrial states of India except Delhi. With this background an attempt was made to examine the quantity of solid wastes generated, collected and treated per day in North Eastern States. It was found that Assam which has the highest number of towns contributed the largest solid waste generated (25.90%). Surprisingly, it was observed that a small populated state like Mizoram was the second highest generator of solid wastes (552 tonne per day). This may be due to the fact that in Mizoram more than fifty per cent of the state population live in urban areas. On the other hand, Sikkim was the least generator of solid waste (only 49 tonne per day) and at the same time it was the only state where 100 per cent collection of solid wastes was done. That is why Gangtok, the capital of Sikkim is the only town in North East India which emerged as one of the top cleanest cities of India (Swachh Sarvekshan, 2016). Arunachal Pradesh which has the lowest population density produced 116 tonne per day of solid wastes but only 60 per cent was collected which it earned the infamous distinction of being the third dirtiest city in India (Swachh Sarvekshan, 2016).

The disposal of urban waste product was generally done by the Directorate of Urban and Housing Department, Government of Arunachal Pradesh till the setting up of the municipal body in 2013. After the enactment of the Itanagar Municipality Act, 2007, the Municipalities came into operation in Itanagar and Pasighat in 2013. In the present study an attempt was made for an in-depth analysis regarding the extent of solid waste accumulation and the households' willingness to pay (WTP) for an improved solid waste management in Itanagar municipal area on the basis of both the primary and secondary data. A contingent valuation method (CVM) is used to identify the determinants of the WTP values. Income, education, age and environmental awareness etc. are the factors which influenced the WTP.

The whole chapter is divided into five sections. The first section dealt with the brief profile of the study area followed by methodology and conceptual framework of the study. The second section examined the socio-economic features of the sampled households. The third section discussed the review of literature of the related studies. The fourth section briefly described the study area and its waste management. The fifth section analysed the results and discussions followed by conclusions and recommendations.

Objectives of the Study

The broad objectives of the present chapter are as follows:

1. To explore the extent of solid waste generation and its management system in Itanagar municipal area including Itanagar and Naharlagun towns.
2. To estimate the maximum WTP among the surveyed households of Itanagar and Naharlagun towns for an improved solid waste management system.
3. To identify the socio-economic variables determining the maximum WTP for an improved solid waste management system.

Brief Profile of the Study Area

Itanagar is the capital town of Arunachal Pradesh. Naharlagun was the earlier capital town of Arunachal Pradesh. Both are twin towns. Itanagar and Naharlagun towns are the centre points of all economic, commercial, trade related activities of Arunachal Pradesh. Shillong was the earlier capital of the then NEFA, which was the capital of the undivided Assam till 1971 (Mitra, 2003). In 1972, Arunachal Pradesh was declared as a union territory and Itanagar was selected as the site for the location of the new capital. Although, it was first shifted to Old Itanagar, i.e. Naharlagun in 1974 but finally it was shifted to New Itanagar, i.e. present Itanagar in 1978. The capital town is situated at the foothills of Himalayas. Administratively, it lies, to the southernmost position of the Papume Pare district bounded between 26°58′N to 27° 10′N latitude which covers an area about 820.50 sq.km (Singh, T., 2003). Itanagar is located between 27°5′4.78″ N latitude and 93°36′18.92″E longitude at an altitude of 320 meters above mean sea level comprising an area of about 11.25 sq. kms while Naharlagun is located between 27°6′31.12″N latitude and 93°41′54.02″E longitude at an elevation of 160 metres above mean sea level covering an area of 12.83 sq. kms. The capital city of Itanagar is a historical place which exists through the ages. Itanagar is a socio-cultural entity instead of its mere geographical character and it manifests the integrative existence since a far past. The term Itanagar stands for the territory of Nyshis and in their language, it is called 'Khita Yokpo', (Begi, 2003). The location map of Itanagar town is shown in Figure 9.1.

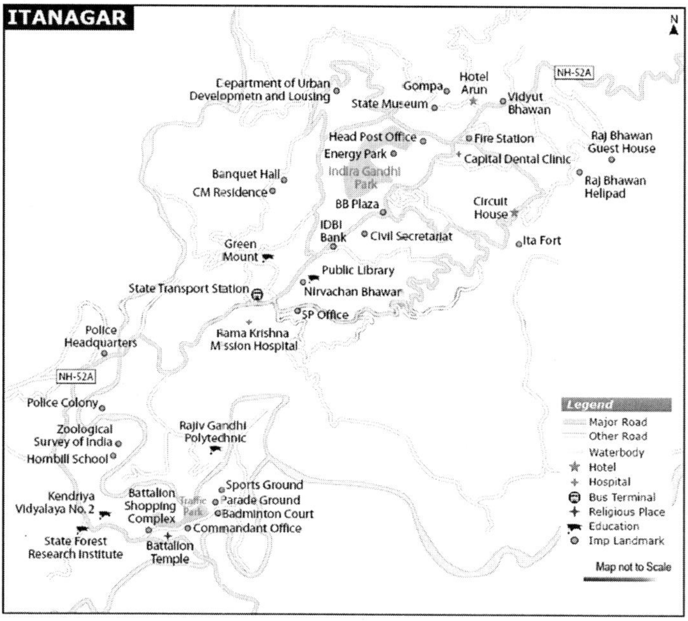

Figure 9.1: Location Map of Itanagar Town of Arunachal Pradesh

Source: www.mapsofindia.com.

Demographic Characteristics of Itanagar and Naharlagun Towns

In this sub-section an attempt was made to examine the demographic characteristics of both the towns which were shown in Table 9.1.

Table 9.1 shows that there was a remarkable increase in the total population of Itanagar and Naharlagun towns. The total population of Itanagar increased to 59490 in 2011 against 6406 in 1981 and that of Naharlagun town increased to 36158 in 2011 against 7710 in 1981. Within the four decades the population in Itanagar town increased by around ten times and that of Naharlagun town increased by around five times. The sex ratio increased from 536 in 1981 to 951 in 2011 in Itanagar town and to 998 in 2011 against 688 in 1981 in Naharlagun town which shows an increasing trend of sex ratio in both the towns, although, in Naharlagun town it increased at a faster rate than that of Itanagar town. It is to be noted that in Itanagar town, the literacy rate increased to 74.25 per cent in 2011 against 53.79 per cent in 1981 and that of Naharlagun town increased to 71.84 in 2011 against 51.21 in 1981.

Table 9.1: Demographic Characteristics of Itanagar and Naharlagun Towns, 1981-2011

Year	Total Population		Sex Ratio		Percentage of Total Urban Population of the State		Literacy Rate (%)		S.T. Population as Percentage of Total Population	
	Itanagar	Naharlagun	Itanagar	Naharlagun	Itanagar	Naharlagun	Itanagar	Naharlagun	Itanagar	Naharlagun
1981	6406	7710	537	688	15.46	18.61	53.79	51.21	18.55	-
1991	16545	14369	808	815	16.53	13.06	65.13	63.15	31.49	-
2001	35022	27020	878	877	15.37	11.86	73.26	69.00	59.00	46.80
2011	59490	36158	950	998	18.98	11.54	74.25	71.84	57.20	57.00

Source: Census of India 1981, 1991, 2001, 2011 and District Primary Abstract of Arunachal Pradesh, 2011.

Data Source and Methodology of the Study

Based on primary data the study was empirical in nature. In fact the study used both primary and secondary data. For collection of primary data, the study used stratified sampling technique. The different stages are as follows: *Firstly,* Itanagar Municipality Corporation (IMC) was the universe of the study which included both Itanagar and Naharlagun towns. It has 30 municipality wards by covering 18 wards for Itanagar and the rest 12 wards for Naharlagun town. *Secondly,* IMC was divided into three different zones in order to cover different groups of people. These were: (1) residential dominated areas, (2) commercial dominated areas, and (3) mixed residential and commercial areas. Further, the stratified zones were divided into three groups like (i) households in Government quarters, (ii) households in private accommodation, and (iii) households in labour colony/*katcha* houses. Finally, the households were selected by using random sampling technique. Attempts were made to include at least twenty five to thirty households from each selected ward. The total sample size was 414 households which consisted of around 2 per cent households of Itanagar and Naharlagun towns as per 2011 Census. In order to conduct survey, a questionnaire was prepared.

The door-to-door sample household survey was carried out for the collection of primary data. To gather proper information, first the market for the product was introduced in front of the households along with a brief idea on the present situation of solid waste management and problems so that if any household was not very familiar with the solid waste management procedures, they might have an idea and inspiration about the reality. Through discussions and conversations, their responses were recorded in the required columns of the designed questionnaire.

The study also used the secondary data collected from various sources like the Census of India Publications, Basic Statistics of North Eastern Region and other published and unpublished data available with Census Authorities, the Directorate of Economics and Statistics and the Directorate of Urban Development, Human Development Report, State Development Report of Arunachal Pradesh, Itanagar Municipal Corporation (IMC), Arunachal Pradesh State Pollution Control Board, Websites of Central Pollution Control Board (CPCB) etc.

Conceptual Framework

To fulfil the main objectives of this study, the Contingent Valuation Method (CVM) was used. The CVM employs survey techniques to ask people about the value they would place on the hypothetical changes in some environmental recourses or non-market commodities. In this study the environmental good was solid waste. The CVM typically consists of three parts (Carson and Mitchell, 1989). This method describes in detail the goods or services being valued and the hypothetical circumstances under which they are made available to the respondents. Here the respondents were informed about the dimension to which the solid waste management problem grew over the years and to what extent it spread its adverse effects in the city. The respondents were informed about the Government run solid waste management and the role of private service providers. *Secondly*, the method entails valuation questions which reflect the respondents' WTP for the good or the service being valued. These questions were asked on the presumption that without the respondents' payment, the good or the service would not be provided. The method was thus aimed at eliciting their WTP in the form of currency. The questions can be reduced to a single question measuring maximum WTP. It could also be used as a bidding game technique wherein a series of offers were made to respondents in an attempt to detect the maximum WTP for the service. This means that if respondent says 'yes' to the initial bid, it indicates his/her WTP greater or equal to that amount.

If he/she answers 'no', then that sum of money was taken as an upper bound on true WTP. Depending on the design of the contingent valuation market, the final bid was the Hicksian compensation or equivalent surplus for the item being valued (Bayle and Bishop, 1998). *Thirdly*, the valuation method contains questions about the respondents' characteristics, their preferences relevant to the service being valued and their use of good and service.

Model Specification

In our present study we used two regression models, i.e. (i) Logistic Regression (Logit) Model and (ii) Ordinary Least Square (OLS) Regression Model.

Logistic Regression (Logit) Model

Logistic regression or logit regression or logit model is defined as a uni and multi-variate technique that permits for estimating the probability that an event will occur or not through the prediction of a binary dependent outcome from a set of independent variables (Niringiye *et al.*, 2010) and it was developed for the first time by David Cox in 1958. For the purpose of our analysis the respondents were classified into two groups -one group comprised those users of 'Improved Solid Waste Management Scheme' who inclined to pay and the other group comprised those users who declined to pay. Surveyed respondents expressed their decisions about the WTP through 'Yes' or 'No' responses. The dependent variable in our analysis was a dummy one. For the purpose of such analysis, Logit or Probit regression model is generally used due to their ability to deal with a dichotomous dependent variable and the model which gives better result is determined by the distribution of the error term. When the error term of the regression model follows the logistic distribution then Logit model is applied. But if the error term follows the normal distribution then Probit model is used (Mazumder, 2013, p. 28). Our study used dichotomous logit regression model with a view to determine the effect of various socio-economic characteristics of WTP for improved solid waste management in Itanagar and Naharlagun towns. Hence, a WTP function for solid waste management services in the study is formulated as given in (9.1):

$$WTP_i = f(Y_i, ED_i, F_i, L_i, A_i, EA_i) \tag{9.1}$$

The mathematical form of the model formulated is given in (9.2).

$$In(WTP) = \frac{1}{1+e^{In(\beta 0+\beta 1\, Yi+\ \beta 2\, EDi+\beta 3\, Fi+\beta 4\, Li+\beta 5\, Ai+\ \beta 6\, EAi+i)}} \tag{9.2}$$

Where,

WTP_i = WTP of households for use of an improved system of solid waste management is assigned with a score of '1' and others with '0' score)

β_0 = Constant term

β_i = Parameters

Y_i = Income of the household

ED_i = Level of educational attainment (in years)

F_i = Family size

L_i = Years of living in the place

A_i = Age of the respondents

EA_i = Environmental Awareness

ε_i = Error term

Ordinary Least Square (OLS) Regression Model

Ordinary Least Square (OLS) Regression Model is defined as a generalized linear modelling technique which is generally applied for modelling a single response variable which is recorded on at least an interval scale. It is used for a single or multiple explanatory variables along with categorical explanatory variables which are properly coded (Hutcheson, 2011). The principal objective of OLS regression model is to minimize the sum of squares of the variations occurred between the observed responses in the given set of data and which are predicted by a linear function of a set of explanatory variables.

As in our structured questionnaire an open-ended question was included, the response was a continuous variable and therefore an OLS technique used was given in (9.3):

$$WTP_i = \beta_0 + \beta_1 Y_i + \beta_2 ED_i + \beta_3 F_i + \beta_4 L_i + \beta_5 A_i + \beta_6 EA_i + \varepsilon_i \quad (9.3)$$

Where,

WTP_i = Maximum WTP for improved solid waste management system
β_0 = Constant term
β_i = Parameters
Y_i = Income of the household
ED_i = Level of educational attainment (years)
F_i = Family size
L_i = Years of living in the place
A_i = Age of the respondents
EA_i = Environmental Awareness
ε_i = Error term

Socio-Economic Features of the Sampled Households

In this section, an attempt was made to examine the socio-economic characteristics of the respondents and the households based on primary survey. The household survey for the present research work was conducted primarily in the morning and evening time so that the interviewees were present at home. The interviews were taken only from among the heads of the households or their spouses or the adult members. Table 9.2 shows the gender-wise classification of the respondents which indicated that males had the lion's shares (80.19%) than females. The data revealed that 82.10 per cent of the respondents were married and the rest 17.90 per cent were

Table 9.2: Gender-wise Classification of the Respondents (Percentage)

Gender	Percentage
Male	80.19
Female	19.81
Total	**100.00**

Source: Field Survey 2013-2016.

single. This was followed by age-wise classification as shown in Table 9.3. Table 9.3 shows that most of the respondents (50.72%) belonged to the age group of 31-45 years, around 26.33 per cent in the age group of 18-30 years and only 21.26 per cent were within the age group of 46-60 years.The educational level of the households was expected to indicate their awareness on cleanliness and solid waste management. Hence an

Table 9.3: Age-wise Classification of the Respondents (Percentage)

Age of the Respondents	Percentage
18-30 years	26.33
31-45 years	50.72
46-60 years	21.26
Above 60 years	1.69
Total	**100.00**

Source: Field Survey 2013-2016.

attempt was made to examine their level of education shown in Table 9.4. Table 9.4 shows that most of the respondents were graduates (31.88%) followed by higher secondary (27.78%), high school (15.22%), post graduates (9.90%), vocational or technically educated (3.86%). The respondents with primary schooling were found to be 7.25 per cent and only 4.11 per cent of the respondents were illiterate. Their occupations

Table 9.4: Highest Educational Attainment of the Respondents (Percentage)

Highest Educational Attainment	Percentage
Illiterate	4.11
Primary School	7.25
High School	15.22
Higher Secondary	27.78
Graduate	31.88
Post Graduate	9.90
Vocational/Technical	3.86
Total	**100.00**

Source: Field Survey 2013-2016.

were classified into different groups and the details were furnished in Table 9.5. It was seen that 32.04 per cent of the respondents were the Government employees followed by 31.52 per cent who were self-employed as traders or businessmen or contractors and 22.22 per cent with employees of private shops or companies. On the other 6.72 per cent were found to self-employed as labourers, 1.55 per cent were retired employees and 5.94 per cent belonged to other category which included housewives, students etc. An attempt was also made to examine the approximate monthly income

Table 9.5: Occupational Classification of the Respondents (Percentage)

Occupational Group	Percentage
Self-employed as labourer	6.72
Self-employed as trader/businessman/ contractor	31.52
Employee of a private company/shop	22.22
Government Employee	32.04
Retired Employee	1.55
Others	5.94
Total	**100.00**

Source: Field Survey 2013-2016.

level data of the surveyed households which was given in Table 9.6. Table 9.6 showed that 33.33 per cent of the households had their monthly income between Rs. 30001-Rs. 40000. 29.95 per cent of the respondents income lied in the range of Rs. 20001-Rs. 30000. 11.35 per cent of the respondents were found having their income in Rs. 40001-Rs. 50000. 4.83 per cent of the respondents had very high incomes which were above Rs. 50000 and

Table 9.6: Approximate Monthly Income of the Households Surveyed (Percentage)

Monthly Income	Percentage
Less than Rs. 10000	3.14
Rs. 10001 - Rs. 20000	17.39
Rs. 20001 - Rs. 30000	29.95
Rs. 30001 - Rs. 40000	33.33
Rs. 40001 - Rs. 50000	11.35
Above Rs. 50000	4.83
Total	**100.00**

Source: Field Survey, 2013-2016.

only 3.14 per cent of the respondents had their monthly income below Rs. 10000. An attempt was also made to know the environmental awareness as well as to analyse the attitude towards solid waste accumulation among the surveyed respondents. For example, Table 9.7 shows the most serious environmental problems faced by respondents in the study area.

Table 9.7: Most Serious Environmental Problems Facing by Respondents (Percentage)

Environmental Problems	Percentage
Inadequate solid waste collection services	42.27
Presence of litter and illegal piles	33.82
Nuisance from solid transfer points	6.76
Problems from liquid waste and its collection/disposition (cleaning up of drains)	14.01
Having no problems	3.14
Total	**100.00**

Source: Field Survey, 2013-2016.

Table 9.7 shows that majority of the respondents (42.27%) reported that inadequate solid waste collection services was the most serious problem faced by them in their neighbourhood, followed by 33.8 per cent of the respondents reported that problems from the presence of litter and illegal piles were the main problems in their neighborhood. On the contrary, some of the respondents (14.01%) were facing the problems from liquid waste and its collection/disposition (cleaning up of drains) in their locality. However, a very small portion of the surveyed households (3.14%) reported that they did not have any such problems in their locality. When the respondents were asked regarding the frequency of clearing the dustbins, a good percentage of respondents (24.64%) replied that they did not know. The details were given in Table 9.8.

Table 9.8: Frequency of Clearing the Dustbins (Percentage)

Frequency	Percentage
Everyday	17.39
Once in two days	30.68
Once in three days	11.35
Once in a week	9.42
Everyday except Sunday	6.52
Do not know	24.64
Total	**100.00**

Source: Field Survey, 2013-2016.

Regarding the knowledge of the respondents about the final disposal of waste products, Figure 9.2 below shows that 49.03 per cent of them were ignorant about it.

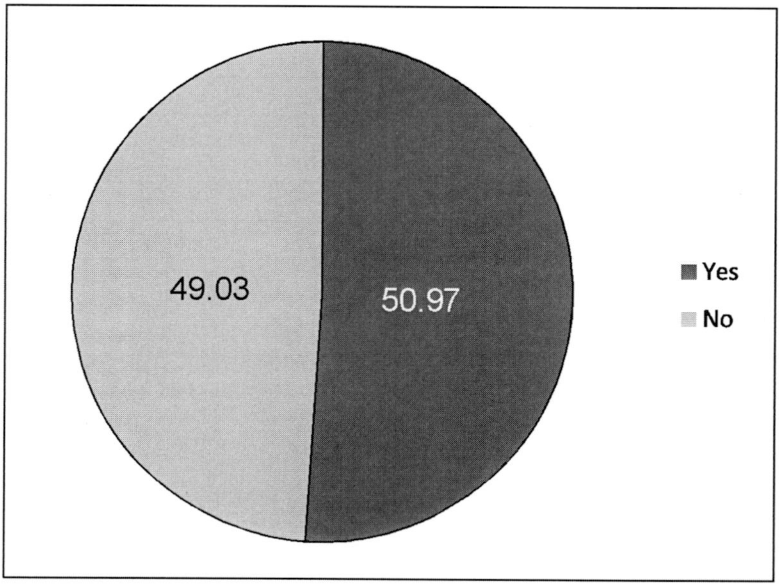

Figure 9.2: Knowledge About the Final Disposal of Wast Products (Percentage)

Source: Field Survey 2013-2016.

Review of Literature

Barai C. Daksha (2007) explained that in Bangalore city, solid wastes were managed by both formal and community-based formal and informal systems. The formal system is looked after by the Health and Engineering Departments. Community based formal system was handled by Bangalore City Corporation (BCC) along with some NGOs like 'Mythri Sarna Samithi'. However, the active participation of private organization and households were not found in the garbage management process. Subhashini Muthukrishnan (2010), in her book, *Economics of Environment* explained that wastes generated both by the households in the form of household waste and the waste generated in production processes by industries in the form of by-products are without reuse value. As a result of increasing population growth along with urbanization and industrialization, the volume of waste increases dramatically in modern societies. Besides, solid waste may fill up landfill sites which become very difficult and costly to maintain. S. Das, E. Birol and R.N. Bhattacharya (2008), in their pioneer work, 'Informing Efficient and Effective Solid Waste Management to Improve Local Environmental Quality and Public Health: Application of the Choice Experiment Method in West Bengal, India' estimated the WTP of households for better solid waste management services provided in Chandernagore and South Dum Dum Municipalities areas of Kolkata in West Bengal. They found that despite the heterogeneity and tight budget constraints, majority of households showed significant WTP for better solid wastes management services. R. Chatterjee (2010), in his article 'Municipal Solid Waste Management in Kohima City-India', explained that it was the level of socio-economic development which determined the amount and composition of wastes in urban places. He explained that enhancing economic development accelerates the composition of wastes. Due to the high population density in towns and rapid urbanization in cities, solid waste management became a mammoth challenge. S. Joel *et al.* (2012), in his article, 'Economic Valuation of Improved Solid Waste Management in Eldoret Municipality', explained that Eldoret town was facing severe solid waste generation and management problems because of increasing rate of population and household disposable incomes. They explained that the solid waste management problem was being tried to solve by supply side of the waste disposal and collection but they tried to solve the problems by demand oriented valuation. They used the contingent valuation technique and multiple regression models to identify the sole factors of WTP for improved quality of environment and found that the residents were willing to pay kshs 363 per months for better services.Muhammad Subhan *et al.* (2014), in their paper 'Urban Community Willingness to Pay for Improved Solid Waste Management in Malaysian Municipality: A Choice Modelling Approach', explained that the problem of solid waste management was a very critical issue in most of the developing countries particularly it was more severe in Asia. They studied the people's WTP for improved solid waste management services in Seremban Municipality-one of the important municipalities in Malaysia and found that the households were willing to pay for improved quality of services for the management of solid wastes. Mazumdhar *et al.* (2013), in their article, 'Sustainable Urban Waste Management in Silchar Municipal Area: An Application of Contingent Valuation Method in Cachar District of Assam', explained that the WTP for sustainable solid wastes management in Silchar municipal area and found that there was a chance of success if proper solid waste management scheme is introduced. For this the municipal authority should make awareness campaigns regarding the goods and bads of proper solid wastes managements and also the benefit of payment for better solid wastes management.Tongam Rina (2012), in her article 'Green Pioneers in A Garbage City' explained that Urban Development department dumps the wastes of the capital city Itanagar near a garbage treatment plant that was under construction for the last many years, at Holongi. The department burned the garbage destroying the vegetation in the area and leaving an unmistakable welcome stench to the neighbouring area and visitors. She mentioned The Green Pioneers comprising people of different groups including students, old people, businessmen, irrespective of sex and caste and age voluntarily cleaned up many landmarks in the city without depending on the Urban Department. She called it as a wakeup call to all concerned. In spite of these efforts, the quantity of garbage generated in the city was growing by leaps and bounds. J. Dutta (2009), in her M.Phil dissertation entitled 'Municipal Waste management in Guwahati City', found that solid waste management services in the city were inadequate and people of the locality were confused about the government imposed 'Integrated Solid Waste Management Scheme'. By applying contingent valuation method (CVM), she estimated the WTP for solid waste management and found that people inclined to pay more to the private organisation rather than to Government-run services.

Brief Description of Present Waste Management Situation

Although in Arunachal Pradesh, the true Figure of solid waste management is not available, it is estimated that a net total of 230 tonnes of wastes is generated per day (State Development Report, 2009). However, the estimates of Central Pollution Control Board (CPCB) 2016, was found to be 116 tonnes per day. The disposal of urban waste product was generally looked after by the Directorate of Urban and Housing Department, Government of Arunachal Pradesh. Although, the services provided by the Department was not at all satisfactory since the accumulated wastes were not disposed properly. The wastes were just taken to an open landfill nearby Holongi (a village outskirt to Itanagar town) and these were dumped and sometimes were burnt openly. Besides, the people of the towns were ignorant about the significance and essential of adequate solid waste management. They simply threw the wastes on the road sides, drains or open piles wastes. With a view to a proper and adequate waste management system, the Itanagar Municipal Corporation (IMC) came into existence w.e.f. 2013 under the IMC Act 2007 which includes both Itanagar and Naharlagun towns. The IMC is now looking after the solid waste accumulation and management services in the towns of Itanagar and Naharlagun, i.e. the Itanagar Capital Complex. In fact, IMC has thirty wards of which eighteen wards fall in Itanagar town and the rest fall in Naharlagun town.

The services rendered by the IMC are somewhat better than the previous system yet the solid waste management services are highly inefficient. There is no door-to-door service in the towns although it was claimed by IMC. Most of the people were unaware of the door-to-door services. It is found that the IMC used to collect the garbages from road sides and dump them and sometimes burn them which pollute the environment. There are no community dustbins in the city. The road side dustbins are also removed from many places. As a result, many people throw their wastes on the roadside heaps of wastes. In certain places, people throw the garbage directly to the collection vehicle (which the IMC termed as door-to-door collection) in the morning from 6 to 7 am. But many people in the town areas do not rise early in the morning and hence, they miss the collection vehicles and ultimately throw the wastes on the roadside heaps and it is lying for next day's collection. Further, for appropriate management of treatment plant, segregation, processing and disposal are some of the important steps for integrated solid waste management. But IMC did not practise such activities. They simply accumulated the waste without segregation and used to dump at the newly constructed dumping site at Chimpu, an outskirt village around 3 to 4 kms away from Itanagar Capital Complex. Hence, the study shows that an adequate waste management system was absent in Itanagar and Naharlagun towns in spite of existence of the municipality corporation.

Present Status of Composition of Solid Waste in Towns

Finally, an attempt was made to estimate the per capita waste generated as well as the composition of waste products from our household sample survey. However, our sample survey in 2013-16 shows that Itanagar and Naharlagun towns produced 670 gm solid waste products per day which was higher than the estimates of 445 gm per day estimated by the Department of Housing and Urban Development, Government of Arunachal Pradesh, 2006-07. This indicates that there was a 50.56 percentage of increase of per capita per day solid wastes generation in both the towns over the decade. Our survey also shows the composition of different types of waste product generated by households in both the towns which was furnished in Figure 9.3.

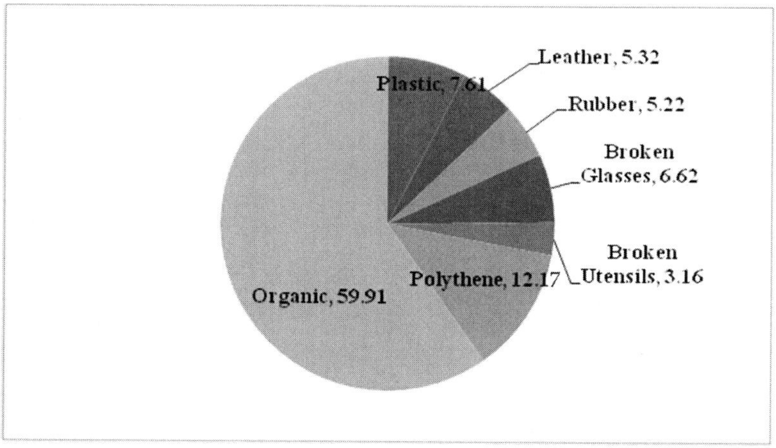

Figure 9.3: Percentage Composition of Different Types of Waste Generated by Households in Itanagar and Naharlagun Towns (Per Day)

Source: Field Survey, 2013-16.

From Figure 9.3 it is seen that organic waste (around 60%) consisted the highest component followed by polythene (around 12.17%). In our survey, plastic and broken glasses consisted of only 7.61 per cent and 6.62 per cent respectively out of total wastes generated by the households. Thus, the analysis shows that per capita waste generation per day in Itanagar and Naharlagun is around 670 gm and there is a shortage of adequate dumping space. The wastes are finally dumped at one designated site where no soil cover is used. The burning of wastes on the side of National Highway is a common practice. Thus the solid waste management in both the towns is creating health problems to the residents. In order to mitigate this problem, the Government and other stakeholders have no doubt an important role to play. The problem is that less importance is given to the problem by both the state and the local governments which results to inadequate provision of storage facilities. Keeping this in view, it is very important and timely to look for the possibility of cost sharing by the households. For this we need to analyse the demand side for improved solid waste management. With this background, an attempt was made to study the WTP from households for an improved solid waste management by applying the Contingent Valuation technique and the details were furnished in subsequent sub-sections.

Results and Discussions

The results of both the logit regression model and ordinary least square model are given below. The estimates of the logit regression model are shown in Table 9.9. The results of the logit regression model showed that age, level of educational attainment and households' incomes had positively determined the WTP for improved solid waste management system in the twin towns. From the result, it was found that age positively influenced the WTP for improved solid waste management and it was statistically significant at 0.01 levels. This could be so because as age increased people were more concerned about environmental hygiene and

Table 9.9: Results of Logit Regression Model

Independent Variable	Coefficients(β)	Wald
Constant	-0.446	0.227
Age of the respondent	0.569	7.687***
Level of educational attainment (years)	0.084	5.829**
Family size	-0.144	2.756*
Income of the household	0.258	3.226*
Years of living in the place	0.055	0.048
Environmental awareness	-0.102	0.140

Hosmer and Lemeshow Test: Degree of freedom = 8, Significance = 0.252 Chi-square = 10.185, Omnibus Tests of Model Coefficients: Degrees of freedom = 6 Chi-square = 34.459***

Note: *, ** and *** indicate 0.10, 0.05 and 0.01 level of significance

sanitation of the locality. Table 9.9 showed that the level of educational attainment was another positively significant determinant of WTP which was statistically significant at 0.05 levels. This shows that the higher the levels of educational attainment the more the people understand the environmental problems and the need of proper solid waste management and they revealed higher WTP for better management services than the illiterate people. Table 9.9 also showed that households' income was another positive determinant of WTP which was statistically significant at 0.10 levels. This shows that the higher the level of income, the higher the amount of WTP they revealed for an improved solid waste management in their locality. Athough it was statistically significant at 0.10 levels of significance, it was also found that there existed a negative or inverse correlation between the family size and the WTP. This means that as family sizes increased, i.e. became larger the WTP for an improved solid waste management decreased which was prbabbly due to budgetary constraints. Surprisingly, it was also observed that environmental awareness was negatively related to WTP but was not statistically significant. However, another variable, i.e.years of living in the place, which was included in the model had a positive coefficient but was not significant. Finally, Hosmer-Lemeshow Test was used and the model was significantly fitted the data since the value was 0.252 which was greater than 0.05. If this value is less than 0.05, it indicates that the data poorly fit in the model.

Result of Ordinary Least Squared Method and Discussions

The results of ordinary least square (OLS) method were furnished in Table 9.10. It is evident from Table 9.10 that except for age all other variables including level of educational attainment, households' income, years of living in the place and environmental awareness were positively significant to the maximum WTP for an improved solid waste management. When years of educational attainment was taken as a proxy variable of the education level, it was found that it positively influenced the WTP for an improved solid waste management and was statistically significant at 0.01 levels. This indicates that when longer time was devoted in attainment of education people understand more about the environmental problems, the need of better solid waste management and reveal their higher WTP for better management services as compared to illiterate people. From the results depicted in Table 9.10, households' income was also found to be another significant determinant of WTP and was statistically significant at 0.01 levels. This indicates that people with higher levels of income, were

Table 9.10: Result of Ordinary Least Square Method

Independent Variable	Coefficients (β)	't' statistic
Constant	-54.418	-2.044**
Age of the respondent	8.625	1.637
Level of educational attainment (years)	2.859	2.654***
Family size	-1.152	-0.460
Income of the household	17.655	4.687***
Years of living in the place	11.633	1.686*
Environmental awareness	40.314	5.348***

Adj.R^2=0.582, F=16.335***

Note: *, ** and *** indicate 0.10, 0.05 and 0.01 level of significance.

willing to pay more for an improved solid waste management in their locality than those with low incomes. Table 9.10 showed that, years of living in the place had positive significant effect on the WTP for an improved solid waste management system in the locality and was statistically significant at 0.10 levels. This shows that living at a particular place for a longer period people become more concerned about the environment and to keep it clean and hygienic and as such their WTP for an improved management of wastes was higher. Finally, the results showed that environmental awareness among the respondents positively determined the maximum WTP for improved solid waste management in the towns of Itanagar and Naharlagun. In order to capture the environmental awareness of the respondents, an index of environmental awareness was constructed. The value of index ranged from 0 to 1 and was statistically significant at 0.01 levels. It is also observed that the higher the awareness level on the environment the higher is the WTP for an improved solid waste management.

Conclusion

The analysis indicated that due to rapid growth of population, the two towns, i.e., Itanagar and Naharlagun were facing acute problems of solid waste management. In the absence of a municipal body, the management and disposal of municipal wastes were looked after by the Directorate of Urban and Housing Department, Government of Arunachal Pradesh till 2013. After the enactment of the IMC Act 2007, the IMC came into existence w.e.f. 2013 for better solid waste management for both the Itanagar and Naharlagun towns. The departmental survey data for 2006-07 indicated that the per capita waste generation per day in Itanagar town was around 445 gm whereas the survey data carried out by us showed that the per capita per day waste generated in the twin towns was approximately 670 gm. This showed an increase of wastes by 50.56 per cent over the decade. The present chapter also attempted to find out the various socio-economic factors determining the maximum WTP for an improved solid waste management in these towns where the data were empirically estimated using the two econometric models, viz. logit and the multiple regression models. The results given by the logit model showed that age, years of schooling and households' income had positive impact on the WTP and were statistically significant. The results given by the OLS estimator also showed that age, years of schooling, household incomes and environmental awareness positively determined the maximum WTP for improved waste management system in the study area. Thus the findings revealed that majority of the residents were not satisfied with the present system of waste management and their WTP inclined for an improved solid waste management system. The average WTP was found to be Rs.106.43 per month which was quite significant. It was observed that the vehicles operated for this purpose were limited and uncovered.

Policy Implications

The following policy recommendations were suggested for proper urban development and improved solid waste management in the urban centres of Arunachal Pradesh:

It is observed that one of the most important environmental issues associated with urbanisation in Arunachal Pradesh is poor urban waste management. Our estimate shows that the waste generated per day in Itanagar and Naharlagun towns was 670 gm which is quite high. Most importantly, the waste generated is not properly cleared and disposed of. We propose that the IMC should introduce clearance of garbage everyday. Hence, it is suggested that the vehicles used by the IMC for transportation of municipal wastes should be covered, more numbers and well equipped.

It was found that majority of the households indicated their higher WTP for an improved solid waste management. Keeping this in view, the IMC may introduce door-to-door garbage collection services daily if necessary on payment basis in order to make the twin towns cleaner and hygienic. To achieve this objective, IMC should concentrate first on awareness campaign about consequences of waste mishandling and benefits of WTP before building up commercial plans for solid waste management in the twin towns of Arunachal Pradesh.

Surprisingly, it was observed that most of the urbanites did not know about the open landfill sites for final disposal of waste products and the ill-effects of such open disposal on environment and health. Hence a mass awareness programme among the residents is necessary to immediately discontinue the current practice of dumping garbages in the open landfill sites and to provide the sanitary landfills at designated points. In fact, the treatment plant at Chimpu should be made functional immediately for final disposal and processing of solid wastes in the capital region.

One of the important components of efficient solid waste management system is the generation of awareness among the urban people about the essence of cleanliness of neighbourhoods and proper solid waste management. Hence such awareness programmes and outreach activities should be held regularly in all the urban centres of the State. It is to be noted that unless the consciousness and awareness of the society grow,

Government's efforts will be of little use. It is expected that through the Government's policy, viz. 'Swachh Bharat Mission' the towns of Arunachal Pradesh will become cleaner and greener.

It is found that around 60 per cent waste generated by our households consisted of organic matters only. Hence, the use of compost machine may be popularised particularly in housing complex as well as institutions for transforming the solid wastes into manures and uses in gardens. To fructify the matter, the three principles of technology, i.e. **Reduce**, **Recycle** and **Reuse** should be applied so that the problems associated with the generation and safe disposal practices of solid wastes are largely minimized.

Thus the study highlighted a number of important issues relating to urban development and emerging environmental problem of the towns of Arunachal Pradesh. However, the fact is that the issues are too broad to be captured in a single framework. Hence, it is expected that the present study will form the basis of future research work on this lesser explored but economically and socially relevant field of study relating to the entire North Eastern Region.

REFERENCES

Anand, P.B. (1999): 'Waste Management in Madras Revisited', *Environment and Development*, Vol. II, No. 2.

Annual Report (2014-15): *Central Pollution Control Board (CPBP),* Delhi, 2016 (Annexure-VIII).

Asnani, P.U. (2006): 'Solid Waste Management', *Indian Infrastructure Report 2006: Urban Infrastructure,* Government of India.

Barai, C. Daksha (2007): *Urbanization, Development and Environment* in C.D. Deshpande Memorial Volume, Rawat Publications, New Delhi.

Bayle, R.J. and Bishop, R.C. (1988): 'Welfare Measurement Using Contingent Valuation: A Comparison of Techniques', *American Journal of Agricultural Economics*, Vol. 70, pp. 20-28.

Carson, R.J. and Mitchell, R.C. (1989): 'Using Surveys to Value Measurement of Goods and Services, The Contingent Valuation Method', *Resources for the Future*, Washington, DC.

Chatterjee, R., (2010): 'Municipal Solid Waste Management in Kohima City-India', *Iranian Journal* of *Environmental Health*, *Science* and *Engineering*, Vol. 7, No. 2, pp. 173-180.

Cox, D. (1958): 'The Regression Analysis of Binary Sequences', *Journal of Royal Statistical Society,* Series-B, Vol. 20, pp. 215-242 (accessed on 21.02.2016).

Das, S., Birol, E. and Bhattacharya, R.N. (2008): 'Informing Efficient and Effective Solid Waste Management to Improve Local Environmental Quality and Public Health: Application of the Choice Experiment Method in West Bengal,

India', *Discussion Paper Series*, Department of Land Economy, University of Cambridge, No. 33, 2008, (accessed on 18.12.2014).

Dutta, J. (2009): 'Municipal Waste Management in Guwahati City', M.Phil Dissertation submitted to the Department of Economics, Gauhati University, Guwahati (unpublished).

Government of Arunachal Pradesh (2006-07): *Departmental Survey (2006-07),* Department of Housing and Urban Development, Itanagar.

Government of Arunachal Pradesh (2009): *Arunachal Pradesh Development Report.*

Government of Arunachal Pradesh (2015): *Statistical Abstract of Arunachal Pradesh,* Directorate of Economics and Statistics, Itanagar.

Government of India (2011): Office of the Registrar, General and Census Commissioner, Census of India, 2011, *Primary Census Abstract Data (Final), General Population Tables.*

Hutcheson, G.D. (2011): 'Ordinary Least Square Regression Model' in L. Mountinho and G.D. Hutchesson, *The SAGE Dictionary of Quantitative Management Research*, pp. 224-228, www.datajob.com (accessed on 24.01.2017).

Kawai, K. and Tasaki, T. (2016): 'Revisiting Estimates of Municipal Solid Waste Generation Per Capita and Their Reliability', *Journal Mater Cycles Waste Management*, Vol. 18, No. 1, pp. 1-13.

Kumar, S. and Gaikward, S.A. (2004): 'Municipal Solid Waste Management in Indian Urban Centres: An Approach for Betterment', in Gupta, K.R. (ed) *Urban Development Debates in the New Millennium*, Atlantic Publication, New Delhi.

Mitra, A. (1995): 'The Trends and Patterns of Urbanisation in Arunachal Pradesh, 1971-91', in Gangly, J.B. (ed) *Urbanisation and Development in North-East India,* Deep and Deep Publications, New Delhi, pp. 126-134.

Mitra, A. (1997): *Internal Migration and Economic Development in the Hills,* Omsons Publications, New Delhi.

Mitra, A. (2003): 'Urbanisation Process in Arunachal Pradesh—A Case Study of Itanagar town', in Begi, Joram (ed) *Itanagar A Profile*, Bharatiya Itihas Sankalan Samiti, Itanagar, Arunachal Chapter, pp. 154-157.

Muthukrishnan, S. (2010): *Economics of Environment*, PHI Learning Pvt. Ltd., New Delhi, pp. 90.

Niringiye, A. and Omortor, G.D. (2010): 'Willingness to Pay for Improved Solid Waste Disposal in Tema Metropolis', *Current Research Journal of Economic Theory,* Vol. 2, No. 3, pp. 119-122.

Nyori, Tai (2003): 'The Capital of Arunachal Pradesh Itanagar: A Historical Perspective', in Begi, Joram (ed) *Itanagar A Profile*, Bharatiya Itihas Sankalan Samiti, Itanagar, Arunachal Chapter, pp. 17-23.

Roy, A.T., Deb, U. and Mazumdhar, R., (2013): 'Sustainable Urban Waste Management in Silchar Municipal Area: An Application of Contingent Valuation Method in Cachar District of Assam', *International Journal of Humanities and Social Science Invention*, Vol. 2, No. 1, pp. 25-33.

Singhal, S. and Pandey, S. (2001): 'Solid Waste Management in India: Status and Future Direction', TERI Information Monitor on Environmental Science, Vol. 6, No. I, pp. 1-4.

Swachh Sarvekshan (2016): Government of India.

World Bank (2006): 'Improving Management of Municipal Solid Waste in India: Overview and Challenges', Washington, D.C. (http://www.mapsofindia.com).

10

Centripetal and Centrifugal Urbanisations in Two Tribal Habitats in Arunachal Pradesh and Assam

Bibhash Dhar

Urbanization is the increase in population in the urban centres or cities due to migration from the neighbouring villages. Aspiring people at first reach a city alone from the hinterlands in search of job and accommodation and subsequently bring their immediate family members to join him and get acclimatized in the city life. Though it is believed that urbanization began with industrial revolution which took its birth in Great Britain in the 18th century still many scholars are of the opinion that urbanization actually started in the banks of Euphrates and Tigris in Mesopotamia.

There are a few types of urbanization as browsed.[1] The writer recognizes four types of urbanization and these are: (1) the metropolitan type evolves in the form of continuous expansion of built-up area in the suburbs of a large city or the increase of commuters coming from the neighbouring rural villages to the city. This type, in either case, is the centrifugal extension of the economic power of the city. (2) the regional centre type comes in the form of appearance of a new urban centre or the development of the existing town at a nodal point of a region. This is the centripetal concentration of the regional economic power; (3) The industrialization type appears in the form of birth and growth of a newly industrialized tract in the country. It is realized through the introduction of economic power from some outer region; and (4) The old-fashioned industry type which is achieved in the form of development of urban industries or old-fashioned local cottage industries in a region. This type is based on the capital brought forth spontaneously from local agricultural production. (https://www.jstage.jst.go.jp/article/grj1925/32/12/3212_629/article).

In the context of urbanization Colby (1933) has coined two specific types of urbanization and these are centripetal and centrifugal types. He expressed that in centripetal types of urbanization, the powerful centripetal forces that hold certain functions in the central zone attract others towards it. On the otherhand, in the centrifugal type there is a movement of some city dwelling families from the central zone of a city towards or beyond the periphery of an urban centre in pursuit of economic interest, spacious and for better living. Though centripetal and centrifugal forces are the theories of Physics but many scholars working on urbanization have found similarities of the two forces of pure science in the studies of urbanization. Centripetal force attracts the bodies towards the centre of the axis of rotation while the centrifugal force pushes the bodies away from the centre. In the present study human rural-urban migration and urban to peripheral region or migration the sub-urban areas from main urban centre along with the other factors related to urbanization are equated with the centripetal and centrifugal forces respectively.

For the present study two tribal habitats located in Arunachal Pradesh and Assam have been considered to examine the centripetal and centrifugal forces in relation to urbanization. One of the realms is the traditional setting

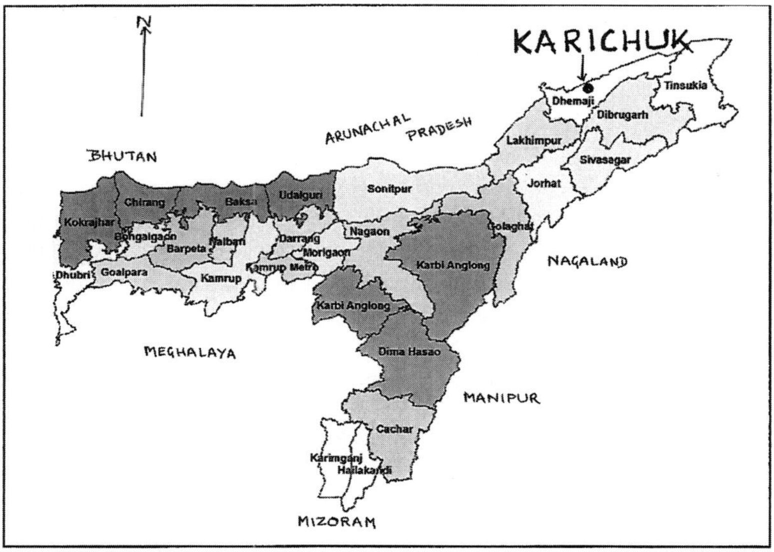

Figure 10.1: Location of Dhemaji in the map of Assam

Courtesy: https://www.google.co.in/search?q=maps+of+assam+district+wise&tbm=isch &source=iu&pf=m&ictx=1&fir=362ZcyyYd0UcAM%253A%252CXJD5fwj

of the Monpa tribesmen group of the Tawang district of Arunachal Pradesh in the district headquarter of Tawang town situated at an elevation of more than 10,000 feet above the mean sea level.

The other habitat is the Karichuk Mishing tribal village located in the Jonai Circle of Dhemaji district of Assam (Location Map 10.1) on the north bank of Brahmaputra. The location map of Dhemaji District is shown in Figure 10.1.

The reason behind selection of the two abodes of the tribal people is to study the types of urbanization that are noticed in the two domains. One is centripetal and the other is centrifugal. Tawang is the habitat of the Monpa, a dominant tribal group of the state of Arunachal Pradesh and its history can be traced from 1681 A.D., the year of construction of the famous Mahayana Buddhist monastery in Tawang. On the other hand, the history of Karichuk village, the habitat of the Mishing, the second largest plains tribal people of Assam next only to the Bodos is quite obscure (https://mishingcult.weebly.com/ about.html).

The Monpas, with their habitats in the highlands of the western-most districts of West Kameng and Tawang is a community of culturally colourful and dynamic group. They are Buddhists by religion and follow the Tibetan-Lamaist type of Buddhism. They have Buddhist temples and monasteries built in higher elevations in their villages. They are expert mountain agriculturists, also subsidize their economy by rearing livestock in the mountain grasslands and carried out caravan-borne trans-Himalayan trade transactions of indigenous items through the mountain passes. The Monpas of Tawang on whom the present work is based, had a non-luminous past as for about three centuries they were under the ecclesiastic rule under the Tibetans. However, following the independence of India and after bringing the Monpa country within the Republic of India, the people heaved a sigh of relief, but again in the subsequent period the people suffered a traumatic experience caused by the infamous Sino-Indian border conflict of 1962. Though it terrorized the people but the succeeding period ushered in a phase of transition in the life and culture of the Monpas of Tawang. It happened because soon after the international border conflict and with the restoration of peace, a large network of roads came up linking the isolated habitats of the Monpas of Tawang with the mainland of India. A large number of people from the pan-Indian region were posted in the Monpa country as well as in other parts of the State for proper administration wherein offices and departments were established by the Central Government and the State Government. The situation ushered in a sea of transformation in all spheres of their life. The hitherto isolated life received the luminosity of formal education, started brisk travels to different parts of the country and carried back the message of transformation and modernization. It shows the dynamicity of the people to a great extent and due to that they have mentally recovered from the shackles of monastic rule and accepted many changes in all spheres of their socio-cultural life.

The Monpas, though had a non-luminous past, but, today are heading towards a promising future through the phases and programmes of transformation launched by the Government agencies which are the main driving forces of urbanization. It is because of transformation which brought in modernization, created employment opportunities, motivated the rural people to move to Tawang proper and additionally developed the opportunities of formal education. All these together acted as a driving force for rapid urbanization with Tawang town as the nodal point. The Monpa habitat of Tawang was rather blessed because urbanization or the process of metropolitanization of the hill town took place at Tawang itself through various progressions of transformation. A large scale migration of the Monpas from the hinterland took place and is still taking place which is the attraction and character of any urban centre of the world. Scholars called it as the centripetal concentration of the regional economic power as the development of the existing town takes place at a nodal point of the region. The young and able Monpas who have already migrated to Tawang in search of opportunities have extended their hands to pull more and more people of their own kin groups or friends to try their luck in the urban centre of Tawang. At the same time there are thrusts from the nearby rural areas to move to Tawang and earn a livelihood. The phenomenon may be termed as the centripetal force of urbanization and the focus is on a nodal point and that is Tawang.

Karichuk the second area of investigation is a small Mishing village in the outskirts of the growing township of Dhemaji. At the time of field investigation in 1975 there were 187 persons in total and distributed through 27 households. It may be stated that the whole area of Dhemaji lies in the basin of the Jiadhol river. The Jiadhol rises somewhere in the undivided Siang district of Arunachal Pradesh in the north of Dhemaji and is famous for its unstable course in the region. It has a tendency to change course every year in its southerly sojourn and inundates large areas of Dhemaji.

The story of urbanization of the Karichuk village of Dhemaji area is a bit different. Here the urbanization has happened in a centrifugal manner. It may mentioned that the village Karichuk as seen in 1975 formed a small pocket of the growing sub-divisional town of Dhemaji under the Lakhimpur district of Assam, but was till then much a village.

The inhabitants of Karichuk, as observed, used to spend nearly half of their days in the township of Dhemaji. Many of these people held certain jobs, such as, peon, watchman, driver etc., in the town proper and others used to roam about in the town in quest of fortune. Such exposure of men-folk of Karichuk has opened their eyes and helped them to develop the idea which propelled them towards inculcating the thoughts of changed and improved living and led to shed their traditional ways. It is nothing but the stage of their initial contact with modernization due to the impact of urbanization. Soon, their urge for accumulation of wealth through trade, commerce and other economic engagements and ultimately the push to lead an urban life became a serious part of their thought process. The concept of urban life which has already emerged in a large way in the minds of the people of Karichuk was further accelerated with the elevation of the sub-divisional town of Dhemaji into the district headquarters of the same name in 2006. Many of the Mishings of Karichuk with the aim of making quick money and become a part of the urban Dhemaji started to sell their landed property to the prospective buyers in spite of expression of unhappiness by the fellow villagers. It may be added here that way back in 1975 a few Mishing villagers of Karichuk were found contemplating to sell their plots of land to the prospective buyers from outside their community. The case of one Mayeng Noroh can be cited as an example. None could debar him from selling his land. As a result, the row of tea and snack shops, State Bank of India, flour mill and small offices of chit funds stood on the land that once belonged to Mayeng Noroh. This is only one example but many of the Mishings of Karichuk slowly parted with their land for want of quick money. As per the traditional tribal norm, the Mishings were required to sell their landed property only to the tribal people so that the plots of land do not fall in the hands of the strangers. Nevertheless, influenced by the ambition of becoming townsmen in the fastest possible way, majority of the villagers of Karichuk preferred to disregard the traditional custom and rule. As a matter of fact, the people of Karichuk were in a tight spot as to what should be their role to save their village from the open flood gates of the urbanization emerging from the growing township of Dhemaji. Karichuk village was guarded by the Ahom villages of Dihingiagaon and Kulapathar and Dhemaji almost juxtaposed where many people of different ethnic-cultural background lived. It was the credit of the Mishings of Karichuk that till then they were able to keep alive their tiny cultural enclave though they were by then formed almost a part of the suburb of Dhemaji. As it was geographically almost a part of Dhemaji thus one hopes to find a semi-urban environment in the village but in reality it was not so. Of course, one cannot deny that the urban influences have not at all entered. Some of them have constructed houses with cement-concrete, young boys developed the habit of enjoying movies at Dhemaji, a change in dress code towards the modern type was also noticed among acceptances of a few other traits of urban life.

Nevertheless, if people of Karichuk were to achieve the real progress and urbanism then they required a massive development in their economic front but that was not an easy task for them. Though their economy was agrarian but most of them did not have enough cultivable land and a good number of them were agricultural labourers. Those who had substantially big agricultural land could not afford to do scientific cultivation for want of money. Moreover, due to their proximity to the growing urban centre, the town had been increasingly taking up more and more of their arable land as the people had no other alternatives but had to succumb to urban pressure and for want of money.

Today, Karichuk is in existence not as the traditional Mishing village but as a hamlet of the district town of Dhemaji. Unlike Tawang, which attracted the Monpas of the nearby villages in search of economic support, the migration of the Mishings of Karichuk was not towards Dhemaji, instead the rising tendrils of the city of Dhemaji swallowed up the sub-urban rural settlement of Karichuk. For the loss of the uni-ethnic tribal habitat of Karichuk in the hands of the emergent urban centre of Dhemaji, though helpless, the resident Mishings were responsible to a great extent.

Generally, people are attracted towards the nearby urban centres due to the availability of many facilities such as exposure to modern living, health care, education for their children, access to jobs in both government and private sectors as the urban economy is more productive than the rural one, living under the jurisdiction of municipality, safe water supply, electricity, easy availability of public transport and many other such aspects that are found in the urban centres but largely unavailable in rural areas. Thus, the centrifugal force or power of urbanization played a major role in bringing under its range the whole Mishing village of Karichuk that was a suburb of Dhemaji since decades disregarding its individual existence.

REFERENCES

Colby, Charles C. (1933): Centrifugal & Centripetal Forces in Urban Geography, *Annals of Association of American Geographers*. Vol XXIII. March 1933, No. 1.

Websites consulted

https://mishingcult.weebly.com/about.html

https://www.google.co.in/search?q=map+of+tawang&tbm=isch&source=iu&pf= m&ictx=1&fir=ir9LeR bYfb6roM%253A%252C96mb_BexOwxB6M%
https://www.google.co.in/search?q=maps+of+assam+district+wise&tbm=isch&source=iu&pf=m &ictx=1&fir=362ZcyyYd0UcAM%253A%252CXJD5fwj

11
Unplanned Growth of Guwahati
Problems and Mitigations

D.D. Mali

Introduction

Planning is important for any kind of activity. It is more so in developing towns and cities. Unplanned growth of towns and cities leads to haphazard growth. This creates lots of problems for the citizens. Planning leads to orderly development of towns and cities. This helps in avoiding the pitfalls of unplanned growth. In this chapter I have highlighted the problems associated with the unplanned and haphazard growth of Guwahati city and the measures needed for mitigations.

Planning

Planning for growth and development of towns and cities are concerned with several aspects of towns and cities:

(i) These include the development and use of land; planning of permission, protection and use of the environment;
(ii) Public welfare, the design of the urban environment including air and water;
(iii) The infrastructure passing into and out of urban areas;
(iv) The infrastructure includes transportation, communications, and distribution networks; and
(v) Urban planning is also known as town planning, city planning and regional planning also known as rural planning etc. Urban planning guides orderly development in urban and suburban areas and is found worldwide. It is mainly concerned with the planning

of human settlements and communities. Besides, urban planning is also responsible for the planning and development of water use, urban agriculture, parks, resources and conserving areas having significance of natural environment.

Urban planners work in tandem with similar fields of architecture, landscape architecture, civil engineering and public administration to achieve strategic, policy and sustainability goals. Today urban planning is a separate and independent professional discipline. There is evidence of urban planning dating back to the Mesopotamian civilization, Indus Valley civilization, Egyptian civilization etc. The importance of the urban planner has been growing in the 21st century. This has happened because of a number of issues a modern society begins to face such as increased growth of population, change of climate and unsustainable development.

Guwahati City

Guwahati is a premier city not only of Assam; but also in the North East India. Guwahati lies between the banks of the Brahmaputra River and the foothills of the Shillong plateau. The city extends to LGB International Airport to the west and the Narengi Township to the east. It is gradually being extended to north Guwahati to the northern bank of the River Brahmaputra. The city is endowed with natural beauty. It is located strategically and has important bio-geographical features. The city is surrounded by 8 hills, 19 reserved forests and 5 major wetlands. There are about 75 villages in hills inhabited mainly by tribal people. The Guwahati Municipal Corporation (GMC) is the local government of the city. The administered area of GMC is 216 square kilometres. The Guwahati Metropolitan Development Authority (GMDA) is the planning and development body of greater Guwahati Metropolitan Area. In the North East India Guwahati is the largest city.

Brahmaputra River has been flowing through the middle of the city. Many ancient Hindu temples are in the city. Therefore, the city is also known as the 'City of Temples'. Guwahati has expanded horizontally and vertically. High-rise buildings have been growing fast in the city. Guwahati has also turned into a major hub of business such as shopping complexes, malls etc. Besides, Guwahati has also become an educational hub. There are also several super specialty hospitals in the city, such as the GNRC, the International Hospital, now known as the Apollo Hospital, Hayat Hospital and so on. Dispur is the capital of Assam and is a part of the Guwahati city.

Growth of Guwahati

Guwahati is the capital city of Assam and also the Gateway to North East India. It is expected that Guwahati will be the Gateway to South East Asia. Guwahati has grown in an unplanned manner for long. Initial effort to develop Guwahati in a planned manner was made in 1836 that is, during the British occupation of Assam. However, thereafter there was practically no effort to develop Guwahati in a planned and systematic manner for long. It was after the lapse of 129 years in 1965 a Master Plan for Guwahati was prepared. It is not known if there were efforts to implement that master plan.

In 1974 Guwahati was declared as a city. After Guwahati becomes a city, in 1987 Guwahati had another Master Plan. The 1965 Mater Plan and 1987 Master Plan did not have detailed plan for water supply and drainage and sewerage systems. Later on these two Master Plans were modified. One aspect of urban planning is inclusion of new areas for the city. The 1987 Master Plan included 262 sq kms. However, though Guwahati became a city in 1974, actual area remains 217 sq kms. Hence, people living in 45 sq kms (262-217) did not get any benefit of city. The modified Master Plan and zoning regulations for Guwahati expired on the 31st March, 2007. Hence, the Guwahati Metropolitan Development Authority (GMDA) prepared a Master Plan for Guwahati Metropolitan Area-2025. The present development is supposed to be on the basis of this Master Plan. This chapter highlights the problems and also suggests measures for mitigations for making Guwahati a better place for living.

Problems

Encroachment: The Government has made efforts to implement the Master Plan. Even then the development of Guwahati still continues to be unplanned. This is reflected in illegal and rampant encroachment of hilly land destroying the scenic beauty of Guwahati. Encroachment is not confined to hilly area only; it has spread to wetland and reserved forests.

Lack of Coordination: There is practically little coordination among the different agencies of the Central and State Governments for proving public utility services. For example, while laying of water supply pipes is done by the State Government agency, the telephone cables laying work is done by BSNL at two different times. This involved digging of public roads. Due to lack of coordination among the different agencies the digging of road is done as per their convenience. The agencies generally do not consider the convenience of common citizens. This creates problems for the citizens. Thus, unplanned growth of the city still continues creating problems for citizens.

Use of Footpaths: Footpaths meant for pedestrians are now mostly occupied by street vendors selling vegetable, fish, meat, milk, varieties of eatables and so on. Though there are occasional efforts to remove the street vendors the situation mostly remains unchanged. Using of footpaths by street vendors create three situations: (a) Pedestrians find it difficult to move freely and comfortably; (b) There is health hazard for those who eat at footpaths. These eating places are open to roadside dusts, and (c) The vendors do not properly clean the garbage they create making it difficult to keep the places clean.

Water Supply: In regard to water supply in the city, less than 50 per cent households only get water supply. There is severe scarcity of water in several localities of the city. As a result these households have to purchase water from private vendors at high price. In many localities water supply pipelines have been laid and water supply awareness programme was launched in 2013. However, even in January 2018 it is not known when the citizens will get supply water.

Street Light: There were no street lights except in a few privileged localities in the city. During the international sport events organised in Guwahati in many localities street lights were installed. It is not known if the street installation of street light is a temporary or a permanent measure.

Road Repair or Reconstruction: People demand for repair or reconstruction of roads because of apathy of the concerned department. Many city roads need repair only. Timely repair of roads can save lot of public money in reconstruction. This is yet to happen.

Traffic Control: In most of the roads, rickshaw pullers, handcart (*thela*) pullers, motor bikes and three wheelers etc. are freely allowed to move. This naturally creates problem of controlling traffic in a better way. As a result traffic control becomes a major problem in almost all the roads.

Movement of Motor-cycles: Motor-cycles are mostly used by younger people. They appear to be less responsible in their movements. At least 10 per cent youth overtake four wheelers by the left side of the vehicles. There are also youth who use footpath for overtaking four wheelers etc. for saving some time without thinking about the elderly people. Besides, many youth drive their two wheelers in a zigzag manner creating hazard for the citizens.

Frequent Accidents: There is hardly a day without accidents leading to death and disability of people. This is a tragic situation where families lose their near and dear ones, apart from spending huge amount of hard earned money. This happens because of high speed, driving vehicle and using mobile at the same time, not using helmets by two wheelers and seat belts by drivers. In addition there is laxity in enforcement of traffic rules by the concerned authority and not checking the licence of drivers.

Social Deprivation: People of several localities feel social deprivation. This happens because of lack of attention from the authorities in road repair or reconstruction, water supply, installation of street light etc.

Mitigation Measures

The following mitigation measures are proposed.

(i) In order to stop encroachment in hills, wetlands etc the circle offices should be made responsible in their respective circles. At least the circle offices can bring the matter to the notice of the competent authority so that appropriate and timely action can be taken. Generally speaking there are some individuals who encourage encroachment in government and forest land with knowledge of authority. Regular reporting to the competent authority and taking quick action for stopping encroachment will help Government. This will also save those who thought of taking a plot of land along with other encroachers.

(ii) There should be coordination and cooperation among different agencies who want to dig roads either for lying of water supply pipes or telephone cables or any other purpose and road should be repaired immediately when the work is over. People of the areas should also be informed about it.

(iii) Footpaths should be kept free for pedestrians only and not for street vendors. Street vendors should be given place in other areas. Besides, fish and meat should not be sold in open areas on the roadside.

(iv) Awareness programmes on water supply were started as far back as in 2013. But efforts should be made to complete the project to mitigate suffering of citizens. Till this can be done the GMC should supply water to those who cannot afford to purchase water from private agencies.

(v) Street lights installed in several areas of the city should be the permanent measure and should not be disturbed even after international sport events or any other national or international events.

(vi) Systematic efforts should be made to repair roads to avoid reconstruction and save public money. This should be done for all the localities.

(vii) In many areas, say, Nepali Mandir, Ganesh Mandir, Lalganesh and such other areas rickshaw should not be allowed to stay since magic, trekker city bus are easily available for transportation of passengers.

(viii) Traffic speed must be controlled in such a manner that there is steady flow of vehicles.

(ix) Zigzag driving of motor cycle should be fully stopped. This should be made a punishable offence. Similarly driving motorcycle on footpath should also be treated as a punishable offence.

(x) Stocking of building materials on the roadside in several places is a regular affair. This creates obstruction to vehicle movement and also to morning workers.

(xi) Government should give equal attention to each and every locality for removing the feeling social deprivation. At present this is visibly absent.

(xii) There should be zebra crossing for pedestrians to cross roads in appropriate places.

(xiii) Roadside parking of car and other vehicles should be in one side of the roads.

Conclusion

Thus, there are many problems. For every problem there are also measures for mitigation. The suggested measures are only a few of many solutions. These are not the only measures. It is hoped that the authority will take appropriate measures to minimize the problems of the city to make it a better place for living.

12

A Legal Study of Slum Dwellers within Shillong

Agglomeration in Context of Sustainable Development Goals

Daiahunlin Mawlong

Introduction

A slum is a heavily populated urban informal settlement characterised by substandard housing and squalor.[1] It differs in size and other characteristics from country to country. It is overcrowded, poorly built congested usually with inadequate infrastructure and lacks proper sanitary and safe drinking water facilities. We noticed in the present situation that the plight of the Scotland of the East has been deteriorating despite the best efforts of the Government. In every seminars and workshops urban planners are deeply concerned about the unplanned growth of towns and cities which, however, resulted into slums or informal settlements. Health issues arise when there is lack of proper sanitation and water facilities, which are unfit for human settlement. The main aim and objectives of all planning programmes focused more on the quality of life (QoL) of every individual. Globally it has been discussed about the need to develop the urban infrastructure so as to keep pace with the ever increasing demand.

Sustainable Development Goal 11 talks about making cities inclusive, safe, resilient and sustainable, as cities are hubs for ideas, commerce, culture, science, productivity, social development and much more. The future we want includes cities of opportunities for all with access to basic services, energy, housing, transportation and more. However, these are challenges that exist in maintaining the cities. Peace, justice, the rule of law and strong and effective institutions as seen in Sustainable Development Goal 16[2] are important for cities and countries. However, in the absence of good governance, strong local institutions, citizen participation and empowerment, it is easy for urban areas to descend rapidly into social, economic and political conflict and then chaos.

The United Nations Conference on Housing and Sustainable Urban Development also known as the Human Habitat III that took place in Quito, Ecuador, from 17th to 20th October, 2016[3] clearly mentioned the need to reduce social inequalities and strengthen drive towards sustainable urbanization in many developing countries and also the need to improve housing conditions and slum upgradation. Furthermore, as per the New Urban Agenda it was discussed about the need to have productive urban centres which are turned into vibrant neighbourhoods that are fully integrated and well managed by the urban management systems rather than remaining as vast islands of informality, social exclusion, poor housing and underdevelopment. It is expected that by 2050, two-thirds of the world's people approximately around 6 billion of them, will be living in cities. As cities are a major hub of national production and consumption, economic and social processes generate wealth and opportunity. However, they also create disease, crime, pollution and poverty[4]. Therefore, cities and towns in a developing country need to look into the sustainable requirements of basic human needs such as decent housing, water and energy supply, sanitation system, education and health care services. Hence, the eradication of poverty, exclusion and inequality is considered very important in making human settlement more liveable and sustainable.

Meghalaya with an estimated population of about 32 lakh as on 2016, it is observed that half of the population migrated to the urban centres and live in an informal settlement. As we can see that parts of the Shillong Urban Agglomeration (SUA) are faced with injustice and dysfunction. Rapid increase of slums or informal settlements has caused severe threats to environment as the living conditions in slums are unhygienic with deplorable conditions and contrary to the norms of planned urban growth. People living in slums are those who are deprived and neglected from their fundamental needs. However, Article 21 of the Constitution of India states that "No person shall be deprived of his life or personal liberty except according to the procedure established by law." *The court in the case of Rural Litigation and Entitlement Kendra versus State of Uttar Pradesh*[5] gave the first indication of the right to wholesome environment. The right to life under Article 21 of the Constitution has been held to include right to healthy environment and right to good environment.

The State of Meghalaya recently witnessed a rapid increase of urban growth and the reasons are mostly due to the migration of people from rural to urban areas in search of a better future. However, people also migrated from Assam, Bangladesh, Nepal, West Bengal and from Tibet. These migrants move into the cities along with their families, culture and their tradition. These groups form their own communities and try to gain access to cities' socio-economic systems. It is observed that most of the migrants live in areas where house rents are less expensive or stay on the land of private individuals who also utilize these people for their personal gain and cheap labour. Parts of the SUA have become a home to extreme deprivation and environmental degradation as many areas are the notified slum areas.

From the records of Shillong Municipal Board, Meghalaya has a total of nineteen slums which are notified and four slums are indentified. Most of these slums locate in the heart of the city like Laimukhrah, Laban, Dhanketi-Malki, Police Bazar etc. Dr. Jemino Mawthoh, the sitting legislator[6] expressed his concern about the unplanned growth in urban centres and if there are no checks and balances the State capital will soon be tagged as one of the North-East slums, which will eventually lead to degradation of environmental quality and sustainable development.

Section 10 of the Meghalaya Slum Areas (Improvement and Clearance) Act, 1973 envisages areas as slums or settlements which are unfit for human habitation when characterised by dilapidation, overcrowding, faulty arrangement and design of buildings, narrowness or faulty arrangement of streets, lack of ventilation, lack of sanitation facilities which are detrimental to safety, health or morals of the people. However, we see Shillong city is struggling to accommodate large population with less affluent people residing in slums and squatter settlements which caused multi-dimensional challenges for the purpose urban development. During the study, 300 respondents were interviewed from six notified slum areas located in the heart of the Shillong City, viz. like Laban, Nongmynsong, Malki-Dhanketi, Laimukhrah, Mawprem and Polo. One common thing found, is that in these six slums all non-tribals are allowed to settle down and work in any part of the SUA provided they have proper documents. It shows that 20.4 per cent belong to the general class whereas 15 per cent belong to the Scheduled Caste, 9.2 per cent belong to the OBC and 55.4 per cent belong to the Scheduled Tribe. However, about 60 per cent of them migrated to Shillong urban centres, 40 per cent migrated from places like Nepal, Bangladesh, Tibet, West Bengal, Assam and from the neighbouring State of Meghalaya. Most of these people work in the informal sectors like hotels, restaurants, shops or as domestic helpers etc. which in many cases are temporary jobs. Hence, they cannot afford to stay in expensive places or rented houses but rather stay in old shack houses where the rents are not expensive and the living conditions are unhygienic and contrary to the norms of planning legislation. However, the State under Section 11[7] has the power to improve any building and land which are unfit for human habitation, hence the state needs to make proper urban planning for the benefit of local people, their QoL and to improve the environment. In Shillong, it is observed that many landed properties are owned by private individuals which becomes very difficult for the government to intrude. However, the objectives of various schemes meant for slum dwellers are:

1. To provide basic amenities, upliftment of the QoL of the urban poor.
2. To create a slum free India the scheme Rajiv Awas Yojana (RAY) was launched in which 50 per cent of the cost of provision of basic civic and social infrastructure and amenties and housing including rental housing for redevelopment would be borne by the centre.
3. To provide the integrated housing under the slum development programme through the scheme Jawaharlal Nehru National Urban Renewal Mission (JNNURM).
4. To promote cities and give a decent QoL to its citizens with a clean and sustainable development through the Smart City Mission of the Ministry of Urban Development.
5. To provide rehabilitation of slum dwellers and to promote affordable housing through the housing-for-all scheme.

Though schemes are available to the people but in order to achieve the goals of adequate shelter and sustainable human settlement, there is a need to develop a comprehensive approach and innovative strategies. Slum settlements have been in existence for a long time, individuals other than the land owners, build their houses in the land which do not belong to them with or without the consent of the landowners. These people live in slums because of internal reasons such as lack of savings and other financial assets and low income. Today, human settlement is mainly a discussion of urban issues since population is growing at a rapid speed which will bring about expansion of cities.

Conclusion

Conditions of people living in the informal settlement or slum areas anywhere in the world would not be considered good. It is more or less same when it comes to the Shillong Urban Agglomeration (SUA). The target for 2030 is to ensure access to safe and affordable housing with better human settlement. But the question is : can we do it? No, it cannot without proper planning and effective implementation of law, whereas Yes, we can do it if there is proper administration and implementation of law. Slum dwellers; also have the right to life as enshrined under Article 21 of the Constitution of India and right to life means the right to live with human dignity and not just mere animal existence. They have the right to access to all the basic amenities. Slum dwellers in municipal slum clearance areas live in a very difficult condition. They fear the constant threat of having their homes bulldozed. Hence, there is a need to upgrade the slum areas and to improve access to municipal basic services and physical infrastructure to create positive social and economic changes in the city. The impact of urbanization on the law and the legal system has not yet received proper attention on an intensive scale. However, the need for making special provisions in the legal system regarding informal settlement is an important matter which requires immediate attention.

Therefore, in order to upgrade the slum areas in Shillong proper planning and legislations are a matter of necessity. Thus, town planning laws have to be looked as a means to an end and not an end itself. Upliftment of slum and informal settlement becomes part of towns or cities broader urban vision to enact the right to adequate housing and living standards for all by focusing on the role of housing at the centre of quality of life and thus a policy action. However, the policy makers need to be extra careful in managing urban growth like infrastructure, investments and urban land use system as once it is done it is very hard to undo. As a matter of fact without proper planning, management and legislations slums may expand and cities may fail to generate employment necessary to improve livelihoods for betterment of human settlement.

To achieve the goals of sustainable development, participation of local government is an effective and powerful tool to mobilize low income communities. Transformation with a better future is what the entire nation wants but with effective implementation of rules and regulations.

NOTES

1. Wikipedia, Slums. Available at: https://en.wikipedia.org/wiki/Slum_housing.
2. United Nations, Sustainable Development Goals. Available at: www.un.org/sustainabledevelopment/sustainable-development-goals.
3. UN Habitat III, United Nations Sustainable Development, 2017. Available at www.un.org/sustainabledevelopment/habitat3.
4. United Nations, Human Settlement, Available at: http://www.un.org/en/sections/issues-depth/human-settlements/index.html
5. AIR 1985 SC 652.
6. The Meghalaya Times, *Without proper intervention, Shillong heading towards NE 'slum' tag.* April 9, 2017.
7. The Meghalaya Slums Areas (Improvement and Clearance) 1973 Act.

13
Problems of Urban Growth and Its Environmental Consequences

Special Reference to Shillong City

Donna Rica Diengdoh

Introduction

Urbanization may be defined as a process of transformation of population, production processes and environment of an essentially rural settlement into urban settlement where people participate more in non-agricultural activities. It also indicates an enormous increase in population size and covers the movement of people permanently or temporarily from village to city. It also includes increase in the number and extent of cities; it symbolizes the movement of people from rural to urban centres. As more and more people, leaves their villages and farms to live in cities, urban growth results. Urbanization occurs naturally from individual and corporate efforts to reduce time and expense in commuting and transportation while improving opportunities for jobs, education, housing and transportation. People move to cities to seek economic opportunities since people in rural areas find it very difficult to improve their standard of living, most of the villagers are dependent on unpredictable environmental conditions and in times of drought, flood or pestilence, survival becomes extremely problematic.

Due to uncontrolled urbanization in India, environmental degradation has been occurring rapidly and causing many problems like land insecurity, worsening water quality and inadequate drinking water supply, excessive water pollution, noise pollution, irregular electric supply, air pollution, traffic congestions and the problems of waste disposal. Major environmental problems are the results of continuation and sharpening of the existing problems that currently do not receive enough political attention. The problems are not necessarily noticed in many countries or nothing has been done even if the situation has been detected. The most emerging issues are fresh water scarcity, deforestation and fresh water pollution and population growth. These problems are very much complex and their interactions are to be defined. It is very important to examine the problems through the socio-economic-cultural system. Even the interconnection of environmental problems is now better known we still lack information on how the issues are linked, on what degree they interact and what are the most effective measures. One problem is to integrate land and water use planning to provide food and water security (UNEP 1999).

This chapter emphasizes on the effect of urban growth on environmental consequences mainly climate, land and water resources. A case study of urbanization in Shillong city has been carried out leading to the conclusions on the existing causes of damage to the environment due to urbanization and preventive measures to keep a check on them. Although it is impossible to restrict urbanization, it has to be ensured that urbanization proceeds the right path causing minimum impact on the environment.

Objectives

1. To study the problem of Shillong city due to population growth.
2. To create awareness of water contamination, noise pollution and problem of waste disposal.

Methodology

To achieve the aforesaid objectives, secondary sources and case study have been used to collect the necessary data and information.

Shillong as an Urban Centre

The urban growth of Shillong can be traced back to the period of 1863-64 when the British shifted their headquarters of Khasi and Jaintia Hills from Cherrapunjee to Shillong (Pakem, 1984). It was from that year that Shillong became the administrative headquarters for the Khasi and Jaintia Hills. Hence Shillong became the administrative centre for the British Raj and has till date preserved its characteristics of an administrative centre essentially being service-oriented. The British felt the need to shift their headquarters from Cherrapunjee to a better centrally located area for adequate water supply and more pleasant weather conditions. Consequently, a committee of enquiry was appointed for the purpose which comprised Colonel Richardson the commanding officer of the British troops who stationed at Cherrapunjee and B.W.D. Morton the then Deputy Commissioner of the United Khasi and Jaintia Hills (Syiemlieh, 1989). The team after studying the surrounding areas like Sohrarim, Mairang, Laitlyngkot and Nongkrem ultimately selected a large open space towards the North-East of Shillong peak as their future headquarters. But it was found that the area did not have sufficient water supply in all seasons of the year, thus such a location was not ideal for sustaining a larger population. Finally, it was decided that the best location would be the northern slopes of Shillong range and the plateau of Iewduh which is the present market centre of Shillong and is now the heart of the city. Hence, it is seen that the British administration gave due weightage to the water supply besides other factors before setting up the station here. Accordingly, on the 8th December, 1863, the British administration signed an agreement with the Syiem of Mylliem and the Syiem of Khyrim (Syiemlieh, 1989).In the year 1866 the then Lieutenant Governor General of Bengal Sir John Peter Grant sanctioned the transfer of the Deputy Commissioner's establishment from Cherrapunjee to Shillong. Thus, on the 20th March, 1874 Shillong was declared as the capital of the Undivided Assam Province that had a population of about 1363 persons (Choudhury, 1998).

As the town grew bigger the British gave due importance to the solid waste management, though the population size was negligible and waste generated was small compared to the present size. Hence in 1878 the township of Shillong came under the Municipal Act by which the town affairs including water supply and solid waste disposal of Shillong by the British were made available (Shullai, 1998). In view of the small population size, the problem of solid waste was not so large in magnitude as of today. With the expansion of the town, it was necessary to acquire more land; consequently, the British Government with other agreements took on perpetual lease from the Syiem of Mylliem, those portions which are now known as European Ward, consisting of Police Bazar, Jail Road and the present cantonment area (Chowdhury, 1998). The Lachumiere Hill was added to the township in 1895 (Chowdhury, 1998). In 1901 the total population of the township was 9621 (Census, 1981). The Shillong Municipality was established in 1910 and the new areas such as Laitumkhrah, Hopkinson Estate, Malki and Mawprem were included under the Municipal boundary just after two years. In 19011, the Shillong's population was 13639 (Census, 1981) showing a growth of 4018 and an increase of 41.76 per cent. The population growth of Shillong before India's Independence is shown in Table 13.1.

Table 13.1: Population Growth of Shillong Before India's Independence (1901-1941)

Year	Population	Increase	Percentage Increase	Remarks
1901	9621			Shillong Municipal Area
1911	13639	4018	41.76	
1921	17203	3564	26.13	
1931	23536	9333	54.25	
1941	38192	11656	43.93	

Source: Census of India, 1981 Provisional Population Total Meghalaya, Series-14.

Within the period of 40 years the population of the Shillong Municipality increased threefold. Shillong emerged not only as an important administrative centre of the British India but also as an important educational and commercial centre. Shillong hill station supports more than 60 per cent of the urban population of the state. Rugged terrains and hilly topography are the constraints of development. A large number of primary streams dominate the landscape and this became the main source of water to the population living here. Under the impact of urbanization, these streams are often the recipients of effluents of the growing population of the city. The streams habitually disappear from the surface due to land reclamation and channelization which leads to environmental problems. Shillong urban centre is growing at a much faster rate which acts as a detrimental to the environment. The city totally lacks of organized solid waste disposal system. In the absence of proper solid waste disposal the effluents generated by this growing population are dumped into streams, streets and road side drains of the localities.

Population Growth

According to 2001, the total population of the State of Meghalaya was 23.06 lakh with an average density of 126 persons per square kms and the level of urbanization is19.36 per cent. The population of the Shillong municipality in 2001 was 132876 persons. The jurisdictional area of Shillong Municipal Board (SMB) which is 10.36 sq kms contains a population of about 1.33 lakh with a floating population of about 40,000 as shown in Table 13.2. Growth of population has increased substantially since the inception of the state recording 18.06 per cent in 1971-1981, 18.57 per cent in 1981-1991, 19.58 per cent in 1991-2001 and 20.07 per cent during 2001-2011. However, the decadal growth rate has gone down to 31.01 per cent in 2001-2011 from 37.59 per cent in 1991-2001 and 37.10 per cent in 1981-1991 in spite of the addition of six more urban localities. As per the 2011 Census, the Shillong Municipal records a density of 13,291 persons per sq km. which is relatively high. Similarly, other constituent units of Shillong urban areas such as Nongthymmai, Cantonment area, Mawlai, Pynthorumkhrah and Madanriting have shown a high increase in population density though they are yet to reach the saturation limit. Growth of population is always considered as a progress of civilization. The growth of township is considered as the growth of the economy. Shillong city had experienced an expansion of residential areas in Laitumkhrah, Laban, Malki, Nongthymmai, Pynthorumkhrah and Nongmynsong. But unplanned development has turned the Shillong city into a concrete jungle. Nongthymmai legislators, Dr. J. Mawthoh (UDP) pointed out on the floor of the August House that random urbanization in Meghalaya, particularly in the State capital of Shillong remained unchecked which led to the growth of slums.

Table 13.2: Population of Shillong Municipality (1901-2011)

Year	Population of Shillong Mucipality
1901	9621
1911	13639
1921	17203
1931	26536
1941	38192
1951	58512
1961	72438
1971	87659
1981	109244
1991	131719
2001	132876
2011	143229

Source: Census of India, Meghalaya Series No. 18, 2011.

Water Pollution

Water quality of our urban water supplies is so important. Majority of the population live in or near the Shillong city which certainly have an impact on the local water supply. Growing population, increased economic activity has resulted in an increased water demand. More and more people are moving into the city especially near the commercial and shopping areas of Iewduh and Police Bazar. Not only land is disturbed when development occurs but the stress on the water resources of the region has increased to supply everyone with water. Construction works in the city demands more water where urbanites are facing shortage of water supply. As the city grew, human activities harm the quality of the local water resources. Many sewer lines are not constructed in a proper manner and most of the houses connected their sewer lines to the adjacent streams to take advantage of the continuous and gradual slopes of stream valley. Blockages, inadequate carrying capacity, leaking pipes often leads to sewage overflows in nearby streams and receiving large amounts of contaminants released from the domestic sewage. This leads to waterborne pathogens which are disease-causing bacteria, viruses and protozoans that are transmitted to people when they consume untreated or inadequately treated water thereby causing severe health problems and life-threatening to the very young and very old persons and to those with damaged immune systems. Therefore, rapid uncontrolled urbanization changed the patterns of consumption and caused a severe misuse of water resources.

Air Pollution

In every state, the State Pollution Control Board informs the citizens about the air quality everyday. Not so in Meghalaya where every information must be literally wrung out of government departments. Meghalaya had registered as the state with the highest density of cars much before anyone could discuss vehicular pollution. Presently, the numbers of vehicles have increased almost a hundred-fold thereby thickening the air with suspended particulate matters. Day-by-day, the fresh air is getting polluted in the city because of the mixing of particulates, biological molecules and other harmful materials. Such polluted air causes health problems, diseases and death. Air pollution is one of the most environmental issues which require solution through concerted efforts of all.

The release of air pollutants in heavy concentrations such as smog, particulates, solid materials etc. gets settled over the city thereby causing air pollution and health hazards to the people. The releases of gaseous pollutants from burning fuel of motor vehicles, burning of garbage etc. contributes to air pollution. Such polluted air never remains at one place but spreads to the whole environment and affects the lives of the people. Most of the air pollution is caused by the automobiles, transport means, cigarettes, paints and batteries as they contain lead and other toxic substances which further aggravate the environmental problem. The release of several harmful gases or dangerous elements from such sources pollutes the whole atmosphere and damages the plants, animals and human beings in many direct and indirect ways.

Noise Pollution

The unwanted sound generated by many sources in our surroundings is commonly known as noise. Noise pollution is one of the big problems in the city as it affects the human lives in many ways. Noise pollution is considered as the environmental pollution due to the excess level of noise emitted by many sources. Excessive noise is harmful to health and causes imbalance to human and animal life. Noise pollution is caused by sources like household machines, household gadgets, road traffic, construction activities, industrial units, loud music, plumbing, generators etc. and noise from consumer products like household equipments, kitchen appliances, vacuum cleaners, washing machines, mixers, pressure cookers, televisions, dryers etc. Unwanted sound generally brings about nuisance to the daily routine activities like sleep at night, conversation, hearing activity etc. Common problems caused by noise pollution are stress-related illness, anxiety, communication problems, speech interferences, sleep disruption, fatigue, headache, nervousness, weakness etc. Continuous exposure to high-level sound causes permanent damage to the eardrum. Poor urban planning such as congested houses also induces noise pollution as members of large families in small spaces produce much unwanted sound. New generation people play music in full volume and dance till late night causes lot of physical and mental disturbances to their neighbours. Such high level of noise slowly affects the health of human beings and as such noise pollution is a dangerous gift of modern industrialized and urbanized societies.

Problems of Waste Disposal

The average resident produces high amount of garbage everyday that is buried down in landfills and litters lands. Now-a-days, people face no more critical trouble than the need to save the environment, mainly in urban areas where solid wastes are uselessly dumped. It has been observed that cities have no controlled structure of garbage disposal. Rubbish growth in Shillong city has been a big problem. Landfills have always been regarded as sources of illnesses and unpleasant smells. The harmful wastes such as paints, chemicals, petrol, diesel, batteries and other toxic chemicals spread on the ground and get into the water pipes which pollute the quality of drinking water. There are also man-made problems as people themselves created the disasters which led to environmental pollution. Thus, man is responsible for his harmful actions and the consequences that he breeds in the society. Environmental concerns have made people more aware of their environmental footprints or the kind of waste they leave during their existence. During the interviews with the members of the civil society organizations and the academicians they revealed that the solid waste management falls among the most poorly rendered services as the systems applied are unscientific and inefficient. There is no specified landfill site and wastes are dumped at the peripheries of the low-lying areas. Heaps of untreated wastes became the root cause for several physical and health hazards. Thus the problems include not only dumping of solid waste but also the mode of transport used and the time of dumping. Mostly uncovered vehicles are used to transport the solid waste which resulted in infrequent droppings besides the absence of a fixed time for dumping. During rainy season, such heaps of environmentally hazardous waste become a cause of water borne diseases. The problem of solid waste management is crucial for Shillong city with no proper storing of waste in a scientifically segregated way. As humanity develops new technology and equipments the level of waste increases everyday and as such public representatives should seriously shoulder their collective responsibility to resolve the issue of garbage disposal.

Preventive Measures

There are a number of measures that can be applied to curb the environmental issues caused by an unplanned city such as air pollution, noise pollution, solid waste and population growth and these are:

1. **Creation of awareness**: We need to raise public awareness and everyone should be conscious of how serious the air became unsafe because the air is being polluted mostly through the activities of irresponsible human beings. Awareness through mass media, seminars, symposia, workshops etc. should be created among the urbanites to propagate the pollution-free measures and to disseminate the information about the impending dangers of air pollution.
2. **Reduction of vehicle-related air pollution:** Air pollution can be cut down by taking fewer trips by cars and commute frequently by public transport. Similarly, to ensure that vehicles comply with the pollution control norms prescribed by the government authorities, regular checking is mandatory.

3. **Prevention of water pollutants:** The pollutants which directly or indirectly discharge into rivers, lakes, streams, canals, etc which cause harmful effects on human beings by transmitting water-borne diseases should be prevented under Section 3 of the Prevention and Control of Pollution Act, 1974.
4. **Promotion of healthy environment in the City**: Solid waste from households and industries pollute the land directly. These include broken glasses, waste papers, rags, plastics, metal scraps, splinters, rinds of fruits and vegetables etc. eventually settle on land and pollute the soils. Solid waste may block the water flows in drain sand stagnate there and then becomes the breeding places for mosquitoes. Dogs, rats, flies, mosquitoes and other creatures which gather on the heaps of dumped solid waste are the carriers of various diseases. Moreover, such heaps of solid waste emit foul smell to the inhabitants of the city. Awareness should be generated among the public and taking of preventive measures for promotion a healthy environment in the city is expedient.

Conclusion

Major environmental problems are the results of continuation and sharpening of the existing problems that currently do not receive any political attention. Though the problems are noticed but no sustainable measures are applied. The most emerging issues are fresh water scarcity, water pollution, deforestation and population growth. It is very important to examine these problems through socio-economic and cultural system and to link these issues with the most effective measures. In Meghalaya, be it in the Municipality Board or in the Meghalaya Urban Development Authority (MUDA); the measures taken by town planners to beautify the city, streamline the development work to meet the demand of the burgeoning city are yet to gain ground. Most of the localities are developing at a very fast pace, buildings constructed for commercial or residential purposes including hostels are mushrooming in an unplanned manner and are cropping up at every corner. But the city lacks the basic necessities like robust solid waste management system, proper footpaths, streetlights, health care facilities and most importantly the acute shortage of water supply to urban dwellers.

REFERENCES

Census of India (1981): Population Total Meghalaya Series 14.

Chowdhury, J.N. (1998): *The Khasi Canvas*. Jetraj Offset, Calcutta, p. 253.

Pakem, B. (1984): Shillong 1971-81 NECSSR Research. *Research India*, Calcutta pp. 1-10.

Shullai L.G. (1998). *Ka Shillong Naduh Ka Snem 1863 Part I & Part II*, pp. 4-5.

Syiemlieh, D.R. (1989): Our City. *Paper Presented at the 10th Annual Conference of NEIHA*. NEHU, Shillong. pp. 9-22.

14

Spatio-Temporal Dynamic Pattern of Urban Centres, Size Distribution and Urban Population Growth in Assam

Kiran Sharma

Introduction

Urbanization is a worldwide phenomenon and by 2050, 66 per cent of the world's population is projected to be urban. Africa and Asia are urbanizing faster than other regions and are projected to become 56 and 64 per cent urban respectively by 2050 (UN, 2014). The 'level of urbanization' refers to the ratio of 'urban' population to total population and the change, if any, over time (Khawas, 2005). "Urbanization is the process by which an increasing proportion of the country's population starts residing in urban areas" (Jha, 2006). In India it is exceptionally dynamic, where unprecedented urban growth rates have occurred over the last 3 decades or so. During the last 50 years the population of India is 1.2 billion which is more than doubled and the urban population 377 million has grown nearly five times (Census, 2011). Population data and socio-economic data have a direct relationship with urban growth. The study of urban growth by size class of towns help us to understand the stages of urban development in a country and the differential growth rates shows the extent of rural to urban migration (Bhagat, 2005). The unprecedented population growth with unplanned developmental activities in India has resulted in the lack of infrastructure facilities (Sudhira *et al.*, 2004) associated with health risks including air pollution, occupational hazards, traffic injury and risks caused by dietary and social changes (Li *et al.*, 2012) and other serious negative effects (Chadchan & Shankar, 2012). Urbanization or the increase in the urban population is determined by three phenomena: natural growth, rural-urban migration and reclassification of areas from rural to urban (Buhaug & Urdal, 2012). Rural-to-urban migration is one of the factors which increased population pressure in town ensuing scarcity of renewable resources like croplands, forests and freshwater (Homer-Dixon, 1999). Environmental degradation including desertification, prolonged droughts and soil salinization are other factors that might deteriorate agricultural livelihoods and push people to the cities (Grimm *et al.*, 2008; Lobell *et al.*, 2011; UK Government Office for Science, 2011, Buhaug & Urdal, 2012). The emerging pattern of urbanization in India is not simply a rural to urban transfer of labour and populations due to the large wage gap (Chauvin *et al.*, 2016), but a complex process of changes in the characteristics of human settlements (Bhagat, 2011a; 2011b; World Bank, 2013; Bhagat, 2014). Generally, urban areas have better access to electricity, drinking water, sanitation and clean fuel compared to rural areas (Mitra & Mehta, 2011, Bhagat, 2017).

Cities in the North-Eastern Hills of India have not emerged as a result of planned intervention; rather they exist as an expanded version of trade centres (Khawas, 2005). The North East is a late comer to development. Geographically, North-East India has never been an easy terrain to reconnoitre and is geo-politically a sequestered region (Nath, 2013). The location map of Assam is shown in Figure 14.1. There were only 12 urban centres in Assam in 1901 and by 1961 the number increased to 53. After the declaration of Guwahati as the capital of Assam in 1972 major structural change took place. The oldest towns to be established by the British are Goalpara, Barpeta, Nowgaon, Jorhat, Dibrugarh, Sibsagar, Golaghat, Silchar and Karimganj. The trauma of partition, political evolution and reorganization of Assam along the present state boundaries and the continuing internal adjustments to achieve decentralized sub-state structures such as autonomous councils punctuated with protest movements and insurgencies have interrupted progress (High level Commission Report, 1997). In the fifteenth census of India, it registered 14 per cent of total population living in urban area in Assam which is much lower than the national average of 31.6 per cent and also lowest among the North Eastern Region States (18.26%). Even after sixty nine years of Independence the level of urbanization in Assam has reached the bottom third of all the States. The present chapter aims at getting an overview of trend of urbanization, spatial organization and hierarchy of urban centres in the state of Assam.

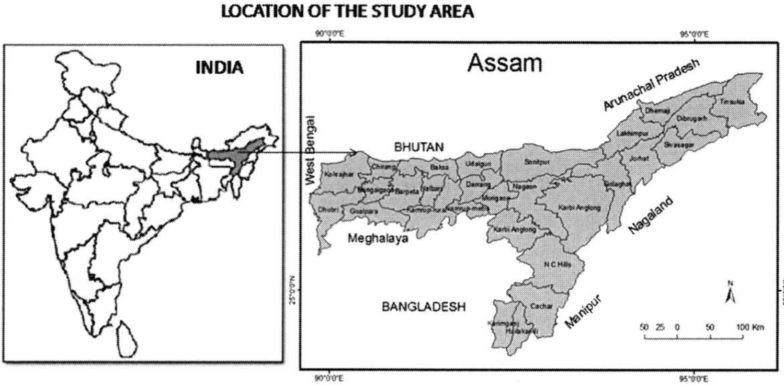

Figure 14.1: Location Map of the Study Area

Database and Methodology

Much of the data required for this study are obtained from secondary sources particularly the analysis is made on the basis of information and data collected from different Census of India publications for the period 1971-2011. The formula used are:

Chi-square Analysis (Mahmood, 2008).

$$\chi^2 \sum_{i=1}^{n} \left[\frac{(Oi - Ei)^2}{Ei}\right] \tag{14.1}$$

where *Oi* and *Ei* are the observed and estimated frequencies respectively of the ith class. The shape of the distribution will vary with (n = 1) which is known as the degree of freedom and the Nearest Neighbour Analysis (Mahmood, 2008) is:

$$R = \frac{\bar{D}_o}{D_r} = \frac{\bar{D}_o}{\frac{1}{2\sqrt{\frac{N}{A}}}} = 2\bar{D}_0\sqrt{\frac{N}{A}} \tag{14.2}$$

where N is the number of urban centres and A is the area of the place. The nearest neighbour index R is the ratio of the actual mean distance between the nearest neighbour points in a given area Do to the mean expected distance of random distribution of the same number of points in the same area. This ratio R ranges from 0 when there is maximum aggregation of the entire urban centre at one location, through 1 which represents a random distribution, up to 2.15 which represents an even distribution. A map showing the spatial distribution of urban centres in Assam as per 2011 census is given in Figure 14.2.

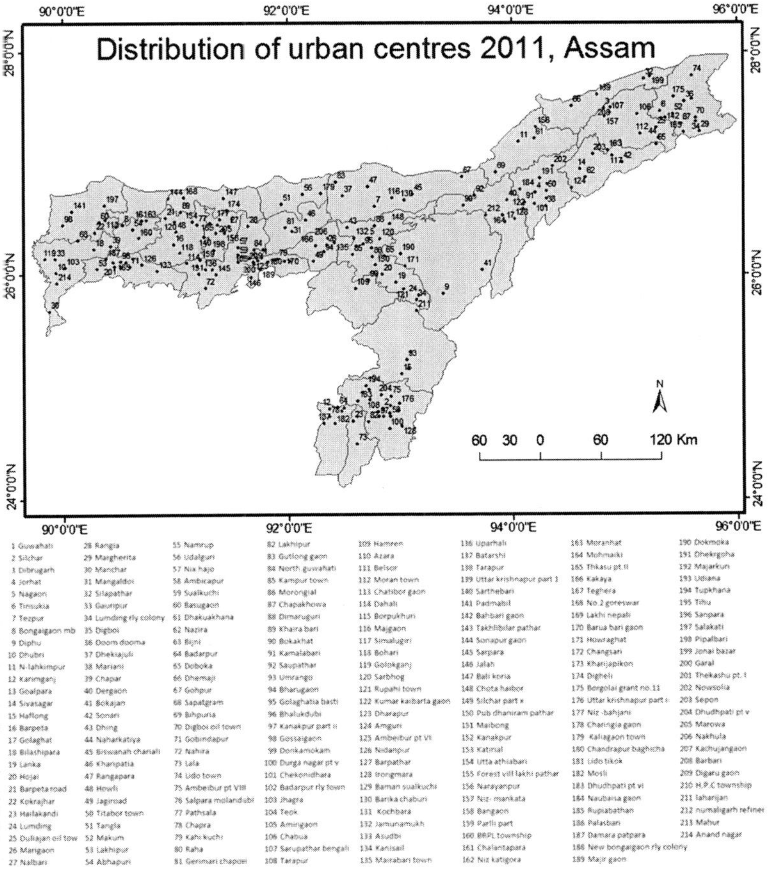

Figure 14.2: Spatial Distribution of Urban Centres in Assam, 2011.

Trends and Patterns of Urbanization

During 1901-2011, the urban population in the state has increased by about 57 times while the number of urban centres has increased by 17 times only. However, over the years there has been an increasing trend towards urbanization and which gained momentum particularly in the post-independence era (Table 14.1). The share of urban population to total population of Assam in 1951 was only 4.29 per cent which has increased to 12.72 per cent in 2001 and 14.10 per cent in 2011 Census.

Table 14.1: Urbanization Trend in Assam (1901-2011)

Census Year	No. of Urban Centres	Urban population	Percentage of Urban population to the total population	National urban population (percentage of total)	Decadal Growth Rate of Urban population (%)	Annual exponential growth rate (%)
1901	12	77,074	2.34	10.84	–	–
1911	14	92,916	2.41	10.29	20.5	1.87
1921	22	1,27,107	2.74	11.18	36.80	3.13
1931	22	1,62,166	2.92	11.99	27.58	2.43
1941	24	2,08,067	3.11	13.86	28.30	2.5
1951	24	3,44,831	4.29	17.29	65.73	5.05
1961	53	7,81,288	7.21	17.97	126.57	8.17
1971	72	12,89,222	8.82	19.91	65.01	5.0
1991	93	24,87,795	11.10	25.71	92.97*	3.28
2001	125	34,39,240	12.72	27.71	36.24	3.23
2011	214	43,88,756	14.10	31.61	27.60	2.43

Note: * Growth rate during 1971-1991 as there was no Census in Assam in 1981.
Source: Census of India, 2001; General Population Tables, Assam, Census of India, 2011, Provisional Population Totals, Vol. 2, Assam.

The annual exponential growth rate for Assam was highest in 1961 with 8.82 per cent. In the case of India the pattern has been somewhat regular it had the peak during 1980s (Census, 2011). In fact at the time of partition a large volume of migrants from within and outside the country has settled in the state. There has been again the pressure of rural to urban migration within the state due to the development initiatives taken under different five year plans, decentralization of administration and slow process of economic diversification and industrialization (Bhagawati *et al.*, 2007) and due to the effect of shift of Assam's capital from Shillong to Guwahati in 1971. The primate city Guwahati with an increasing urban population has experienced the faster urban growth primarily due to migration from infrastructure deficient areas which led to the unregulated expansion of the urban informal sector (MoDONER & ADB, 2006). The trend and growth rate of urban population in Assam for 110 years (1901-2011) is given in Figure 14.3.

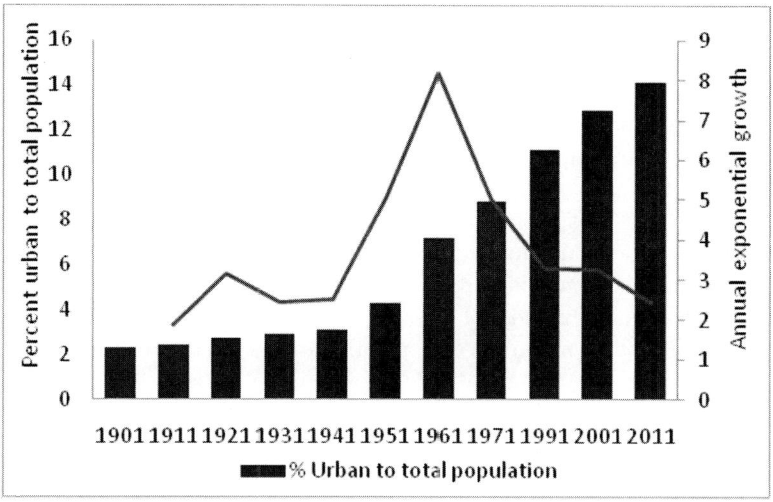

Figure 14.3: Percentage and Growth Rate of Urban Population (1901-2011)
Source: Census of India, 2001 and 2011, Provisional Population Totals, Vol. 2, Assam.

Growths in urban centre are apparent from Table 14.1. The Statutory Towns (STs) increased from 80 in 2001 to 88 in 2011 Census. However, the Census Towns (CTs) have tremendously increased from 45 in 2001 Census to 126 in 2011 Census showing an increase of about 180 per cent. On the other hand, the total of both STs and CTs shows an increase of over 70 per cent. The districts which register a rise of STs in 2011 Census are Nagaon, Lakhimpur, Tinsukia, Sibsagar and Jorhat whereas the rise of CTs is almost in all the districts. The districts recorded with no CT are Lakhimpur and Dima Hasao. The variation in growth rates of STs and CTs raises a potential conflict, whether the towns actually provide goods facilities and services or they simply fulfil the criteria of township. The growth of unplanned towns and cities in Assam severely demands for basic services and infrastructural development (Deka & Devi, 2017).

Unevenness of the distribution was another common phenomenon of India's population in the geographical studies (Chandna, 2002). To study the distribution pattern of urban centres in Assam, a null hypothesis assumed that a number of urban centres in five regions i.e. upper Assam, middle Assam, lower Assam, Barak valley and hills tend to be equally distributed. To test the assumption made, the chi-square values are calculated for the three census years 1971, 1991 and 2011 which are 17.14, 14.14 and 41.88 respectively. At degree of freedom 4, the tabulated value of chi-square at 1 per cent level of significance is 13.28 which is much less than the calculated value. Thus, the null hypothesis is rejected and the distribution of urban centres in Assam for the last three decades is found to be uneven. The uneven urbanization suggests a high potential for a more balanced pattern of urbanization in future. Table 14.2 indicates the spatial distribution pattern of urban centres in all the regions of Assam from 1971 to 2011 which is found to be approaching towards cluster except for NC Hills and middle Assam region in 1971 which is found to be slightly approaching towards random. Variation in distribution is due to the low urbanization in hilly region with inaccessible terrains, less fertile lands for agriculture and low infrastructural development which create all possibilities for migration of population from rural to urban for better opportunities.

Table 14.2: Nearest Neighbour Analysis of Distribution Pattern of Urban Centres in Assam (1971-2011)

Region	R, 1971	R, 1991	R, 2011
1. Upper Assam	0.42	0.49	0.65
2. Middle Assam	0.90	0.55	0.36
3. Lower Assam	0.36	0.52	0.43
4. Barak Valley	0.31	0.45	0.44
5. Hills	0.96	0.40	0.40
6. Assam	0.42	0.49	0.46

A Class Size Analysis

The study of hierarchy of towns gives a clear idea about the functional complexity of towns. The higher the level of hierarchy of a town, the higher is its functional complexity and the reverse is equally true (Singh, 2006; Manta *et al.*, 2013). The Census of India categorizes the urban centres into six groups on the basis of the population size as shown in Figure 14.4.

An analysis of the distribution of urban population across size categories reveals that the process of urbanization in Assam has been large city oriented. This is manifested in a high percentage of urban population being concentrated in class I cities which has gone up systematically over the decades in the last century and which can lead to serious infrastructure deficiencies in the urban development pace. Guwahati has maintained its dominance and lead as the prominent town over the other towns of the region. A number of lower order towns has graduated to class I category, the process of rural settlements acquiring urban characteristics has been weak. The foregoing analysis gives a clear understanding about the state having a wide variation in urban population, a close relation with the

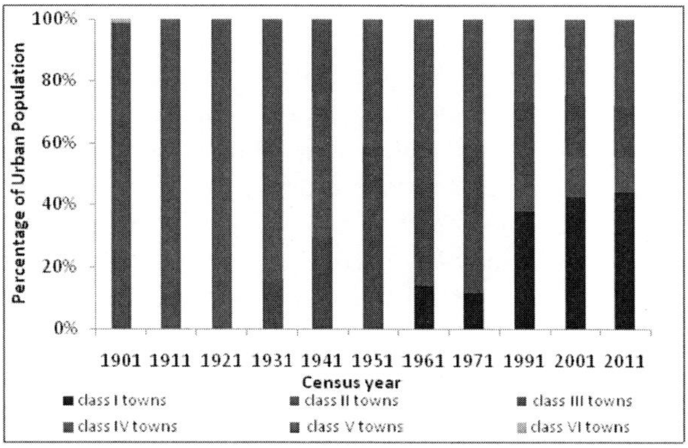

Figure 14.4: Proportion of Urban Population in Different Size Categories
Source: Census of India 2001 and 2011, Provisional Population Totals, Vol. 2, Assam.

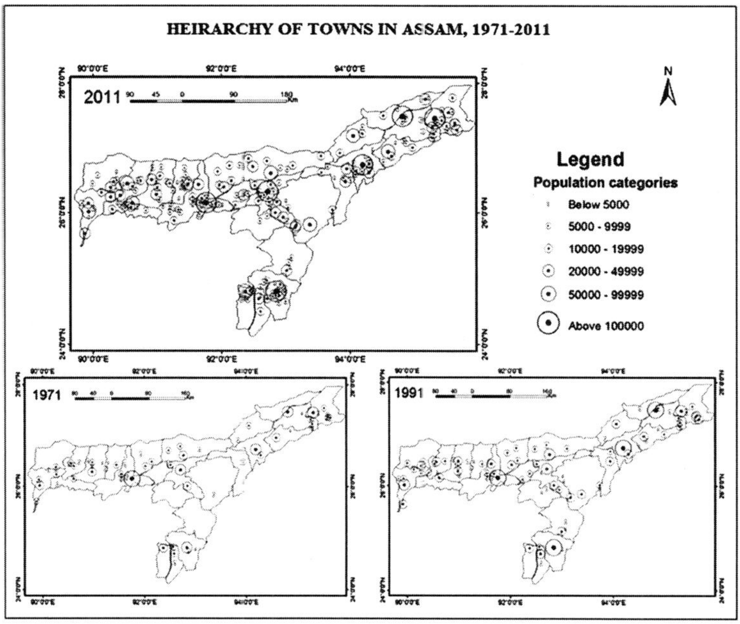

Figure 14.5: Changing Hierarchy of Urban Centres in Assam (1971-2011)
Source: Computed by author from census data 1971, 1991 and 2011.

inequalities in urbanization among the districts of Assam. Kamrup metro district constitutes 83 per cent of urban population as it includes Guwahati city which has the highest 22 percentage share of urban population against 0.04 per cent in Anand Nagar town within Dhubri district which has 10.04 per cent urban population and which is the lowest in the state (Census, 2011). Therefore, there is a need for proportionate distribution of urban population in the different size category of urban centres which is necessary towards bringing a balanced urban and regional development in the state (Bhagawati *et al.,* 2007). The hierarchy of urban centres in Assam (1971-2011) is shown in Figure 14.5.

Spacing Between the Urban Centres

Figure 14.6 shows that the higher the category of urban centres, the longer is the spacing. For example Guwahati city, the largest urban centre in the study area has also the longer spacing which acts as a central place in providing the essential services to the surrounding areas. The spacing between the class I towns which decreased by 37 per cent from 1991 to 2011 indicated the emergence of new large urban centres in Assam. The spacing for other classes also simultaneously decreases. Thus, the overall spacing between the classes of urban centres in Assam is decreasing over the periods. The spacing decreases when there is increase of urban centres which shows the pattern of development in the state as a whole and which incentivise further provision of facilities and services in a proper manner.

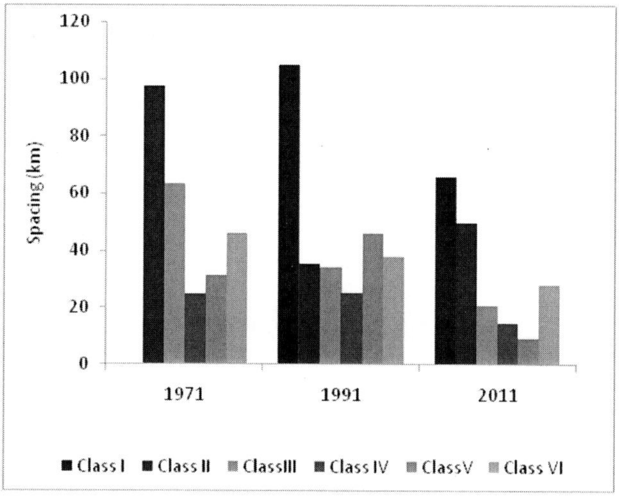

Figure 14.6: Class-wise Spacing of Urban Centres in Assam (1971-2011)

Conclusion

The inequalities of urbanization among the districts of Assam may be addressed by giving impetus for a balanced infrastructural development in small and medium towns. Spatial distribution of urban centres in the study region reveals an uneven pattern and a high concentration around the primate city and industrial town. Guwahati has maintained its dominance and lead as the prominent town in terms of both high urbanization and high population growth rate. It ensures a perfect central position in providing essential services to a large complimentary areas. The urban amenities in Assam are ones of the lowest in the country (Dwivedi & Jha, 2012). It is also found that the Assam accounted for about 43.22 per cent as the largest road network but it is to be noted that the expansion of road network is not in proportion to the surge in population and motorization in the country. However, the state account for 10 per cent of rural roads in India. In terms of urban roads, it has less than 20 per cent of the total roads in the state (Basic Road Statistics of India, 2016) and so is the per-capita consumption of electricity (Government of India, Power Sector, 2017) which are among the most important indicators of development. Investment in industrial sector is poor as in the state as it is affected by insurgency problems. Urbanization in Assam highlights a merely rise in urban population rather than a significant urban development. There is a strong need for improvement of infrastructural services and a vibrant environment which is conducive for more investment in industrial sector in order to accelerate the progress of urbanization in Assam. Hence, they need to be guided and directed onto a sustainable growth trajectory.

REFERENCES

Basic Road Statistics of India (2016). A report on basic road statistics of India 2013-14 and 2014.

Government of India Ministry of Road Transport and Highways Transport Research Wing, New Delhi. Retrieved from: http://aiggpa.mp.gov.in/images/files/KAIR/Knowledge-Resources/10-Infrastucture/Statistics/Basic%20Road%20Statistics%20of%20India.pdf

Bhagabati, A.K., Kar, B.K., & Bora, A.K. (2001). *Geography of Assam*. Rajesh Publications.

Bhagat, R.B. (2004). Dynamics of urban population growth by size class of towns and cities in India. *Demography India*, *33*(1), 47.

Bhagat, R.B. (2005). Urban growth by city and town size in India. [Unpublished] 2005. Presented at the 2005 Annual Meeting of the Population Association of America Philadelphia Pennsylvania March 31-April 2 2005.

Bhagat, R.B. (2011a). Emerging pattern of urbanisation in India. *Economic and Political Weekly*, 10-12.

Bhagat, R.B. (2011b). Urbanisation and access to basic amenities in India. *Urban India*, *31*(1), 1-13.

Bhagat, R.B. (2014). Urban migration trends, challenges and opportunities in India. *World Migration Report*: Migrants and Cities, International Organization for Migration.

Bhagat, R.B. (2017). Migration and Urban Transition in India: Implications for Development. Retreived from: http://www.un.org/en/development/desa/population/events/pdf/expert/ 27/papers/V/paper-Bhagat-final.pdf

Census of India (1971). General Population Tables, Assam.

Census of India (1991). Primary Census Abstract Assam, Series IV, Part II-B.

Census of India 2011: General Population Totals, Census of India – 2011 Manipur. Census of India website: http://www.censusindia.net.

Chadchan, J. & Shankar, R. (2012). An analysis of urban growth trends in the post-economic reforms period in India. *International Journal of Sustainable Built Environment*, *1*(1), 36-49.

Chandna, R.C. (2002). *A Geography of Population: Concepts Determinants and Patterns*. New Delhi: Kalyani Publishers.

Chauvin, J.P., Glaeser, E., Ma, Y., & Tobio, K. (2016). What is Different About Urbanization in Rich and Poor Countries? Cities in Brazil, China, India and the United States. Retrieved from: http://scholar.harvard.edu/files/chauvin/files/chauvin_etal_urbanizationrichandpoorcountries_wp.pdf

Deka, P.P., & Devi, M.K. (2017). Problems and Prospects of Development in Guwahati, Assam. In *Sustainable Smart Cities in India* (pp. 109-122). Springer International Publishing.

Dwivedi, R. & Jha, P. (2012). Pura: A Vision & Its Implementation (Phase I). *Management Insight*, *7*(2).

Government of India Power Sector (2017). Government of India Power Sector January-2017. Ministry of Power Central Electricity Authority, New Delhi.: http://www.cea.nic.in/reports/ monthly/executivesummary/2017/exe_summary-01.pdf

Government of India. Planning Commission (1997). Transforming the North East. Accessed on April 5, 2013 Retrieved from http://planningcommission.nic.in/reports/genrep/ne_exe.pdf

Grimm, N.B., Faeth, S.H., Golubiewski, N.E., Redman, C.L., Wu, J., Bai, X., & Briggs, J.M. (2008). Global change and the ecology of cities. *Science*, *319*(5864), 756-760.

Homer-Dixon, T.F. (2010). *Environment, scarcity, and violence*. Princeton University Press.

Jha, V.N. (2006). *Small Towns and Regional Development*. Rajesh Publications.

Khawas, V. (2005). Urbanisation in the North-East: Patterns, trends, and policy prongs. *Social Change*, *35*(2), 47-69.

Li, X.H., Liu, J.L., Gibson, V., & Zhu, Y.G. (2012). Urban sustainability and human health in China, East Asia and Southeast Asia. *Current Opinion in Environmental Sustainability*, *4*(4), 436-442.

Lobell, D.B., Schlenker, W., & Costa-Roberts, J. (2011). Climate trends and global crop production since 1980. *Science*, *333*(6042), 616-620.

Mahmood, A. (2008). *Statistical Methods in Geographical Studies*. Rajesh Publications.

Manta, R., Borah, J. & Borah, J. (2013). Growth of Small Towns in the Surroundings of Guwahati City, Assam, India. *International Journal of Scientific & Engineering Research*, 4(12), 1135-.1150.

Mitra, A. & Mehta, B. (2011). Cities as the engine of growth: Evidence from India. *Journal of Urban Planning and Development*, *137*(2), 171-183.

MoDONER & ADB (2006). Report of North Eastern Region Urban Development Project, (TR-18), Ministry of Development of North Eastern Region (MoDoner) and Asian Development Bank, accessed on April 1, 2013.:http:// mdoner.gov.in/sites/default /files/ silo2_content/ ner_vision/Vision_2020.pdf

Nath, A. (2013). Cohesive Urbanisation in North-East India: Issues & Concerns. *Journal of Politics & Governance*, Vol. 2(1/2), pp.66.

Singh, K. (2006): *Small and Medium Towns: A Geographical Perspective*. Rajat Publications, New Delhi.

Sudhira, H.S., Ramachandra, T.V., & Jagadish, K.S. (2004). Urban sprawl: metrics, dynamics and modelling using GIS. *International Journal of Applied Earth Observation and Geoinformation*, *5*(1), 29-39.

UK Government Office for Science, (2011). Foresight – Migration and Global Environmental Change: Future Challenges and Opportunities. Government Office for Science, London.

United Nations, Department of Economic and Social Affairs, Population Division (2014). *World Urbanization Prospects: The 2014 Revision, Highlights (ST/ ESA/SER.A/352).*

World Bank (2013). *Urbanization beyond Municipal Boundaries: Nurturing Metropolitan Economies and Connecting Peri-Urban Areas in India*, Washington, D.C.

15

Quasi and Open Land Market in the Context of Liberalisation, Using the WPI Method

A Comparative Study of Shillong and Guwahati

Nabanita Kanungo

The rates of land as fixed by the respective State Governments indicate their assessment of the revenue potential and transaction taxes of an area in the city, referred to as 'circle rates'. This is reiterated by the fact that the rates are fixed by revenue departments of the State Governments. The higher the revenue potential of an area, the greater is the value of land. This is exemplified in broad rural-urban biases of investment which tend to gravitate towards the cities and which, even within cities, create distinct zones of high and low investment. The central city areas and even axial transport corridors of trade tend to draw and support high end services and create the imperatives for the emergence of commercial retail spaces of consumption, pushing urban land values higher. In terms of the non-commercial and residential built environment, such locations tend to become sites of private property development or real estate development which tend to be largely owned and occupied by high income groups. On the contrary, land values grade lower into interior areas which have not experienced such changes in the built environment.

The two study areas, namely the cities of Guwahati and Shillong were selected for this research to enable a comparison of their built environments especially with focus on the different land-market conditions. Guwahati has an open land market without any laws restricting the purchase and sale of land as long as he or she is a citizen of India. Thus, there is an unlimited number of buyers and sellers, giving its land-market the true character of a market in the economic sense. The Guwahati Municipal Corporation Area (GMCA) is the area selected as a representative of an open land-market.

It is located in the South-Eastern part of the Kamrup District of Assam, between 25° 43′ and 26° 51′ N and 90° 36′ and 92° 12′ E, comprising an area of 216.00 sq. km and encloses 60 Wards (Table 15.1). It excludes the North Guwahati Town Committee area, Amingaon and other revenue areas which otherwise are together known as the Guwahati Metropolitan Area (GMA). The largest urban centre of the North-East India, the GMCA commands a population 9,63,429 (2011 Census) which is 32.20 per cent of the total population of the Kamrup district and about 23.89 per cent of the total urban population of the state. Contrarily, the land-market of Shillong is restricted, with laws permitting transaction of land to the indigenous tribal (ST) population only. The area identified to represent the restricted or quasi land-market is the Shillong Municipal Area (SMA), the commercial and administrative core of the Shillong Urban Agglomeration (SUA) (25° 35′ to 25° 32′ N and 91° 51′ to 91° 54′ E), which serves as the headquarters of the East Khasi Hills District and the capital city of Meghalaya.

Table 15.1: Ward Numbers with Corresponding Ward Names and Areas in GMCA

Ward No.	Ward Name/Area	Ward No.	Ward Name/Area
1	Satmile/Sadilapur/ Kamakhya Road	11	T. Road (North)
2	Railway Road	12	R.K.Ch.Road
3	Railway Colony Road	13	Sualkuchi Road
4	Facing A.T. Road/ Barabazar– Citybus Terminus	14	A.K. Deb Road/Cycle Factory/A.K.Azad Road
5	Maligaon Chariali-Overbridge	15	A.K. Azad Road (West)
6	Malabar Road	16	A.K. Azad Road(E)/ Lalganesh Mandir
7	Maligaon/A.T. Road/ Kamakhya	17	N.H.37
8	A.T. Road (North)	18	Kaliram Ch. Road/R.K. Ch. Road
9	A.T. Road/(North)	19	Machkhowa
10	Gotanagar Road/N.H.37 (N&S)	20	Bishnupur

contd...

Ward No	Ward Name/Area	Ward No.	Ward Name/Area
21	Subhash Road/Pital Karkhana	41	R.G.B. Road/Zoo-Narengi Road
22	A.K. Azad Road (Main)	42	R.G.B. Road/ G.S. Road-Bhangagarh-Ganeshguri
23	Birubari	43	R.G.B. Road/G.S. Road/ Medical Col.
24	R.P. Road/Ganeshguri-Kahilipara	44	R.G.B. Road/Zoo-Maniknagar
25	G.S. Road/B.K.K. Road	45	Noonmati Road
26	Bora Service/Rajgarh Road	46	Noonmati Road/Chandrapur Road
27	Md.Shah Road	47	Refinery/Noonmati Road
28	Md.Shah Road/Chatribari/ Athgaon Road	48	Noonmati Road/Jyotinagar
29	Fancy Bazar Road/M.G. Road/A.T. Road	49	Zoo-Narengi Road/ Chandrapur/Satgaon Road
30	M.N. Road/A.T. Road/ H. Road/Fancy Bazar	50	Hegrabari Road
31	G.S. Road/N.C.B. Road/ G.N.B. Road	51	Daranda Road/Sarumotoria Road
32	Md. Shah Road/A.K. Azad Road/G.S.Road	52	Chandrapur Road/Bonda
33	G.S. Road	53	Narengi Road/G.S. Road
34	M.G. Road/H.C.G. Road/ Jorpukuri	54	Narengi Road/Khanapara Road
35	M.G. Road/L.P.B. Road	55	G.S. Road/Khanapara Road/N.H. 40
36	B. Baruah Road	56	Basistha Road/Patharkuchi
37	M.R.D. Road/Chandmari-Silpukuri area	57	G.S. Road/Basistha Road
38	M.R.D. Road/Chandmari-Silpukuri area	58	Basistha Road/Hathigaon Road
39	P. Sarania Road/G.N.B. Road/Lachitnagar Road	59	Kahilipara Road/Hathigaon Road
40	Noonmati Road/Jyotinagar Road.	60	Hatigaon Road

Source: Guwahati Metropolitan Corporation (GMC); Department of Land Revenue, Deputy Commissioner's Office, Guwahati Metropolitan District, Assam.

The SMA has a total area of 10.36 sq. km only and contains 27 Wards (Table 15.2), with a population of 1,43,229 (2011 Census) which is 24.05 per cent of the total urban population of the state. The SUA as a whole constitutes 59.14 per cent of the total urban population of Meghalaya and SMA being a part of it, plays a significant role in terms of commercial and administrative influence it has for the state. This opens up a case for examining as to how the same could ramify into differential development of the built environment and how the same exacerbates peculiar aspects of the housing markets, especially in terms of home ownership and buyers' responses towards availing home loans.

Table 15.2: Ward Numbers with Corresponding Ward Names and Areas in SMA

Ward No.	Ward Name/Area
1	Laitumkhrah-Nongirmbah-Lumsohra- Nongrimaw- Demsniong
2	Upper and Lower New Colony
3	Upland Road, Upper Lachumiere
4	Lummawrie
5	Dhankheti-Kharmalki-Risa Colony-Khlieh Shnong-Wahkdait
6	Umshirpi-Chinapatty-Mission Pdengshnong
7	Red Cross-Keating Road-Barik Secretariat Hill-Temple Road-European Ward
8	Quinton Road-Oakland-Ward's Lake-Pine Wood Hotel-Lower Lachumiere
9	Police Bazar
10	Upper Jail Road
11	Mawlai Nongmali-Forest Colony
12	Umsohsun-Mawkhar
13	Wahingdoh-Riatsamthiah
14	Jaiaw Shyiap-Lumpyllun-Jaiaw Pdeng
15	Jaiaw Laitdom-Lumsyntiew-Jaiaw Pdeng
16	Jaiaw Langsning
17	Mission Compound-Wahthapbroo
18	Sunny Hill-Qualapatty-Wahthapbroo
19	Lower Mawprem
20	Upper Mawprem

contd...

Ward No.	Ward Name/Area
21	Naspatighari-Mawprem
22	Rilbong-Kench's Trace
23	Bishnupur-Kench's trace
24	Laban West
25	Laban East
26	Lumparing-Lumsohphoh
27	Lumparing-Riat Laban-Madan Laban

Source: Shillong Municipal Board (SMB).

The comparison attempted is thus largely based on a scheme of comparing dissimilar units. However, the fact that both these cities are located in the India's North East, traditionally considered to be on the periphery of development in relation to the rest of India, also give us a vantage point to study them in the context of liberalisation, especially in terms of their selection for the ambitious JNNURM scheme in 2004-05. If the JNNURM era is assumed to bring the rhetoric of the new economic imperative and its attendant city-development programmes, a process begun with the Look East Policy in 1992, cities with their differential land-market conditions offer the scope to investigate the truth of certain overarching assumptions regarding liberalisation's homogenising effects. This gets highlighted when we consider the fact that in Shillong, a Sixth Scheduled area, the 74th Constitutional Amendment Act does not apply and where the land tenure system and local governance are defined by traditional laws and customary practices unlike in Guwahati, where no such laws prevail.

Land Market in SMA and GMCA: A Brief Historical Overview

The traditional land tenure system in Meghalaya initially did not allow for the development of land as private property. Traditionally, land belongs to the community with families and clans having only occupancy and user rights over it. However, long years of occupation of a particular piece of land converted the occupancy right into ownership right. "Thus, in terms of ownership two classes of land can be identified in the Khasi-Jaintia society—*Ri Raid* (commune or community land) and *Ri Kynti* (private land). The latter (i.e. *Ri Kynti*) refers to land that is under the effective control of the holder, who enjoys proprietary, heritable and transferable rights over it. *Ri Raid*, on the other hand, refers to that class of land, which is under the control of the community and over which members have only right of use and occupancy but no proprietary right. Ideally *Ri Raid* land cannot be transferred to an heir or leased or transferred as property. And, if a person leaves the land unoccupied for three consecutive years it reverts to the community. This, however, does not always happen in practice" (Nongbri, 2001:1895). Thus, although formally heritable rights are not formally recognised, wherever the occupant has made permanent improvement on the land in the form of permanent buildings or has planted perennial trees, in the course of time, his/her family acquires heritable rights as *de facto* owners of that parcel of land (Nair, 1986; Nongbri, 2001; Mukhim, 2011). A third category which came into existence during the British period may be recognised, which is the "Crown Land" or land that was purchased or "ceded" to the British Crown. In such areas, traditional laws did not apply and this category implicitly introduced for the first time, the concept of land as a commodity in selected areas. The British entered into an agreement (hundred year leases) with the *Syiem (king)* of Mylliem in 1861 to procure land for civil and military stations. Territories such as the present European Ward, Police Bazar and Jail Road were 'ceded' by the Syiem of Mylliem and his Durbar to the British in exchange for money. The Cantonment was established on the purchased territories and land in these areas came under the sole administration of the Ministry of Defence. In 1883, more land was purchased from the Syiem for the purpose of building sites. The land tenure system in Shillong was thus divided into three distinct administrative divisions, namely (i) areas which were directly under the British administration where the then government Acts and rules applied (freed of traditional land relations for administrative purposes), (ii) cantonment areas where only selective rules and Acts applied, and (iii) other administered areas which were quasi-autonomous and less important in terms of administration and where the (British) laws and Acts were not applicable (JNNURM CDP Appraisal Report, *Indian Institute of Public Relations*, New Delhi). However, the true nature of the restricted land-market in SMA owes itself to the Land Transfer (Regulation) Act which the Meghalaya Assembly enacted in 1971 and which received the assent of the President of India in 1979. The Act designed to protect the indigenous Scheduled Tribes from land alienation and legally restricted the transaction of land between the indigenous Scheduled Tribes only.

Owing to the fact that there are no restrictions on the number of buyers and sellers, the land market of GMCA on the other hand allows normal market processes to prevail. Under the Assam Land and Revenue Regulation Act, 1886, the rights which may be acquired over land and legal procedural rules of acquirement of the status of land holder do not restrict the number of buyers and sellers on the basis of caste, creed or community—conditions essential to the operation of a free or open market. The Act also grants that legal land holders "... shall have a permanent, heritable and transferable right of use and occupancy, subject to the payment of all revenue taxes, leases and rates from time to time legally assessed or imposed in respect of land..." (Das, 2009: 23). In Assam and thereby in GMCA, there have been concrete laws of land transaction, registration and revenue regulations since 1886 which have been revised from time to time. This guaranteed documentability of land transaction allowed for competitive bidding of land to prevail under free market conditions. While the former added to the commodification of land, vouchsafing it as a legal guarantee for home and other loans from banks, the latter enabled the State Government to assess land values more accurately over time. However, in Meghalaya and thereby in SMA, land tenureship and ownership rights were customarily indeterminate being 'non-revenue' in character, without necessitating any cadastral surveys of land nor vesting of permanent property rights to the owners. Such conditions allowed for the development of an anomalous transaction system in the subsequent years. It was observed that "...customary laws [of land] [were] not codified and leave ample scope for arbitrary application" (Mukhim, 2011: 285). This severely affected the documentability of land transaction which both devalued land as a commodity and reduced the legal strength and authenticity of transaction deeds as guarantees for loans.

Methodology: Database and Techniques of Analysis

Database

The analysis of the land-market in SMA and GMCA is based on calculating the percentage rate of real change in the land prices of different wards in both these study areas over a period of five years, from 1999 to 2004 for SMA and four years, from 1999 to 2003 for GMCA. The analysis is based on the data on land values (Rs./sq. ft.) for the respective periods from the Department of Land Revenue, District Commissioner's Office, Guwahati Metropolitan District, Assam and East Khasi Hills District, Meghalaya. Since the data for a systematic slab of zonal land valuation, as created by the Revenue Department of Assam, is available only for 2003, the rates of a previous period have been obtained from Guwahati Municipal Corporation (GMC) records which only specify a term as 'existing prices of land' of the different Wards. These rates have been considered relevant to the year 1999 and published by way of Government's notification. It may be noted that these prices are not current market prices but valuated by the respective revenue departments for the minimum prices on which the taxation for transaction are levied by the respective registrars of land registration, as 'circle rates'. It is difficult to obtain the actual transaction prices which the buyers and sellers are reluctant to divulge. The parties generally register the transactions on the basis of the circle rates though the actual transaction prices are considerably higher. The Governments, however, do revise the circle rates once the market prices appreciate considerably, but there is invariably a considerable lag between the market prices and the circle rates fixed by the civic authorities.

In order to gauge changes in land values within the municipal limits of both the cities, a longitudinal evaluation has been adopted which has mainly involved deflation of the respective current year land prices (the 2004 prices for SMA and 2003 prices for GMCA) of commercial and non-commercial areas in the Wards. The method of deflation was adopted to derive real prices of land in order to make them comparable over a period of time while accounting for the effect of inflation on the prices of land. The changes in land values and the subsequent derivations of the nature of the two land-markets have been assessed by calculating the percentage rate of change in real prices of land in the respective periods for both the study areas. The spatial aspect of changing land values in the period has been attempted to be shown by projecting the computed results on maps. Thus, a picture has been attempted to show the nature of the land-markets in terms of changing land values in particular areas *within* the individual municipal limits of the cities and also how they differ in these respects *between* themselves.

Standardisation of Data and Technique

The first step was to standardise the unit price of land which was quoted in terms of Rs. per sq. ft. for Shillong and Rs. per *katha* for Guwahati. Thus, it was required that the land values of Guwahati be converted into Rs. per sq. ft. to make them comparable with prices in Shillong. One *katha* in Assam is four times the standard equivalent of 720 square feet. As 20 *kathas* equal to 1 *bigha* in the local sense, 5 *kathas* equal to 1 *bigha* in the standard sense in Assam. Hence, to convert the rates of land given in per *katha* to square feet, the price per *katha* was divided by 2880 (720×4). It may be also be mentioned that in the study, the upper limit of land values pertain to leading commercial, road frontage or prime urban locations and the lower limit relate to areas of low investment characterised by their distance from the prime road frontage areas. These include fringe areas, which may be commercially undeveloped areas, depressed areas or peripheral areas, non-retail and residential areas and bye-lanes, hill areas and villages. The gradation in land prices appears to follow the principle of accessibility to commercial sites and the main road and motorability of roads.

Further, it was required that the values over the two time periods (base and current), be stabilized by price deflation and thus made comparable over the time interval. This was done to incorporate the role of inflation on prices by basing the comparison on real rise in land values. For this, the current prices for both categories were deflated using the WPI for related years. The reason for using the WPI and not the CPI is that the latter is used for different working groups. In case of inter-country comparisons, CPI is ideal. However, for intra-India analyses, the WPI is considered more appropriate. The WPI for the related years were obtained from the *Indian Economic Survey*, 2010-11. The technique used is given in (15.1).

$$x/wcy*wby \tag{15.1}$$

where x is the current price to be deflated, wcy is the WPI of the current year and wby is the WPI of the base year. Using this mathematical relationship, the percentage rate of change in real price over the respective periods of time for the two study areas was calculated using the equation (15.2).

if x/wcy*wby=DP and DP-byp =RR then,

$$RR/byp/t*100=PRC \tag{15.2}$$

where DP=Deflated Price of current year, RR = Real Rise, byp = base year price, t (time) = 4 years (in the case of Guwahati) and 5 years (in the case of Shillong) and PRC = percentage rate of change in real land prices.

**Note*: For both SMA and GMCA, the WPI for the base year was 140.7. The WPI for the current year for SMA was 187.3 and in case of GMCA it was 175.9 for the related years.

The values obtained were then assigned classes which denoted areas of maximum, moderate and minimum change in the period. However, due the fact that land price slabs differ vastly in the two areas, comparison on a common classification of rates of change in the period could not be done. Thus, the methodology of comparing the two different land markets elucidates a case of comparison of dissimilar units and justifiably lends itself to two case studies which are then compared.

A Brief Overview of Land Values of SMA and GMCA during the Base and Current Years

Before attempting a comparative assessment of the change in the land values of the two study areas, it would be worthwhile to consider the trends of land values pertaining to both during the base year and the respective current year. The price of land (Rs./sq. ft) in the SMA and GMCA for the respective period for which they have been studied, (that is between 1998-99 to 2003 for GMCA and between 1998-99 to 2004 for SMA) reveals at first glance the very high base price of land in SMA. Subsequently, the range between the highest values in GMCA and those in SMA in both commercial and non-commercial categories is also very high. In other words, the highest values of land in GMCA amount to some of the lowest in SMA. For instance, in terms of current year prices of commercial sections for both the study areas, (that is 2003 for GMCA and 2004 for SMA), the highest value of land was registered at Rs. 347.22/sq. ft. in GMCA, whereas in SMA, it was Rs. 800/sq. ft. Again, the lowest value in GMCA in the same category stood at Rs. 27.78/sq. ft whereas in SMA, it was Rs. 60/sq. ft. In terms of the base year for both study areas, that is 1998-99, the highest land value in the commercial sections of GMCA was registered at Rs. 121.53/sq. ft. whereas in SMA, it was Rs. 500/sq. ft. Again, in the non-commercial category, the highest value in GMCA was Rs. 6.94/sq. ft., while in SMA, it stood at Rs. 60/sq. ft (Tables 15.3, 15.4, 15.5 and 15.6). It is clear from the above that relatively, land values have been consistently higher in SMA compared to those in GMCA in both commercial and non-commercial areas right from the base to the current year. As has been already observed, the wide differences in values for both commercial and non-commercial sections of the two areas during the base and the current period justify the adoption of an individual evaluation of each area to show the significant dynamics that may be unique to that area. The differences being pertinent, the values as they were recorded for the periods in both areas even after due standardisation would not allow for a comparison on a common range of class intervals. Thus both areas have been studied individually in terms of a suitable range of land values for commercial and non-commercial categories which best represents the unique dynamics of change in land values in the period. This also reveals to some extent the scarcity of land in SMA which may have allowed prices to soar whereas, in its more extensive counterpart, the GMCA, land prices have been much lower. However, more interestingly, the effects of the high base prices of land in SMA translate visibly into the evaluation of percentage rate of change in land values in the area for the period studied which puts it in stark contrast against GMCA, where base prices are lower. This is shown in the following sections.

Table 15.3: Percentage Rate of Real Rise in Land Prices in SMA (1999-2004) (Commercial Areas)

Ward No.	Base Year (1998-99) Prices (Rs./sq.ft)	Current Year (2003) Prices (Rs./sq.ft)	Deflated Prices (Rs./sq.ft)	Real Rise (Rs./sq.ft)	Rate of Real Rise between 1998 and 2003 (%)
1	400	500	375.60	–24.40	–1.22
2	250	300	225.36	–24.64	–1.97
3	300	400	300.48	0.48	0.03
4	400	500	375.60	–24.40	–1.22
5	250	400	300.48	50.48	4.04
6	250	300	225.36	–24.64	–1.97
7	200	500	375.60	175.60	17.56
8	200	500	375.60	175.60	17.56
9	500	800	600.96	100.96	4.04
10	300	500	375.60	75.60	5.04
11	150	250	187.80	37.80	5.04
12	300	300	225.36	–74.64	–4.98
13	200	300	225.36	25.36	2.54
14	200	300	225.36	25.36	2.54
15	200	300	225.36	25.36	2.54
16	200	300	225.36	25.36	2.54
17	300	300	225.36	–74.64	–4.98
18	200	300	225.36	25.36	2.54
19	200	250	187.80	–12.20	–1.22
20	250	250	187.80	–62.20	–4.98
21	250	250	187.80	–62.20	–4.98
22	200	300	225.36	25.36	2.54
23	200	300	225.36	25.36	2.54
24	250	300	225.36	–24.64	–1.97
25	250	300	225.36	–24.64	–1.97
26	80	100	75.12	–4.88	–1.22
27	250	250	187.80	–62.20	–4.98

Source: Base and Current Prices obtained from Land Revenue Department, Office of the District Commissioner, East Khasi Hills, Meghalaya.

Table 15.4: Percentage Rate of Real Rise in Land Prices in SMA (1999-2004)
(Non-Commercial Areas)

Ward No.	Base Year (1998-99) Prices (Rs./sq.ft)	Current Year (2003) Prices (Rs./sq.ft)	Deflated Prices (Rs./sq.ft)	Real Rise (Rs./sq.ft	Rate of Real Rise between 1998 and 2003 (%)
1	160	250	187.80	27.80	3.48
2	160	200	150.24	–9.76	–1.22
3	180	200	150.24	–29.76	–3.31
4	160	250	187.80	27.80	3.48
5	160	200	150.24	–9.76	–1.22
6	160	160	120.19	–39.81	–4.98
7	120	300	225.36	105.36	17.56
8	120	300	225.36	105.36	17.56
9	300	600	450.72	150.72	10.05
10	180	300	225.36	45.36	5.04
11	100	150	112.68	12.68	2.54
12	180	180	135.22	–44.78	–4.98
13	120	150	112.68	–7.32	–1.22
14	120	150	112.68	–7.32	–1.22
15	120	150	112.68	–7.32	–1.22
16	120	150	112.68	–7.32	–1.22
17	180	150	112.68	–67.32	–7.48
18	120	150	112.68	–7.32	–1.22
19	120	150	112.68	–7.32	–1.22
20	160	160	120.19	–39.81	–4.98
21	160	150	112.68	–47.32	–5.91
22	120	200	150.24	30.24	5.04
23	120	200	150.24	30.24	5.04
24	160	160	120.19	–39.81	–4.98
25	160	160	120.19	–39.81	–4.98
26	60	60	45.07	–14.93	–4.98
27	60	60	45.07	–14.93	–4.98

Source: Base and Current Prices obtained from Land Revenue Department Office of the DC, East Khasi Hills, Meghalaya.

Table 15.5: Percentage Rate of Real Rise in Land Prices GMCA in 1999-2003 (Commercial Areas)

Ward No.	Base Year (1998-99) Prices (Rs./sq.ft)	Current Year (2003) Prices (Rs./sq)	Deflated Prices (Rs./sq.ft)	Real Rise(Rs./sq.ft)	Rate of Real Rise between 1998 & 2003	Ward No.	Base Year (1998-99) Prices (Rs./sq.ft)	Current Year (2003) Prices (Rs./sq)	Deflated Prices (Rs./sq.ft)	Real Rise (Rs./sq.ft)	Rate of Real Rise between 1998 & 2003
1	13.89	27.78	22.22	8.33	14.99	31	69.44	347.22	277.74	208.29	74.99
2	17.36	45.14	36.11	18.74	26.99	32	121.53	347.22	277.74	156.21	32.13
3	13.89	34.72	27.77	13.88	24.99	33	69.44	347.22	277.74	208.29	74.99
4	17.36	69.44	55.55	38.19	54.99	34	52.08	173.61	138.87	86.79	41.66
5	17.36	69.44	55.55	38.19	54.99	35	41.67	208.33	166.64	124.98	74.99
6	17.36	69.44	55.55	38.19	54.99	36	34.72	173.61	138.87	104.15	74.99
7	27.78	69.44	55.55	27.77	24.99	37	34.72	173.61	138.87	104.15	74.99
8	27.78	69.44	55.55	27.77	24.99	38	31.25	173.61	138.87	107.62	86.10
9	27.78	69.44	55.55	27.77	24.99	39	52.08	173.61	138.87	86.79	41.66
10	17.36	45.14	36.11	18.74	26.99	40	31.25	69.44	55.55	24.30	19.44
11	27.78	69.44	55.55	27.77	24.99	41	41.67	173.61	138.87	97.20	58.32
12	27.78	69.44	55.55	27.77	24.99	42	52.08	173.61	138.87	86.79	41.66
13	27.78	52.08	41.66	13.88	12.49	43	52.08	173.61	138.87	86.79	41.66
14	34.72	69.44	55.55	20.83	14.99	44	41.67	173.61	138.87	97.20	58.32
15	34.72	69.44	55.55	20.83	14.99	45	41.67	69.44	55.55	13.88	8.33

contd...

contd...

Ward No.	Base Year (1998-99) Prices (Rs./ sq.ft)	Current Year (2003) Prices (Rs./sq)	Deflated Prices (Rs./sq. ft)	Real Rise (Rs./ sq.ft)	Rate of Real Rise between 1998 & 2003	Ward No.	Base Year (1998-99) Prices (Rs./ sq.ft)	Current Year (2003) Prices (Rs./sq)	Deflated Prices (Rs./sq. ft)	Real Rise (Rs./ sq.ft)	Rate of Real Rise between 1998 & 2003
16	34.72	52.08	41.66	6.94	5.00	46	31.25	69.44	55.55	24.30	19.44
17	27.78	52.08	41.66	13.88	12.49	47	31.25	69.44	55.55	24.30	19.44
18	69.44	347.22	277.74	208.29	74.99	48	31.25	69.44	55.55	24.30	19.44
19	121.53	347.22	277.74	156.21	32.13	49	27.78	69.44	55.55	27.77	24.99
20	42.68	173.61	138.87	96.19	56.34	50	27.78	45.14	36.11	8.33	7.50
21	34.72	173.61	138.87	104.15	74.99	51	27.78	69.44	55.55	27.77	24.99
22	41.67	52.08	41.66	-0.01	0.00	52	27.78	69.44	55.55	27.77	24.99
23	27.78	34.72	27.77	0.00	0.00	53	45.14	69.44	55.55	10.41	5.76
24	52.08	173.61	138.87	86.79	41.66	54	41.67	69.44	55.55	13.88	8.33
25	34.72	173.61	138.87	104.15	74.99	55	45.14	69.44	55.55	10.41	5.76
26	34.72	173.61	138.87	104.15	74.99	56	27.78	45.14	36.11	8.33	7.50
27	121.53	347.22	277.74	156.21	32.13	57	52.08	173.61	138.87	86.79	41.66
28	121.53	347.22	277.74	156.21	32.13	58	34.72	69.44	55.55	20.83	14.99
29	121.53	347.22	277.74	156.21	32.13	59	31.25	173.61	138.87	107.62	86.10
30	121.53	347.22	277.74	156.21	32.13	60	31.25	45.14	36.11	4.86	3.88

Source: Current Prices of Land (2003): Department of Land Revenue, Deputy Commissioner's Office, Guwahati Metropolitan district, Assam; Base prices (1998-99): Guwahati Municipal Corporation (GMC).

Table 15.6: Percentage Rate of Real Rise in Land Prices in GMCA (1999-2003) (Non-Commercial Areas)

Ward No.	Base Year (1998-99) Prices (Rs./ sq.ft)	Current Year (2003) Prices (Rs./sq)	Deflated Prices (Rs./sq. ft)	Real Rise(Rs. /sq.ft)	Rate of Real Rise between 1998 & 2003	Ward No.	Base Year (1998-99) Prices (Rs./ sq.ft)	Current Year (2003) Prices (Rs./sq)	Deflated Prices (Rs./sq. ft)	Real Rise (Rs./ sq.ft)	Rate of Real Rise between 1998 & 2003
1	6.94	27.78	22.22	15.27	54.99	31	41.67	347.22	277.74	236.07	141.64
2	6.94	27.78	22.22	15.27	54.99	32	24.31	121.53	97.21	72.90	74.99
3	13.89	34.72	27.77	13.88	24.99	33	24.31	121.53	97.21	72.90	74.99
4	10.42	27.78	22.22	11.80	28.33	34	17.36	173.61	138.87	121.51	174.97
5	6.94	52.08	41.66	34.72	124.98	35	13.89	69.44	55.55	41.66	74.99
6	13.89	52.08	41.66	27.77	49.99	36	13.89	69.44	55.55	41.66	74.99
7	13.89	69.44	55.55	41.66	74.99	37	10.42	52.08	41.66	31.24	74.99
8	10.42	45.14	36.11	25.69	61.65	38	10.42	52.08	41.66	31.24	74.99
9	6.94	45.14	36.11	29.16	104.98	39	24.31	45.14	36.11	11.80	12.14
10	13.89	27.78	22.22	8.33	14.99	40	13.89	45.14	36.11	22.22	39.99
11	20.83	52.08	41.66	20.83	24.99	41	17.36	45.14	36.11	18.74	26.99
12	6.94	34.72	27.77	20.83	74.99	42	38.19	69.44	55.55	17.35	11.36
13	6.94	27.78	22.22	15.27	54.99	43	38.19	69.44	55.55	17.35	11.36
14	10.42	69.44	55.55	45.13	108.31	44	20.83	45.14	36.11	15.27	18.33
15	20.83	52.08	41.66	20.83	24.99	45	20.83	45.14	36.11	15.27	18.33

contd...

contd...

Ward No.	Base Year (1998-99) Prices (Rs./ sq.ft)	Current Year (2003) Prices (Rs./sq)	Deflated Prices (Rs./sq. ft)	Real Rise(Rs. /sq.ft)	Rate of Real Rise between 1998 & 2003	Ward No.	Base Year (1998-99) Prices (Rs./ sq.ft)	Current Year (2003) Prices (Rs./sq)	Deflated Prices (Rs./sq. ft)	Real Rise (Rs./ sq.ft)	Rate of Real Rise between 1998 & 2003
16	13.89	45.14	36.11	22.22	39.99	46	10.42	45.14	36.11	25.69	61.65
17	27.78	52.08	41.66	13.88	12.49	47	17.36	45.14	36.11	18.74	26.99
18	13.89	173.61	138.87	124.98	224.96	48	20.83	45.14	36.11	15.27	18.33
19	41.67	347.22	277.74	236.07	141.63	49	13.89	45.14	36.11	22.22	39.99
20	17.36	173.61	138.87	121.51	174.98	50	27.78	45.14	36.11	8.33	7.50
21	27.78	104.17	83.32	55.54	49.99	51	27.78	34.72	27.77	0.00	0.00
22	27.78	45.14	36.11	8.33	7.50	52	10.42	45.14	36.11	25.69	61.65
23	20.83	34.72	27.77	6.94	8.33	53	34.72	69.44	55.55	20.83	14.99
24	27.78	34.72	27.77	0.00	0.00	54	27.78	45.14	36.11	8.33	7.50
25	10.42	52.08	41.66	31.24	74.99	55	41.67	69.44	55.55	13.88	8.33
26	17.36	86.81	69.43	52.07	74.99	56	27.78	45.14	36.11	8.33	7.50
27	41.67	173.61	138.87	97.20	58.32	57	34.72	45.14	36.11	1.38	1.00
28	52.08	347.22	277.74	225.65	108.31	58	31.25	69.44	55.55	24.30	19.44
29	41.67	347.22	277.74	236.07	141.64	59	31.25	52.08	41.66	10.41	8.33
30	27.78	347.22	277.74	249.96	224.96	60	27.78	45.14	36.11	8.33	7.50

Source: Current Prices (2003): Department of Land Revenue, Deputy Commissioner's Office, Guwahati Metropolitan district, Assam; Base price (1998-99): Guwahati Municipal Corporation (GMC).

Percentage Rate of Change in Land Prices in SMA (1999 to 2004): Implications of a Quasi Market Upon Land Values

The effects of a restricted land market on land transaction reflect starkly on the computation of the percentage rate of change in land values in SMA. Here a high incidence of negative growth or fall in land values is observed in the period between 1999 and 2004 in both categories of prime commercial or road frontage areas and interior residential or non-commercial areas.

Commercial/Road Frontage Areas in SMA

The overall positive rise in commercial/road frontage sites of the different wards in SMA tends to be low ranging from 0 to more than 7.0 per cent only. Wards which have experienced more than 7.0 per cent rise in land values in the period which is the highest rise recorded in SMA include areas where land became a commodity after the British purchased the areas from the local *Syiems* (technically ceded from the Syiem of Mylliem in favour of the British Crown). These areas are Red Cross, Keating Road, Barik and Secretariat Hill of the European Ward and Quinton Road, Oakland, Wards Lake, Pine Wood and Lower Lachumiere. Most of SMA's administrative functions (Barik, Secretariat Hill, Lower Lachumiere) are located in the buildings of this area apart from commercial (Keating Road, Pine Wood) and residential functions (Oakland). It is these areas where some kind of open transaction is made possible as in these areas, having been purchased by the British, traditional laws did not apply. Thus, the price of land increased owing to their exclusive marketability. Areas which experienced low rise in land values but which recorded high base year prices include the core commercial area and some straddling of market areas, viz. Police Bazaar, Laitumkhrah, Dhankheti, Upper Lachumiere and Upland Road. This appears to be the result of very high base year values which have in effect locked these areas out of frequent transaction and devalued them considerably over time. The other areas where devaluation is observed are largely those where previously land values were high. These are by and large settled by minorities and areas characterised by old settlements, depressed, ghetto-like features consisting of slums and shacks such as Lumparing, Upper Mawprem, Naspatigarhi, Mission Compound, Sunny-Hill, Qualapatty (Table 15.3 & Map 15.1).

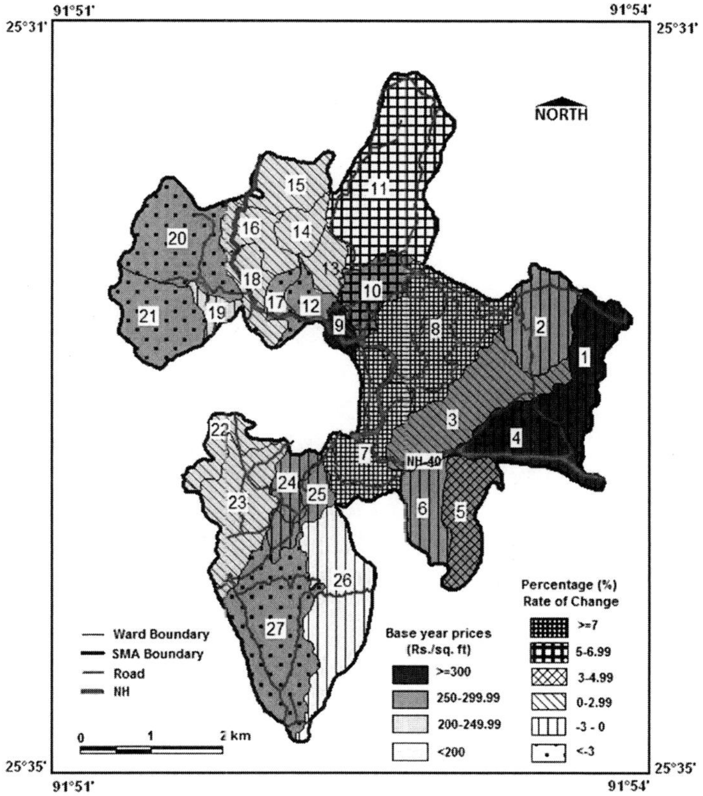

Figure 15.1: Per cent Rate of Change in Land Values of Commercial Areas of SMA (1999-2004).

Source: Original Map: Directorate of Census Operations, Shillong; reproduced with computed values from Kanungo, N., 2014. Consumption and the Urban Morphology: A Comparative Study of the Re-creation of Space in Shillong and Guwahati, Ph.D. Thesis, Department of Geography, North-Eastern Hill University, (unpublished).

Non-Commercial/Residential Areas

The non-commercial areas reflect almost the same trends as their commercial counterpart in SMA where the rate of real rise also tends to be very low, ranging from 0 to more than 7.0 per cent only. This reiterates the preponderance of low to negative change in land values. Areas which have experienced relatively high positive rise in land values (more than 7.0 per cent rise) are those where some kind of open transaction is made possible. In this aspect too, the non-commercial areas behave similarly to their commercial counterparts. Depressed areas, settled by minorities and the lower income groups such as Sunny Hill, Mawprem and Lumparing continued to experience negative change in land values in their interior or non-commercial sections (Table 15.2 & Map 15.2).

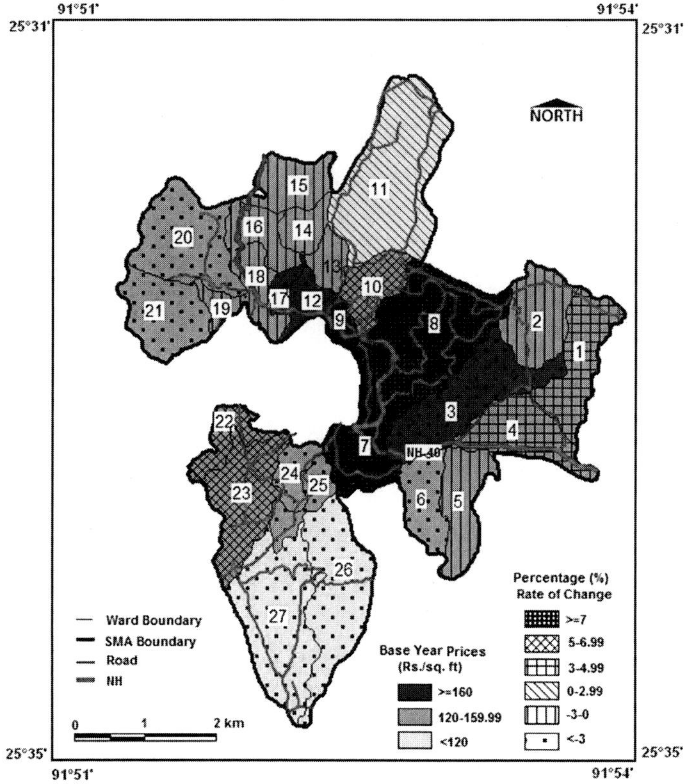

Figure 15.2: Per cent Rate of Change in Land Values of Non-Commercial Areas of SMA (1999-2004).

Source: Original Map: Directorate of Census Operations, Shillong; reproduced with computed values from Kanungo, N., 2014. Consumption and the Urban Morphology: A Comparative Study of the Re-creation of Space in Shillong and Guwahati, Ph.D. Thesis, Department of Geography, North-Eastern Hill University, (unpublished).

Implications of an Open Market upon Land Values

In stark contrast to SMA, the percentage rate of change in land values in commercial sections of the GMCA, an open market, leans towards very high positive change ranging from 80 to 100 per cent and the non-commercial areas even exceed the 100 per cent mark. The most significant feature of this rise is that it tends to concentrate in areas where land values for the base year were high, unlike in SMA, where areas with high base price have mostly experienced very low to negative change.

Commercial Areas in GMCA

Here, the commercial axis of the G.S. Road appears to have attracted most of the commercial investments which may have been decisive in raising the value of land. Areas which have recorded high rise (80 to 100 per cent) in GMCA are found to invariably straddle the main road axial corridors such as the M.R.D. Road-Silpukuri stretch and the Kahilipara-Hathigaon areas. This group is closely followed by areas which recorded 60 to 80 per cent rise in land values during the period of reference, which include Kaliram Ch. Road-R.K. Chandra Road, Subhash Road and almost the entire stretch of G.S. Road barring the Khanapara section, M.G. Road, B. Baruah Road, Rajgarh Road, M.R.D. Road.Interestingly, most of these areas (within GMCA's individual range of land prices) had relatively high land prices in 1999, between Rs. 35 to more than Rs. 50 per sq. ft. The above confirms that values have risen particularly and persistently in high-value commercial areas along the main roads unlike the trends observed in SMA. This partially explains increased transactions or investment in these areas for commercial ventures which significantly transformed the skyline of the city from 1999 to 2003. Areas away from this axis have had low land values in 1999 and record the lowest rise in land values. The only exception is the Pandu-Maligaon complex where despite relatively low base prices of land, there has been a considerable rise in land values owing to its location along a convergence of major roads and rail routes (Table 15.3 & Map 15.3).

Non-Commercial Areas in GMCA

There has been spectacular rise in land prices in the non-commercial locations as compared to the commercial areas of the wards in the GMCA. The highest rates of change exceed 100 per cent in areas. These areas also coincide with their commercial counterparts and share proximity, though not immediate to S.R.C. Road, Jorpukuri,Maligaon-Chariali over-bridge, A.T. Road (North), A.K. Azad Road, Kaliram Ch. Road, Machkhowa, Bishnupur, Chatribari, Fancy Bazar and G.N.B. Road.This axis marks the northern, traditional, old commercial area incorporating Ulubari-Fancy-Bazaar-Pan Bazaar complex and the Chandmari-Silpukuri area. The western pocket in the Pandu-Maligaon area makes a remarkable presence in this category owing to the convergence of major railway and road network. However, what is equally remarkable is that most of the Wards straddling the G.S. approach road up to the Ganeshguri crossing which registered very high prices in 1999 show a low percentage rise in land values (less than 40 per cent). This may indicate that the non-residential areas along this axis did not experience as many transactions in the period as did the commercial sections of those wards. Also, since the base year prices were very high in these areas, it is possible that land may have been bought earlier by individuals and locked for redevelopment in the current year in terms of function, contemporary aesthetics and efficiency of design. Residential areas straddling the G.S. Road axis, which had a high base year price, show a low rise (less than 40 per cent) which may be ascribed to either the operation of the base effect or decline in transaction related to residential activity (Table15.4 & Map 15.4).

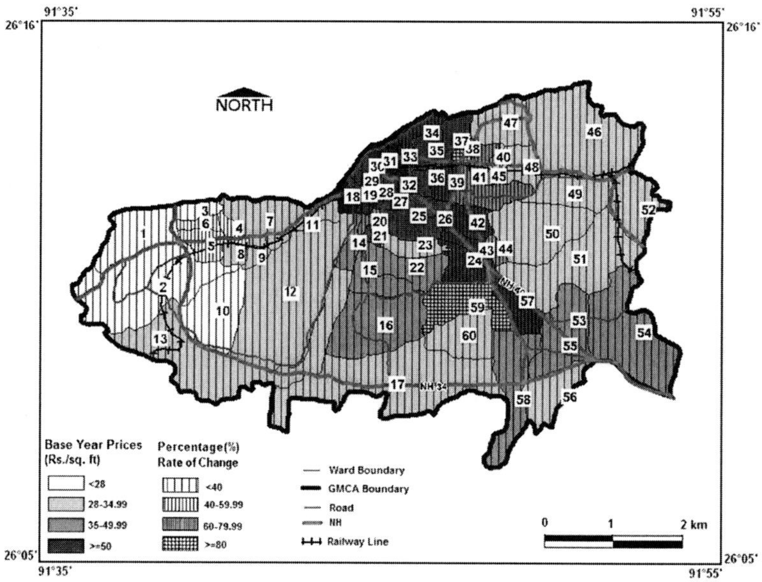

Figure 15.3: Per cent Rate of Change in Land Values of Commercial Areas of GMC (1999-2003).

Source: Original Map: Guwahati Municipal Corporation (GMC) & Guwahati Metropolitan Development Authority (GMDA); reproduced with computed values from Kanungo, N., 2014. Consumption and the Urban Morphology: A Comparative Study of the Re-creation of Space in Shillong and Guwahati, Ph.D. Thesis, Department of Geography, North-Eastern Hill University, (unpublished).

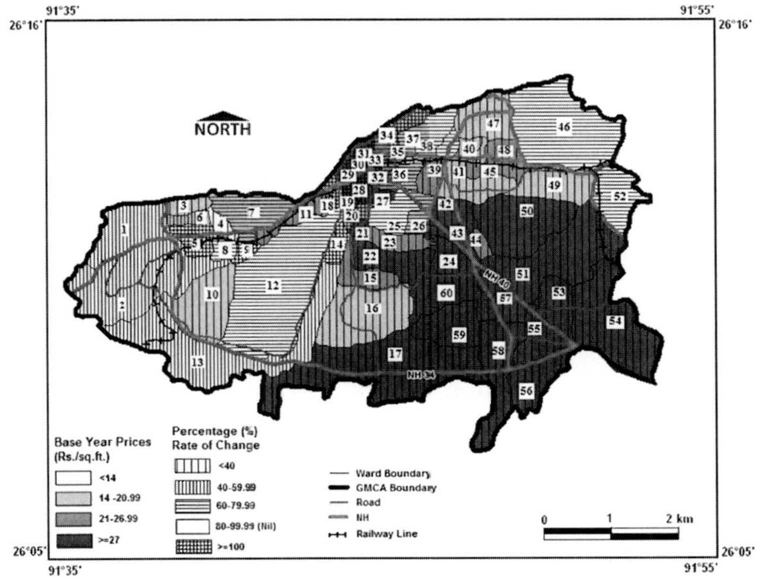

Figure 15.4: Per cent Rate of Change in Land Values of Non-Commercial Areas of GMC (1999-2003).

Source: Original Map: GMC & GMDA; reproduced with computed values from Kanungo, N., 2014. Consumption and the Urban Morphology: A Comparative Study of the Re-creation of Space in Shillong and Guwahati, Ph.D. Thesis, Department of Geography, North-Eastern Hill University, (unpublished)]

Home Loans and Its Relation to Nature of Land Market

In the post-liberalised financial climate, private sector banks gained considerable ground in terms of direct housing finance disbursements whereas investments in National Housing Bank (NHB)/HUDCO by banks have been decreasing in the recent period. More recently, the housing finance market has evolved as a largely oligopolistic market with three dominant players, namely HDFC (which began operating in 1977), the largest housing finance company, ICICI Bank, the largest private sector bank and State Bank of India, the largest public sector bank in the country; these three leading housing finance players accounted for approximately 75 per cent of the housing finance market in 2005 (Sodhi, 2008). Increased competitiveness among banks have spurred the housing finance market and home loans have thus emerged as a driving factor behind the potential and proclivity of consumers to own homes (Gupta and Varma, 2008).

Easy access to home loans has indeed been found to be significantly correlated with increased home ownership rates among the high and middle income groups. Thus the profile of home loans not only acts as a quotient of income and consumption, it underlines a key feature of the associated land-market in terms of the location of financial outlets, banks, offices and related services and also how it finally translates into the built environment by enabling consumers to fulfil their financial requirements for home ownership (Kanungo, 2015).

In terms of home ownership, the surveyed areas in GMCA reveal a much higher rate of home ownership than those in SMA. The high rates of home ownership in GMCA may be related to the prevalence of apartment-type of dwelling which offers ownership to people who were formerly tenants. This indicates that whereas the nature of land market reflects foremost on the physical built-environment in terms of how it plays as a base for housing activity, it also has a significant bearing upon home-ownership rates. In SMA, conversely, a higher percentage of tenancy in the surveyed area may indicate the effects of a restricted land-market upon home ownership (Table 15.7). It is probable that such a land-market appears to allow ownership to a small number of people. Further, there appears to be a significant difference between the respondents of the two cities in terms of their behaviour in accessing and utilising home loan facilities. Generally, GMCA has a much higher percentage of home owners who have availed of home loans (49.47 %) compared to a mere 27.92 per cent in SMA (Table 15.8). It may be inferred that the open land-market in GMCA not only facilitates the burgeoning of the housing market, it also creates financial avenues for consumers to fulfil their demand for housing. Another very important differentiating feature in availing home loans among the two sets of respondents is the fact that in GMCA the popularity of nationalised bank loans has been observed whereas almost all of the creditors in SMA (97.7% of 43 respondents) have availed housing loans from their offices (Table 15.9).

Table 15.7: Home Ownership Profile of SMA and GMCA

	SMA	**%**	**GMCA**	**%**
Total Home Owners	154	57.0	190	70.4
Tenants	116	43. 0	80	29.6
Total	**270**	**100.0**	**270**	**100.0**

Source: Fieldwork, 2009-10.

Table 15.8: Home Owners Who Have Availed Home Loans in SMA and GMCA

	SMA	%	GMCA	%
Availed Home Loans	43	27.92	94	49.47
Not Availed	111	72.08	96	50.53
Total	**154**	**100.00**	**190**	**100.00**

Source: Fieldwork, 2009-10.

Table 15.9: Sources of Home Loans in SMA and GMCA

Sources of Home Loans	SMA	%	GMCA	%
Emolument from Govt. Office	42	97.7	0	0.0
Relatives	1	2.3	4	4.3
Bank, HUDCO, LIC, Housing Board	0	0.0	86	91.4
Private Financing Agency	0	0.0	4	4.3
Total	**43**	**100.0**	**94**	**100.0**

Source: Fieldwork, 2009-10.

In SMA, and perhaps this would be true of other Sixth Schedule areas as well, banks insist on guarantee vouched by the Autonomous District Councils (ADCs) that in case of default would have the right to mortgage the land of the borrower. However as per the provisions of the Land Transfer Act of Meghalaya, 1971, the bank is required to sell the property to a tribal only. The anomalous regulations of land tenure and nature of land transfer in the state subjects the legal documentation process to vagueness and reduces its legal credibility as a guarantee against which loans can be disbursed. The restricted land-market thus bears upon the system of issuing *pattas* to potential loaners, which, as legal documents, are crucial for procuring home loans. This may be the most probable reason as to why the number of people taking loans is very less in SMA. Banks and even the Meghalaya Housing Board have had a high default rate due to this problem which hinders their recovery rates and discourages them from disbursing further housing loans. Further, the potential loanees are limited to the local Scheduled Tribe community only, since non-tribals living in SMA cannot get landed property transferred in their name and therefore, hold no security for financial institutions for mortgaging the land or built property against sanction of housing loans in their favour. This illuminates a socio-political angle to the restriction of the land-market, beyond the purely economic sense, contributing nonetheless to the latter. Contrary to this, the open land-market in Assam and thus in GMCA allows for free and open transaction which follows a much more definite, coherent and transparent regulatory system and which in turn allows for easy legal documentation of the process.

Summary and Conclusion

Generally, the manner in which the nature of the land-market effects change in land values over a period of time is manifest in both the areas. While the land market in the SMA reveals a preponderance of negative change in the real land prices over the time period for which it has been studied, in GMCA, no negative change has been observed. While the overall rate of positive change in both categories of land (commercial, road frontage sites and non-commercial areas) of the different wards in SMA tends to be low (ranging from 0 to more than 7% only), in GMCA, the same ranges from 0 to above 100 per cent in the non-commercial and 0 to 100 per cent in the commercial categories. This appears to be the result of very high base year values in SMA which have in effect locked these areas out of frequent transaction and devalued them considerably over time. The other areas where devaluation (negative change) is observed, and where previously land values were high, are areas by and large, settled by minorities and areas characterised by old settlements, depressed, ghetto-like features consisting of slums and shacks. However, the most significant point of difference this situation has with the GMCA is that in the latter, the rise in prices (especially evident in the case of commercial areas) occurs even where land values for the base year were high.

In the SMA, the spatial patterns for positive change in prices of land are observed to be similar for both commercial and non-commercial areas, that is, wherever commercial areas of a ward have shown positive change in land prices, the non-commercial areas of the same ward have also risen to some extent in the period. The consistent rise has been observed largely in areas where some open transaction is allowed owing to historical reasons. In GMCA on the other hand, the rise in prices of non-commercial areas is far more spectacular and extends to even interior areas which are far from the main commercial axis. Thus the most important observation that comes forth from the above analysis is that selected areas where some kind of open transaction is enabled (owing to historical reasons, in the case of SMA) have experienced any, even if relatively low rates of rise in real land prices in the period. This condition is better understood in the case of GMCA where an open land-market (which prevails throughout its area), enables transaction between an unlimited number of buyers and sellers and fosters the high appreciation of real values of land over time.

Further, the nature of the land-market is found to have significant bearings on the number of people availing home loans. Since land transaction deeds and pattas serve as legal documents in procuring home loans, any restriction in the documentability of land transaction (as obtains in a restricted market) may on one hand tend to limit the number of individuals availing home loans and/or wanting to opt for home loans and on the other, increase the default rate among banks and housing agencies. Contrary to this, the open land-market in GMCA, allows for free and open transaction which in turn allows for easy legal documentation of the process, thus leading to a thriving housing and home loan market. Also, due to the fact that in a restricted land-market as SMA, the ethnic ceiling on land-transaction enables private land-ownership to remain restricted to a few, it is these few individuals who become owners of large parcels of urban land as it keeps circulating (*via* transaction) among them, ultimately leading to their official devaluation over time.

It may be worthwhile to mention certain factors which may have influenced the findings on the land market in the two study areas. Primary among them is what has been mentioned as 'the base effect'. It may be noticed that wherever the base year prices have been high, the subsequent calculations of the percentage rate of change in real prices have been low. This is especially true for SMA where the base year prices (even of the areas with the lowest land prices) have been much higher compared to the most prime areas in GMCA.The other reason behind such findings could be the time period for which computation was done, which was too short. Thus, although there may have been a rise in real values over this period of time, the *rate of change* has been calculated to be very low in real terms. Once the land prices of the current year are deflated, the percentage rate of change shows negative growth over the period concerned which is surprising considering the highly appreciating actual market values of land in the area.The study has not been able to take into consideration a parallel comparison of prevailing market prices owing to their extreme fluidity and other practical difficulties. However, it is worthy of mention here that as elsewhere, market prices are extremely high in comparison to the circle rates fixed by the respective authorities in the study areas. Nevertheless, the nature of the land market is found to play a very significant role in determining land values over time. It may be inferred that a quasi or restricted land-market lowers the bidding capacity of other potential buyers and affects in turn the estimates of values made by local civic authorities which are dismally low compared to the market prices of those very areas. So while actual transaction may happen on much higher prices (even if its volume is reduced considerably by restricting the gamut of buyers and sellers), the rates fixed by local authorities give us only a minimum estimate of the same and are thus unable to show the actual behaviour of the land market. However, due to the sheer volume of transaction and its open nature, the values of land tend to show a picture closer to reality than in a restricted market. Also, the same parcel of land exchanging hands between a limited number of buyers, over time results in general devaluation of land in these areas; the situation over an extended period of time, may, as Mukhim has maintained, lead to the concentration of the greater part of urban land in the hands of a few, mostly the landed political elite. While this is true of open land-markets as well, in comparison to their restricted counterparts, they may exhibit a much starker contrast, enabling swift privatisation of land which in turn brings in its wake some of the most conspicuous features that typify a liberalised built environment. The issue of urban primacy (where large urban centres under such a competitive financial climate benefit the most out of from prevailing developmental schemes); the predominance of HIG schemes in the housing market; the financial preponderance of single, expensive and one-time iconographic projects; the emergence of Urban Local Bodies (ULBs) as entrepreneurial entities, are some aspects of liberalised privatisation which have been observed in the extended research to prevail in both the study areas, especially where open transaction of land prevails. Thus, while the dynamics of land in Guwahati allows us to locate it with other liberalised Indian cities, the same sets it apart from cities within the North-East, where land transaction, being restricted by law to protect indigenous tribals from land alienation, has rather led to the emergence of a hybrid-condition which, as Rata has explained, may be better understood as a case of neo-tribal capitalism.

REFERENCES

Das, B.N., (2009). *Land Laws of Assam*, Assam Law House, Guwahati, pp. 21-24, 38-46.

Gupta, S. and R. Varma, (2008). Comparative Analysis of Financial Performance of Private Sector Banks in India: Application of CAMEL Model, *Journal of Global Economy*, 4 (1):144-156.

Indian Economic Survey, 2010-11, pp. A62-A64.

JNNURM CDP Appraisal Report, *Indian Institute of Public Relations*, New Delhi, http:// jnnurm.nic.in/nurmudweb/cdp_apprep_pdf/CDP_APPRAISAL_IIPA/ Shillong_IIPA.pdf

Kanungo, N., (2015). Aspects of Liberalised Privatisation of the Housing Market in North-East India: A Case Study of the Guwahati Municipal Corporation Area (1998-2008), *Urban India*, Vol. 35(1), pp. 30-44

Mukhim, P., (2011). Land Ownership among the Khasis of Meghalaya: A Gender Perspective, in *The Oxford Anthology of Writings from the North-East*, Misra, T. (ed.), Oxford University Press, pp. 285-296.

Nair, M.K.S., (1986). Constraints on the Development of a Land Market in Meghalaya, *Economic & Political Weekly*, Vol. 21 (30): 60-67, Stable URL: http://www.jstor.org/ stable/ 4375936 (accessed on 13th October, 2009).

Nongbri, T., (2001). Timber Ban in North-East India: Effects on Livelihood and Gender, *Economic & Political Weekly*, Vol. 36. (21), pp.1893-1900, Stable URL: http://www.jstor. org /stable/4410670 (accessed on 21st August, 2009.

Rata, E., (1999). *The Theory of Neotribal Capitalism*, Research Foundation of SUNY for and on behalf of the Fernand Braudel Centre, Vol. 22, No. 3, pp. 231-288, Stable URL: http:// www.jstor.org/stable/40241459. Accessed: 15/03/2012 04:02

Sodhi, I.S., (2008). Development Of Housing Finance in India, *Shelter: Housing and Finance Policy*, HUDCO, Vol. 11 (1), pp. 34-44.

Other Reading and Sources

Kanungo, N., 2014. Consumption and the Urban Morphology: A Comparative Study of the Re-creation of Space in Shillong and Guwahati, *Ph. D. Thesis*, Department of Geography, North-Eastern Hill University, (*unpublished*).

Study on Urbanisation of Shillong, Final Report, 1994, Socio-Economic Research Foundation, *(SERF),* New Delhi, pp. 1-66.

16
Town Morphology
A Case Study of Selected Towns in Meghalaya

P.K. Ryngnga

Introduction

Town Morphology is the spatial structure, change and characteristics of city and town by examining the patterns of its component parts and the process of its development. It is also an analysis of physical form that focuses on streets, buildings and land use patterns. Morphological studies often deal with development of forms and pattern of the present city or other urban areas through time, in short with evolution. In fact, an urban settlement is apparently a physical entity and a morphology it acquires is a result of a long process of growth. In a more restricted sense, the terms of morphology refers to the internal structure of various land uses in urban areas. The functional structure, functions and forms, constitute the principal and intimately related aspects of urban morphology. In a specific period of time, the structure of a town passes through various developmental stages and is the consequence of the processes it undergoes. In general, morphology of a town is quite different from that of a biological organism, to the extent of its individuality with the function. But the process of formation of a town and the development of an organic form pass through three stages, viz. (i) Histogenesis, (ii) Patternogenesis, and (iii) Morphogenesis. In the process of town formation 'histogenesis' refers to the origin of historical nucleus of a town and it forms some definite means of intercommunication between individual human agglomerations. During this stage, nucleus development of a town takes place. Settlement starts concentrating around a religious site, fort, lake etc. where centripetal force is active in this process. The pattern formation or 'patternogenesis' may be regarded to be the phase of development of various nuclei of human settlements and their interactions within, ultimately providing a pattern of skeleton to the town. More precisely, the development of roads and structures can be put into this heading. Thus, the sectoral development of town takes place and the centrifugal force, to some extent, is active. The state of 'morphogenesis' can be perceived in the morphological character, to be closely associated with the functional character of present day city.

Urban morphology is the study of the physical form of a city which consists of street patterns, building sizes and shapes, architecture, population density and patterns of residential, commercial, industrial and other uses among other things. Special attention is given as to how the physical form of a city changes over time and how different cities compare with each other. Another significant part of this subfield deals with the study of the social forms which are expressed in the physical layout of a city and conversely, how physical form produces or reproduces various social forms. This approach challenges the common perception of unplanned environments as chaotic or vaguely organic through understanding the structures and processes embedded in urbanization. The term 'morphology' includes various internal forms and structural patterns and characteristics of a spatial unit. In brief, urban morphology is the distribution of different functions in a city. Morphology is concerned with plans and builds of the habitat, viewed and interpreted in terms of its origin, growth and function. It is a description of their nature, their relative disposition and their social interdependence which constitutes a geographical analysis of an urban area. There are three basic models in urban morphology, namely (i) the Burgess' Concentric Model (1923), (ii) the Hoyt's Sector Model (1939), and (iii) the Ullmann & Harris' Multi-Nuclei Model (1945).

Morphology of Indian cities with respect to the existing layout of streets, arrangement and characteristics of buildings and associated patterns of land uses can be perceived both in terms of historical and as well as in geographical settings. Coming to the Indian context, it is seen that no Indian town purely follows these urban morphological models. The most salient feature of urban morphology of Indian towns includes at least four types of cities. Though a lot of variations in the city structure is observed—ranging from fully planned and modern westernized cities to more or less indigenous cities, but a varying blend of the orient with the occident and with the distinctive Indian culture is a common feature. The Indian culture still has an upper hand in most of the cities. The four common types of cities found in India, are: (i) the indigenous cities with one dominant node which follow in general the Bleicher-Clark Model of urban density gradient which are more in numbers, (ii) the Anglicized port cities, viz. Mumbai, Kolkata and Chennai which have lower densities in the city centre as contrasted with the indigenous cities, (iii) the two-node cities cities like Hyderabad-Secunderabad and Bangalore and (iv) the planned cities like Chandigarh, Jamshedpur and Bhubaneswar where population density is lower throughout and the density crest is not necessarily at the centre.

Generally towns and cities in India's North East follow an indigenous pattern with one node, but the classification of towns varies from one to the other. The urban social pattern in North East Indian cities and towns are very complex due to the influence of a variety of factors. The presence of many religions, languages, castes and classes produces a more heterogeneous pattern. The existence of multiple physical urban patterns is caused by the presence of indigenous settlements of course British influence shape the social patterns of the region. Thus, in the light of the above preliminary discussions the chapter explores the characteristics of town morphology and further accentuates the forces behind the gradual change of towns of Meghalaya.

Functional Classification of Towns

The towns in Meghalaya are classified based on the functions they perform varying from political to economic activities along with their roles within urban systems. The classifications are as under:

Administrative Towns: These towns are the headquarters of administrative departments of central or state governments such as Shillong, Tura and Jowai. The main function is to administer the state, districts and sub-divisions of the state. However, when compared among the three towns, evidences revealed that Shillong attained the highest level order as administrative towns.

Educational Towns: In this category of town, Shillong secured the highest form of educational town followed by Jowai and Tura respectively. Shillong till today which grew at a faster rate is, *inter alia,* due to its educational set up. It is still the best place for education in the North East which attracted a large number of student population.

Economic Towns: Apart from the above two, to some extent these three towns are still the best places for trade and commerce. In terms of hierarchy, Shillong dominates in this category perhaps due to its proximity to Guwahati.

Resorts: Over the years, Shillong has witnessed a transformation in the field of tourism due to the physiography, natural beauty that God has bestowed upon. After 2001, rural tourism development has opened a wider prism to tourism industry which then triggered population flow into the State of Meghalaya.

Urban Land Use

The study of urban land is made in three ways: (1) How much part of the land is used and for what purposes? (2) In what types of works are the buildings located on that land? (3) How many people are involved in various types of work inside the town? In fact, these three things are correlated with their original relations of land-use. The number of buildings is highest that are involved in the largest type of work that develops on the urban land and in this profession people's involvement is numerically significant. There is only a difference of attitude in these three aspects. Land-use is very wide because in it we also include residences and land. Although it is not considered as commercial, yet it has great importance for a section of population falls under the category of dependents. Land-use presents the classification of urban land according to the category of utilization. In it, along with the study of all-round expansion of town land, perpendicular expansion is also studied. Therefore, the study of land-use has a very important place in urban morphology (Bansal, S.C., 1999). The following emphasizes the town-wise morphological study of Meghalaya:

Shillong, the District Headquarters of East Khasi Hills, which is the capital of the State, is located at 25° 35′ north latitude and 91° 53′ east longitude occupying a valley called Shillong valley of about 45 sq. kms. in area. It is about 103 kms to the south of Guwahati and is located at the altitude of 1500 above the mean sea level. It is an agglomeration of seven urban centres viz. Shillong Municipality, Shillong Cantonment, Madanrting, Mawlai, Nongthymmai, Pynthorumkhrah and Nongmynsong. It has a population of about 2,67,662 according to the 2001 census. Shillong owes its importance due to its administrative function and about 55 per cent of the total workers of the town are engaged in non-agricultural activities. The percentage of workers engaged in industry is 10.5 per cent in trade and commerce 17.7 per cent in transport and communication etc. Shillong is also a very important educational centre in the North East India as a whole and it is a place of attraction for tourism industry. The study area, therefore, is suitable for such kind of studies in order to evaluate the impact of these activities on land use land cover (LULC) changes in the past thirty years. As far as the morphology of the city is concerned, it is found that the residential areas account for 74 per cent of the total area of the city and defense14 per cent. The commercial area occupies 3.5 per cent of the city. The main commercial areas of the city are Bara Bazaar and Police Bazaar. Late 1990s saw other areas such as Laitumkhrah, Polo, etc. which emerged as the secondary commercial centres. Invariably all the towns of Shillong Urban Agglomeration (SUA) developed their respective commercial nodes. Human activities such as agriculture, tourism, transport infrastructure and urban development have significant influence on land use/land cover (Carsjen and van Lier, 2002). The service sector attracts population increases from year to year which affects urban development in Shillong and in turn shapes and transforms land use land cover (henceforth to be known as LULC). The broad LULC categories in Shillong have been outlined in Table 16.1 indicates that the LULC of Shillong since 1970's embraces a general trend of LULC categories. The population growth of Shillong city since 1971 up to 2011 is given in Table 16.2.

Table 16.1: Major Land Use Land Cover Categories and Its Description Used for the Study

Land Use/Cover Classes	Description
Built-Up Area	Residential, urban built-up
Vacant land	Shrub, Construction Site
Forest	Reserved Forest, Protected forest

Source: Author's Construct.

Table 16.2: Growth of Population in Shillong City (1971-2011)

Year	Total Population	Decadal Variation	Decadal Growth Ratio
1971	1,22,752	+20.350	19.88
1981	1,75,180	+52.428	41.08
1991	2,23,336	+47.570	27.85
2001	2,67,881	+44.545	19.94
2011	3,54,325	+86.444	32.26

Source: Census of India 1971, Meghalaya, Part II-A, Census of India 1981, Meghalaya Part of 1981 Vol.II, Census of India 1991, Meghalaya, Census of India 2001, Meghalaya & Census of India 2011, Meghalaya, Provisional Paper).

From Table 16.2, it is observed that there is a population increase since 1970s to the 2011 in Shillong which indicated that increase of its population resulted in the transformation of land from other uses to urban built-up in order to cater to the growing demand in housing and service sectors. The study area has undergone significant transformation since the 1970s. The town was once covered by nearly 90 per cent of evergreen pine trees because of its location is quite far from the mainland India and its hilly topography. However, it is very rich in cultural heritage and natural beauties which compelled the Britishers to convert the study area into summer station. Gradually the study area became the desirable destination for migration of peoples from far and nearby places such as other states of India, Bangladesh, Nepal, Bhutan and these factors later contributed towards population congestion which change the LULC of Shillong. It is timely, therefore, to assess the impact of such development on local environment. This includes evaluating the LULC changes and measuring the annual urban expansion intensity index from 1970s till the present time. It will provide significant indicators to assess the sustainability of tourism development in the state. The study monitored land use changes in from 1971 to 2011 in order to evaluate the impact of increase of population. Time series data were collected from various sources such as maps, tables, field surveys and reports. LULC was divided into three broad categories as shown in Table 16.3. This classification was used in order to ensure uniform category of all LULC maps.

Table 16.3: Land Use Land Cover of Shillong City (1970-2010)

Category	1970 Sq. Km (%)	1986 Sq. Km (%)	1991 Sq. Km (%)	2010 Sq. Km (%)
Built Up Area	27.240 (31)	37.242 (28)	38.043 (29)	42.4127 (36)
Vacant/ Barren Land	30.051 (34)	48.930 (36)	39.9206 (30)	34.0961 (26)
Forest	31.884 (35)	48.375 (36)	54.68 (41)	54.63 (42)
Total	**89.1753 (100)**	**134.5483 (100)**	**132.6263 (100)**	**130.9718 (100)**

Source: Author's Construct from the calculated Area of land use land cover using Arc GIS.

Table 16.3 and Figure 16.1 show the LULC changes from 1970 to 2010. Built-up area category increased quite significantly where LULC activity covers only 27.24 sq. kms in 1970 and increased to 38.04 sq. kms in 1991. By 2010, an additional built-up area of 4.37 sq. kms was recorded. Areas which underwent significant changes mostly centred around Pynthorumkhrah, Mawlai, Madanrting and near the existing population centres such as in Laitumkhrah and Laban. Urban built-up areas centred around IGP and Laitumkhrah which are the administrative and commercial-*cum*-residential areas of the case city. Evaluation of annual urban expansion index, however, revealed more interesting results. This index shows the speed of urban expansion per unit area.

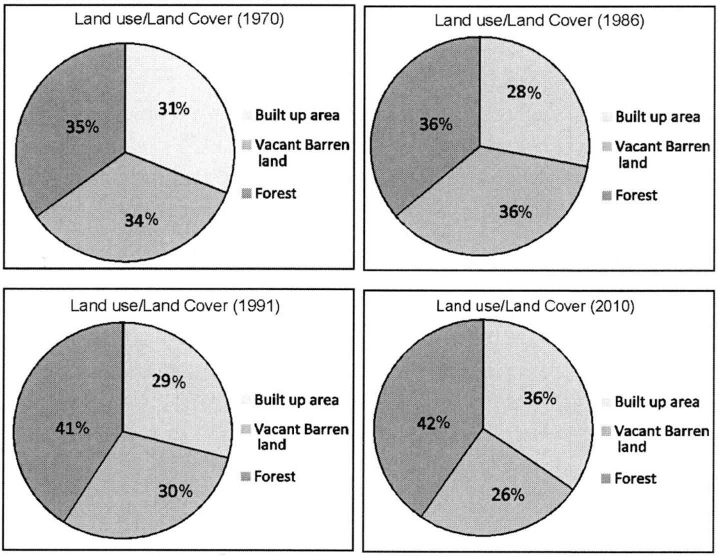

Figure 16.1: Land Use Land Cover of Shillong City (1970-2011)

Source: Author's Construct- Change detection from 1970-2011 using Arc GIS.

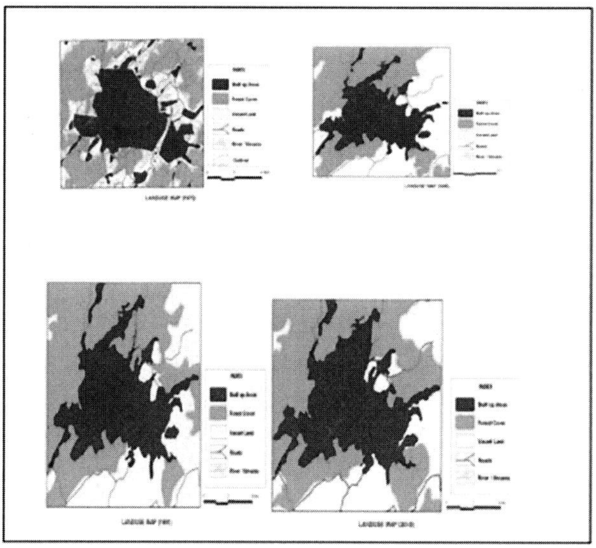

Figure 16.2: Areas Showing High Speed of Urban Expansion

Source: Author's Construct using Arc GIS.

The statistics showed that many parts of the study area experienced high-speed of annual urban expansion. During the first phase (1970-1986), few areas of Shillong experienced a high speed of urban expansion which included Laban, Laitumkhrah and Mawkhar (Figure 16.2). This period was the period of impact due to the bifurcation of the State from Assam where administrative set up played a major role in shaping this new town. LULC transformation during that era was mainly due the change of forest into urban area in order to house the new service centres. During the second phase (1986-1991), fast speed to medium speed urban expansion took place in which rural migration plays the major role in influencing the rate of change. The study area had experienced more population due to the augmentation of administrative and educational set up. During the third phase (1991-2010), the city underwent a tremendous speed of urban expansion and in 2010 it was seen that urban expansion has reached the saturation point which necessitated the Government to develop a corridor to the east called Mawdiangdiang to form a new township popularly known as the New Shillong. However, apart from the built-up area, other types of LULC categories did not change much in the last thirty years.

Table 16.3 is indicative that after 1986, vacant land area decreased from 48.930 sq. kms to 39.9026 sq. kms in 1991 to approximately 34.0961 sq. kms in 2010. On the other hand, the area under forest did not reveal much change since Shillong is a tribal town where rules and regulations prohibited people to cut trees indiscriminately. It is seen that forest in 1970 covered 31.884 sq. kms increased to 48.375 sq. kms in 1991 and further increased to 54.68 sq. kms and remained constant till 2010 except for a decrease of .05 sq. kms.

Jowai is the Headquarters of West Jaintia Hills District and is home to the Pnar tribe. It is a scenic place located on the plateau surrounded on three sides by the Myntdu river bordering Bangladesh to the south at a spatial distance of about 50 kms from the Indo-Bangladesh border. Due to its high altitude of 1380 m above the mean sea level, Jowai is an important business and education hub of the entire district catering to the needs of students from all over the district and as well as from the adjacent parts of Assam and Bangladesh. It is well equipped with amenities such as schools, colleges, hospitals, post offices etc. The functional classification of this town is somewhat difficult to describe, since time immemorial, there was a market called law Musiang which lies in the heart of the town itself and all activities revolved around this market. The segregation of functional zone of the town even does not follow any definite pattern but it is clear that all the functions are concentrated around the market. In fact the morphology of the town is very much affected with the presence of the market.

Table 16.4: Land Use Land Cover of Jowai Town

Land Use/Land Cover	**Area in Hectare**	**Per cent to developed land**	**Per cent to total master plan**
Residential	63.70	63	3.43
Commercial	1.25	1.24	0.07
Public/Semi Public	1.40	1.38	0.08
Church/Religious	1.12	1.11	0.08
Burial & Cremation Ground	11.75	11.62	0.63
Industrial	0.08	0.87	0.05
Roads	19.75	19.54	1.36
Open Space (Parks & Playgrounds)	1.25	1.24	0.07
Agricultural land	262.50	–	14.15
Forest & other barren land	1491.5	–	80.40
Total	**1855**	**100**	**100**

Source: Jowai Master Plan 1991-2001.

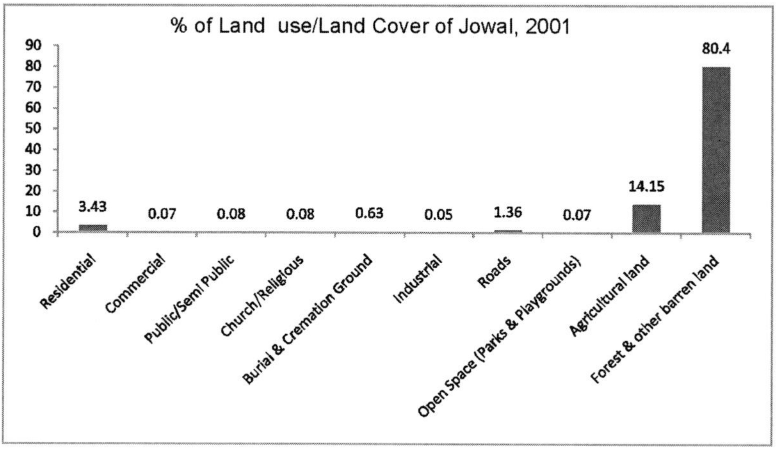

Figure 16.3: Land Use Land Cover of Jowai Town.

Note: Author's Construct from Table 16.4.

From Table 16.4 and Fig 16.3, it revealed that forest and other barren land constituting 80.40 per cent is still a dominating land cover followed by agricultural land of 14.15 per cent and residential areas of 3.43 per cent. However, the Master Plan Area of Jowai is 18.55 sq. kms. All villages around periphery now form part of the planning area. Jowai town is being administered by a Municipality headed by the state civil service officer as the Chief Executive Officer. The prime functions of Municipality are maintenance, repair of roads and footpaths, provision of drinking water and sanitation.

Tura is a hilly town and a municipality in West Garo Hills District and is one of the largest towns in the State. Tura is a valley located at the foothills of the Tura range and right below the Tura Peak. Tura is a cultural and administrative centre of the Garo tribe. Tura super market is directly related to the genesis of Tura town and is located adjacent to the traditional bazaar. Tura has never been given any perceptible importance and impetus to be a tourist destination. The Municipal area of 18.32 sq. kms is proposed to increase to 39.16 sq. kms by including nearby villages including Danakgre, Badagongre, Agilangre, Doldegre, Bokmagre, Robagre, Dobgre and Walbakgre. The LULC of Tura can be visualized from Figure 16.4 which is indicative of the fact that residential areas dominate the eastern part of Tura and commercial land use are seen dotted in and around Tura whereas the periphery of the town is still dominated by forests.

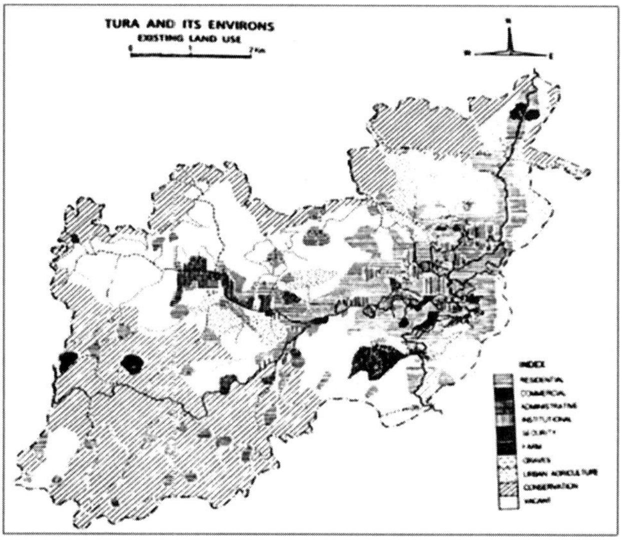

Figure 16.4: Land Use Land Cover of Tura Town.

Source: Ryngnga & Sarma Meghalaya.

Discussions

The phases of development in every town is characterized with the growth of additional functions and resulted in the growth and extension of these towns. Because of cool and healthy climate and peaceful environment, the three towns need to be fully developed as tourist resorts and educational centres. Shillong is visited every year by not less than 5000 tourists. It has a High Court, Universities, head offices of both Central and State departments. It has a number of hotels, inns and restaurants. It is the only urban centre in the State which has a golf course. Jowai is a main connecting town between the State of Meghalaya and Assam and Mizoram, Tripura. Due to this function, this town gradually developed to a full-fledged Municipality.

However, classification of functions has impacted the towns which are discussed as under:

Impact of Educational Institution on the Morphology: In modern times, Shillong, Jowai and also Tura are equipped with big educational institutions of higher learning, medium and public schools. Some of these have nationwide fame. The Missionary schools are run in a very congenial atmosphere with sufficient space and good hostels, in open areas with peaceful atmosphere, although some institutions like St. Anthony's College, St. Joseph's College, St. Mary's Convent and All Saints' etc. are at the heart of the congested residential and business areas. Besides these, the training and technological institutes have also been added to the town morphology. These training institutions have hostels and facilities for games. In all the three towns, though these institutions are handicapped by limited area at their commands, they have helped in the growth and expansion of the towns on modern lines.

Impact of Trading and Commercial Establishment: Shillong is growing fast because of the growth of trade and commerce. Business centres have developed in the central parts of Police Bazaar along the main roads. In Jowai and Tura, the business areas have become over-crowed.

Impact of Tourism Development: All the three towns have felt the impact of tourism development. The town morphology has taken a fast turn with the development of this sector particularly after 2000. It has a prospect of attracting large number of people.

Impact of Administrative Functions: Shillong, Jowai and Tura town grew to perform administrative functions particularly Shillong because it was the summer capital of the erstwhile Assam Government and also the headquarters of different government offices. Thus, the establishment of these administrative set up has also added to the growth and expansion of towns.

Impact of the Policy of the Government: The governmental development activities after the year 2000 injected new inspiration to the resort towns and planned development took place in them. Thus, the towns have better future prospects of growth as well.

Impact of Town Forming Forces: Two forces, viz. centripetal and centrifugal are the most important factors for the formation and development of town morphology. For the origin of the towns in Shillong, some nuclei have worked as the centripetal forces, particularly administrative and educational set up. They have attracted and concentrated the population and various establishments. Colby (1959) has termed the centripetal forces as functional magnetism and functional prestige.

Prospects and Problems: The growth of towns is affected by centripetal forces and forms commonly the concentric growth pattern. At this stage, the centrifugal force ensues and establishments occur towards the peripheral zones. The congestion and suffocation in the heart of the towns have caused the search of open space which is termed as spatial force. When the oppressed class tends to move outward due to the increased land value and high taxes, it is termed as 'the force of social evolution'. Shillong, Tura and Jowai and its surrounding towns attract a number of tourists during the summer season. Because of this, population of towns is growing very rapidly and the related problems are also growing very rapidly. For want of basic facilities such as water, electricity, residence etc. problems are being noticed in the growth of the towns. Even then people are migrating to the cities in search of employment and other facilities. Consequently, unauthorized encroachments and illegal constructions are going on public land. These encroachments and illegal constructions are being made not only by poor class but also by rich and prosperous class due to which the problems of towns are growing rapidly. In these towns the central parts are narrow and crowded where residential areas are adjacent to the commercial areas characterized by narrow lanes and rickety houses with two to three storeys. Due to the continuous process of rural-urban migration, the growth rate of urban population is galloping and the residential density is too high and consequently illegal residential areas in various parts of towns have come up. The construction of residential areas has been rapid in the encroached areas of the town. In these towns, commercial area is also centralized. There is also a sufficient evidence to show migration of functions from one town to the other town. In these towns each activity appears to seek a site at which it may flourish best and the people of the community appear to determine how they wish the land to be used.

Conclusion

Urban Morphology is a phenomenon that urban areas experienced with the change in pattern, form and structures. The spatial arrangement of internal form appraoches human settlements as generally unconscious products that emerge gradually. Of the three towns, Shillong has reached a saturation point and urban sprawling process is more evident. However, the other two towns, viz. Jowai and Tura are still growing and are in the process to take their final form. Nevertheless, the overgrown towns if not properly checked in time pose problems to the residents due to inadequate residential houses and other civic amenities that will be rampant. The urban centres will then be highly congested and will lack element of civic infrastructure planning such as layout of roads, open spaces, differentiating commercials and residential landuse etc. which will then chock the healthy development of towns and cities.

REFERENCES

B. Harris, and M. Batty, (2001): Locational Models, Geographic Information and Planning Support Systems, in Brail, R.K and Klosterman, R.E. (eds) *Planning Support Systems*, ESRI Press, California pp. 25-57.

D. Simon, D. McGregor, and K. Nsiah-Gyabaah, (2004): The changing urban-rural interface of African cities: definitional issues and an application to Kumasi, Ghana, *Environment and Urbanization*, 16(2), 235-248.

ESRI. (1998): Using the Arc View Spatial Analyst. Redland: Environmental Systems Research Institute.

G.J. Carsjen, and H.N. van Lier, (2002): Fragmentation and Land-Use Planning-An Introduction, *Landscape and Urban Planning*, 58, pp 79-82.

Gita Singh, (2001): *Urban growth and changing land use pattern in Shillong*, Unpublished Thesis, NEHU, Shillong.

Goh Ban Lee, (1991): *Urban Planning in Malaysia: History, Assumption and Issues*: Tempo Publishing House, Kuala Lumpur

Government of India, (2000): *Manual on Nationwide Land Use/Land Cover Mapping using satellite imagery*, NRSA, Dept. of Space, Balanagar, Hyderabad.

Government of India, (1994): Mapping and monitoring Urban Sprawl (Hyderabad city using remotely sensed and satellite data) Project Report NRSA, Hyderabad Urban Development Authority.

Government of Meghalaya, (1991): *Master Plan of Shillong 1991-2011*, Directorate of Urban Affairs Shillong, Meghalaya.

H.B. Chauchan., Nayak, and Shailesh, (2005): Land use/ Land cover changes near Hazira region, Gujarat, Using Remote Sensing Satellite Data, Volume no. 33(3), September, *Indian Society of Remote Sensing*, Dehradun.

J. Stillwell, S. Geertman, and S. Openshaw, (1999): Developments in Geographical Information Systems and Planning in Stillwell, J., Geertman, S. and Openshaw, S. (eds.) *Geographical Information and Planning*, London, Springer. pp. 3-22.

J.A., Atauri, M. Mugica, & Ramirez-Sanz, L. and J.V. De Lucio, (2000): Assessment of nature conservation scenarios: Species or landscape structure? A case study in the Madrid region (Spain). in Mander, U, Jongman, R.H.G. (Editors) *Landscape Perspectives of Land Use Changes*: WIT Press, pp. 167-190.

J. Malczewski, (1999): *GIS and Multicriteria Decision Analysis*, New York, John Wiley & Son.

L. Poelmans, and A. van Rompaey, (2010): Complexity and performance of urban expansion models, Computers, *Environment and Urban Systems*, 34(1), pp. 13-27.

Narimah Samat, (2010): Assessing Land Use Land Cover Changes in Langkawi Island: Towards Sustainable Urban Living, *Malaysian Journal of Environmental Management* 11(1).

P.J. Harding, M.W. Jackson, and S.M. Otterstrom, (2007): Mapping, Measuring and Modelling Urban Growth, In Jensen, R.R., Gatrell, J.D., and McLean, D. (editors) *Geo Spatial Technologies in Urban Environments: Policy, Practices and Pixels*, 2nd edition, Berlin: Springer, pp. 141-176.

P.K., Joshi, G.S. Rawat, H. Padiliya, and P.S. Roy, (2005): Land use/land cover identification in an Alpine and Arid Region (Nubra valley Ladakh) Using Remote Sensing Satellite Data, Volume 33 (3) September Indian Society of Remote Sensing, Dehradun.

P.K. Ryngnga & S. Sarma, (2016): *Meghalaya*, Geophil Publishing House, Guwahati, India.

P.K. Ryngnga, (2007): *Patterns of Urban Development in Shillong since Independence*, Jawaharlal Nehru University, New Delhi, Unpublished Thesis.

S. Geertman, and F.J. Toppen, (1990): Regional planning for new housing in Randstad, Holland. In Scholten, H.J. and Stillwell, J. (eds.) *Geographical Information Systems for Urban and Regional Planning*. Dordrecht, Kluwer Academic Publishers, pp. 95-106.

Sarma, S., Meghalaya (2001): *The Land and Forest a Remote Sensing Based Study*, Geophil Publishing House, Guwahati, India.

Shetty, Amba, Nandagiri, Lakshman, Thokchom, Sangeeta, and M.V.S. Rajesh, (2005): Land use/ Land cover mapping using Satellite data for a forested & watershed, UDUPI District Karnataka state of India, *A Journal of the Indian Society of Remote Sensing*, June, Volume 3, IIRS, Dheradun.

Sudhir Mahajan & Pankaj Panwar, (2005): Land use changes in Ashwani khad watershed Using GIS Techniques. *The Indian Society of Remote Sensing*, Volume 33, June, Dehradun.

T. McGee, (2009): Building Liveable Cities in the Twenty First Century Research and Policy Challenges for the Urban Future of Asia, International Symposium on Sustainable Living, 4th June, Seremban, Malaysia.

T. McGee, (2009): The Spatiality of Urbanization: The Policy Challenges of Mega-Urban and Desakota Regions of Southeast Asia, Lestari Public Lecture, No. 8, Bangi Universiti Kebangsaan Malaysia.

17
Road Safety and Patterns of Road Accidents
A Case Study of Guwahati-Shillong National Highway in Ri Bhoi District, Meghalaya

Phiralin Amy Marsing and *Vinitoli H. Zhimo*

Introduction

Right to life and safety is the fundamental right of any citizen. This is guaranteed under the constitution of every country in the world including India. However, more people die every year from road accidents all over the world than the number killed during the whole of the Second World War. Road fatalities are due to a number of reasons, primary among them are bad condition of roads and traffic violations, poor implementation of various laws governing road traffic and safety issues and last but not the least, the faulty engineering of road mechanics, be it road design or traffic lighting etc. Furthermore, lack of awareness of road safety issues among the masses and apathy of the policy makers and implementers add to the increasing problem of road safety.

India has the dubious distinction of being one of the countries with highest number of road accidents which yield a cart-load of case law, which, of course, is not an elegy on the dead but a real tribute on this threatening piece of legislation. Each case, however, bears its own imprint which cannot be universalized. A look at some of the statistics on road safety presents a very grim picture worldwide and especially in developing countries like India. Road fatalities now leads the list of accidental death in India much more than any other such as by droning, fire, rail mishaps. The magnitude of road accidents in India is increasing at an alarming rate. About 60,000 people are killed every year in India which tops the world in the number of road fatalities. National level of fatalities per kilometre is 0.025.

Significance of Study

There is a fast increase in the number of commercial and as well as personal vehicles and the gradual improvement in the automotive technologies also in the district day by day where the number of accident cases also increases. Serious accidents of passengers, drivers, conductors, highway pedestrians and shop keepers near the highway have occurred in recent years. Such accidental deaths have badly affected the family members especially the bread earners. Different types of accident cases took place in the District from time to time. Due to the increase in the number of vehicles and the frequency of their movement, sometimes, it was found that the whole family died in the road accident leaving behind the kids only. In some cases, road accidents made the victims permanently disabled which caused irrepairable loss of earnings as they were no longer able to carry out any works. Such accidents have affected the family members and the society. Hence the significance of the study for this national highway number 6.

Objective of the Study

The present study aims at understanding the main reasons, patterns and impacts of accidents which occured in the Guwahati-Shillong highway connecting the two capitals of Assam and Meghalaya and to come out with safety measures for all road users.

Methodology

The methodology used in the study comprises four stages, viz. literature review, data collection, data analysis, identification of causes, problems and issues, proposed safety measures, conclusion and recommendations.

Review of Literature

Dr. R.G. Chaturvedi (2010) in "Law of Motor Accident Claims and Compensation" focuses on different aspects of Motor Accidents and discusses the concept of awarding compensation to victims of Motor Accidents. He says, "If the Government opts for mandating the automobiles to carry a statutory inscription that birding kills or maims, because it is unimpeachable truth that Indians motorized mayhem has officially made it the most dangerous place to drive in the world. Suffice this to betray the Division Bench decision of the High Court of Madras in B. Govinda Rajaju Chetty (1966) V.M.L.A. Goondaraja Mudaliar that a motor vehicle without which modern life would become impossible, cannot or should not be held to be inherently a dangerous thing." Kunal Mehta (2010) in his article "An Analyze of Law Relating to Accidents Claims in India" nicely wrote focusing the aspects of accident arising out of use of motor vehicles such as no fault liability, claims applications, assessment of claims, legal defence available to the Insurance Companies towards third party, gratitude passengers, dishonour of cheque of insurance premium, right to recovery from owner to Insurance Company Claims Tribunal and Appeal etc. P.K .Sarkar (2004) in his book "*The Motor Vehicles Act*, 1988" has explained the philosophy behind awards of compensation as far as pain and suffering proceeds on the footing that even though no monetary loss is occasional because of this situation, that is, because of the physiological aspect which the law takes cognizance of and which has been dealt with in some detail in the *Jhulun Rani Saha's case* where both the English and Indian laws have been analyzed in some detail. M. Stanley Fernandez (1995) in his article "Road Accidents" explains the duty of care in case of accidents required from owners and drivers of motor vehicles. He mentioned that there are numerous and extensive categories of situations which are treated by the courts as imposing a duty of care. By way of illustration merely, makers or repairs of chattels owe duty to those who use those chattels, teacher owes a duty to his chill-pupil, an occupier of land to visitors there and those engaged in skilled occupations to their customers, those carrying out activities on a highway to others highway users. The increased in road accidents is the poor condition of roads and disproportionate number of vehicles. A defendant who owed a duty to another was held to owe a duty also those who owe might attempt to rescue that other from acute peril in which the defendant's negligence had placed him. K.C. Dutt and Sunita Dadhich (1988) in their article "Motor Accidents Claims" focused on different aspects of motor accidents and discussed the concept of awarding compute to involvement of motor vehicles and law relating to compensation to victims of motor accidents. The book deals with the accidents which occurred due to involvement of motor vehicles and law relating to compensation to victims of such accidents. The authors also explained the concept of liability of owners and insurance of vehicles associated with the accident and broadly discussed the concept of vehicles involved and their criminal liability in case of motor accident under the Motor Vehicles Act.

Profile of the Study Area

Nongpoh town is located in the midway of Shillong-Guwahati highway. According to the 2011 Census Nongpoh is known as the fastest growing town in the State of Meghalaya. In recent years, development in the field of economic, political, social and in transportation has been taking place in this District at a faster pace than others. In the absence of railways, waterways and other modes of transportation; motorways or vehicular traffic is the only mode of transporting pasengers and freight means and is thus a lifeline for mobility in this part of the region. This NH number 6 is a 4-lane road constructed by the National Highway Authority of India (NHAI) which also serves as a bypass for the two cities. Prior to this, the highway was a 2-lane road which was constructed during the time of the Undivided Assam where vehicular traffic commuted between the two cities regularly. With the passage of time, traffic survey indicated that the volume of vehicular traffic has increased beyond the designed capacity of the 2-lane road and seeing this condition the Government of India converted it into a 4-lane highway. As this highway does not end itself within the urban peripheries of the two capitals but extends to other parts of the NE Region, the numbers of vehicles traveling through this road increase day by day and to a large extent, due to the erratic behaviour of drivers, the number of accidents also increase. It is unfortunate that despite being a planned national highway with smooth surface, it took a toll of human lives such as passengers, pedestrians, old persons and students mainly caused by reckless drive.

Data Base

The data on causes of accidents, numbers of accidents, numbers of injured persons, numbers of dead persons both males and females were the secondary data collected from the Superintendent of Police's office, Nongpoh and drawn from books, journals and Government records for the years 2014, 2015 and 2016 and supplemented by limited field studies.

Findings and Discussions

Based on the secondary data, the details of vehicular accidents which occurred on this highway for the years 2014, 2015 and 2016 are given in Table 17.1.

Table 17.1: Details of Road Accidents for Years 2014, 2015 and 2016

Year	Nos. of Accidents	Nos. of Injured Persons	Male	Female	Nos. of Dead Persons	Male	Female	Causes of Accidents Either of the Following
2014	51	65	60	5	34	31	3	Overtaking, careless, over speeding etc.
2015	40	42	36	6	23	20	3	Overtaking, careless, over speeding, driving under influence of drug, alcohol, physical fatigue of drivers etc.
2016	47	60	46	14	38	27	11	Influence of drug, alcohol overtaking, careless, over speeding etc. driving under bad weather condition, other causes physical fatigue of drivers.
Total	**138**	**167**	**142**	**25**	**95**	**78**	**17**	

Source: S.P. Office Nongpoh, Ri Bhoi District.

Table 17.1 indicated that during the period under the study, the cumulative figures of road accidents registered were 138 numbers, injured persons were 167 out of which 142 numbers were males and 25 were females. The dead persons recorded were 95 numbers comprising 78 males and 17 females. The data showed that the numbers of injured and dead persons were mostly males and the causes of accidents were mainly due to overtaking, carelessness, over speeding, influence of drugs, alcohol, physical fatigue of drivers, driving under bad weather condition. Road accidents occurred in all types of transport modes such as taxis, cars, buses, trucks, two-wheelers etc. In the year 2014, heavy vehicles like trucks and lorries which were the prime carriers of consumer goods, trailers, containers etc. and buses both government and private including school buses mostly involved in accidents. In the year 2015, accidents were met mostly by vehicles like three wheelers, auto rickshaws both passenger and goods carriers followed by two wheelers such as motor cycle, bikes and scooters and by Jeeps both government and private. In the year 2016, accidents were met mostly by SUVs of 7 & 8 seater capacities, station wagons etc. including vehicles like trucks, lorries, cars and taxis. Road accidents classified according to place of occurrence revealed that accidents mostly occurred in places near the educational institutions, residential areas, religious places, recreation places, industrial areas and at pedestrian crossings. In recent years, it was found that the frequency of accidents was more near the schools, colleges, educational institutions and pedestrian crossings and the victims either injured or dead were mostly schools students. Accidents near the residential areas along the national highway which took away lives of innocent people in the form of 'hit-and-run' drive occurred mostly during night time due to physical fatigue, reckless drive and overspeeding. In the case of public transportation like buses, tourist cabs; accidents occurred mainly due to overspeeding and over-taking of the leading vehicles. Accidents met by private vehicles like cars and two-wheelers such as scooters and bikes were mainly due to drunk driving and overspeeding. In case of two-wheelers, it was also reported that non-use of helmets was the deciding factor for fatality. Such types of accidents resulted mostly either in spot deaths or serious injuries with less chance of survivals. In our study of this highway we identified some of the places where accidents used to occur or the accident-prone locations and called "black spots" and these were Dwarksuid, Bhoirymbong, Umroi Madan, Nongtraw and Umdohbyrthi on the Shillong bypass and Umling, Shangbangla, Mawtnum, Quinine, Nongpoh proper, Mawdiangum, Downgate Nongpoh, Umlyngkdait, 12th Mile, 14th Mile, 15th Mile Byrnihat, 17th Mile and 18th Mile Byrnihat on the NH number 6. During the years 2014, 2015 and 2016, it was reported that the maximum numbers of accidents which occurred on the 'black spots' were Shangbangla, Umdohbyrthi, Bhoirymbong and Dwarksuid followed by Umroi madan, Nongtraw, Umling, Mawtnum Quinine. During the period of study, traffic police of this District detected certain types of driving cases which involved violation of Motor Vehicles Act. These were: (i) driving/pillion riding without helmet, (ii) driving under the influence of alcohol and drugs, (iii) over-speeding, (iv) non-use of seat belts, (v) use of mobile phones while driving, (vi) overloading, (vii) rash and negligence driving, (viii) driving without driving licence and (ix) driving by minor local drivers in and around the nearby segments of highway. From the temporal point of view, it was observed that accidents used to occur on different spots of the highway in the month of December, January and February mostly due to inebriated driving and overspeeding as people were in festive mode and in full working season during these months.

In ensuring safety of the society and in carrying out the order passed by the Apex Court banning the sale of liquor along the national highways, it was observed that Ri Bhoi police in collaboration with personnel from Excise Department used to intensify regular checking of vehicles to detect drunken driving, rash driving and illegal sale of liquor on the highway. The Superintendent of Police, Nongpoh informed us that there were no more wine stores along the national highway and vendors were allowed to set up their wine stores beyond 100 metres from the outer edge of the National or State Highway (SH). Despite such enforcement of law, it was observed that many wine shops were actually selling liquor illegally within the radius of 100 metres from the highway which was contrary to the claim of the law enforcing authorities. It is really unfortunate in our country that over one lakh persons lose their lives every year due to road accidents thereby affecting the properties and families of the deceased persons. This underlines the urgency for evolving and adopting various road safety measures. As a part of the advocacy campaign for road safety, "Road Safety Week" is being observed throughout the country every year in the month of January wherein stakeholders are actively involved through various activities to highlight and promote safe roads to the citizens.The Ministry of Road Transport and Highways (MoRTH), Government of India in the meeting of the Advisory Committee held on the 18th March, 2013, which was attended by all the Chief Secretaries of States and Union Territories (UTs) had informed that in 2011, 1.42 lakh persons were killed in 4.9 lakh road accidents. It was also identified that 24,655 road accidents were caused by drunken driving which resulted in 10,553 deaths and 21,148 injuries of persons. The meeting had resolved to remove all liquor vends on NHs and banned the issuance of fresh licences in consonance with the popular adage "prevention is better than cure". The occurrence of a large number of road accidents leading to injuries and fatalities is not a phenomenon confined to NHs alone but also to the SHs. Both the NHs and SHs share a common experience of an unacceptably high number of road accidents, injuries and fatalities where drunken driving is one of the major causes. Hence, the content of the advisories issued by the Union Government as well as their basis, rational and foundation would equally apply to SHs. Human life is precious. As an integral part of economic development as road network expands, the rate of accidents also increases which has a profound impact on the lives of common citizens. In strengthening the safe road movement, the Transport Research Wing, MoRTH brought out a publication titled "Road Accidents in India, 2015". It was portrayed that in 2015 a large group of persons which assembled on the foreground was the leading cause of 27,152 road accidents under the influence of alcohol. The advisory meeting of the Chief Secretaries of all States and UTs held on the 1st December, 2015 organised by the said Ministry had noted the report that as on 2009, India had the highest number of road accident fatalities in the world. This is indicative of the fact that road accident in India occurred every four minutes. In curbing drunken on driving, the Parliament had legislated law with a zero-tolerance policy towards driving under alcholic influence. For a nation on the cusp of economic development, India can well avoid the tag of being the accident capital of the world. Our highways and expressways are expanding to provide seamless connectivity and unheralded opportunities for the growth of trade and industry, movement of goods, persons and capital. They are the backbone of freedom for trade, commerce and communication as guaranteed by the Article 301 of the Constitution. Our highways are dotted with cautionary or warning signs and informatory signs where the impending danger of combining speed and alcohol constituting a heady cocktail is also made prominent.

Conclusion

The details of patterns of road accidents that occured in NH 6 for the three years was collected from the Office of the Superintendent of Police, Ri Bhoi, Nongpoh. In the year 2014, 2015 and 2016 the number of cases was registered mostly for the accidents met by heavy vehicles, cars and two wheelers apart from the pedestrians. The study reckoned the average numbers of both males and females who were injured and also the total number of dead persons where males were significantly more than females. It was also found that the main causes of accidents were over speeding and drunk driving. It was also observed that in the month of January, February and December; the accidents cases both injured and dead were at their peak level. The spots of accidents were mostly near the schools and pedestrian crossings. From the crime records maintained by the Police of this District, it was evident that violations of the Motor Vehicles Act during the last three years such as pillion riding without helmet, driving under the influence of alcohol or drugs, over speeding, non-use of seat belts, using of mobile phone while driving, over loading, rash and negligence driving, driving without driving licence, driving by minor local drivers in around the areas were rampant. The Ri Bhoi Police have tried their best to mitigate the accident cases by organising every year the awareness programme on road safety, drugs abuse and addiction, application of Juvenile Justice Act, band on sales of tobacco and alcohol by persons below the age of 21 years and complete ban on drugs. They used to organize refresher trainings for drivers on road safety rules, various signs/signages and rendering of first aid services in case of accidents. They also used to hold special meetings with the local drivers especially with local Sumo and auto drivers and discussed the essence of Road Safety and made them aware about the meanings written in the signboards like "Go Slow in Accident Prone Area", "Market Area", "Blind Curve", "School Area", "Obey Traffic Rules" etc. so to avoid accident while driving on the highways. Hence the study clearly established the rising prevalence of road accidents in the area and how to make it a safe place for driving. The Ri Bhoi police identified some venues which they called them 'black spots' where accidents used to occur regularly and took away many lives. The study also noted the role played by the Ri Bhoi police in dealing with the accident cases which was laudable. However, to seriously address this issue, the following measures are proposed.

Recommendations

1. Construction of speed breakers at some designated places especially near the school areas.
2. Installation of signboards at some portions of the highway.
3. Provision of zebra crossings in many places especially the places near the villages and small towns.
4. Provisions of quick services to drivers like two-away of the damaged vehicles, ambulance services for quick medical help be made in the highway project to aid during accidents or break down of vehicles.
5. Scientific methods such as guidance for traffic conditions through mobile phones and internet facilities, availing hospitals with trained medical staff at specific intervals with supply of oxygen and life saving medicines be made available while managing the unfortunate happenings like traffic congestion, accidents, vehicles break down etc.
6. Installation of cameras at the appropriate spots and right intervals for identification of vehicles breaking the traffic rules and criminals should be carried out on the highway.
7. Timely payment of compensation and treatment to the victims.
8. More prompt and effective functioning of police for accidents cases.
9. Treatment of accident cases not as regular civil matters.

10. Awareness programme on the menace and aftermath of drunk driving should be conducted from time to time.
11. Strict implementation of road safety policy and rules.
12. Regular check up and inspection of vehicles.
13. Strict adherrence to rules nd procedures while issuing driving licences.
14. Supervision and control of speed of vehicles.
15. Establishment of Literacy Programmes Centres and First Aid Centres for the victims of road accidents.
16. Strong actions should be taken against the law breakers.

REFERENCES

Ahliwalia, Isher, J., (1992): *Redefining the Role of the State; India at the Cross Roads*, N.D: Centre for Policy Research.

Bakshi, P.M.'s, (1989) : "Accident Victim and the Criminal Law" *Law 3 JILI*, p. 566.

Central Instutute of Road Transport, Pune, "Accident Analysis of Selected Indian Cities /States/ Corridors" published by Centre for Road Safety.

Dalvi, M.Q., (1997): *Transport Planning and Policy in India*, Himalaya Publishing House, Mumbai.

Gupta. D.P., (1999): *Moderning Road Infrastructure and Road Transport*, India Merchant Chamber, Mumbai.

K. Guptewar's (1995): "Comparative Negligence in Motor Accidents", *11 JILI* (1969), 413.

M. Stanley Fernandez's, "Road Accidents", *Cri. L.J.* 49.

Books

A.B. Majumder, (1998): *Motor Accident Claims*.

B.N. Chaudhuri, (1990): *Motor Vehicles Act*, 1988.

D.K. Gaur, (2001): *A Textbook on the Indian Penal Code*.

G. Ison Terence, (1989): *Accident Compensation: A Commentary on the New Zealand Scheme*.

Jaggis Motor Vehicles Laws & Rules (1978).

K.C. Dutt and Sunita Dadhich, (1988): *Motor Accident Claims*.

Matadin, (1984): *State Monopoly of Road Transport in India*.

P. Leekrishnan, (1997): *Legal Aspects of State Carriage Licening in India*.

18
Urbanisation in Sikkim
A Case Study of Gangtok Sub-Division

Pranay Jyoti Goswami and *Biswajyoti Das Gupta*

Introduction

Sikkim is a tiny hilly state in the North Eastern Himalayan region which joined the Indian Union as the 22nd state on May 16, 1975. The state is located between 27°04′46″ and 28°07′48″ North latitude and 88°00′58″ and 88°55′25″ East longitude covering an area of 7096 km^2. The state has international borders with Bhutan, China and Nepal and the national border with Darjeeling District of West Bengal. The state is famous for its lush green vegetation, verdant forests ranging from tropical to temperate and alpine zone, scenic valleys and majestic mountains. The administrative jurisdictions of the state are divided into four districts and nine sub-divisions as on 2011.The state is thinly populated with only 610577 persons, out of which, 456999 (74.85%) persons live in rural areas and 153578 (25.15%) persons live in urban areas. The density of population is 86 persons per sq. km. which is much below the national density of 382 persons per sq. km. Agriculture is the primary activity of the people of the state.

The state has witnessed a rapid increase in establishment of hydel power projects, construction works, industries, service sector enterprises, viz. hotels and transport etc. in the post liberalization period since 1991. Industrialization and modernization concerted as a centripetal force which resulted in the gradual migration of people from rural to urban areas. It is observed that there was a net migration of 2540 persons from urban to rural areas in the state in 1991 and the reverse trend is noticed in the state since 2001. The net migration of population from rural to urban areas in the state was 494 persons in 2001 which increased to 28424 persons (18.51%) in 2011. It is also observed that only 38.25 sq. km (0.54%) is an urban area which shares 25.15 per cent of the total population. The density of population in the urban area is 4015 persons per sq.km whereas the corresponding density of population in the rural area is 65 persons per sq. km. as on 2011. It is observed that one of the reasons for rural-urban migration is the search for work opportunities. Data on net migration of 252 persons from urban to rural area in search of work opportunities in 1991 and the reverse trend since 2001 corroborate this fact. Similarly, it was observed that there was a net migration of 2197 persons from rural to urban areas in search of job opportunities in 2001 which increased to 12872 persons in 2011. This constituted 45.29 per cent to the total net migration from rural to urban areas in the state and 8.38 per cent to total urban population. The continuous increase in net migration of population from rural to urban areas in search of work opportunities may be due to the decline of opportunities in agricultural activities. It was observed that the total area under cultivation for food grains (including cereals and pulses) and oilseeds has gradually declined. However, it was observed that a slight increase in area under horticultural crops occurred. On the other hand, the state depends on the supply of almost all agricultural produce, viz. food grains, oilseeds, vegetables, fruits etc. from the neighbouring states, viz. West Bengal and other states in the country. Among its four districts, East District has a high concentration of urban population of 122487 persons which is almost 80 per cent of the total urban population. The East District has three sub-divisions, viz. Pakyong, Rongli and Gangtok where Gangtok which is the capital of the State situates here. All the urban areas in the district fall under the Gangtok Sub-division. The Gangtok sub-division has three urban local bodies (ULBs), viz. Gangtok Municipal Corporation, Singtam Nagar Panchayat and Rangpo Nagar Panchayat. Of the total area of 563.00 sq. kms of this sub-division, only 21.17 sq. km. (3.76 %) is urban with a population of 116604 persons which constitutes 53.13 per cent of the total population of this sub-division. The percentage share of urban population in all the other sub-divisions in the state is less than even 22 per cent of the total population of the respective sub-divisions. The density of population of the Gangtok sub-division is 390 persons per sq. km., whereas the corresponding population density in urban areas of the sub-division is as high as 5508 persons per sq. km. Hence, an attempt is made in the present study to examine the level of urbanization in the Gangtok sub-division in the post liberalization period since 1991 and the state of sanitation facilities over the period in the urban areas of this sub-division.

Objectives

The objectives of the present study are:

1. To examine the level of urbanization in Gangtok sub-division since 1991.
2. To investigate the state of sanitation facilities over the same period in the urban areas of Gangtok sub-division.

Methodology

For the present study, census data for different years are used. Different urbanization level and tempo measurement techniques are applied, viz. per cent of urban population, urban/rural population ratio, annual exponential growth rate of urban population, annual exponential change in percentage share of urban population, annual exponential change in urban/rural ratio of population etc. to understand the level of urbanization in the area of study. On the other hand, percentage of households having different sanitation facilities, viz. latrine, drainage and bathroom facilities within the house premises are calculated to find the state of sanitation facilities in the urban areas. Percentage of slum population to total urban population is also calculated in the present study. Appropriate statistical tools such as correlation, regression etc. are used to establish the relationships among the urbanisation parameters. Tables and charts are for used data representation.

Level of Urbanisation

It is observed that population in the urban areas of the Gangtok sub-division has been continuously increasing since 1991. This sub-division has a population of 31872 persons in 1991, which rose to 52852 persons in 2001 and further rose to 116604 persons in 2011 and rural population declined by (-) 32819 persons between 2001-2011. This is indicative of the fact that the share of population in the urban areas continuously increased from 23.25 per cent in 1991 to 28.04 per cent in 2001 and to 53.13 per cent in 2011. To understand the level of urbanisation in the sub-division, the urban/rural ratio of population is also calculated over the period and it was found that the ratio was 30.30 per cent in 1991 and increased to 38.96 per cent in 2001. The ratio was so high in 2011 (113.38%) when the urbanites had overpopulated the ruralites. The level of urban population in the sub-division is presented in Table 18.1 and Figures 18.1 and 18.2.

Table 18.1: Level of Population in Gangtok Sub-Division

Year	Total Population	Rural Population	Urban Population	Per cent Share of Urban Population to Total Population	Urban/ Rural Population Ratio (in %)
1991	137070	105198	31872	23.25	30.30
2001	188517	135665	52852	28.04	38.96
2011	219450	102846	116604	53.13	113.38

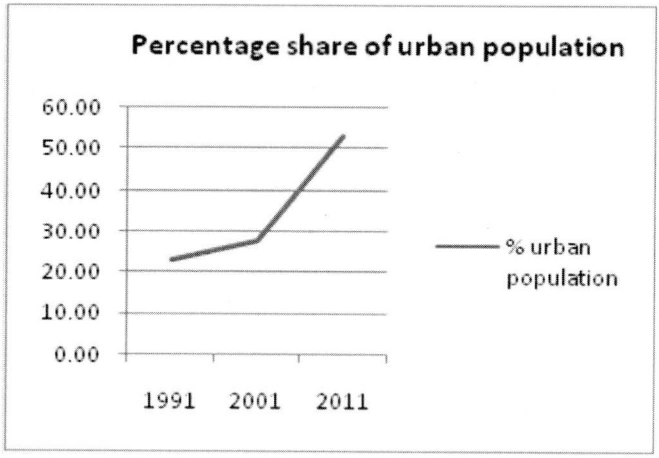

Figure 18.1: Percentage Share of Urban Population

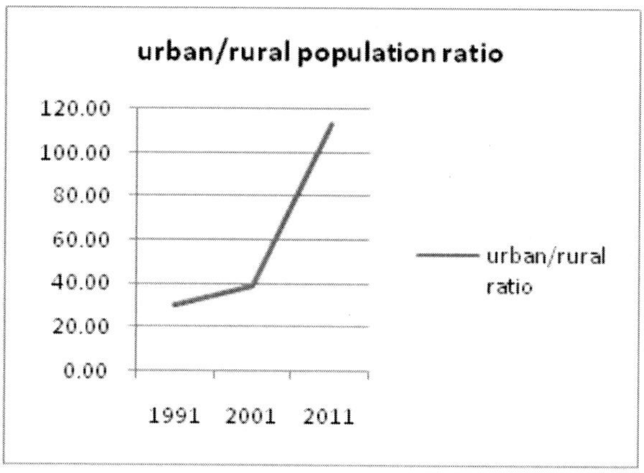

Figure 18.2: Urban-Rural Population Ratio

The sub-division underwent a high tempo of urbanization over the period since 1991. The annual exponential growth rate of urban population stood at 5 per cent during 1991-2001 and rose to 8 per cent during the decade of 2001-2011. Further, the annual exponential change in urban/rural population ratio has also sharply increased from 3 per cent during 1991-2001 to 11 per cent in 2001-2011. This has caused a rapid change in the annual exponential percentage share of urban population in the sub-division from 2 per cent between 1991 and 2001 to 6 per cent between 2001 and 2011. The same tempo of urbanization is observed in the constituent towns of the sub-division. It is observed that the annual growth rate of population has rapidly increased from 1.6 per cent between 1991 and 2001 to 12.3 per cent between 2001 and 2011 in Gangtok Municipal Corporation and from 2.2 per cent between 1991 and 2001 to 10.4 per cent between 2001 and 2011 in Rangpo Nagar Panchayat. However, there is a decline in annual exponential growth rate of population in Singtam Nagar Panchayat town from 3.4 per cent during 1991-2001 to 0.8 per cent during 2001-2011 as can be seen in Table 18.2.

Table 18.2: Growth of Population in Towns of Gangtok Sub-Division (1991-2011)

Towns	**Total Population**			**Annual Exponential Growth Rate of Population**	
	1991	**2001**	**2011**	**1991-2001**	**2001-2011**
Gangtok Municipal Corporation	25024	29354	100286	0.016	0.123
Singtam Nagar Panchayat	3868	5432	5868	0.034	0.008
Rangpo Nagar Panchayat	2980	3709	10450	0.022	0.104

Urbanization is a social phenomenon relating to changes in the economic structure of population when it moves from agricultural society to a non-agricultural society. This is reflected in this sub-division when we observe the gradual fall in the work participation rate (WPR) in agricultural activities from 13.64 per cent in 1991 to 12.90 per cent in 2001 and further declined to 12.17 per cent in 2011. On the other hand, a continuous increase in percentage share of urban workers to total workers from 24.59 per cent in 1991 to 25.37 per cent in 2001 and soared higher to 46.77 per cent in 2011 is found in this sub-division. The decline in the work participation rate in the agricultural sector and the increase in the percentage share of the urban workers are given Table 18.3 and Figures 18.3 and 18.4.

Table 18.3: Level of Workers in the Gangtok Sub-Division

Year	Total workers	Workers in rural areas	Workers in urban areas	Agricu-ltural workers	Per cent share of workers in rural areas to total workers	Per cent share of workers in urban areas to total workers	Work particip-ation rate (WPR) in agri-culture
1991	51068	38509	12559	18698	75.41	24.59	13.64
2001	83575	62374	21201	24323	74.63	25.37	12.90
2011	107521	57236	50285	26705	53.23	46.77	12.17

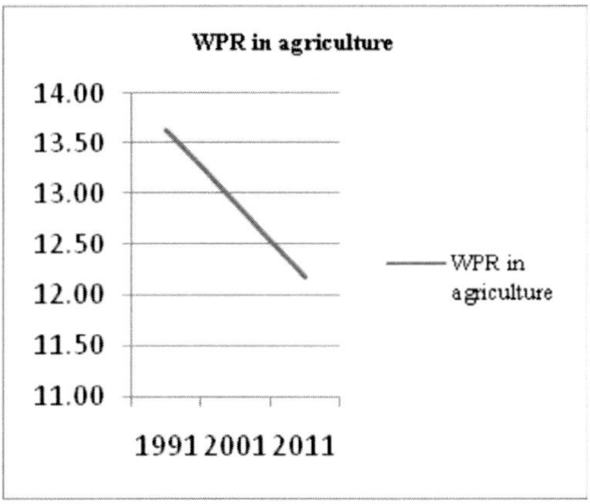

Figure 18.3: WPR in Agriculture

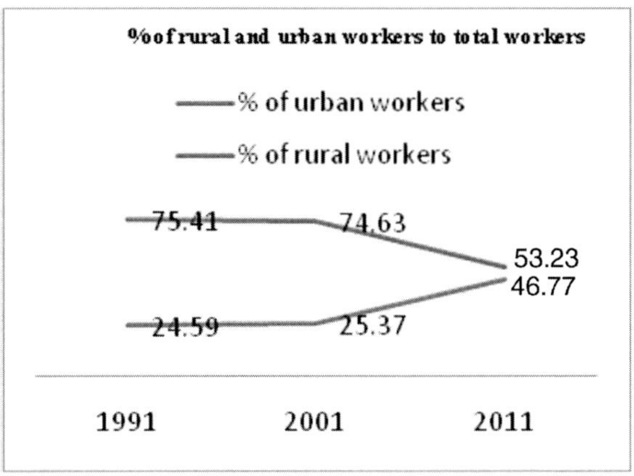

Figure 18.4: Per cent of Rural and Urban Workers to Total Workers

It is observed that there is a high degree of negative correlation (-0.88) between the work participation rate in agriculture and the percentage share of workers in the urban areas. Similarly, a high degree of negative correlation (-0.96) between the work participation rate in agriculture and the urban population in the Sub-division exists. To investigate the cause of urbanization in the sub-division, the relation between the WPR in agriculture and the percentage share of population in urban areas is tested using the linear regression analysis. The analysis reveals that when the percentage share of urban population is a dependent variable Y and the work participation rate in agriculture is an independent variable X, the multiple correlation R is 0.93 (93%) and the coefficient of determination R^2 is 0.864 (86.40%) and the adjusted R^2 is 0.728 (72.80%). The analaysis reveals that the relationship between the parameters has a high degree of determination. The regression coefficient (b) of the WPR in agriculture (X) is -20.30. The coefficient value of the constant (a) is 296.68. The simple regression line stands as $Y = a + b X = 296.68 - 20.30 X$. The regression line shows that with each unit increase in work participation rate in agriculture, percentage share in urban population falls by -20.30.

State of Sanitation Facilities

The urbanites in the sub-division do not have adequate sanitation facilities. For the study, three parameters of sanitation are taken into account, viz. availability of latrine facility, bathroom within premises and drainage facilities. The data for the census years of 2001 and 2011 are analyzed to investigate the state of sanitation facilities over the period. It is observed that there is an improvement in the bathroom within the premises and latrine facilities to the households in the urban areas of the sub-division during the period under study; however, there is deterioration in the drainage facility. It is found that the percentage of households without drainage facility in the urban areas has increased from 5.3 per cent in 2001 to 5.5 per cent in 2011. On the other hand, out of the three constituent towns in the sub-division, Singtam Nagar Panchayat and Rangpo Panchayat have improved in all the above facilities, but Gangtok Municipal Corporation has observed deterioration in latrine and drainage facilities. The percentage of households without latrine facilities within the premise of the houses has increased from 2.4 per cent in 2001 to 3.6 per cent in 2011and the percentage of households without drainage facility has deteriorated from 2.0 per cent in 2001 to 5.0 per cent in 2011 in Gangtok Municipal Corporation.

It is evident that deterioration in sanitation and housing facilities over the years results in the generation of slum dwellers in any urban area. Sikkim has witnessed slum population for the first time in 2003. The percentage share of slum population in the sub-division is almost one-fourth (23.55%) of the total urban population in 2011 whereas the percentage share of slum population from the total population in Gangtok in the same year is 21.55 per cent which is high as can be seen from the Table 18.4.

Table 18.4: Slum Population in Gangtok Sub-Division

State/Sub-division/Town	Slum Population (2011)	Urban Population (2011)	Share of Slum Population to Urban Population (in %)
Sikkim	31378	153578	20.43
Gangtok Sub-division	27466	116604	23.55
Gangtok Municipal Corporation	21610	100286	21.55

Conclusion and Suggestions

Thus, it is observed that there is a high level of urbanization in the Gangtok sub-division and its constituent towns since 1991. The high level of urbanization in the sub-division is caused by the fall in the WPR in the agriculture sector. It is found that the availability of some sanitation facilities in the urban areas of the sub-division deteriorates and the concentration of slum population in the sub-division also occurred during the period of study. Proper intervention is required from the State and the local Governments to arrest further escalation of urbanization in the sub-division. To revamp the agriculture sector in the state in general and in the Gangtok sub-division in particular, to mitigate further rise in urbanization and to eradicate the sanitation problems, some policy prescriptions are proposed below:

1. Adoption of skill development measures among the rural youth by providing alternative work avenues in the rural areas.
2. Applications of appropriate measures in agriculture sector for supporting the farmers such as provision of minimum support price, supply of high yielding variety seeds and seedlings to the peasants etc.
3. Extension of crop insurance facility as well as establishment of more soil testing centres.

4. Establishment of more seed processing units in the sub-division to facilitate more accessibility of farmers to these units for upgrading the seed quality.
5. Undertaking of more training programmes through Krishi Vigyan Kendra to the practicing farmers, rural youth for improvement of their skill and knowledge in farming and cultivation.
6. Applications of town planning principles in areas such as drainage and latrine facilities for the uncovered households of all urban areas.
7. Establishment of multiple public toilets in the slum areas of the towns.

With the introduction of organic farming in the State of Sikkim in 2016, it is expected that soil fertility of the cultivable land will be sustainable and agricultural production cost will be reduced. However, in the entire State, the fruits of organic farming are yet to yield the expected returns. It is imperative on the part of the State Government and the local self-governments to explore more appropriate measures in addition to those already outlined above, to prevent rural-urban migration of population in search of work in the Gangtok Sub-division. Keeping in mind the rate of population growth, vehicular growth and the sanitation problems in the urban areas of the sub-division, putting in place of a robust master plan is inevitable.

REFERENCES

Agriculture Census and EARAS Unit, *Hand Book on Agriculture in Sikkim 2014-15*, Food Security and Agriculture Development Department, Government of Sikkim, Gangtok.

Census of India (2011), Sikkim, *District Census Handbook*, Series 12, Part XII-B, Directorate of Census Operations, Sikkim, Ministry of Home Affairs, Government of India, Gangtok, 2014.

Census of India (2001), Sikkim, *District Census Handbook*, Series 12, Part A & B, Directorate of Census Operations, Sikkim, Ministry of Home Affairs, Government of India, Gangtok, 2003.

Census of India (1991), Sikkim, *District Census Handbook*, Series 22, Part XII-A & B, Directorate of Census Operations, Sikkim, Ministry of Home Affairs, Government of India, Gangtok, 1993.

Deb, Bimal J., Keya Sengupta and B. Datta Ray (ed.), (2008): *Globalization and North East India*, Concept Publishing Company, New Delhi.

Dewan, M.L., (2009): *Agriculture and Rural Development in India: A Case Study on the Dignity of Labour*, Concept Publishing Company, 3rd ed., New Delhi.

Dorji, N.J. (ed.), (2010): *Sikkim A to Z*, Gushing Torrent International Pvt. Ltd., Gangtok.

Kothari, C.R., (2004): *Research Methodology: Methods and Techniques* 2nd ed., New Age International Publishers, New Delhi.

Srinivasan, K., (2013): *Training Manual on Demographic Techniques*, Office of Registrar General and Census Commissioner, India, Government of India, New Delhi.

http://www.censusindia.gov.in-*Percentage of households to total households by amenities and assets*, Table HH-14, Houselisting & Housing Census, Office of Registrar General and Census Commissioner, India, 2011.

http://www.censusindia.gov.in-*Distribution of households by availability of bathroom & type of latrine within the house and type of drainage connectivity for waste water outlet*, Table H-10, Office of Registrar General and Census Commissioner, India, 2001.

http://www.censusindia.gov.in-*Migrants by place of last residence, Age, Sex, Reason for migration and duration of residence-2011*, Table D-5 (Provisional), 2011 Census, Office of Registrar General and Census Commissioner, India.

http://www.censusindia.gov.in-*Migrants by place of last residence, Age, Sex, Reason for migration and duration of residence*, Table D-5, 2001 Census, Office of Registrar General and Census Commissioner, India.

http://www.censusindia.gov.in-*Migrants by place of last residence, duration of residence and reason for migration*, Table D-3 (S), 1991 Census, Office of Registrar General and Census Commissioner, India.

http://www.censusindia.gov.in-*Primary Census Abstract Data for Slum (India & States/UTs - Town Level)*, A Series, 2011 Census, Office of Registrar General and Census Commissioner, India.

19
Unplanned Growth of Guwahati City

A Geographical Study

Siddheswar Sarma

Introduction

Study Area

Guwahati is the premier urban centre of North East Region of India, known as the Gateway of North-East. It lies as the point of intersection of 26°10′45″ north latitude and 91°45′00″ east longitude. The Master Plan indicates that the Guwahati Metropolitan Area (GMA) is approximately 262.00 sq.kms and additions of Sila-Matiya-Najirakhat-Bhulung area as New Town-I, Charmajulipam-Gamdhmau-Ambari-Bamum Soalkuchi area as New Town-II, Panchniyapara-Sajjanpara-Gariyapara-Alibari-Tarapatipara area as New Town-III and marginal adjustments in boundary including Pamohi village as special scheme area comprising 66 sq.kms is under consideration.

Drainage

The master drain Brahmaputra River has been aligned longitudinally and it flows east to west direction segmenting Greater Guwahati into North Guwahati in the north and the core city in the south. On the north bank of the river Brahmaputra, the river Ghorajan and Barnadi are maintaining their natural courses and discharge into Brahmaputra. These two rivers are not harmful to the dwellers of the North Guwahati. On the south bank of the river Brahmaputra there are as many as five tributaries such as Bharalu, Mara Bharalu, Barapani, Khanajan and Bondajan. Bharalu is the most harmful tributary to the city dwellers which flows through the alluvial depression of Guwahati Municipal Corporation area to meet at Bharalumukh. Bondajan in the east and Khanajan in the west both rivers originate from Silsako Beel and Dipar Beel respectively. Backflow of water from Brahmaputra River through Bharalu, Khanajan and Bondajan cause floods frequently in every summer.

Relief

The original city is located within a crescent shaped basin, surrounded by a number of hillocks. The hills are outliers of the Meghalaya Plateau, predominantly residual in character. They are composed of granites and gneissic rocks with the outer surface fairly weathered and contain red soil. The hills have steep slope but from the base, the slopes become gradual up to the river bank on the north. As a result, an undulating topography has emerged with swamps and low-lying areas in between. The original settlements were mostly located on the elevated plains and the foothill zone. Thus, the low-lying areas, smooth terrain and some hillocks of different elevations present a peculiar relief to the area. The benchmark of G.T.S. (Great Trigonometrical Survey) near Deputy Commissioner Office is 54.75 metres. While 52.20 metres is recorded near the Railway Station above the M.S.L. with an average elevation of 51.3 metres for the southern bank of Brahmaputra and it rises up towards Kharghuli and Chitrachal (Nabagraha) hills in the east (216.00 metres) and Nilachal Hill (303.00 metres) in the central part. The average elevation of low-lying areas is 49.00 metres and the lowest is 41.16 metres above the M.S.L. This land gradually rises to Khasi and Jaintia Hills to a maximum elevation of 575.00 metres which ends in the southern boundary of Guwahati. Again, there are areas near Chitrachal hills with a general elevation of 182.00 metres towards the east and to the southern plains of 49.00 metres elevation. In between the Khasi hills and the Brahmaputra River situates the Sarania hill (250.00 metres), Fatashil hill range (358.00 metres) and the Kalapahar Narakasur Hills (200.00-300.00 metres). A vast low-lying area of Dipar Beel occupies more than 54.00 sq.kms situates on the western part of the city. Moreover there are low lying plains intervened by scattered swamps and marshes in between the hills, extending from east to west. These low-lying areas are inundated often at the time of heavy rainfall.

Database and Methodology

For geographical location of the study area, Survey of India's topographical sheet No. 78 N/12 and 78 N/16 of R.F. 1:63360 (scale 1 inch to a mile) are used to prepare the map of Greater Guwahati. It depicts various features of topography, characteristics of rivers, tributaries, settlement pattern and transport network etc. To find out the average slope of the area, the C.K. Wentworth formula given in (19.1) is applied on a contour map of the above mentioned sheets.

$$\tan\theta = \frac{N \times I}{3361\ (constant)} \qquad (19.1)$$

where tan θ = average angle of slope, N = average numbers of contour crossings per mile and I = contour interval in feet.

For rainfall analysis hourly data of seven years were collected from the Indian Metrological Department. Average hourly variations of rainfall during monsoon period (May to September) of a few consecutive years are tabulated and calculated using the formula given in (19.2).

$$R = \frac{r}{n} \qquad (19.2)$$

where

R= average rainfall per hour

r= total rainfall of the hour of the month

n = total number of rainfall occurrence of the hour of the month

To adopt a pragmatic approach, the standard deviation and co-efficient of variations of hourly data are calculated using the following formula given in (19.3) and (19.4).

$$\sigma = \sqrt{\frac{\Sigma(x - \bar{x})^2}{n}} \qquad (19.3)$$

where,

σ = standard deviation,

x = hourly rainfall,

$\bar{x}$ = mean hourly rainfall,

n = number of observation and

$$CV = \frac{\sigma}{\bar{x}} \times 100 \qquad (19.4)$$

where

c.v = coefficient of variation of mean hourly rainfall

σ = standard deviation

$\bar{x}$ = mean hourly rainfall

The data regarding various levels of water in Brahmaputra were collected from Brahmaputra Flood Control Department for the monsoon period of 150 days (May to September). The average water level percentage of 150 days and cumulative percentage of 150 days are also calculated. This way most of the parameters have been analysed and presented with the help of suitable diagrams and other cartographic aids. A few secondary data relevant to the problems were collected from the Town and Country Planning Department, Assam and Guwahati Municipal Corporation.

Results and Analysis

Average Slope Analysis

The term slope is used for the land surface which inclines from the horizontal. The average slope of Greater Guwahati has been studied with the help of average slope determination of C.K. Wentworth[2]. It is found that the average slope of Greater Guwahati varies from zero degree to 18 degrees. The maximum slope is 18 degrees as noticeable in the Nilachal Hill (6° to 18°), Kalapahar-Narakasur Hill (9° to 18°) and the Khanapara Hill side (6° to 18°) areas and is shown in Figure 19.1. In the same way Hengrabari, N.C., Modgharia, N.C., Ramcha Hill Grant, Sunsali Grant, Clearance Garden, Noonmati Garden which all are in the North-Eastern part of the Greater Guwahati, it is noticed that the average slope varies from 9° to 18° or above. In the Kalapahar-Narakasur Hill and Hengrabari-Modgharia hill areas, the slope declines to 3 degrees towards Ganesguri. Beyond these areas the plains extend from Saolkuchi, Sijubari and Hatigaon to Satgaon. A corridor is less than 3 degrees of average slope is found between the westward slope of Nilachal Hills and the eastward slope of Jalukbari Hill area.

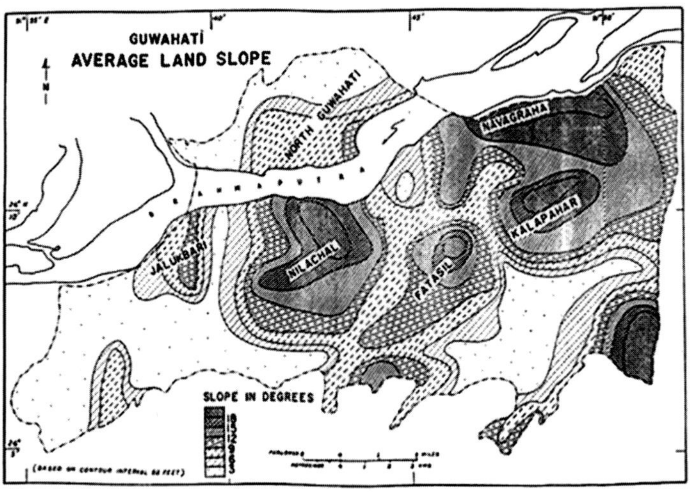

Figure 19.1: The Average Land Slope of Guwahati City

Source: Author's Ph.D. Thesis.

Further, it is noticed that the 3 degrees isopleth encircles the Dipar Beel and extend along the Pub-Bora Gaon to Borjhar-Azara area which ends the western limit of Greater Guwahati. It is also observed that the Mora-Bharalu plains extend south to north between the Fatashil and Kalapahar Hills. An isolated spot near Mikirpara with slopes varying from 3 to 6 degrees and another spot near Kakatipara with varying slope of 3 to 12 degrees are found in the South-West periphery of Guwahati. These isolated hills are actually outliers of the Meghalaya Plateau. The three tributary basins of Greater Guwahati are of contrasting characters. The Bondajan basin is found at higher altitude which has a 9° slope; the Bharalu basin has a 6° slope while the Khanajan basin lies below the 3° slope. Thus, it is observed that the average slope of the urban complex gradually falls towards west with exceptional inter-basin separation. The intervening hills dividing the basins are the residual outliers of the Maghalaya Plateau. Over the years, these are considerably eroded and they demonstrate only the relict monadnocks. The relief and slope characteristics of Greater Guwahati region indicate that while the natural inclination of the relief is from east to west, the drainage of three tributaries to Brahmaputra has been at right angle to the natural inclination. Moreover, the orientation of the city is axial along the Brahmaputra in the East-West direction and the natural drainage courses again intersect the city at the right angle. Viewed from this aspect, the typical form of Guwahati city is analogous to the concept of a linear city propounded by James Craig and put forward by Don Arturo Soria Mata in 1882 (Ratcliffe, 1981). Therefore, the natural courses are intersected by roads, bridges, culverts and other man-made hindrances.

Rainfall Analysis

The water logging and inundation problems may be looked into from the point of view of rainfall intensity and rainfall regime of the city. Rainfall data for each hour for 7 years (1980-1986) of 5 monsoon months, i.e. May to September are used and analysed as can be seen in Table 19.1. The average rainfall per hour for each monsoon months and for the season has been plotted in the graphs. The graphs are not smooth and show many primary and secondary peaks. To make the curve smooth three points moving average as seen in Table 19.2 is used. Yet some of the smoothed curves have shown oscillatory character (Figure 19.2).

Table 19.1: Average Variation of Rainfall per Hour for the Monsoon Season (1980-1986)

(*Rainfall in mm*)

Hours	May	June	July	August	Septe-mber	Seasonal (Monsoon)
1	3.9	3.7	3.4	3.2	3.6	3.6
2	5.0	3.0	6.5	2.9	2.0	3.9
3	3.1	2.7	3.4	3.4	5.5	3.6
4	3.3	2.1	1.3	1.2	3.0	2.2
5	2.9	1.9	1.7	4.0	1.7	2.4
6	1.7	1.5	1.9	4.4	1.1	2.1
7	3.0	1.2	2.1	3.3	1.0	2.1
8	1.2	1.0	2.1	3.1	2.7	2.0
9	2.5	2.1	2.9	3.4	1.6	2.5
10	1.5	2.6	2.4	3.0	1.5	2.2
11	1.8	3.0	3.1	2.3	2.0	2.4
12	1.6	4.3	1.9	2.5	2.3	2.5
13	1.7	3.4	1.1	2.6	1.5	2.0
14	1.2	10.0	1.2	1.4	1.1	3.0
15	2.9	1.7	1.6	1.8	1.9	2.0
16	1.0	5.8	1.3	2,5	1.7	2.5
17	1.2	5.0	4.6	2.4	3.3	3.3
18	2.1	1.4	1.5	3.7	1.4	2.0
19	2.6	1.3	2.3	1.9	2.2	2.0
20	2.8	2.0	2.4	2.1	4.1	2.7
21	1.4	2.0	5.1	4.1	4.5	3.4
22	3.0	5.1	2.4	3.2	3.0	3.3
23	8.8	1.8	3.3	2.2	4.0	4.0
24	4.8	2.2	2.7	2.5	2.0	2.8

Source: Author's Computation and Indian Meteorological Department.

Table 19.2: Three Point Moving Average of Rainfall per Hour for the Monsoon Season 1980-1986

(Rainfall in mm)

Three Point of the Hours	May	June	July	August	September	Monsoon Season (Average)
1, 2, 3	4.0	3.1	4.4	3.1	3.7	**3.7**
2, 3, 4	3.8	2.6	3.7	2.5	3.5	**3.2**
3, 4, 5	3.1	2.2	2.1	2.9	3.4	**2.7**
4, 5 6	2.6	1.8	1.6	3.2	1.9	**2.2**
5, 6, 7	2.5	1.5	1.9	3.9	1.3	**2.2**
6, 7, 8	2.0	1.2	2.0	3.6	1.6	**2.1**
7, 8, 9	2.2	1.4	2.4	3.2	1.8	**2.2**
8, 9, 10	1.7	1.9	2.5	3.1	1.9	**2.2**
9, 10, 11	1.9	2.6	2.8	2.9	1.7	**2.4**
10, 11, 12	1.6	3.3	2.5	2.6	1.9	**2.3**
11, 12, 13	1.7	3.6	2.0	2.5	1.9	**2.5**
12, 13, 14	1.5	5.9	1.4	2.2	1.6	**2.3**
13, 14, 15	1.9	5.0	1.3	1.9	1.5	**2.5**
14, 15, 16	1.7	5.8	1.4	1.9	1.6	**2.6**
15, 16, 17	1.7	4.1	2.5	2.2	2.3	**2.6**
16, 17, 18	1.1	4.0	2.5	2.9	2.1	**2.4**
17, 18, 19	2.0	2.5	2.8	2.7	2.3	**2.2**
18, 19, 20	2.5	1.5	2.0	2.6	2.6	**2.7**
19, 20, 21	2.3	1.7	3.3	2.7	3.6	**3.1**
20, 21, 22	2.4	3.0	3.3	3.1	3.9	**3.6**
21, 22, 23	4.4	2.9	3.6	3.2	3.8	**3.4**
22, 23, 24	5.5	3.0	2.8	2.6	3.0	**3.4**

Source: Author's Computation.

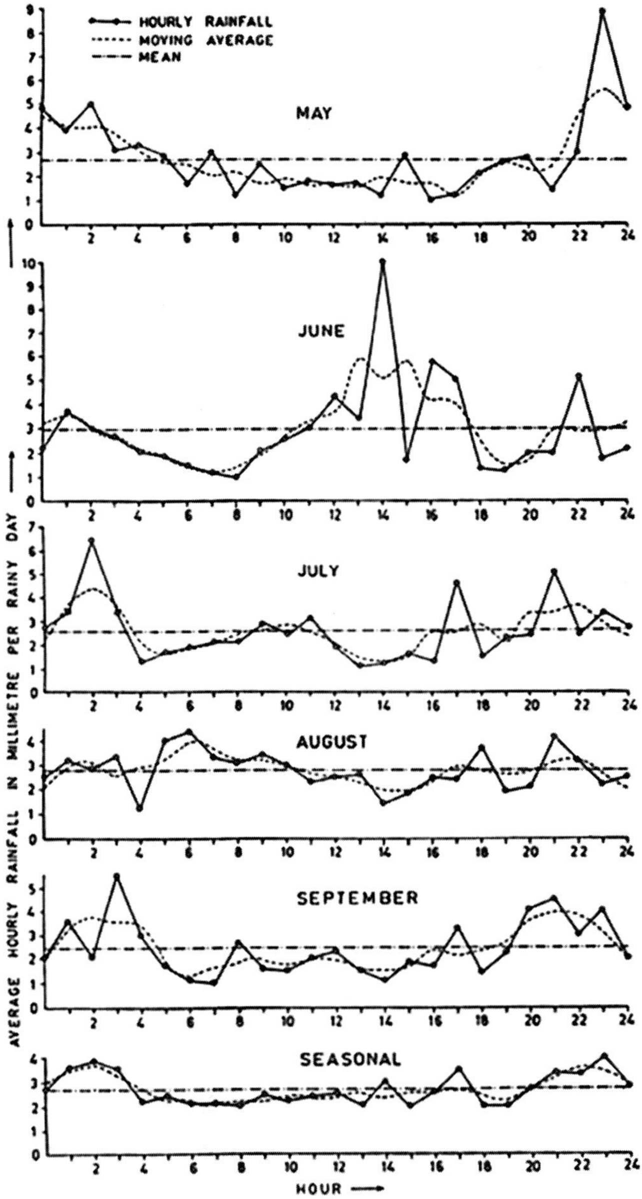

Figure 19.2: Hourly Variation of Rainfall at Guwahati City.

Source: Author's Computation.

The curve for the month of May indicates few peaks, out of which two are greater than the mean rainfall of 24 hours. May, June and July curves show prominent peaks. The characteristic feature of high peak of May 2300 hour IST corresponds to afternoon peak of June 1400 hours IST and then to early hour peak to July 0200 hour IST. The peaks are conspicuously smooth in the month of August. Significantly, both yearly peak 0300 hour IST and late peaks 2000 to 2300 hour IST occur in September. During the monsoon season as a whole the rainfall curve shows three prominent peaks each at 2300 hours IST, 1400 hour IST and 0200 hour IST. Along with these three prominent peaks five other mild peaks rainfall exist. From the above analysis it is apparent that Guwahati experiences about eight peak hours of high intensity rainfall periods in one monsoon season. The rainfall curve shown in Figure 19.2 clearly depicts that mostly rainfall occurred in the afternoon and during night which is less ranging from 0400 hour to 1300 hour IST. The mean hourly rainfall per rainy day is maximum and incessant in June and minimum in September. The co-efficient of variation of mean hourly rainfall is also maximum in the month of June. Hence, June rainfall is always alarming as soils absorb by the rain water reach the saturated point. The other peaks (primary and secondary maximum) from June to September, is a sensitive period with full of potential of flooding the city through runoff water.

Behaviour of River Water Inside Greater Guwahati

The tributaries of Brahmaputra inside the Greater Guwahati are rendered inactive in discharging their water load because of the higher water level in the master drain. On the contrary, backflow from the river Brahmaputra enters through the outlets of natural drainage and increases both the level and volume of water in these tributaries. Normally, backflow through Bondajan on the East, Khanajan on the West and Bharalu in the central part, causes flood inside the Greater Guwahati almost at every spate of high water in Brahmaputra. From observations over a period of 10 years, it is found that the water level of Brahmaputra rises above the danger level (49.68 metres) for seven times during the above period. It means that hardly one year was free from flood out of every three years. Monthly water level of the Brahmaputra adjacent to the D.C. court area was studied and plotted in the graph as shown in Figure 19.3. From this curve it was observed that the water level has crossed the danger mark twice in 1980, once in 1981, thrice in 1987 and twice in 1985. In the year 1982, 1983 and 1986 the water level did not cross the red mark (49.68 metres) at all. The water level that crossed the danger level is generally, in between July, August and September only.

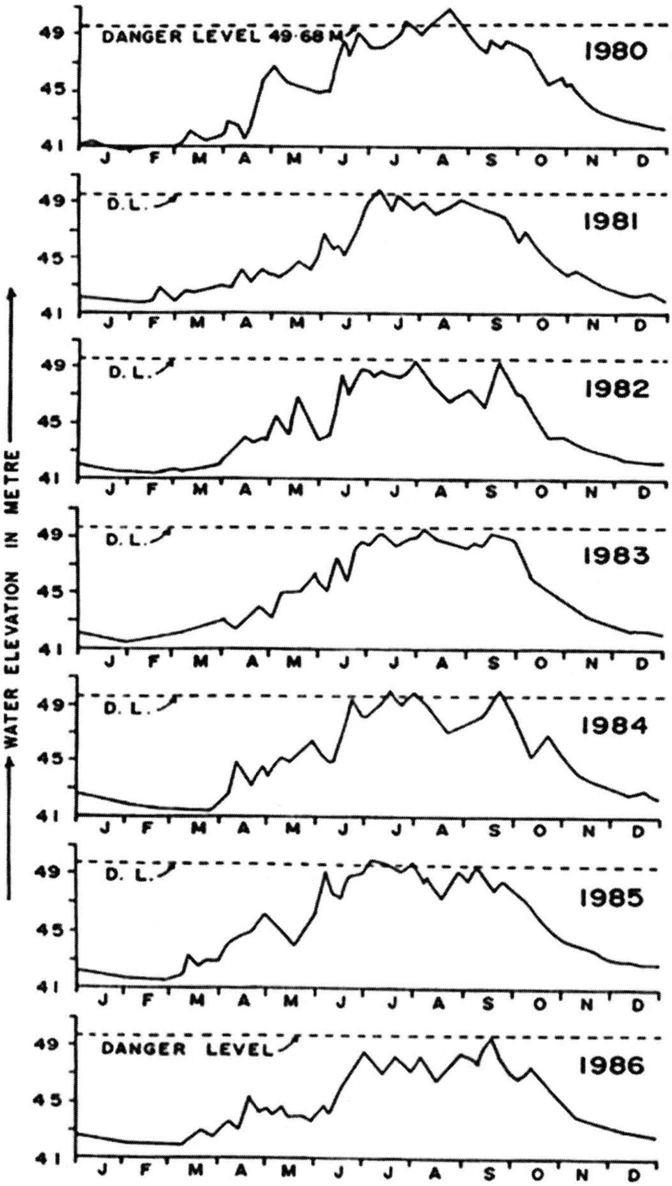

Figure 19.3: Monthly Water Level of Brahmaputra at D.C. Court Site.

Source: Author's Computation.

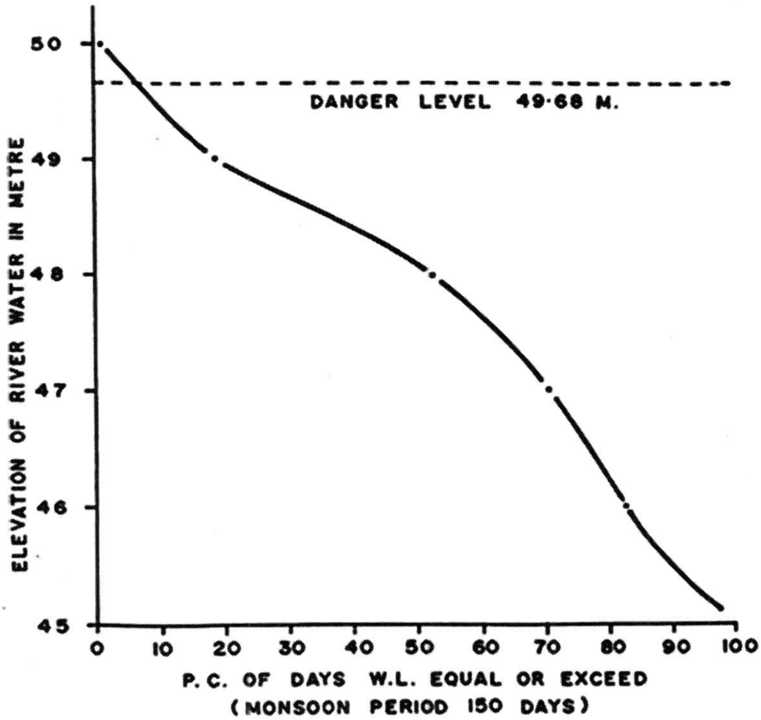

Figure 19.4: Danger Level of Brahmaputra River at D.C. Court Site.

Source: Author's Computation.

An observation was made on the daily water level of Brahmaputra at D.C. Court site for the period of seven years and tabulated in percentage for 150 days (May to September) and represented in cumulative graph shown in Figure 19.4. It shows that for about 7 per cent of 150 days (10.5 days) the water level of Brahmaputra equals the danger level or exceeds it during the monsoon period. During this period when the water level exceeds or equals the danger level, the sluice of Bharalu used to be closed to stop the backflow from Brahmaputra and to avoid inundation of the city area. "Gradient or slope of the stream channel is the angle between the water surface and the horizontal plane." In general, the gradient of a stream decreases from its source towards the mouth. But in case of Bharalu River, the gradient of the river bed does fall progressively and at certain meanders, the river bed is found to be of higher elevation than the upper course. This is mainly due to the sluggish movement of water in the lean season and the deposition of silt on the bed. This is another reason for rapid rise of water level in the river. The closure of the sluice gate near the Pragjyotish College results in the accumulation of the rainwater from the catchment area in the drain. As water cannot flow out through its mouth at the time of high waters in Brahmaputra, the accumulated water takes a reverse course and slowly drains out through the Mora-Bharalu (Dead River) to Dipar Beel. Unfortunately, the shallow and narrow channel of Mora Bharalu fails to clear off the accumulated water with any great speed. This keeps the water level of the Bharalu River high for weeks together and causes water logging in the entire low-lying areas of the basin.

Water Logging and Inundation Problem

Water logging is a colossal and continuous problem of Guwahati. In order to locate and verify the vulnerable water logging spots, constant personal observation was made by the researcher for the last few consecutive monsoons. Empirically speaking, few causes which attributed to this phenomenon are:

1. Topography of Guwahati is significantly undulating.
2. Both natural and artificial drains are not capable of carrying the storm water due to their shallowness and narrowness.
3. Encroachments over the low-lying areas by new settlers on either side of the natural drains choked the natural flow of flood water to the drains.
4. Construction of building and roads over the man-made drains are also responsible for bottlenecking the drainage.
5. Indiscriminate cutting of hillside for filling up the low-lying areas is also responsible for sheet wash and blockage of channels. Hills exposed to heavy rain supply enormous loose soil and silt up the drains rapidly.
6. The filled-up areas possess high seepage capacity because of lower compactness and saturate at a faster rate and therefore, do not allow flow of flood water.
7. Most of the original swamps and natural water reservoirs are filed up for residential, official, industrial and institutional purposes. Consequently, the rain water spread over the built-up areas causing flash flood.
8. Rising of the ground water table with the rise of Brahmaputra level saturates the entire plain area and reduces the rate of percolation.

The topography of Guwahati controls the natural drainage. As mentioned earlier the relief of the city gradually slopes from east to west. Two major natural drains of Greater Guwahati originate in the hills and others two major drains originate from the lakes. Mushrooming of settlements on either side of the perennials drains, the presence of depressed area usually prompts the tendency of collection of water in scattered areas after every heavy shower. The culture morphology of the city has undergone tremendous changes and new settlements particularly, the unplanned ones have created many bottlenecks to the system of natural drainage. Within the busy functional areas of the city, drain-*cum*-footpaths are not adequate to carry all storm waters. Besides, most of the drains are relentlessly constructed against the natural direction of flow. In addition, the broad gauge railway line passing through the heart of the city constrains the existing inadequate drainage system of the city. Ignoring the city's Master Plan, construction of broad gauge line across the natural courses added to the problem. Enormous sheet wash from Nabagraha hill slopes constantly fills up the existing drains and inundates the road from Silpukhuri to the Flood Control Commission Office at Chandmari. Similar situations are also seen over the road near Assam Engineering Institute. In matters of water logging, soil consumption of the city area has a major role to play. At one hand, the depressed areas are composed of transported soil from the hilly areas and at the other, much of the built up areas have come up over the newly filled soils. In the absence of effective soil conserving cover, the rain-water erodes the high land and deposits the materials over the monsoon period. Two specific reasons may be attributed to this phenomenon, viz. (i) the low-lying areas composed of transported soil or silt and (ii) wide spread saturation of soil due to the rise of Brahmaputra level and due to nature of its soil composition as noted earlier. Consequently, the surface flow progressively increases with the advance of monsoon season resulting in the collection of rain water in the depressed regions. The best example of such a situation is Kumarpara area. The elevation of this area is comparatively low (49 metres above the MSL whereas the danger level of Brahmaputra at the D.C. Court site is 49.68 metres). Being nearer to the Brahmaputra and Bharalu, soil of the area gets rapidly saturated with the advent of monsoon. The sub-soil of this region hardly gets time for complete desiccation in between the wet seasons and the monsoon coupled with high water in the Brahmaputra completely stops percolation. Hence, the entire Kumarpara area is submerged during heavy showers.

Illegal encroachers fill up most of the natural water reservoirs of Greater Guwahati. The swampy areas in between Fatasil and Lakhra road are packed with settlements. The Bishnupur area and the low-lying areas of Gopinath Nagar are also filled up for the construction of residential quarters, resulting in permanent blockade of rain-water. The areas in between the Rajgarh road and R.G. Baruah road significantly lie below 49.00 metres contour. This part of the city is also subjected to continuous earth filling for new construction of residential houses. In the absence of effective outlets, the water in unfilled areas remains stagnant causing water-logging for weeks together. Looking into the growth momentum of the city, establishment of industrial areas and capital complex in and around the city, various government agencies have offered suggestions for alleviation of this problem. The notable suggestion offered by the Town and Country Planning Department, Assam and the Brahmaputra Flood Control Commission, perhaps, would ease the situation to a certain extent provided that these schemes are effectively implemented. Nevertheless, it is comprehended that urban renewal for the case city is required to be undertaken on a war footing and multi-pronged strategies.

Conclusion and Remedial Measures

From the above analysis of various aspects of the city environs, three prime issues emerged and these are: (i) the natural drainage problem, (ii) the silting problem, and (iii) the artificial drainage problem.

The Natural Drainage Problems

The main natural drainage of the city is the Bharalu river. Prolonged silting and encroachment upon its banks have reduced the load discharge capacity of the drain especially in the lower part starting from R.G. Baruah Road bridge (Zoo road bridge) to Lakhra road bridge point. Bed of the middle part of Mora-Bharalu is at higher elevation falls to carry off normal discharge. At the time of high water level of the Brahmaputra, the water back flows into the city through the existing channels and open culverts. Dipar Beel needs to be excavated to enable it to absorb the city runoff through the existing drain. Barchala Beel connected through open drains cannot accommodate all the water received at the time of peak discharge. There is also no practical use of Chala Beel (Chatribari Swamp) due to its shallowness. Hence, both the beels need to be excavated to enable them to reserve the excess storm water.

The Artificial Drainage Problems

Existing drainage facilities of Guwahati are not adequate to carry all storm waters from each of the localities. Hence, some more new drains could be constructed along with the natural slope of the area. Moreover, existing drains can be renovated for easy flow of rainwater with provision of annual clearance. As most of the roads, inside the city are very narrow, underground drains are desirable. These roads should not be utilized for drain-cum-foot path indiscriminately. Existing manholes of drain-*cum*-foot path are not adequate. More manholes and inlet holes are required for the quick disposal of silt and stagnated water. The size of the inlet holes and their positions need to be re-oriented.

Silting Problems

The problem of silting is very serious, especially in high rainfall intensity areas, as it is related with the hill cutting and earth filling. Even, well-designed drainage systems may not cope up with the huge volume of silt load carried along with the runoff, unless some scientific and technological measures are put in place. It is seen that clearing silt from the existing drains do not help as the high intensity of rainfall from surrounding hills with silt overflow towards the city dwellers. For this, deep drain may be constructed along the foothills of all the hills located in and around the Guwahati. Tunnel like drains should be constructed through Nilachal, Nabagraha hills connecting drains of foothills to outlet into the master drain Brahmaputra so that runoff with silt would be released immediately. In the same way, a few more silt traps may be constructed at the designated sites along the foothills of Sarania hills, Kalapahar, Narakasur, Fatasil, Sonaighuli and Ramcha hills. These silt traps need to be cleaned after each storm. For this special labour force should be employed therein. Before making any remedial measures for construction of drain, tunnel and silt traps aerial photographs of two seasons of Greater Guwahati should be obtained. An aerial photograph covering water logging area of summer season and another aerial photograph of winter season should be obtained so that construction work could be taken up in a planned and phase manner. These strategies are only the humble suggestions of the author and should not be taken as overall pervading and complete in all respects. I hope that this article will serve as a heuristic base for further investigation in this field by research scholars, geomorphologists, hydrogeologists, civil engineers, town planners and other professionals in their respective fields and will also be helpful in tackling this age-old problem.

REFERENCES

Calcutta Metropolitan Planning (1971): *A Report on Master Plan for Water Supply, Sewerage and Drainage for Guwahati Metropolitan District (1971-2001)*, Calcutta.

Guwahati Metropolitan Area (2009): *Master Plan for Guwahati Metropolitan Area,* Guwahati.

Ratcliffe, J. (1981): *An Introduction to Town and Country Planning*, Reprinted 1989, Hutchinson Education Limited, London, p.45.

Strahler, A.N. (1971): *Physical Geography*, Willy Eastern Pvt. Ltd., New Delhi.

The Constant Figure 3361 is derived from a formula which is explained fully by Wenworth; it is 5280 × 0.6366, which Figure is the mean of all possible values of Sin θ is the angle between the grid-lines and contours.

Wentworth, C.K. (1930). "A simplified method of determining the average slope of land surfaces" in *American Journal of Science,* Vol. 220.

20
Guwahati City in Evolution

Siddheswar Sarma

During the Classical Age

Guwahati is an ancient and famous town of Assam. The historical antiquities of the city are gleaned from various sources, viz. (i) ancient scriptures, (ii) earlier inscriptions, (iii) earlier literature and (iv) accounts of early foreign travellers and historians. Ancient scriptures like *Kriskindhya Ramayana*[1] described *Pragjyotisha* as the city built on an extensive seaside mountain known as *'Varaha'* with golden peaks. The whole city was built with gold and was ruled over by a *Danava* known by the name of Naraka. *Kalikapurana* explains *Pragjyotishpura*[2] as the abode of *Bramha*, god of creation, who created stars and planets here in *Pragjyotishpura*. This signifies that this was the city where the study of astrology on a scientific basis was initiated. The word *Pragjyotishpura* derived as *prag*—pre, *jyotish* – astrology and *pura* is a sanskritised Dravidian word which means a town or city or place of 'old astrological centre'. The present *Nabagraha Temple* stands as the evidence of the ancient seat of astrological studies in the city. The temple of nine planets with *'tole'* epitomizes the ancient heritage of the city for *'tole'* is a place of learning in old age, i.e. school or institution. The inscription on the copper plate of Dharmapala Raja depicts certain Sanskrit verses which refer to the name of Kamrup Nagar[3]. Different sources ascertain and refer to both *Kamrupa* and *Pragjyotisha* as the kingdom and as the capital city which underwent changes at different periods. Specifically, it is known that the name '*Pragjyotishpura'* is much older than the name *'Kamrupa'*. In the classical literature, references regarding the ancient city are abundantly found. The great classical poet, Kalidasa, in his epical literature, *Raghuvmsa*, mentioned about the foundation of the *Pragjyotishpura* and as well as *Kamrupa* along with the river *Lauhitya.* The verse Raghu IV: 81-83 reads:

> *Chakampe Tirualauhitya Tasmin Pragjyotishesvarah*
> *Tamisah Kamrupanamtyakhandalabikramam.*

Huen Tsang, a Chinese explorer, visited Assam in 640 A.D. He recorded his observations in his travel diary about *Kamrupa*. At that time Kumar Bhaskar Verma was in the throne of *Kamrupa* as Baruah (1933) wrote, "The kingdom came to be known as *Kamrupa* during the *puranic* time based on the legend that *Kamdeva*, the God of love – the Indian Cupid – who was destroyed by the fiery glance of *Shiva* returned to life in this country". In this connection, S.K. Chatterji (1951) wrote that the region around the *Kāmākhyā* identified as Prāgjotisha-*Kāmarupa* was mainly inhabited by the *Kirāta*[4] or Indo-Mongoloids. The beginning of Indo-Aryan settlements in *Kāmarupa* is generally traced from the foundation of *Prāgjyotisha* kingdom by Naraka, a Kshatriya prince from Videha, who had eliminated the reigning *Kirāta* chief Ghataka. The *Purānas* described Naraka as the son of *Visnu* (Lord *Visnu*) and *Bhumi* (Mother Earth) although King Janaka of Videha brought him up as his own son and credited him with a settlement of a large number of Brahmins and members of other *varnas* in *Prāgjyotisha*. The eulogies in some of the *Kāmarupa* inscriptions also mention that Naraka and his son Bhagadatta settled in *Kāmarupa*.[5] After analysing the literatures found in the writings of M.M. Sharma (1978) and the Role of *Tambula* in Assam's Social Life' by M. Neog (1978), The capital city of *Prāgjyotisha*, it was affirmed that the modern name Gauhati was derived at a later stage. The following verse corroborates this fact.

> *tambulavalliparinaddhapuga*
> *krishnagauruskandhanivesitailam.*[7]

This meant that there were arecanut (*tambula*) trees, which used to be covered by encircling betel leaf creepers and the trunks of the black sandal trees which used to be encircled by the cardamom trees. From these rows of the arecanut the name of Guwahati seems to be originated. The '*Guwa*' is an Assamese pronouncing word of '*Guvuka*' (*tambula*) of Sanskrit and '*Hati*' is a row of trees, i.e. '*Guwahati*' means rows of arecanut trees. This name Guwahati embraces both sides of the bank of Brahmaputra. It is obvious that the name of Gauhati is a corrupt offshoot of the word Guwahati – which was coined by the British. This English name of Gauhati was again recoined as Guwahati to revive the tradition.[8]

The main evidence of classical age to know a particular place, the abandoned ancient citadel, curved stones, stone pillar, beautiful finished slab, remains once famous temples, bricks, mortar and earthen ware etc. are utilized by the archaeologists and antiquarians. This, however, helped to find the missing links between the past and the present city in evolution. Fortification of this capital city was done by joining almost all hillocks on the north and the south bank of the city for protection from external aggression. This amply exhibits the remarkable engineering skill of the ancient planners and engineers. The temples of Kamakhya, Umananda, Nabagraha, Manikarneswar and Asvakranta which were built on the hillocks also amply demonstrate the pristine glory of the ancient architecture. Likewise, Sukreswar, Banesvar, Ugratara and Chatrakar were built on planning basis. All these temples of both the north and the south bank of Guwahati indicated immense monumental value and serve the religious thirst of the people. The scattered relics of the old monuments clearly indicate that Guwahati was definitely famous for religious and cultural activities of the region.

Guwahati During Ahom Period (1625 A.D-1826 A.D.)

Prior to the invasion of the Ahoms in 1625 A.D. Guwahati remained as a prominent centre of the western plain of Assam Valley. For a short period, Guwahati was the capital of the Koch Kingdom. Ahom occupied both the banks of Brahmaputra and in the place of Pragjyotishpur the Ahom rulers used the name Guwahata or Guwahati. Perhaps during the early part of Ahom reign, the functional centre was shifted to the south bank where the present Guwahati is located. From the historical records, it may be mentioned that almost all the battles against the Mughals were fought from this headquarters. For strategic reasons, the capital was shifted from north bank to south bank thereafter. Guwahati—during Ahom period comprised the area between the foot of the Kamakhya hill and Nabagraha hill including Kharghuli. In the north-south direction, Guwahati extended from the river Brahmaputra to Chalabil as can be visualised in Figure 20.1[9]. There were as many as ten *Chowkies* (Garrison Gateway) constructed around Guwahati, including North Guwahati for its security and protection. *Karoipani Chowki* and *Kanaibarshiboa chowki* are on the north bank; while Pandu, Duargaria, Dharamduar, Jaiduar and Latasil Pani *Chowki* are on the south bank.[10] Both the *Kanaibarshiboa Chowki* of north bank and *Jaiduwar Chowki* of south bank were the eastern most gateways to Guwahati. The *Chilar Chowki* on *Momaikata garh* of the north bank and *Pandu chowki* on the south bank of the Brahmaputra were the western gateways to Guwahati.The *'garh'* which means the fortification of wall like embankment encircles capital town of pre-Ahom period were renovated and made strong to defend against the invasions of Muhammedans. *Mumaikata garh* is known for its great historic events along with the Rangmahal and Narakasur garh on the north bank, Jalukbari, Tetelia, Fatasil, Rajgarh on the south bank are still found in a dilapidated condition (Figure 20.1). There were regular boat services between the *ghats* at Rajduwar, Avaskranta and Pandu. Boats were the only means of communication between north and south bank. As Guwahati was the regional headquarters of the Ahom rulers, the office of *Barphukan* (Chief Commander) was located on the west of the confluence of the Bharalu and the Brahmaputra River. Near Uzanbazar, there was a place of royal armory, known as Kharghuli. This was the strategically important garrison of the chief commander of Guwahati.

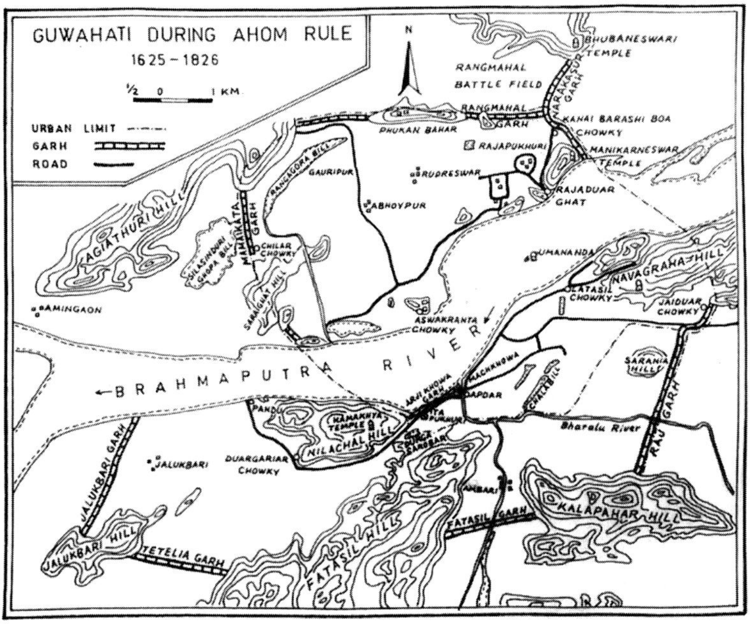

Figure 20.1: Guwahati during Ahom Rule.

Source: Author's Construct based on the Survey of India's topo sheet and reconnaissance survey.

Guwahati During British Period (1886 A.D. - 1947 A.D.)

After the treaty of Yandabo, Assam came under the control of East India Company in 1826. However, till 1836, the British could not establish any effective administrative control over Guwahati. In the absence of civic amenities and poor hygienic condition, the British soldiers suffered from various diseases. The British officers, however, constituted a town improvement committee to look after the affairs of the town, and perhaps for this reason the capital was shifted from Guwahati to Shillong.[12] Though the capital was shifted to Shillong, Guwahati remained as administrative headquarters of Assam. In the year 1878, Guwahati Municipality Board was formed and the first task of the Municipality was to construct a water supply plant. At that time the municipal area was constituted of eight wards, covering 6.5 sq.km. and Shillong was linked with Guwahati by a narrow cart road.

By the year 1897 railways were extended from North Bengal to Guwahati and Upper Assam, Cachar was also linked by rail line in stages. Several other roads were also constructed by the public works department to and from Guwahati joining various important places.[13] The major road links noteworthy of their importance were constructed. These were : (1) Guwahati to Shillong (G.S. Road), (2) Guwahati to Agia (A.T. Road), (3) Guwahati to Kalong River (A.T. Road), (4) Guwahati to Digaru River

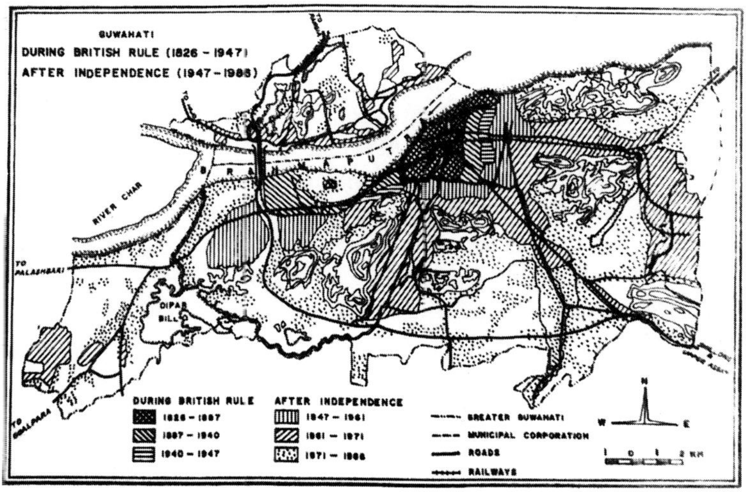

Figure 20.2: Guwahati during British Rule and After Independence.

Source: Author's Construct Based on the Settlement Pattern and Transport Network of GMC Area.

(Old Nowgong or Sonapur road) and (5) Guwahati to Mawphlang via Nongkhlaw. Educational and cultural function of the town was geared up during the British period. Cotton College in 1901, the Curzan Hall (Nabin Bordoloi Hall) in 1903, the Assam State Museum in 1940 was established in stages at Guwahati. Gradual growth of urban population was responsible for improvement of the amenities in the town. Subsequently, the municipality was expanded in 1940 and the area was extended to 7.5 sq. km.[14] Guwahati witnessed the horrors of the Second World War. During this period, Guwahati was used as a stronghold of the British army. Civil lines and Cantonments were constructed in the heart of the town, besides there was a face lift of the town with the addition of new lines of transport and communication as can be seen in Figure 20.2.

Guwahati During the Post-Independence Period (1947 A.D.-1986 A.D.)

There is difference between pre-independence and post-independence India. In the pre-independenence period the British administration was busy in consolidation of their power and little interests were shown for improvement of the towns. The multifaceted growth and development were envisaged only in the post-independenence period. During the post-independence period, especially in planning periods the following additions were made : (i) High Court of Assam, (ii) All India Radio, (iii) Guwahati University and (iv) Railway Headquarters. Besides these, The State Central Library, The Assam Engineering College, The Guwahati Medical College etc. have been established in stages. All these new additions in the urban functions have naturally enhanced the administrative as well as commercial functions in the city.

Consequently, the population of the town increased from 48,615 in 1951 to 1,00,707 in 1961.[15] The municipal jurisdiction was also increased from 7.68 sq. km. in 1951 to 14.24 sq. km. in 1961 by including three more wards. In the mean time, multiple nuclei was developing from the core of the town towards the periphery. The station at New Guwahati, Industrial State at Bamunimaidan, the Oil Refinary along with subsidiary industry at Noonmati, Military Cantonment at Satgaon, Military Hospital at Basistha, The State Police Battalion at Kalapahar, The Airport with Airforce Headquarters at Azara, all these have cumulatively expanded the spatial dimension of the Guwahati City (Figure 20.2). The landmarks in the history of Guwahati was the construction of the Saraighat Bridge across the Brahmaputra in the year 1962. The significance and functional importance of Guwahati radically changed and magnified, when north-eastern states were politically reorganized in seven states. The North-Eastern states were linked with the mainland by a narrow corridor of about 14 km. Guwahati is the major centre of this link, and serve as the main gateway to the areas east of Guwahati. Growth of Guwahati accelerated with the shifting of capital from Shillong to Dispur in the year 1973 (in eastern outskirt of the city).[16]

After independence, a large number of migrants (particularly refugees) from neighbouring countries like Bangladesh, Nepal, Burma and job seekers from other states of India came to Guwahati, besides having spread themselves in the whole N.E. region and the region which added to the growing complexity of the problem.[17] Ultimately, Guwahati Municipal Corporation, had to extend its area jurisdiction to 216.19 sq. km. (in the year 1974).

At present, Greater Guwahati is composed of one Municipal Corporation, two town committees, fifteen special areas like Railway, Refinery, Guwahati University and Defence areas with 82 villages covering a total area of 243.2 sq. km. (95 sq. miles).[18] Radical changes in its functional behaviour has not only made the city life uncomfortable, but also created innumerable problems. The abrupt growth of population, encroachment upon the open land and disturbance caused to ecosystem led to serious consequences that are familiar to unplanned city development.

The trend and rendencies of its past history profusely indicated the expansion of Guwahati Municipal Corporation into a metropolis in the near future and if the problem faced by it, particularly those that are connected with drainage, are not resolved immediately, it will compound its growth.

NOTES

1. Sarma, D. (1981): *Kamrupa Sasanavali*, edited, Publication Board, Assam, Guwahati, pp. 8-9 (from *Kiskindhya VIII* in original *Devanagari*'s script).
2. *Ibid,* p. 10.
3. Baruah, K.L. (1933). *Early History of Kamrupa*, K.L. Baruah, Shillong, p.11.
4. Chatterji, S.K. (1951): *Kirāta-Jana-Kriti: The Indo-Mongoloids, Their Contributions to History and Culture of India*, The Asiatic Society, Calcutta.
5. *Bisnupurāna*, pt. v, ch. 29; *Bhāgavata Purāna*, x.59; *Mārkandeya Purāna*, ch. 7; *Harivamsa*, ch. 63, *Kālikā Purāna* 38.101, 81.2.
6. Sharma, M.M. (1978): *Inscriptions of Ancient Assam,* Gauhati University Publications, Gauhati.
7. Neog, M. (1978): *Role of Tambula in Assam's Social Life.*
8. Government of Assam (1985): Instruction to all Departments to use the spelling of Guwahati in place of Guwahati in all official correspondences, notification etc. with effect from the 15th August, 1985.

9. Bhattacharyya, N.N. (1977): *Guwahati: A Study in Urban Morphology*, An unpublished Ph.D Thesis, Department of Geography, Gauhati University, Guwahati, p. 52.
10. Das, M.C. (1987): "Yuge Yuge Guwahatir Ruprekha" in *Paura Bichitra*, a Journal of G.M.C., Gauhati, 1st Issue, 1987, (Assamese Section), p. 15.
11. Rao, V.V. (1978): "Early History of Gauhati Municipal Board" in *Paura Bichitra*, a Journal of G.M.C. Gauhati, 1st issue, (English Section), p. 9.
12. Hunter .W.W. (1879): *A Statistical Account of Assam*, Trubner and Co., London p. 55.
13. Bhattacharyya, N.N. (1977): *Ibid,* p. 65.
14. Census of India (1971): Assam, Series -3, part V-B, Special Survey Reports on Selected Town – Gauhati, p.4.
15. The Assam Gazette (1986): Extraordinary Issue, No. 129, Dispur, 24th December, p. 925.
16. Gopalkrishnan, R. (1984): "Some Theoritical Considerations in the Analysis Immigration into the Brahmaputra Valley", *Journal of Social Science and Humanities,* Vol. II, No. 4, October-December, North-Eastern Hill University, p. 39.
17. Calcutta Metropolitan Planning Organsiation (1971): *Report on Master Plan for Water Supply, Sewerage, and Drainage for Gauhati Metropolitan District, 1971-2001*, Submitted to the Government of Assam, pp. 2-3, 2-4.
18. A Revised Report of the Town and Country Planning Department, Government of Assam, 1981.

21

Deprivation and Rights to Education of Slum Children in Shillong

Sumana Paul

Introduction

Slums are the habitations which located on disputed as well as unused government, municipal and private lands characterized by a serious lack of basic amenities and sanitation with dense and overcrowded housing conditions. It is a place where mostly the below-the-poverty-line (BPL) people reside. Such people experience the worst conditions of sanitation and health. The BPL people are those people who do not have enough money to pay the rent, eat a healthy meal and so on. In India, a BPL person is someone who cannot afford one square meal a day. Education is the only means of escape for these deprived children of India's slums. The recent rapid urban population growth and the relative lack of attention to urban poverty have possibly exacerbated deprivation in urban areas. As population of urban areas grew, that of slums accounted for 17.37 per cent of the total urban population as per the Census of India 2011. There is often a reluctance to regularize the informal settlements and to provide the basic infrastructures and services to such areas because rural-urban migrants are often regarded as temporary urban residents.

The most common problem facing the urban population in a majority of the developing countries is the limited access to almost all the basic services such as health, shelter and particularly water supply and sanitation facilities. The Central and the State governments have been introducing a number of urban welfare programmes for improving the socio-economic conditions of the urban slum dwellers in India. In most of the cities, 1/4th to ½ population lives in poverty and deprived of the basic needs. The basic poverty continuum demonstrates itself in low incomes, inadequate nutrition levels and basic services, limited means of education and low skills. A number of studies reveal that urban poor in India are those households whose income is in between Rs. 650 and Rs. 700 a month and who live in low income settlements which mostly lack of adequate sewerage facilities, water supply and health care.

Meaning and Types of Slums

In defining a slum, the office of the Registrar General of India (RGI), write, "a slum, for the purpose of census, has been defined as residential areas where dwellings are unfit for human habitation by reasons of dilapidation, overcrowding, faulty arrangements and design of such buildings, narrowness or faulty arrangement of street, lack of ventilation, light, or sanitation facilities or any combination of these factors which are detrimental to the safety and health." The RGI classified slums into three categories, viz. (i) Notified Slums are all the notified areas in a town or city notified as 'slum' by State, UT Administration or Local Government under any Act including a 'Slum Act', (ii) Recognized Slums are all the areas recognised as 'Slum' by State, UT Administration or Local Government, Housing and Slum Boards, which may have not been formally notified as slum under any Act and (iii) Identified Slum is a compact area of at least 300 population or about 60-70 households of poorly built congested tenements, in unhygienic environment usually with inadequate infrastructure and lacking in proper sanitary and drinking water facilities (Identified).

Slum Conditions in Shillong

In Meghalaya too, a huge chunk of population live in the urban slums, besides the slums in the rural areas. This rapid urban population growth and relative lack of attention to urban poverty, has possibly exacerbated multi-dimensional deprivation, including deprivation of education. Shillong known as the "Scotland of the East" is found to be the only State capital in the entire north-eastern region which has a slum population of over 50,000 persons. In Shillong, a large chunk of population lives in urban slums and it has the highest slum population.Viewed terms of good urban sanitation and cleanliness Shillong earned the 18th rank among the Indian cities. The emergence of slums in Shillong is mainly due to the high growth and unplanned development of Shillong urban area which is one of the oldest, largest and fastest growing hill stations in the country. This high growth is mainly attributed to migration of poor sections of the population in search of better economic opportunities. Further, there is hardly any effective mechanism of Government supervision or intervention in the slums.

Move to Reduce Slums in Shillong by 2021

In 2012, the Meghalaya Government has set a target of a decade to reduce slum areas as there are as many as 12 locations in the city alone which have been notified as slums. Unplanned expansion of urban areas without adequate facilities, population explosion, rural-urban migration, influx and an intricate land tenure system limiting the Government control over usage of land are some of the reasons which have been identified as factors behind the growth of slums in Shillong. Since 2004, the Urban Affairs Department which also looks after the municipal administration has notified 12 areas in Shillong alone as slums. These include Laitumkhrah, Nongmynsong, Demseiniong, Pynthorbah, Jhalupara and Mawbah. The specified indexes used for declaring areas as slums include sanitation, drinking water, dwelling homes, economic status of the residents, conditions of roads, drains and sewerage system.According to the Meghalaya State Development Report, 2008, "slums have emerged in the urban areas of the state purely because of lack of infrastructure. Most of the slum pockets are located in low-lying and water-logged areas amid poor sanitary conditions and unhygienic surroundings." The Minister has announced that a target of a decade has been set to reduce slum areas by at least 75 per cent and by 2021, the Government should be in a position to de-notify some of the notified slums. Such announcement came in the backdrop of the department's eagerness to inaugurate the first phase of the residential units meant for slum dwellers. The construction of the 64 dwelling units (DUs) at Lumphira in Nongmynsong on the outskirts of the city was completed and the first phase of beneficiaries belonging to the BPL families would be given accommodation on priority basis. The Minister further informed that a committee was constituted to identify and select the beneficiaries where only "deserving" families would be given preference without 'personal favours'. Apart from the 64 units, construction of the remaining 536 units was still going on. The total cost of the project, under the Jawaharlal Nehru National Urban Renewable Mission, is around Rs. 30.44 crore. The Government had initiated the construction of these 600 DUs for the urban poor since September 2008.

City Slums Selected for Upgradation

Under the Central Government's scheme of Basic Services to Urban Poor (BSUP), five slums of Shillong were selected for upgradation. The selected slums were Mawbah, Demseniong, Lower Mawprem, Pyntohrumkhrah and Kynjatphutbol. The Urban Affairs Minister Ampareen Lyngdoh said that the total project cost has been estimated at Rs 2129.73 lakh of which the Centre's share would be Rs. 1658.05 lakh. The rest would be borne by the State Government. Under the scheme, altogether 168 DUs would be constructed while the construction of the 48 DUs has already begun in lower Mawprem and she added that 'the remaining 120 DUs would be constructed depending on the availability of land'.The Government is expecting to complete the implementation of the scheme by the end of 2013. The Scheme is being implemented by Meghalaya Urban Development Authority (MUDA) which is the designated nodal agency at the State level. The main thrust of the BSUP is focused on the integrated development of slums through projects for providing shelter, basic services and other related civic amenities with a view to provide utilities to urban poor. The ever increasing number of slum dwellers causes tremendous pressure on the urban basic services and infrastructure. In order to cope with the massive problems emerged as a result of rapid urban growth; the Government of India has launched this project in selected cities on mission mode.

Objectives of the Study

The primary objectives of the study are:

(i) to find out the basic educational status of the slum children,
(ii) to find out the major constraints faced by the slum children in the process of attaining education, and
(iii) to suggest how these slum children can access to quality education.

Sample Size of the Present Study

For the purpose of the present study the investigator had to draw up samples of children living in different urban slums located in East Khasi Hills District of Meghalaya. A random sampling technique has been adopted to choose the locations of the slums in order to ensure that there is no systematic bias in our analysis. Of the 23 identified slums of Shillong, a list of 5 randomly chosen slum locations has been taken included in the sample space as shown in Table 21.1. A sample of 100 children was randomly drawn so as to provide an unbiased estimate of the numbers, composition and the condition of the children in the slums.This constituted the *sampled population* which represented the *target population* where data and information have been sought for analysis.

Table 21.1: Slums Targeted for the Present Study

Sl. No.	Area	Name of the Slum
1	Anjali	Harijan Colony
2	Naspatigiri	Naspatigiri
3	Jhalupara	Mathura Compound
4	Paltan Bazaar	Paltan Bazaar
5	Punjabi Line	Punjabi Line

Source: Author's Field Study.

Data Analysis

Analysis of data has been done on the basis of (i) sex, (ii) age group, (iii) category, (iv) social grouping, (v) economic status and (vi) educational status.

Findings

The following findings were obtained from the study.

Educational Level of Slum Children

The study revealed that 37 per cent of the children were the first generation learners while remaining 63 per cent were not. It is encouraging to see that 60 per cent of the children were the school-going children in both formal and non-formal education while only 40 per cent were the drop-outs. With regard to the interest of the children in different fields of activities, it was found that 22 per cent of the children had expressed their interest to study while 16 per cent in playing cricket, 14 per cent in dancing and the remaining 48 per cent had expressed their interests in different activities. It is very encouraging to find out that these children too had high aims in life and desired to become the learned citizen of the country. Out of the total respondents, 22 per cent of them wanted to become doctors while 29 per cent expressed their desire to become teachers and spread the light of knowledge. Besides, some of them aimed to become police and army officers while others showed interest in games and sports and government jobs as well.

Causes of Dropouts of Slum Children

The attendance ratio of slum children was much lower than that of the non-slum children in Shillong as a whole. Low perception level of the value of education by the parents and limited financial means for educating their children were the major constraints. Even if children were attending schools, majority of them were already over-aged. These were some of the reasons which discouraged slum children from attending schools. Lack of friendly learning environment at home had largely forced urban slum primary school-going children out of schools. The present study also revealed that children who worked as garbage pickers had higher school dropout rates.Aparently, one of the reasons could be engaging them as rag-pickers by their parents or family members were labelled as 'dirty' and 'unwanted' children by others. Children from these families were unable to get integrated into the nearby schools owing to poor social acceptance.It was also found that unless robust measures were adopted by the government, NGOs and other stakeholders; education of urban deprived children would continue to remain a challenge because they were constrained by poor feeding, accommodation, poverty, hunger, early orphanage in life, poor drainage and sanitation, inadequate health services, congestion, petty trade, violence, sexual abuse, slum area business, unconducive learning environment and lack of sufficent sleep.

Observations and Ground Realities

The study identified a wide gap between the urban slum primary school children and those children living in better urban settings for attainment of quality education. It is disheartening to observe that very few of these Government schemes have reached in those slums and there is hardly any initiative taken by the NGOs to help and support these slum children.

Proposed Measures for Accessibility of Slum Children to Quality Education

Based on the findings of this study, the following measures are proposed for accessibility of slum children to quality education.

- The Government or some NGOs could step up their efforts for provision of quality education to the slum children.
- Different programmes and activities undertaken by the Government if Meghalaya such as the Sarva Shiksha Abhiyan, Integrated Child Development Services (ICDS) etc. could be properly extended to all the slum children.
- The existing national programme for education of girls at elementary level such as the Kasturba Gandhi Balika Vidyalaya, the mid-day meal scheme and other incentives could be extended to them.

- The recent promulgation of Right to Education Act for all enabled any child to get the benefits of education for his/her overall development irrespective of his/her place of habitation. Also, the RTE Act has a provision for every child who is above six years of age and who has not yet been admitted to any school or could not complete his/her elementary education due to any reason, to be admitted in a class appropriate to his or her age.The underage child who is admitted in school has the right to receive special training or additional instruction in order to keep him/her at par with other children in the class. Such laid down principles could be implemented in real practice more effectively.
- Shishu Shiksha Ghar (renamed as Sparks) is an organisation which has put the RTE Act into implementation by initiating the non-formal educational centres in different slums to provide education to the slum and other under-privileged children. Shishu Shiksha Ghar (SSG)/Sparks was started by adopting a right-based perspective to address to the educational needs of the children in distressful situation. It emphasized on the need for inclusion of all children in education thereby ensuring their Right to Education and finally mainstreams them in full time formal schools. The stress is to "Make Education a Reality for Every Child". A group of individuals joined the initiative and helped in teaching-learning process. The organization has started in January 2010 at Anjali as the first centre of learning. The centre comprised children of all categories such as rag pickers, domestic helpers, child labours, street children, slum, children, cow boys, and others. From its humble inception of one centre with 73 children, presently, four SSG centres with around 350 children enrolled in these centres are functioning and showing utmost interest in learning and actively involving themselves in the various activities of the centres. The classes are divided into Nursery and KG for new learners and Class I to VII for quick learners and school drop-outs. The teaching-learning timing has been fixed according to the flexibility of the children since many of these children are engaged in supplementing support of their families. The school timings thus vary from 12:30 p.m. to 3:30 p.m.; 2:00 p.m. to 5:00 p.m. and 6:00 p.m. to 8:00 p.m. accordingly. SSG could extend their activities further by working closer in tandem with the Education Department.
- Ways and means could be properly devised so as to ensure quality education for slum children to stop this self-perpetuating cycle of poverty.

- The Government could, at least, revamp its system of slum education in the education policy.
- Government schools should be opened with better-trained personnel and reasonable infrastructure.
- Their English speaking skills can be, worked on, since English is a global language.
- Urban slum conditions impede the efforts to increase pupil enrollment, participation, retention and attaining quality education for primary school pupils. It is recommended that government should upgrade slum areas and invest in health, economic, social programmes and projects that enhance quality education for slum children.
- Children need their parents to expose them to a wide variety of areas for opening up the opportunities and developing the interests among the children.
- Parents' awareness programmes could be organised by NGOs to get support and encouragement of their children in putting more efforts for better education and to enable them to face the world with confidence.
- NGOs could organise awareness programs for raising sponsors by taking out peaceful demonstrations and carrying out street plays in raising support for their cause.
- The Government should work hand in hand with NGOs *to "Make Education a Reality for Every Child".*

Concluding Remarks

The study sheds light on the prevailing conditions of primary education in slum urban areas and to create awareness about the need for policy reforms in education and Urban Local Bodies (ULBs). The investigator feels that this research document can be an important tool for advocacy with the Government to address to the problems faced by the slum dwellers especially the children who often fall prey to various social issues due to the vulnerability of life in slums. Slum pockets characterized by low education and literacy levels are more vulnerable to poor child health. Emphasis on education creates avenues for gaining information, capabilities, confidence and eagerness to try alternative approaches of earning. We need to join hands for ensuring every basic right of the children and make education a reality for every child. As every concerned citizen let us try our best to provide quality education to the slum children which will enable them to break the bondage of poverty and live a life with purpose and meaning. Let us do our bit to light their world and shape their future through the light of education as the children of today are the future of tomorrow.

REFERENCES

Adinarayanappa, N.A. (2008): *Urbanization Slums and Environmental Health*, Anmol Publication Private Limited, New Delhi.

Aggarwal, J.C. (2012): *Child Development and Process of Learning*, Shipra Publications, Delhi.

Prasad, Janardan & Kaushik, Vijay Kumari (2012): *Child Education and Social Development*, Kanishhka Publishers, Distributors, New Delhi.

Sinha, Rekha & Sinha, U.P. (2007): Ecology and Quality of Life in Urban Slums, Concept Publishing Company, New Delhi.

http://www.theshillongtimes.com/2013/05/18/ampareen-for-blanket-ban-on-child-labour

http://www.ncbi.nlm.nih.gov/pmc/articles/PMC2483298

http://www.telegraphindia.com/1111120/jsp/northeast/story_14775278.jsp

http://www.telegraphindia.com/1110907/jsp/northeast/story_14473085.jsp

http://www.indiaenvironmentportal.org.in/news/shillong-has-highest-slum-population

http://www.indiaenvironmentportal.org.in/news/shillong-has-highest-slum-population

22
Urbanization and Transportation
A Study of Shillong City and its Suburbs

Utpal Kumar De and *Gitumoni Rajbongshi*

Introduction

Shillong, the capital city of Meghalaya has steadily grown in size both in structure and form since 1864. The city also known as the "Scotland of the East" is in the midst of rapid urbanization as can be evident by higher income opportunities and employment generation, high literacy rate, rapid industrialization, improved level of infrastructure, easier access to information etc. Like any other urban area, the population of Shillong Urban Agglomeration (SUA) has been growing at an increasing rate since 1971. From 122752 in 1971, the population of SUA rose to 354759 in 2011. It is perceived that with the rapid growth in its population and many other related factors, more outlying areas are becoming urbanized day by day resulting in the formation of SUA.

The city is the hub of various administrative, commercial and educational activities. The city has also shown prospects in the field of trade and commerce during the last two decades. With increasing population and improvement in the standard of living; demand for transportation in the area increases. But it is to be noted that urban road infrastructure always fall short short of the rapid population growth and therefore, this chapter aimed to highlight various problems associated with urbanization and its relation withthe transportation sector. The urban centres of Shillong are affected by urban sprawl which thereby imposes severe demand on road transportation that further leads to the problem of traffic congestion. Apart from narrow road and yearly growth of vehicles, the signs of traffic congestion are evident in most of the town roads. In addition to that, the major highway that is the national highway-6 (former NH 40 & 44) which passes through the heart of the city further adds to the problem of traffic congestion.

Transport sector in Shillong has undergone substantial change over time. The number of vehicles registered per year has shown an increasing trend. As per the record of the District Transport Office in Shillong, the number of registered vehicles during 1990-91 was only 30456 which increased to 40645 during 2000-01 and further increased to 117934 in 2013-14 (Government of Meghalaya, 2016). In the 2009-10 alone 6477 vehicles were registered and that increased to 8595 in 2011-12.

These Figures indicate that there is an accelerated growth of registered vehicles in Shillong city and its surrounding regions. As it is true that some of the registered vehicles move out of the region every year, many old cars also come from outside every year and many of them do not get them registered in the regional transport office of Shillong. So, a net import of old vehicles every year may safely be argued as many old cars (more than 15 years old) are not allowed to run in many metro areas of the country and those are transferred to rural areas and to North-Eastern part of the country where no such strict rule is followed. Therefore, logically the number of registered vehicle can be considered as the minimum number of vehicles being present in and around the town.

Road length of Shillong was about 356.00 kms in 2009 with a road density of 2.05 km/sq. km. The total road length (sum of all types) of SUA was only 250 kms. Table 22.1 reveals the drastic rise in pressure of cars on the available road network of the city and its vicinity. Table 22.2 reflects the very low road density in Shillong as compared to several other cities in India. Moreover, due to hilly terrain roads are narrower in Shillong.

Table 22.1: Area, Population Density, Registered Vehicle and Road Density of SUA

Year	Area (sq. kms)	Population	Density of Population (per sq. km)	Number of Registered Vehicle	Road Density (Road Length per sq. km of area)	Number of Cars per km of Road
1981	25.40	174643	6877	NA	NA	NA
1991	25.40	223366	8794	30465	NA	NA
2001	25.40	267662	10538	40645	0.12	155.04*
2011	27.19	354759	13047	117934	0.10	303.81**

Source: Census Report, 1981, 1991, 2001 & 2011, Government of India, Statistical Handbook, Meghalaya, Government of Meghalaya.

Note: *Figures corresponds to 2005-06 and **Figures correspond to 2009.

Table 22.2: Road Length and Density of Shillong

Urban Component	Length of road	Area in sq. km	Density per sq km
SMB	111	10.36	10.71
SUA	139	17.04	8.16
PUA	106	146.06	0.72
Total GSPA	**356**	**174.00**	**2.05**

Source: DPR for Procurement of Buses Shillong 2009.

Table 22.1 reveals that along with increase in population and functional diversification of the town, there has also been a sharp increase in the number of vehicles registered in Shillong regional transport office, thereby led to the problem of traffic congestion. However, it is important to note that gradual increase in population and vehicles registered over time are not the sole causes of severe traffic congestion. Unplanned growth educational institutions and administrative centres across places within the town compound the traffic congestion problem during school or office opening and closing hours.

Objectives of this Study

The prime objectives of the study are:

- To highlight the current trend of urbanization in SUA.
- To examine the impact of urbanization on the transportation sector in Shillong.

Hypothesis

Growth of vehicle population and its density is much higher as compared to the growth of road density.

Data and Methodology

To examine the trend of urbanization over the years data on population, rural urban concentration of population, workers participation, housing characteristics, number of bank offices, credits and deposits etc. have been collected from various issues of *Statistical Handbook of Meghalaya* and *Census Reports*. Data regarding road lengths, types of road in Greater Shillong Planning Area (GSPA), number of Passenger Car Units (PCUs) etc. were collected from the City Development Plan Report, Meghalaya 2007. For analyzing the aforesaid hypothesis, the data regarding number of vehicles registered and road length have been collected for East Khasi

Hills District to represent the SUA from where road density and vehicle density have been computed. Shillong falls under the East Khasi Hills District of Meghalaya and a larger proportion of people are residing in SUA. As data for SUA is available only for population, most of the data relating to rural urban concentration of population, vehicle population, road lengths, housing status and bank details have been presented pertaining to the East Khasi Hills District. Tabular and graphical illustrations are given to depict the trend of urbanization.

To study the second objectives, i.e. the impact of urbanization on transportation, the traffic related data as given by the JNNURM Report and the Detailed Project Report (DPR) for Procurement of Buses in Shillong (2009) are used to show the volume of traffic on various road stretches in Shillong. The Urban Affairs Department, Government of Meghalaya has engaged a firm and has prepared the City Development Plan (CDP), 2007. The CDP indicated that surveys have been carried out for the peak period of traffic and the volume/capacity (V/C) ratios of different urban roads have been worked out and such findings have been considered in this chapter. To test the above-mentioned hypothesis, log of number of registered vehicles and road length have been regressed overtime for the period 1999-2014. Their trend coefficients have been compared to examine whether road length has grown faster than that of the registered vehicles. If growth of vehicle density is higher than road density, it clearly shows the rising problem of traffic congestion in Shillong. This further reveals that these two variables are statistically correlated and are the main factors of traffic congestion. The equation of regressions is $LnY_t = \beta_1 + \beta_2 t + U_t$, where Y_t is the number of registered vehicles or road length, t is the annual exponential growth rate, β_1 and β_2 are the regression coefficients representing the intercept and slope of the linear regression line and U_t is random disturbance term with all classical linear regression properties.

Current Urbanisation Situation

Population in Shillong

The population in GSPA has increased significantly from 155600 in 1971 to 397883 in 2011. This, however, is expected to increase to 914261 by 2041. As per the Census of India 2011, SUA consists of 12 towns (2 Statutory Towns and 10 Census Towns). The urban population of GSPA has increased from 78 per cent in 1971 to 89 per cent in 2011 and only 11 per cent of the population fall under the sub-urban vilages. Consequently, the number of towns in SUA has also increased significantly from 2 census towns in 1971 to 10 census towns in 2011. Table 22.3 shows the population growth of GSPA from 1971 to 2011. It is seen that over the years,the population has been increasing in all the urban and peripheral areas including the sub-urban villages of GSPA. In 1971 the number of towns were limited to only two census towns, i.e. Nongthymmai and Mawlai. Gradually with the population growth other peripheral areas have joined in urban agglomeration and presently, the SUA has 10 census towns and two statutory towns, i.e. Shillong Municipality and Shillong Cantonment. According to 2011 census, 32 numbers of villages are included in GSPA and the urbanisation rate of these sub-urban villages is also observed over the years. As per 2011 census, the population of Shillong Municipality was the highest among all the GSPA components followed by Mawlai, Nongthymmai and by others. Table 22.4 revealed that the population density of Shillong Municipality was the highest among all the GSPA components followed by Madanrting, Pynthorumkhrah and by others.The population trend of SUA, sub-urban villages and GSPA from 1971 to 2011 is diagrammatically presented in Figure 22.1.

Table 22.3: Population of GSPA

Sl. No.	**GSPA Component**	**Population**				
		1971	**1981**	**1991**	**2001**	**2011**
1	Shillong Municipality	87659	109244	131719	132867	143229
2	Shillong Cantonment	4730	6520	11076	12396	11930
3	Nongthymmai	16103	21558	26938	34292	38004
4	Mawlai	14260	20405	30964	38303	55012
5	Madanrting	NA	6165	8987	16318	29194
6	Pynthorumkhrah	NA	10711	13682	22115	27219
7	Nongmynsong	NA	NA	NA	11371	15017
8	Mawpat	NA	NA	NA	4663	6184
9	Umpling	NA	NA	NA	9796	8529
10	Nongkseh	NA	NA	NA	4931	4846
11	Umlyngka	NA	NA	NA	4696	7381
12	Lawsohtun	NA	NA	NA	6386	8214
	Shillong Urban Agglomeration	122752	174703	223366	298134	354759
13	Villages	32848	42571	47747	63711	76474
	GSPA	155600	217274	271113	331373	397883

Source: City Development Plan, 2007 & Census, 2011.

Table 22.4: Population Density of GSPA

Sl. No.	GSPA Component	Population Density (per sq. km.)				
		1971	1981	1991	2001	2011
1	Shillong Municipality	8461	10545	12714	12825	13825
2	Shillong Cantonment	2570	3543	6019	6737	6025
3	Nongthymmai	5496	7358	9194	11704	10984
4	Mawlai	2322	3323	5043	6238	8960
5	Madanrting	NA	3051	4449	8078	12975
6	Pynthorumkhrah	NA	5076	6484	10481	11583
7	Nongmynsong	NA	NA	NA	5686	10078
8	Mawpat	NA	NA	NA	565	750
9	Umpling	NA	NA	NA	389	347
10	Nongkseh	NA	NA	NA	398	392
11	Umlyngka	NA	NA	NA	673	1059
12	Lawsohtun	NA	NA	NA	674	866
	SUA	4832	6878	9794	11728	12999
13	Villages	220	286	320	428	513
	GSPA	894	1248	1558	1904	2289

Source: Authors' Calculation.

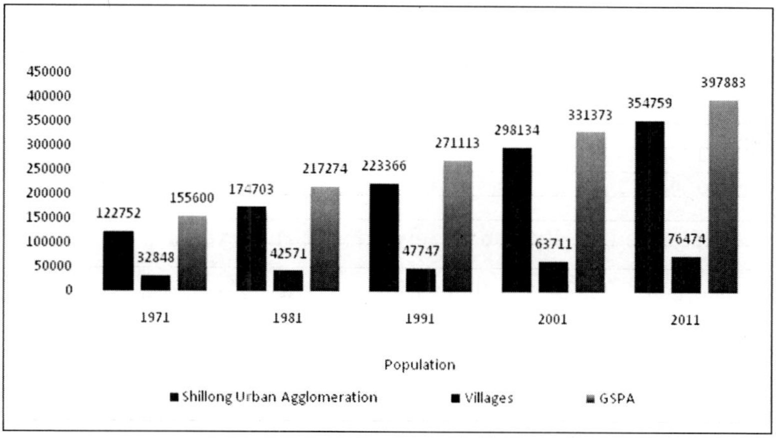

Figure 22.1: Population Trend of SUA, Villages and GSPA (1971-2011)

Source: Authors' Construction.

Rural Urban Concentration of Population

The concentration of total population in rural and urban areas in East Khasi Hills District is presented in Figure 22.2. In 1971, the total population in rural areas was 368457 and was much higher than the population of the urban areas i.e. 122753. But the trend of population growth over the period of four decades revealed that the growth in both the rural and urban population were positive but growth rate of urban population was much higher and continued to be higher as on 2011. Figure 22.2 revealed that the growth of population of rural areas was not impressive.

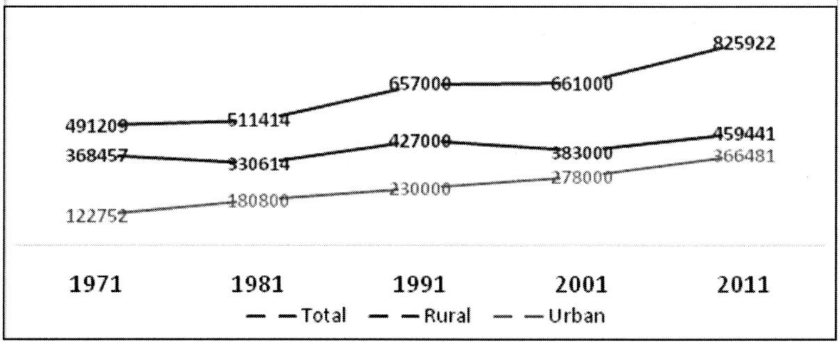

Figure 22.2: Trend of Total, Rural & Urban Population of East Khasi Hills (1971-2011)

Source: Authors' Construction.

One important inference drawn from this Figure is that day by day the concentration of population in urban areas continued to increase at a faster rate as compared to the rural areas. This may be due to the rural-urban migration of population caused by a number of factors like for better job opportunities, education attainment etc. This has further added to the population of SUA which ultimately pressurised on the road transport and compounded the problems of traffic congestion.

District-wise Distribution of Towns and Urban Areas

As per the CDP 2007, of all the districts of Meghalaya, East Khasi Hills, West Khasi Hills and East Garo Hills, have two towns each and the rest of the districts have one town each. The highest contribution is made by East Khasi Hills District which accounted about 60 per cent of its population in the urban areas as compared to rural areas. The lowest concentration of urban population is in South Garo Hills which has only 2 per cent of urban population. The highest level of urbanisation is in the East Khasi Hills District of Meghalaya which is evident from the fact that nearly 42 per cent

Table 22.5: Population of Sub-Towns in Shillong

GSPA Component	2001	2002	2003	2004	2005	2006	2007	2008	2009	2010	2011
Shillong Municipality	132867	132973	133079	133185	133292	133399	133506	133613	133720	133827	143229
Shillong Cantonment	12396	12532	12670	12809	12950	13092	13236	13382	13529	13678	11930
Nongthymmai	34292	35115	35958	36821	37705	38610	39537	40486	41458	42453	38004
Mawlai	38303	39107	39928	40766	41622	42496	43388	44299	45229	46179	55012
Madanrting	16318	17313	18369	19490	20679	21940	23278	24698	26205	27804	29194
Pynthorumkhrah	22115	23199	24336	25528	26779	28091	29467	30911	32426	34015	27219
Nongmynsong	11371	NA	NA	NA	NA	NA	NA	NA	NA	NA	15017
Mawpat	4663	NA	NA	NA	NA	NA	NA	NA	NA	NA	6184
Umpling	9796	NA	NA	NA	NA	NA	NA	NA	NA	NA	8529
Nongkseh	4931	NA	NA	NA	NA	NA	NA	NA	NA	NA	4846
Umlyngka	4696	NA	NA	NA	NA	NA	NA	NA	NA	NA	7381
Lawsohtun	6386	NA	NA	NA	NA	NA	NA	NA	NA	NA	8214
SUA	267662	260239	264340	268599	273027	277628	282412	287389	292567	297956	354759

Source: Statistical Handbook of Meghalaya, 2001.

of its total population lives in urban areas. Table 22.5 depicts the yearly population of the components of SUA from 2001 to 2011.The growth rate of population of SUA has been 18.99 per cent during the period 2001-2011. Within the SUA, the growth rate of Shillong Municipality was less than 1 per cent which was minimal but the growth rate of other smaller census towns within SUA was considerably high.

Housing Status of East Khasi Hills District

Census of India defines institutional population as a group of unrelated persons who live in an institution and take their meals from a common kitchen called an institutional household. Examples of institutional households are boarding houses, messes, hostels, hotels, rescue homes, jails, ashrams, orphanages etc. Houseless population are the households who do not live in buildings or census houses but live in the open roadside, pavements, in hume pipes, under flyovers, or in open places of worship, mandaps, railway platforms, staircases etc. and are treated as houseless households. A cursory look at the status of population as houseless and institutional population as given in Tables 22.6 and 22.7 reveals that for

Table 22.6: Houseless Population in East Khasi Hills District

	1971		1991		2001	
	No of house-holds	**Persons**	**No of house-holds**	**Persons**	**No of house-holds**	**Persons**
Total	265	291	58	221	65	266
Rural	244	244	NA	36	NA	245
Urban	21	47	NA	184	NA	21

Source: Statistical Handbook of Meghalaya, 1971, 1991 & 2001.

Table 22.7: Population in East Khasi Hills District

	1971		1991		2001	
	No of house-holds	**Persons**	**No of house-holds**	**Persons**	**No of house-holds**	**Persons**
Total	120	2881	269	4756	729	13333
Rural	11	206	NA	525	NA	6847
Urban	104	1992	NA	4321	NA	6486

Source: Statistical Handbook of Meghalaya, 1971, 1991 & 2001.

over four decades from 1971 to 2001, the number of households with houseless population has decreased from 265 to 65 households. It is important to note that the number of persons without houses is found to be more in rural areas as compared to urban areas thereby corroborates the fact that urban areas are getting more urbanised and developed with better standards of living. This is possible because better employment opportunities are available in urban areas which facilitate more people to get better job opportunities thereby enabling them to live a good quality of urban life. The increase in the number of deposits and credits over the years as given in Table 22.8 is evident of such urban amneities. The deposits have increased from 90140 lakh in 1981 to 96135 crore in 2001. Similar increase is observed in credits which buoyed up from 513 lakh in 1981 to 25340 crore in 2001. Such quantum jump of increase is indicative of the increasing rate of urbanisation with better living standards of the urbanites.

Table 22.8: Bank Offices, Deposits and Credit in East Khasi Hills District (1981-2001)

	1981	1991	2001
No. of Bank Offices	21	75	126
Deposits	90140 (lakh)	31489 (lakh)	96135 (crore)
Credit	513 (lakh)	5324 (lakh)	25340 (crore)

Source: Statistical Handbook of Meghalaya, 1981, 1991 & 2001.

Current Urban Transport Situation in SUA

Over the years, there has been a gradual increase in the population of Shillong from 223366 in 1991 to over 267662 in 2001 which further increased to 354759 in 2011 (Census Reports 1991, 2001 and 2011).

Road Network Characteristics in Shillong

Road Width of GSPA

Table 22.9 reveals that out of total road lengths of GSPA which is 356 kms, about 70 per cent of the roads are with road widths of 3.75 metres. About 16 per cent are classified as Intermediate Lane and 13 per cent only as Double lane which is relatively very small. Had provisions for wider road widths been made, that would have eased the traffic congestion problem to a greater extent as compared to the present situation.

Table 22.9: Road Classification by Widths in GSPA as on 2007

Classification of Road	Single Lane	Intermediate Lane	Double Lane	Total
	Up to 3.75 metres	3.75-6.9 metres	Above 7.00 metres	
National Highway			33	33
State Highway	0	0	0	0
Other district roads	66	10	0	76
Village roads	45	0	0	45
Urban roads	140	35	24	199
Total road length	251	58	47	356
Percentage	70.5	16.3	13.2	100

Source: City Development Plan for Shillong, 2007.

Types of Roads

The classification of roads by types in GSPA is given in Table 22.10. The Table indicates that as on 2007, 93.12 per cent are blacktopped roads, 0.08 per cent are concretre roads, 2.56 per cent are gravel roads and 4.24 per cent are kutcha roads.

Table 22.10: Road Classification by Types in GSPA as on 2007

Classification	Blacktopped	Cement concrete	Gravel	Kutcha	Total
National Highway	33	0	0	0	33
State Highway	0	0	0	0	0
Other District Roads	59.4	0	9.1	7.5	76
Village Roads	37.4	0	0	7.6	45
Urban Roads	198.7	0.3	0	0	199
Total Road Length	331.5	0.3	9.1	15.1	356
Percentage	93.12	0.08	2.56	4.24	100

Source: City Development Plan for Shillong, 2007.

Vehicle Growth in Shillong

Table 22.11 depicts the number of vehicles registered in Meghalaya. It is seen that the number of two wheeler vehicles registered were the highest followed by cars, taxis and jeeps respectively. This reveals an increase in the purchasing power of the people leading them to use their own private vehicles for meeting daily mobility needs. This signifies their economic prosperity if the developed urban roads are useable by the motorists in accordance with their designed capacities. But it is found that over the years, road infrastructure development has not been able to keep pace with the vehicular growth as can be seen from the traffic jams that motorists and other road users face day by day. Table 22.12 shows similar characteristics of the number of vehicles registered by types in the East Khasi Hills District. The number of vehicles registered in Meghalaya from 2001 to 2013 and the types of vehicles registered in the East Khasi Hills District from 2001 to 2011 are presented in Figures 22.3 & 22.4 respectively.

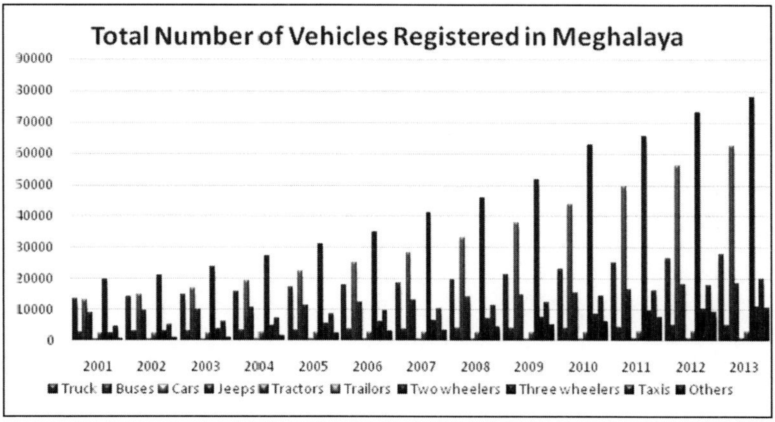

Figure 22.3: Total Number of Vehicles Registered in Meghalaya (2001-2013)

Source: Authors' Construction.

Table 22.11: Number of Vehicles Registered in Meghalaya

Year	Truck	Buses	Cars	Jeeps	Tractors	Trailors	Two wheelers	Three wheelers	Taxis	Others
2001	13464	2463	12853	8930	434	2250	19395	2196	4514	577
2002	14028	2827	14595	9401	441	2304	21050	2934	5030	772
2003	14780	2955	16638	9919	447	2370	23793	3514	5985	984
2004	15817	3244	19186	10490	466	2504	27238	4575	7150	1525
2005	17058	3456	22351	11386	487	2607	31008	5231	8338	2194
2006	17898	3587	25163	12358	517	2612	34721	5943	9387	2796
2007	18569	3733	28335	13098	525	2649	40954	6451	10204	3471
2008	19712	3859	32995	13911	567	2680	45748	6976	11171	4258
2009	21337	3962	37981	14594	609	2713	51710	7617	12426	5163
2010	23029	4071	43901	15541	665	2765	62791	8525	14326	6123
2011	25202	4280	49728	16355	751	2794	65713	9399	16024	7592
2012	26577	4902	56209	18166	786	2833	73093	10337	17952	9166
2013	27777	4981	62545	18378	818	2842	78022	10935	19925	10583

Source: Statistical Handbook of Meghalaya, 2001 to 2013.

Table 22.12: Number of Vehicles Registered in East Khasi Hills

Year	Truck	Buses	Cars	Jeeps	Tractors	Trailors	Two wheelers	Three wheelers	Taxis	Others
2001	6954	1484	8955	6057	255	1983	11346	213	3196	268
2002	7506	1521	8964	6402	263	2012	11961	293	3773	374
2003	7516	1609	11029	6651	269	1933	12703	398	3813	423
2004	8320	1784	13223	7352	280	2126	14044	832	5265	617
2005	8704	1876	16418	7910	293	2163	15757	961	6181	746
2006	8720	1891	17174	7965	295	2179	15886	1023	6354	817
2007	8883	1917	18099	8299	301	2163	16598	1128	6837	908
2008	9226	2079	22460	9131	314	2211	18407	1347	7824	1034
2009	8883	1917	18099	8299	301	2163	16598	1128	7988	609
2010	9616	2150	25570	9565	324	2234	19861	1441	8596	1153
2011	10031	2201	29687	10035	342	2281	21911	1534	9654	1427

Source: Statistical Handbook of Meghalaya, 2001 to 2013.

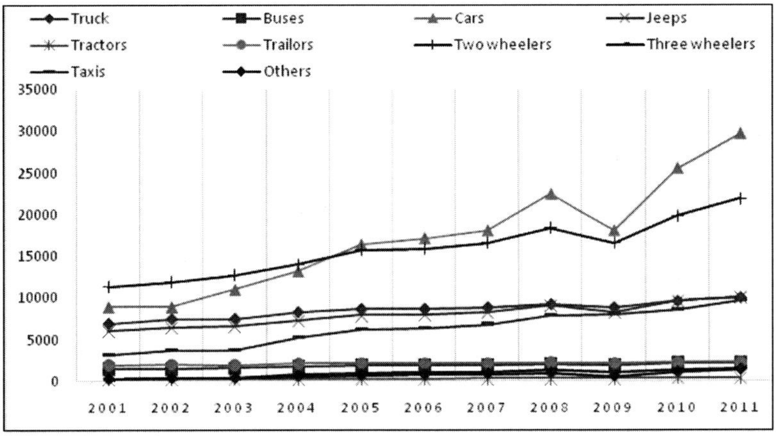

Figure 22.4: Types of Vehicles Registered in East Khasi Hills (2001-2011)
Source: Authors' Construction.

Current Traffic Congestion Condition in Shillong City

Shillong being the State capital of Meghalaya is the busiest administrative centres of the State. It is one of the main commercial and institutional centres of the State. It is an important centre of education, administration and tourism. SUA consists of 7 urban units i.e. Shillong Municipality, Shillong Cantonment, Mawlai, Nongthymmai, Pynthorumkhrah, Madanrting and Nongmynsong. Continuous and rapid increase in the number of registered vehicles with rising affordability of the people has resulted in chaotic traffic situation. Majority of the road corridors suffer from several inadequacies like capacity constraints in the road networks, poor definition of road hierarchy, on street parking, mixed traffic, poor traffic management, slow journey speeds, poor safety situations, inadequacy enforcement of traffic rules, lack of pedestrian facilities and other street furniture. Further, the existence of the national highway i.e. NH-6 through the heart of the city, construction activities, shops and other ribbon developments along the already congested road puts additional pressure on the urban traffic. Some of the critical road stretches where traffic congestion is evident are: (i) Police Bazar (Down from Centre Point Hotel G.S. Road), (ii) Civil Hospital (P.W.D. Road main Highway), (iii) Police Bazar (Hotel Pegasus Crown Road), (iv) Police Bazaar (7th way to Jail Road), (v) Keating Road to Police Bazar (Centre Point Hotel), (vi) Dhankheti (Main N.H. Road), (vii) Nongmynsong (3rd way Road to Nongmynsong), (viii) Anjalee Road (Anjalee Petrol Pump to

Mawlonghat), (ix) Bara Bazaar (Syndicate Stand Road to Bimola Road, (x) Bimola Road to Motphran Road (Motphran Bridge), (xi) Motphran Bridge to Garikhana Road and (xii) Garikhana Road to Jhalupara Road.

The DPR for Procurement of Buses Shillong (2009) indicates the traffic volumes on different sections of arterial roads as can be seen in Table 22.13.

Table 22.13: Traffic Volumes on the City's Arterial Roads

Name of the Road	Total Volume	Peak Hour Volume	Peak Hour Share (%)
Dhankheti Road	30958 (12 hour)	3450	11.0
Firebrigade Road	23017 (12 hour)	2416	11.0
G.S. Road (Near Centre Point)	22967 (12 hour)	2535	11.0
G.S. Road (Near IGP)	25853 (24 hour)	3201	12.0
G.S. Road (Near NEDFI Office)	16539 (24 hour)	1712	10.0
Secretariat Road	37249 (24 hour)	5668	15.0
Polo Road	12204 (12 hour)	1432	12.0
Rhino Point	22320 (12 hour)	2427	11.0

Source: DPR for Procurement of Buses Shillong, 2009.

The main peak hours of severe traffic congestion are during morning 8:00 to 10:00 a.m. and evening from 4:00 to 8:00. It is found that the time of occurrence of traffic congestion on different arterial roads are of distinct categories. Most of the traffic is found to concentrate in areas where educational and administrative institutions exist. The hub of educational centres i.e. Don Bosco square centre is found to be highly congested with vehicles during morning school and office hours. It is observed that starting from Dhankheti point till Nongthymmai the road is congested with many private vehicles which come to drop the school students in time during morning hours. Similar situation is observed during the closing times of schools. It is also observed that most of the parents prefer to drop their school going children in their respective private vehicles rather than on the sharing basis or carpooling. As evident from the above table, about 30958 numbers of vehicles are recorded in 2007 to be running on Dhankheti Road. It is important to note that the figures correspond to year 2007 which would have been more by now. From the data and the day-to-day experiences, it is evident that the services of the existing arterial roads are no longer able to accommodate the increasing numbers of vehicles which grew at the exponential rate over the years. Thus, we witness the alarming pressure of vehicles on arterial roads in the present day situation. The V/C ratios of the city's arterial roads are given in Table 22.14.

Table 22.14: Volume-Capacity Ratios of City's Arterial Roads

Name of the Road	Width in mts	PCUs	Capacity (PCUs)	V/C Ratios
Dhankheti Road	7.5	31590	18200	1.7
Firebrigade Road	8	29471	18200	1.6
G.S. Road (Near Centre Point)	8.5	32877	18200	1.8
G.S. Road (Near IGP)	10	25853	25200	1.0
G.S. Road (Near NEDFI Office)	10	16539	42000	0.4
Secretariat Road	10	37249	42000	0.9
Polo Road	4.7	18876	12600	1.5

Source: DPR for Procurement of Buses, Shillong (2009).

Impact of Traffic Congestion on the People of Shillong

Shillong, which was once a peaceful and quite town, now has turned into a crowded city.The major traffic congestions are witnessed all over the city especially in those areas where educational institutions are located. With schools and colleges resuming, the situation of traffic congestion is becoming worst day by day, making it difficult for the people to reach their destinations in time. Everyday, people and mainly parents of school students have to experience unpleasant experiences of traffic jam while dropping their children. Everyone staying in Shillong witness long lined up cars every morning and afternoon. In addition to that parking space is a major problem. Shillong has come up with constructions of large buildings of educational institutions, administrative offices and shopping complexes but without proper provision of parking spaces and footpaths. Shillong though witnessed a rapid rate of urbanization in terms of population growth, structural transformation etc. but the scope of expansion of the existing roads is very limited due to the existence of shops, residential buildings, hotels, restaurants on both sides of the roads. Though the Government has been exploring every possible means to ease the problems of traffic jams, but the urban setting demands more cooperation and collective responsibility from the urbanites so that traffic congestion problem will not turn into a free rider problem.Common experiences and people's opinion indicate that reckless driving such as haphazard overtaking, taking U-turns on impermissible road sections, illegal on-street parking added by pedestrians' random crossings and erratic beheaviour of road users are the prime causes of traffic congestion rather than the road width factor. The main cause of traffic jams as highlighted by the urban dwellers include (a) hold up at cross roads, (b) pedestrians crossing at cross roads and anywhere along the roads, (c) The 'Me' first attitude of some or most drivers, (d) jumping lanes by 'Me' first drivers and taxi drivers, (e) stopping of taxis and buses on the middle of the road to let off or pick up passengers by drivers and (f) non-stopping of vehicles by drivers before the entrance to in-roads and fuel stations unless they see a traffic police ahead. Such actions of the drivers block the opposite flow of traffic if some vehicles intend to cross into the in-roads or fuel stations (*The Shillong Times*, February 16, 2017). Some of the measures put forward before the government by the urbanites to ease the traffic congestion are construction of overhead walkway near the main secretariat, flyovers over the main cross-roads and expansion of the roads. Figure 22.5 shows the traffic congestion in the city. Further, parking of vehicles right near the road is found to affect the smooth movement of people as well as vehicles which created the problems of traffic congestion (*Meghalaya Times*, June 9, 2017). The busiest centres identified are Malki-Dhankheti and Fire-Brigade-Jingkieng where vehicle-pedestrian conflicts are regularly witnessed and other areas like Laitumkhrah, Bara bazaar and Jail roads vendors are found to make petty shops on the foothpaths meant for pedestrians which is illegal. It has been observed that disorderly parking of vehicles is also contributing to traffic congestion besides lack of parking spaces. As most of the commercial establishments lack parking arrangements, shopkeepers are often seen parking their vehicles in suburbs like Quinton Road, Quinton Lane, Dr. P.B. Deb Road, Jail Road, Traverse Lane, Oakland and Keating Road.

Figure 22.5: Traffic Congestion on Police Bazaar and Dhankheti Roads

The main Police Bazar junction, particularly the erstwhile plaza in front of the O.B. Shopping Mall meant for two wheelers is then mixed with the food vendors which occupied more than half of this side of the junction meant for vehicles and pedestrians. Besides numerous one Way and No Entry barricades with embarkation and disembarkation of commuters of local cabbies; public transport contributes weight heavily on the city's traffic congestion. This traffic situation has taken its toll on other smaller roads of the city as these are now used frequently to avoid traffic jams thereby turned them into traffic congested roads where jams regularly occurred.

Despite such severe level of traffic congestion the city has been facing, the Shillong Traffic Police have been putting in their efforts to manage traffic congestion problem by monitoring vehicles on the road, time-to-time diverting traffic in coordination with the situation, rigorously clamping vehicles for violating traffic rules and imposing fines etc. However, application of demand-side traffic countermeasures is always concomitant with the supply-side countermeasures. Lack of supply-side measures are scarcity of proper parking places, inconveniences of locations of parking sites which resulted into illegal on-street parking. Sometimes, the traffic congestion on the highway affects the students in attending classes and sometimes during various board examinations they reach the examination halls late. To quote the state Education Minister Ampareen Lyngdoh "There are seven cases of students—two for higher secondary examinations and five for secondary examinations—who arrived late today at the exam centres in Shillong because of the traffic jam", the news published in *The Telegraph* on 11th March, 2010. In the past few years, since the beginning of the peak coal business season in November not a single issue of *The Shillong Times* was without any reference to the traffic jam on the national highway-44 passing through the town, which connects Tripura and Mizoram. Apart from recurrent traffic congestion, non-recurrent traffic congestion like during Durga Puja Festival or related events adds to the traffic congestion in Shillong. Figure 22.6 highlights traffic congestion on Barik-Civil Road stretches this year.

Figure 22.6: Rush on Durga Puja Eve Creates Heavy Traffic Congestion in Shillong

Source: The Shillong Times, Monday, 25.09.2017. Photo: Sanjib Bhattacharjee.

Results and Discussions

This chapter aimed at identifying the impacts of urbanization on the transportation sector of East Khasi Hills District of Meghalaya. As per most of the commuters' view, traffic congestion is one of the worst problems faced by the people everyday. This indicates that due to urbanization and better standards of living of the people, people now can afford to buy private vehicles. This increase in the purchasing power of the people has led to more number of vehicles registered and thereby leading to increasing numbers of vehicles plying on Shillong Roads. Given constrained road infrastructure, the number of vehicles has been increasing much faster as compared to road lengths of the region. This, however, indicates that there is traffic congestion in Shillong.

Table 22.15 depicts the regression results of number of vehicle registered and road length on time to examine their growth. It reveals that annual exponential growth of vehicles in the area was about 7 per cent while that of road length was only 1 per cent during the period under study. This gives an important insight that infrastructure; particularly road infrastructure always falls short of the growing urbanization. It means that vehicle density has increased at 7-1 i.e., 6 per cent annual exponential rate during the period. Therefore, it is necessary to undertake some effective policy measures to expand existing road infrastructure through construction of flyovers wherever needed, which will lead to overall growth of the region. As there are constraints of expanding road or widening, through better traffic mechanism at least the existing roads can be made more effective and redress the pressure of growing vehicles.

Table 22.15: Regression Results of LN Registered Vehicles, LN Road Length, Road Density and Vehicle Density on Time

LN Registered Vehicles = 10.37 + 0.07 t	R- Square = 0.96
(17.09) (16.99)	Adjusted R-Square= 0.95
LN Road Length = 7.38 + 0.01 t	R- Square = 0.84
(47.15) (8.28)	Adjusted R-Square = 0.83
Vehicle Density = 18.36 + 1.88 t	R- Square = 0.95(17.09) (16.99) Adjusted R-Square= 0.95
Road Density=0.57+ 0.01 t	R- Square = 0.83
(47.15) (8.28)	Adjusted R-Square = 0.81

Source: Calculated by the authors.

Conclusions and Policy Recommendations

The following concluding remarks can be made from this present study. The towns under Shillong Urban Areas have been increasing over four decades from 2 census towns in 1971 to 10 census towns in 2011. This indicates an increasing rate of urbanisation over the years. Apart from population, other indicators of urbanisation considered include, population with institutional and houseless population, bank account details etc.

It has been found that vehicular growth was much higher as compared to infrastructural growth thereby indicated that people faced the problems of traffic congestion. Apart from this aspect of considering traffic congestion problem, there are many other aspects like delay measurement, traffic count etc. but due to time constraint two parameters have been looked in the analysis that is vehicle density and road density.

The following recommendations can be suggested:

1. Institutions mainly schools and colleges should plan for buses for dropping and picking of students as well as teachers.
2. Government should make provision for flyovers wherever necessary.
3. Construction of proper parking arrangements.

REFERENCES

Census of Meghalaya (2011): *District Census Handbook East Khasi Hills*. Directorate of Census Operation, Meghalaya.

City Development Plan (2007): Department of Urban Affairs. Shillong, Meghalaya.

DPR for Procurement of Buses Shillong (2009): Urban Affairs Department, Government of Meghalaya.

Lim, T. (Undated): *Traffic Congestion and Parking Space is a Nightmare*. Retrived from http://meghalayatimes.info/index.php/editorial/20665-traffic-congestion-and-parking-space-is-a-nightmare-in-shillong

Statistical Abstract of Meghalaya (1971 to 2016): Government of Meghalaya. Directorate of Economics and Statistics, Meghalaya, Shillong.

Websites

http://www.theshillongtimes.com/2017/09/25/rush-on-durga-puja-eve-creates-heavy-traffic-congestion-in-shillong/

https://thenortheasttoday.com/the-sticky-jam-of-shillong/

https://thenortheasttoday.com/meghalaya-gears-up-to-ease-traffic-congestion/

https://thenortheasttoday.com/tag/shillong-traffic-police/

https://www.nelive.in/meghalaya/opinion/meghalaya-urban-congestion-where-shillong-heading

23
Factors Behind Urban Housing Demand in Dimapur

Utpal Kumar De and *Vitsosie Vupru*

Introduction

The centre of most people's lives is their home. Generally, their residence is the place where they spend maximum time and where they mainly need to get comfort and security. Apart from providing shelter, privacy and storage of possessions, it is also the primary base for a family and social activities and a forum for expression of personality and taste. Moreover, it serves as the centre for gratification of leisure activities for many people. Abiodun (1976), however, asserted that the most outstanding of all the problems of urbanization is that of providing ample housing facilities for the residents.

Households attempt to maximize well-being by their location decisions (Blomquist, Berger and Hoehn, 1988). The deep connection between urban change and housing stock is evident in the strong correlation between population levels and housing units. But residential houses are randomly constructed in an unplanned town or city which leads to various problems apart from congestion. Unlike other consumption goods, the housing market is unique since it manifests the characteristics of heterogeneity, durability and spatial fixity which satisfy several wants. The market price of a housing unit can be influenced not only by the cost of construction, but also by the buyers' evaluations of the innate attributes of housing unit. The attributes of housing can be broadly classified into Structural, Locational and Neighbourhood characteristics and those fulfil a number of requirements of the residents (Freeman, 1979). The estimation of price has been done in a number of studies by fitting a demand function for housing attributes (Shimizu, 2014; and Hulagu *et al.*, 2016). Price of residential properties is found to vary across space and time depending on the characteristics of houses as well as on preferences of the potential buyers and their capabilities.

As per locational attributes, distance to central business district (CBD) and accessibility to job are supposed to affect housing prices. Several studies have found significant impact of distance to city or job centre on house prices (Soderberg and Janssen, 2001; Frew and Jud, 2002; Frew and Wilson, 2002; Welch, 2010; McMillen and McDonald, 1998). Orford (1999) also considered distances to multiple employment centres with distances to other regional amenities in estimating housing prices (see Ottensmann Payton and Man, 2008). Cost of travel, travelling time, convenience and availability of different modes have all been used to measure accessibility to CBD, which impact housing prices (Vessali, 1996; Kockelman, 1997; So, Tse and Ganesan, 1997). But Kain and Quigley (1970) established that better educated and higher income households tend to reside farther away from CBD.

Some studies have shown the implicit price of views, such as a good view (Li and Brown, 1980; Rodriguez and Sirmans, 1994); sea view (Tse, 2002), lake view (Lansford and Jones, 1995; Kruse and Ahman, 2009), ocean and lake view (Benson, Hansen, Schwartz and Smersh, 1998), valley view (Corell, Lillydahl and Singell, 1978) and found positive impacts; while cemetery view negatively affect property value (Tse and Love, 2000).

Structural attributes such as floor area or size (Carroll, Clauretie and Jensen, 1996), number of rooms, bedrooms and bathrooms (Garrod and Willis, 1992; Rodriguez and Sirmans, 1994), floor level (So, Tse and Ganesan, 1997), provision of balcony (Chau, Wong and Yiu, 2004), have been found to affect house prices positively. Good architectural design also commands a price premium (Millhouse, 2005). Researchers also surmised that age of building is negatively related to property prices (Kain and Quigley, 1970; Rodriguez and Sirmans, 1994). However, Li and Brown (1980) found a positive effect of age on some buildings due to historical significance or vintage effects of those buildings. Also availability of garage is found to positively affect house prices (Forrest, Glen and Ward 1996). Other empirical works found that structural quality, such as exterior structure and condition of floors, windows and walls to influence housing prices significantly (Kain and Quigley, 1970; Morris, Woods and Jacobson, 1972).

In respect of neighbourhood attributes, the quality of public schools tends to appreciate the value of neighbourhood residential property (Haurin and Brasington, 1996; Black, 1999; Max, 2004). However, it was pointed out that there are also negative externalities of 'year-round school' on the neighbouring residential properties (Clauretie and Neil, 2000). Proximity to shopping complexes exerts both positive and negative externalities (Des Rosiers, Lagana, Theriault and Beaudoin, 1996). But the size of a shopping centre and values of surrounding residential properties are found to have a positive relationship (Sirpal, 1994; Des Rosiers, Lagana, Theriault and Beaudoin, 1996). Also, places of worship, such as churches, appears to impact residential houses in a positive way (Carrol, Clauretie and Jensen, 1996). Urban forests also exert positive externalities (Tyrvainen, 1997).

Ridker and Henning (1967), Anderson and Crocker (1971), Chay and Greenstone (1998), Chattopadhyay (1999), Zabel and Kiel, 2000 and Murty and Gulati (2004) examined the relationship between air quality and property values and observed significant impact of air pollution on residential property values. All these studies found significant willingness to pay for improvement in ambient air quality and thus the enhanced house prices. Preference for environmental or natural resource quality can thus be reflected in the variation in house prices and would be suitably estimated by using hedonic pricing techniques [(Ketkar, 1992 (cited in Kiel, 1995)], Leggett and Bockstael (2000) and Deaton and Hoehn (2002).

Hazards, security etc. are also important criteria for people's preference of residential houses. The influence of other negative externalities such as crime rates (Thaler, 1978), traffic noise (Nelson, 1982); airport noise (Nelson, 1980; McMillan, Reid and Gillen, 1980; Pennington, Topham and Ward, 1990; Espey and Lopez, 2000); hazardous waste sites (Deaton and Hoehn, 2002); industrial sites (Vor and Groot, 2011), all are found to have reduced neighbouring property values.

Since housing comes as a bundle of attributes and it is very difficult to separate them. Here we make an attempt to determine which attribute(s) has significant impact(s) on the demand for housing in the study area. Due to some basic differences in attitude, conveniences and constraints with respect to demand for housing attributes, the analysis is done separately for Tenants and House Owners.

It may be noted that frequent construction of residential buildings are difficult and it is observed that rarely residential buildings are sold or purchased every year in the study area. Most house owners who inherited their houses are constrained to live there since it is too difficult for many of them to buy or construct a new residential building. Not only that, many a time, several family members share the same property (by virtue of inheritance law) and stay with difficulty in the same building (for locational advantage) instead of moving to a remote area where land is plenty.

On the other hand, for tenants, given their income and other preferences, it is relatively easier to change accommodation as per their needs and capabilities. A large number of service holders from outside the region, prefer to stay in rented accommodation till the end of their service period or they get residential accommodation from their employers. Also, due to special provision under the 6th Schedule category of state in India, the non-tribal people working in the study area hailing from other region are debarred from owning houses in major part of the area. Also, preference pattern in respect of various attributes may differ between the purchase for (construction of) own house and rented accommodation by the tenants. For tenants, it is temporary and some of the attributes they cannot change but accept for the convenience of their work and the owners may like to add many features to their houses for their long term objectives of maintaining livelihood and/or enjoying amenities.

Here we tried to examine the determinants of the demand for housing and its price in case of owner-occupied and tenant households in Dimapur town, Nagaland.

Background and Study Area

The strategic location of Dimapur town (Figure 23.1) on the rail, air and road ways has given it a growing importance as manifested by the commercial prosperity during the last few decades. It is one of the fastest growing urban centres in India and performs the role of a transportation nodal point in Nagaland (GOI-UNDP Project, 2013). It has been experiencing a steady flow of immigrants since the statehood of Nagaland in 1963 (Town Planning Organization, 1975). The town recorded a heterogeneous mix of people hailed from all over India, unlike other places of Nagaland for which it is also known as "mini India" (DMC). The population of the town continuously increased over time that put much pressure on the housing sector as spatial expansion of the town has stopped since 1991, which is clear from the rapid growth of density during previous two decades. Over 60 per cent of the households stayed in rented accommodations as they mostly came from various places of the country for different opportunities including government services, businesses and daily labourers.

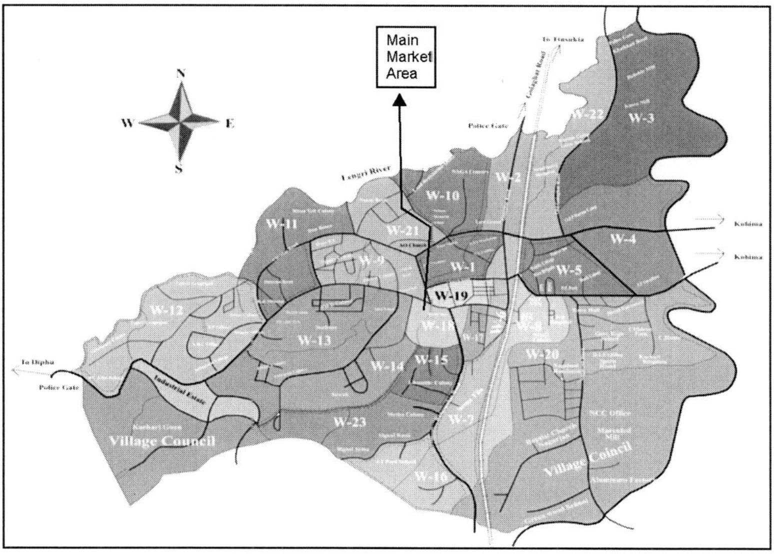

Figure 23.1: Location Map of Dimapur Town, Nagaland

Source: Dimapur Municipal Council.

Data and Methodology

The analysis is based on the primary data collected during 2015-16 in the study area. On an average, twenty (20) households each were selected by simple random sampling without replacement from all the 23 wards in the study area. However, from the larger ward proportionately more numbers were also selected. From the list of the total households in each ward, sample respondents have been selected by simple random sampling procedure. After proper scrutiny for the erratic and incomplete information, finally 490 interview schedules are used for the analysis. Out of 490 total sample units 414 are tenant households and 76 are owner-occupied households. The information has been collected through an interview schedule from the respective sample respondents in each ward. From both the tenants and owners, information on structural attributes, locational attributes and neighbourhood attributes in regard to the residential building were collected. Availability and quality of floor, wall, roof, number of rooms, toilet, water supply in the house, sewer type, overall condition of house etc. (structural characteristics), quality of approach road, location of the house near river, distance from workplace, business centre, rail station, shopping centre etc. (locational characteristics), household perception of security, pollution and proximity to local amenities such as departmental shop, worship place, educational institution etc. (neighbourhood characteristics) are collected from each respondent.

From the data collected, we first selected some important structural, locational and neighbourhood attributes based on earlier empirical studies. Then we checked the problem of multi-collinearity and dropped some variables having high Variance Inflation Factor (VIF) even though they were considered important in other studies (Maddala, 2001). Next, in order to reduce the problem of heteroscedasticity a double-log form of the hedonic price function is chosen for the estimation by transforming the quantitative data into their natural log form (Wooldridge, 2013). Thus, the hedonic price equation with *n* housing attributes is given by

$$\log P_i = \alpha_1 + \sum_{i=1}^{n} \beta_i \log z_i + \sum_{i=1}^{n} \gamma_i X_i + U_i$$

where P_i represents the monthly rent paid by the ith respondent, z_i represents quantitative explanatory variables like age of house, carpet area, distances to places of importance etc. and X_i represents categorical variables like floor material, quality of approach road, security standard etc., α_1 represents the intercept and U_i the random disturbance term with usual classical regression properties. Here β_i represents the elasticity of P_i with respect to ith explanatory variable Z, while γ_i the impact of a marginal change in the ith categorical variable on the rate of changes in P_i.

Results and Discussions

The regression results in Table 23.1 represent combined impacts of all the three housing attributes on the housing prices (or rent). In case of tenants, it is observed that floor quality, water connection and carpet area of the house positively impact the monthly rent whereas distance from train station and proximity to heavy traffic road negatively impact the monthly rent at one per cent level of significance. Also, the number of floors of the building, age of house (in years), house exterior wall material and the location convenience index positively affect the monthly rent, while coefficient of median distance from workplace, market, school and government office, and view quality index is negative and significant.

On the whole, it is observed that six structural attributes significantly affect the monthly rent, four locational attributes and one neighbourhood attribute have significant impacts on the monthly rent. Structural characteristics play the most dominant role in the housing price followed by the locational characteristics. All the coefficients of the variables or attributes which significantly impact the monthly rent are found to have the expected signs except for view quality index. Though most people prefer to enjoy good scenic views from their house, it appears that there is some compromise in choosing their place of residence in favour of other structural and locational attributes to stay within the main town area. Neighbourhood attributes, which also significantly influence people in their housing choices, is observed to be insignificant except for proximity to main roads when all the housing attributes are combined. This may be because neighbourhood qualities are not significantly different across the different wards of the town.

In case of owner-occupied respondents, it is found that carpet area, quality of floor, water connection and exterior wall material have significantly positive impacts on housing price (implicit rent). All the coefficients of the variables or attributes which significantly affect the housing price are found to have the expected signs.

Table 23.1: Results of Regression of Log of Rent Paid on All Housing Attributes According to Status of Ownership

		Tenants	**Owners**
Variable		Coefficient	Coefficient
(Constant)		4.048 (8.31)***	4.193 (4.16)***
Structural	LnNo of Floors	0.039 (2.03)**	0.048 (0.97)
	Floor Type	0.106 (4.60)***	0.165 (2.72)***
	Veranda/Balcony	-0.007 (-0.31)	0.063 (0.48)
	Water Connection	0.124 (5.74)***	0.279 (2.42)**
	House Condition	0.027 (1.13)	-0.042 (-0.85)
	LnAge of House	0.054 (2.51)**	0.054 (1.00)
	LnCarpet Area	0.745 (28.94)***	0.482 (5.77)***
	House Exterior Material	0.040 (1.73)*	0.199 (1.88)*
Locational	Located Near River/ Lake	-0.009 (-0.30)	-0.009 (-0.13)
	Quality of Approach Road	-0.016 (-0.90)	0.031 (0.54)
	LnMedDist_WMSGO	-0.058 (-1.72)*	0.013 (0.14)
	LnDist_Forestcover	0.029 (0.78)	-5.7E-06 (-0.17)
	LnDist_Trainstation	-0.114 (-5.04)***	-5.3E-06 (-1.14)

contd...

contd...

		Tenants	Owners
	View Quality Index	-0.062 (-1.94)*	0.127 (1.19)
	Location Convenience Index	0.115 (1.81)*	0.012 (0.06)
Neighbourhood	LnMedDist_WpDsH	0.016 (0.56)	-0.028 (-0.39)
	Security Standard	0.019 (1.33)	0.010 (0.22)
	Neighbour House Structure is Temporary	-0.027 (-0.85)	0.013 (0.16)
	Neighbours' Community	-0.034 (-0.50)	-0.009 (-0.13)
	Education Level of Neighbours	-0.031 (-1.48)	-0.020 (-0.35)
	Near Garbage/Waste Yard	-0.018 (-0.79)	0.055 (0.54)
	Near Heavy Traffic Road	0.066 (2.73)***	0.082 (1.24)

Dependent Variable: LNMonthly Rent

Note: (1) *, ** & *** indicate significance at 10 per cent, 5 per cent and 1 per cent level respectively

(2) Values in the parentheses represent t-values

(3) MedianDist_WMSGO represents the median distance from workplace, market, school & Govt. Office.

(4) MedDist_WpDsH represents the median distance from worship place, departmental shop & hospital.

R^2, Adj.R^2& F-stat. (sig.)	0.88, 0.88 & 135.82 (.000)	0.74, 0.63 & 6.70 (.000)
White Heteroskedasticity Test:		
F-Statistic (prob.)	1.57 (0.001)	1.14 (0.342)
Obs* R-squared (prob.)	309.52 (0.070)	40.04 (0.337)

Dependent Variable: Squared Residual.

Source: Field Survey conducted during 2015-16.

Overall, six structural attributes affect housing price. Though locational attributes such as distance from workplace and market, quality of view from house etc. are important in housing choices, the result revealed that coefficients of these attributes are not significant in case of owners. This may be because the average distances from workplace and market are not much. The average distance to workplace for those who commute on foot is recorded to be about 179 metres (with an average time of six minutes) and for vehicle users it is 1563 metres (with an average time of 15 minutes). The average distance to market is recorded to be 1280 metres and most owner-occupied respondents are found to possess a personal vehicle (89.47 per cent) as mentioned earlier. Moreover, it is also observed that owner-occupied respondents have an average view quality index of 0.527 as against the overall average of 0.478. This implies that since most of them have quite a good scenic view, its coefficient is found to be insignificant when other important attributes are also considered together. Coefficients of neighbourhood attributes are also found to be insignificant in this case when all housing attributes are taken together. As some of the explanatory variables already captured the variation in price (Dependent variable) the coefficients of neighbourhood variables became insignificant as they offer little more explanation only.

Conclusion

The analysis of the determinants of the demand for housing in the study area has revealed several important insights. The combined impact of all the three housing attributes on the housing prices (or rent) reveals that with respect to tenants, six structural attributes and four locational attributes significantly affect the monthly rent. In case of owner-occupied respondents, however, only three structural attributes have significant impacts on housing price. This implies that in a small town like Dimapur structural attributes impact demand for housing most significantly. This may be because, though locational attributes and neighbourhood attributes are also important, the average distance to places of importance and places of regular visit are relatively less and because neighbourhood qualities are not significantly different across the different wards of the town.

Spatial variation in monthly rent is also observed across the wards and it is found that households residing in wards closer to the main market pay significantly higher rent as compared to those living in wards farther away from such central places.

Policy Implications

From the overall analysis and the knowledge gathered from the survey, certain important policy implications may be highlighted:

(1) Apartment/Flats system of housing may be promoted to mitigate the rising scarcity of housing in Dimapur if horizontal expansion

is not feasible. In this regard, banks should promote housing loans with attractive EMIs.

(2) As distance from workplace, market and other places of importance affects house price significantly, proper distribution of such facilities can distribute the housing preferences across the areas and help in avoiding congestion of some central areas.

(3) Good communication facilities can reduce the travel time further and development of all wards with major common amenities can make the pricing space neutral.

(4) Proper waste disposal management is essential since presence of garbage dumping sites in close proximity to residential houses significantly reduces house price (rent). As there is willingness to pay for cleanliness in the form of more rent or price that can be charged from the residents and the revenue can be utilized for the proper garbage treatment.

(5) Proper records of all house/land transactions should be maintained for better future research and policy making.

REFERENCES

Abiodun, J.O., (1976): "Housing Problems in Nigerian Cities" in *The Town Planning Review*, 47 (4), 339-347.

Anderson, R.J.Jr. and Crocker, T.D. (1971): Air pollution and residential property value. *Urban Studies,* 8, 171-180.

Benson, E.D., Hansen, J.L., Schwartz, A.L. Jr. and Smersh, G.T. (1998): Pricing Residential amenities: The value of a view. *Journal of Real Estate Finance and Economics*, 16 (1), 55 – 73.

Black, S.E. (1999): Do better schools matter? Parental valuation of elementary education. *Quarterly Journal of Economics*, 114 (2), 577-599.

Blomquist, G.C., Berger, M.C. and Hoehn, J.P., (1988): New Estimates of Quality of Life in Urban Areas. *The American Economic Review*, 78 (1), 89-107.

Carroll, T.M., Clauretie, T.M. and Jensen, J. (1996): Living next to Godliness: Residential property values and churches. *Journal of Real Estate Finance and Economics*, 12(3), 319-330.

Chattopadhyay, S. (1999): Estimating the demand for air quality: New evidence based on the Chicago housing market. *Land Economics*, 75(1), 22-38.

Chau, K.W., Wong, S.K. and Yiu, C.Y. (2004): The value of the provision of a balcony in apartments in Hong Kong. *Property Management*, 22(3), 250-264.

Chay, K.Y. and Greenstone, M. (1998): *Does air quality matter?Evidence from the housing market.*NBER Working Paper 6826. Retrieved from: citeseerx. ist.psu.edu/ viewdoc/download? doi =10.1.1.199.480&rep= rep1&type=pdf.

Clauretie, T. M. and Neill, H.R. (2000): Year-round school schedules and residential property values. *Journal of Real Estate Finance and Economics*, 20(3), 311-322.

Corell, M.R., Lillydahl, J.H. and Singell, L.D. (1978): The effects of Greenbelts on residential property values: Some findings on the Political Economy of Open Space. *Land Economics*, 54(2), 207-217.

Deaton, B.J. and Hoehn, J.P. (2002): The effect of hazardous waste sites on property values in zones of high industrial activity: a hedonic approach. *Paper submitted for the AAEA 2002 Annual Meeting,* Long Beach, California. Retrieved from: http://ageconsearch.umn.edu/bitstream/ 19612/1/sp02 de01. pdf on the 25/1/2014

Des Rosiers, F., Lagana, A., Theriault, M. and Beaudoin, M. (1996): Shopping centres and house values: An empirical investigation. *Journal of Property Valuation and Investment*, 14(4), 41-62.

DMC official website – dmcnagaland.nic.in/SSL/login.aspx.

Espey, M. and Lopez, H. (2000): The impact of airport noise and proximity on residential property values.*Growth and Change*, 31, 408-419.

Forrest, D., Glen, J. and Ward, R. (1996): The impact of a Light Rail system on the structure of house prices: A hedonic longitudinal study. *Journal of Transport Economics and Policy*, 30(1), 15-29.

Freeman, A.M. (1979): Hedonic prices, property values and measuring environmental benefits: A survey of the issues. *The Scandinavian Journal of Economics*, 81(2), 154-174.

Frew, J. and Jud, G.D. (2002): Estimating the value of apartment buildings. *Paper presented at the 2002 American Real Estate Society Annual Meeting.* Retrieved from: aux.zicklin.baruch.cuny.edu /jrer/papers/pdf/past/vol25n01/05.77_86. pdf on 15/6/2014.

Frew, J. and Wilson, B. (2002): Estimating the connection between location and property value. *Journal of Real Estate Practice and Education*, 5 (1), 17-25.

Garrod, G. and Willis, K.G. (1992): Valuing goods' characteristics: An application of the Hedonic Price Method to environmental attributes. *Journal of Environmental Management*, 34(1), 59-76.

Government of India, UNDP Project (2013): *District Human Development Report, Dimapur*, Nagaland. Government of Nagaland, Department of Planning and Coordination.

Haurin, D. and Brasington, D. (1996): *The impact of School quality on real house prices: Interjurisdictional effects.* Working Papers 010, Ohio State University. Retrieved from: www.econ.ohio-state.edu/pdf/haurin/haurin.pdf on 11/2/2014.

Hulagu, T., Kizilkaya, E., Ozbekler, A.G. and Tunar, P. (2016): A Hedonic house price index for Turkey.Working Paper No. 16/03, Central Bank of the Republic of Turkey. Retrieved from: https://www.unece.org/fileadmin/DAM/ stats/documents/ece/ces/ge.22/2016/Session_6_Hedonic_House_Price_ Index_for_Turkey.pdf on 27/11/2017

Kain, J.F. and Quigley, J.M. (1970): Measuring the value of housing quality. *Journal of the American Statistical Association*, 65(5), 532-548.

Kiel, K.A. (1995): Measuring the impact of the discovery and cleaning of identified hazardous waste sites on house value. *Land Economics*, 71(4), 428-435.

Kockelman, M. (1997): The effects of location elements on home purchase prices and rents: Evidence from the San Francisco Bay area. *Transportation Research Record* No. 1606, pp. 40-50.

Kruse, S.A. and Ahmann, J. (2009): *The value of Lake adjacency: A hedonic pricing analysis on the Klamath River, California*. Ecotrust Working Paper Series No. 5. Retrieved from: www.ecotrust. org/workingpapers on 18/1/2014.

Lansford, H. Jr. and Jones, L.L. (1995): Marginal price of Lake recreation and aesthetics: An hedonic approach. *Journal of Agricultural and Applied Economics*, 27 (1), 212-223.

Leggett, C.G. and Bockstael, N.E. (2000): Evidence of the effects of water quality on residential land prices. *Journal of Environmental Economics and Management*, 39, 121-144. Retrieved from: http://www.idealibrary.com on 24/11/2013.

Maddala, G.S. (2001): Introduction to econometrics (2nd Ed.). New York, Macmillan Publishing Company.

Max, S. (2004): Schools, what is it good for? When it comes to home prices, school matters. Buyers will pay a premium to live near top schools. CNN. com, August 27, 2004. Retrieved from http://money.cnn.com/2004/08/27/real_estate/buying_selling/schools/ on 12/2/2014.

McMillen, D. and McDonald, J.F. (1998): Suburban subcentres and employment density in metropolitan Chicago. *Journal of Urban Economics,* 43(1), 157-180.

McMillan, M.L., Reid, B.G. and Gillen, D.W. (1980): An extension of the hedonic approach for estimating the value of quiet.*Land Economics*, 56 (3), 315-328.

Millhouse, J.A. (2005): *Assessing the effects of architectural design on real estate values: A qualitative approach.*(Masters Dissertation), Rice University.

Morris, E.W., Woods, M.E. and Jacobson, A.L. (1972). The measurement of housing quality. *Land Economics*, 48(4), 383-387.

Murty, M.N. and Gulati, S.C. (2004): A generalized method of hedonic prices: Measuring benefits from reduced urban air pollution. *Natural Resources Accounting*, CSO, GOI. Retrieved from: http://www.iegindia.org/workpap/wp254.pdf on 24/11/2013.

Nelson, J.P. (1980): Airports and property values: A survey of recent evidence. *Journal of Transport Economics and Policy*, 14(1), 37 – 52.

Nelson, J.P. (1982): Highway noise and property values: A survey of recent evidence. *Journal of Transport Economics and Policy*, 16(2), 117-138.

Ottensmann, J.R., Payton, S. and Man, J. (2008): Urban location and housing prices within a hedonic model.*The Journal of Regional Analysis and Policy*, 38(1),19-35.

Pennington, G., Topham, N. and Ward, R. (1990): Aircraft noise and residential property values adjacent to Manchester International Airport.*Journal of Transport Economics and Policy*, 24(1), 49-59.

Ridker, R.G. and Henning, J.A. (1967): Determinants of residential property values with special reference to air pollution.*The Review of Economics and Statistics*, 49(2), 246-257.

Rodriguez, M. and Sirmans, C.T. (1994): Quantifying the value of a view in single-family housing markets. *The Appraisal Journal*, 62, 600-603.

Shimizu, C. (2014): Estimation of hedonic single-family house price function considering neighborhood effect variables. *Sustainability*, 6, 2946-2960. DOI: 10.3390/su6052946.

Sirpal, R. (1994): Empirical modelling of the relative impacts of various sizes of shopping centres on the value of surrounding residential properties. *Journal of Real Estate Research*, 9(4), 487-505.

So, H.M., Tse, R.Y.C. and Ganesan, S. (1997): Estimating the influence of transport on house prices: Evidence from Hong Kong. *Journal of Property Valuation & Investment*, 15(1), 40-47.

Soderberg, B. and Janssen, C. (2001): Estimating distance gradients for apartment properties.*Urban Studies*, 38(1), 61-79.

Thaler, R. (1978): A note on the value of crime control: Evidence from the property market. *Journal of Urban Economics*, 5(1), 137-145.

Town Planning Organization. (1975). *The Master Plan for Dimapur*, Department of Urban Development, Government of Nagaland.

Tse, R.Y.C. (2002): Estimating neighbourhood effects in house prices: Towards a new hedonic model approach. *Urban Studies*, 39(7), 1165-1180.

Tse, R.Y.C. and Love, P.E.D. (2000): Measuring residential property values in Hong Kong. *Property Management*, 18(5), 366-374.

Tyrvainen, L. (1997): The amenity value of the urban forest: An application of the hedonic pricing method. *Landscape and Urban Planning*, 37, 211-222.

Vessali, K.V. (1996). Land use impacts of rapid transit: A review of the empirical literature. *Berkeley Planning Journal*, 11(1), 71-105.

Vor, F. de & Groot, H.L.F. de (2011): The impact of industrial sites on residential property values: A hedonic pricing analysis from the Netherlands. *Regional Studies*, 45(5), 609-623, DOI: 10.1080/00343401003601925.

Welch, T.F. (2010): *Estimating the effects of transportation infrastructure proximity using multiple longitudinal regression methods: The case of Atlanta* (Master's dissertation), Florida State University.

Wooldridge, J.M. (2015): *Introductory econometrics: A modern approach*. Nelson Education.

Zabel, J.E. and Kiel, K.A. (2000): Estimating the demand for air quality in four U.S. cities.*Land Economics*, 76(2), 174-194.

Index

SCC00021/9431/27.8.25/21T

(7452500574)